Internationalizing the Communication Curriculum in an Age of Globalization

Globalization and the resulting internationalization of universities is driving change in teaching, learning and what it means to be educated. This book provides exemplars of how the communication discipline and curriculum are responding to the demands of globalization and contributing to the internationalization of higher education.

Communication as a discipline provides a strong theoretical and methodological framework for exploring the benefits, challenges and meanings of globalization. The goal of this book, therefore, is to facilitate internationalization of the communication discipline in an era of globalization. Section one discusses the theoretical perspectives of globalism, internationalization, and the current state of the communication discipline and curriculum. Section two offers a comprehensive understanding of the role, ways and impact of internationalizing teaching, learning and research in diverse areas of study in communication, including travel programs and initiatives to bring internationalization to the classroom. The pieces in this section will include research-based articles, case studies, analytical reviews that examine key questions about the field and themed pieces for dialogue/debate on current and future teaching and learning issues related to internationalizing the communication discipline/curriculum. Section three provides an extensive sampling of materials and resources for immediate use in internationalization in communication studies: sample syllabi, activities, examples and readings will be included. In sum, our book is designed to enable communication curriculum and communication courses in other disciplines to be internationalized and to offer different approaches to enable faculty, students and administrators to incorporate and experience an internationalized curriculum regardless of time and financial limitations.

This book is notable as a professional development resource for individuals both inside and outside the communication discipline who wish to incorporate a global perspective into their research and classrooms.

Paaige K. Turner (PhD Purdue University) is Dean of the College of Communication, Information, and Media at Ball State University. She was the recipient of the NAFSA: Association of International Educators Region IV 2012 Dorothy Brickman Outstanding New Professional Award and a 2013 Fulbright-Nehru International Education Administrators Award to India. For the past six years, she has co-led the Campus Internationalization Track at the Institute for Campus and Curriculum Internationalization. She has been an external reviewer for the American Council of Education: Center for Internationalization and Globalization Internationalization Laboratory and served as the program coordinator for the AIEA: Association of

International Education Administrators Senior Advisor Program. She also served on the National Communication Association's Task Force on Fostering International Collaborations.

Soumia Bardhan is assistant professor at University of Colorado Denver. She earned her BA (with Honors) in English Literature from the University of Calcutta, her MA in Communication from University of Madras, and her PhD in Communication from the University of New Mexico. Her research interests are informed by intercultural/international communication and Islamic/religious studies and she has conducted grant-funded fieldwork in Egypt, Turkey, Morocco, and India. Her research has appeared in peer-reviewed journals and books by leading academic presses. Soumia has directed seven travel study courses in Spain, France, Morocco, and India. She serves as a director on the board of the International Communication Association and is chair of its Intercultural Communication Division (2019–2021). She also served on the National Communication Association's Task Force on Fostering International Collaborations in research, teaching, and service.

Tracey Quigley Holden is an assistant professor in the Department of Communication and academic director of the Middle East Partnership Initiative Student Leaders Program and an affiliate faculty member with the Center for Political Communication at the University of Delaware. Dr. Holden earned her PhD from the Pennsylvania State University. She also served on the National Communication Association's Task Force on Fostering International Collaborations.

Eddah M. Mutua is a professor in the department of communication studies at St. Cloud State University, Minnesota. She teaches and researches in the area of intercultural communication with a special interest in intercultural and interethnic conflict, post-conflict peace communication and African culture and communication. She coordinates an award-wining service-learning project nationally recognized for its efforts to promote internationalization of intercultural communication curriculum. Dr. Mutua earned her PhD from University of Wales, Aberystwyth. She also served on the National Communication Association's Task Force on Fostering International Collaborations.

Routledge Research in Communication Studies

Populist Political Communication in Europe
Edited by Toril Aalberg, Frank Esser, Carsten Reinemann, Jesper Strömbäck, and Claes H. de Vreese

Setting Agendas in Cultural Markets
Organizations, Creators, Experiences
Philemon Bantimaroudis

Communication, Advocacy, and Work/Family Balance
Jenny Dixon

Integrative Framing Analysis
Framing Health through Words and Visuals
Viorela Dan

The Discourse of Special Populations
Critical Intercultural Communication Pedagogy and Practice
Edited by Ahmet Atay and Diana Trebing

Interrogating the Communicative Power of Whiteness
Edited by Dawn Marie D. McIntosh, Dreama G. Moon, and Thomas K. Nakayama

Media in War and Armed Conflict
The Dynamics of Conflict News Production and Dissemination
Edited by Romy Fröhlich

Mediated Intercultural Communication in a Digital Age
Edited by Ahmet Atay and Margaret D'Silva

Queer Communication Pedagogy
Edited by Ahmet Atay and Sandra L. Pensoneau-Conway

Intercultural Communication, Identity, and Social Movements in the Digital Age
Edited by Ahmet Atay and Margaret D'Silva

Internationalizing the Communication Curriculum in an Age of Globalization
Edited by Paaige K Turner, Soumia Bardhan, Tracey Quigley Holden, and Eddah M. Mutua

Internationalizing the Communication Curriculum in an Age of Globalization

Edited by Paaige K. Turner, Soumia Bardhan, Tracey Quigley Holden, and Eddah M. Mutua

NEW YORK AND LONDON

First published 2020
by Routledge
52 Vanderbilt Avenue, New York, NY 10017

and by Routledge
2 Park Square, Milton Park, Abingdon, Oxon, OX14 4RN

Routledge is an imprint of the Taylor & Francis Group, an informa business

© 2020 Taylor & Francis

The right of Paaige K. Turner, Soumia Bardhan, Tracey Quigley Holden, and Eddah M. Mutua to be identified as the authors of the editorial material, and of the authors for their individual chapters, has been asserted in accordance with sections 77 and 78 of the Copyright, Designs and Patents Act 1988

All rights reserved. No part of this book may be reprinted or reproduced or utilised in any form or by any electronic, mechanical, or other means, now known or hereafter invented, including photocopying and recording, or in any information storage or retrieval system, without permission in writing from the publishers.

Trademark notice: Product or corporate names may be trademarks or registered trademarks, and are used only for identification and explanation without intent to infringe.

Library of Congress Cataloging-in-Publication Data
A catalog record for this book has been requested

ISBN: 978-0-367-21794-5 (hbk)
ISBN: 978-0-429-26612-6 (ebk)

Typeset in Sabon
by Apex CoVantage, LLC

Contents

Acknowledgements x
Foreword: Notes on, Confessions About, and Hopes for Globalization xi
STEPHEN JOHN HARTNETT

PART I
Theoretical Perspectives of Globalism, Internationalization, and the Current State of the Communication Discipline and Curriculum 1

1 Introduction: The Relevance of Communication in Internationalization 3
  PAAIGE K. TURNER AND EUNKYONG LEE YOOK

2 Internationalizing the Communication Curriculum: State of the Field 11
  SOUMIA BARDHAN

PART II
Internationalizing the Communication Discipline and Curriculum 21

3 Intercultural Communication: A 17-Year Analysis of the State of the Discipline 23
  SOUMIA BARDHAN, JANET COLVIN, STEPHEN CROUCHER, MOIRA O'KEEFFE, AND QINGWEN DONG

4 The Internationalization of a Communication Studies Major: A Global Redesign 36
  JOSEPH P. ZOMPETTI, JOHN R. BALDWIN, AND LANCE LIPPERT

5 Integrating the Goals of Global Learning Into the Learning
  Outcomes of the Communication Curriculum   50
  ELIZABETH M. GOERING

6 Internationalizing Intercultural Competence Instruction
  in the Community College Basic Course   64
  WEI SUN, DONNA OTI, ANDREW JARED CRITCHFIELD,
  AND TARYN K. MYERS

7 Internationalizing the Communication Center: Rhetorical
  and Multilingual Frameworks   76
  LAURA A. STENGRIM

8 Internationalizing Rhetorical Studies   84
  ALBERTO GONZÁLEZ AND AMY N. HEUMAN

9 The Internationalization of Scientists' Communication:
  An Essential Literature Review   99
  HELENA TORRES-PURROY AND SÒNIA MAS-ALCOLEA

10 Internationalizing Public Relations Education   113
   MAUREEN TAYLOR

11 Internationalization Opportunities for Strategic
   Communication: Engaging With Latin America and the
   Latino Communities in Public Relations and Advertising
   Courses   130
   JUAN MUNDEL, ESTHER QUINTERO, AND MARIA DE MOYA

12 Internationalizing Public Relations From the Global South:
   "Thinking Globally, Acting Locally"   143
   B. SIBANGO AND M. TABANE

13 Adapting to Students From Different Family Backgrounds
   on Campus   153
   SEOKHOON AHN

14 Examining the Intercultural Outcomes of Internationalized
   Education in the Arabian Peninsula   165
   MARTA TRYZNA, MARIAM ALKAZEMI, AND FAHED AL-SUMAIT

15 Internationalizing and Decolonizing the Classroom   185
   AHMET ATAY

16 The Value of a Fulbright: Internationalizing Education One
    Person at a Time   196
    WENDY LEEDS-HURWITZ

17 The Three Pillars of Short Course-Abroad Experiences   207
    ISMAEL LOPEZ MEDEL

PART III
Internationalization Promising Practices: Sample Syllabi,
Critical Incidents, and Activities   221

18 Connecting Local and Global Communication Contexts
    in the Classroom: Intercultural Engagements With University
    and K–12 Students   223
    EDDAH M. MUTUA

19 Internationalizing the Communication Classroom via
    Technology and Curricular Strategy: Pedagogical Takeaways
    From a Three-Way Online Collaboration Project   235
    RITA KORIS, SUSHIL K. OSWAL, AND ZSUZSANNA B. PALMER

20 Translating Tasks for International Classrooms   243
    REBECCA M. TOWNSEND AND TRUDY MILBURN

21 Contact and Context(s): Cultural Discourse Analysis
    of Internationalized Activities in a Blended Media
    Studies Course   250
    BARBARA RUTH BURKE AND LIENE LOČMELE

22 Internationalizing Interpersonal Organizational Communication   259
    ANN ROGERSON AND L. CELESTE ROSSETTO

23 Introduction to the Course Face-to-Face Communication   267
    TESSA VAN CHARLDORP, MARIJE VAN BRAAK, AND
    ARANKA AKKERMANS

24 Thriving in the Globalized Communication Environment:
    Teaching Resilience to Digital Culture Shock   278
    KATE DUNSMORE

    List of Contributors   284
    Index   292

Acknowledgements

The editors are grateful for the support and inspiration provided by the National Communication Association Task Force on Fostering International Collaboration in the Age of Globalization. We also thank Isabella Fuller for her administrative support.

Foreword

Notes on, Confessions About, and Hopes for Globalization

Stephen John Hartnett

CU Denver Department of Communication

1984/85: When I was an undergraduate at Rutgers, I applied for an exchange program with the University of Southampton, England. Like so many Americans, I was monolingual, so going abroad meant England. And then there was the question of the Beatles, the Stones, and Pink Floyd, those three pillars of my youthful, white, mass-mediated consciousness, so I figured what the hell, let's go to England and see about meeting Paul and Mick and David. There had been a particularly fantastic English teacher as well, Bill Keach (now at Brown), who made it seem like Chaucer and Shakespeare were punk rockers, so I wasn't opposed to having a pint with fellow poets and rabble rousers. And there was a love interest too, as the smartest woman in my cohort, Andrea Slane (now at the U. Ontario), had made it known that she was applying; if I had any hopes of winning her heart, I could not do it from New Brunswick, so . . . I share these confessions of youthful naivety by way of saying that in 1984, when I first left America, folks were not yet talking about globalization as an unstoppable force of human development. The internationalization of higher education was neither an imperative nor an unavoidable reality but simply a choice. It sounded like a kick, so I went to England.

Biking to Stonehenge in the snow was pretty cool. Working at the local socialist bookshop was where I first learned about Antonio Gramsci and Theodore Adorno and Stuart Hall. Visiting the museums and galleries in London cracked open my provincial New Jersey consciousness about ways of seeing the world. Andrea and I would go dancing at the local Rasta club, where the DJ would spin tunes from the altar of an abandoned church while dancers from around the world smoked giant spliffs and melted into a whirl of sweaty bodies. The faculty at Southampton rocked me with experimental poetry, feminist theory, and my first baffling taste of Derrida in a "seminar" that consisted of three students meeting in the professor's office, where we drank tea and tried to sound smart. I marched with the striking coal miners and saw British police riding giant horses, smashing heads with billy clubs as they splattered the streets with blood and snot and broken teeth.

I spent nine months in England and came home in love, broke, and—thank you Drs. Middleton and Crowley!—committed to a new sense of the larger world. The day after I returned, May 13, 1985, the Philadelphia police dropped a bomb on the MOVE house, killing 11 innocents and torching three blocks of houses. I spent that summer driving a truck up and down the Jersey Turnpike, reading Andrea Rich and Aijaz Ahmad after work, training into NYC with Andrea, and wondering why we had returned to a nation that bombs its citizens.

1996: After the tearing down of the Berlin Wall and the implosion of the USSR, the Cubans went hungry. A former "client state" of what Reagan called "the Evil

Empire," the Cuban economy had stagnated for years under Castro's inept management and America's merciless embargo, so when the Russians stopped sending money and oil and food, the local world collapsed. And so the Radical Philosophy Association began sending teams of scholars to Cuba for front-line experiences, where we could witness the revolution firsthand, bring down medical supplies, work shoulder to shoulder with Cuban colleagues, and try to make sense of how the global economy was interconnected. I had been studying Spanish while working on my PhD at UC San Diego, and I was terrible. Jumping into the revolution seemed like a great idea, and I needed an immersive experience to help improve my garbled Spanish.

I was stunned to learn that the historic Malacón, the curving beachfront boulevard that graces downtown Havana, was so destroyed that you could stand on the street, look up into the houses, and peer straight into the indigo Caribbean sky—for all the roofs of all the houses had either blown away or crumbled into piles of debris. One afternoon while driving across the island, we hit a pig. We scrambled out of the 1950s-era jalopy to see the poor beast wiggling on the ground, squealing. Then a cowboy came riding over the hill, hollering in Spanish, waving his weapon, demanding payment for his lost livestock. Then the damn pig got up and waddled away. The cowboy laughed, pulled out a flask, and we sat there on the side of the road drinking. Then an old school bus came bouncing along, full of other cowboys, who were getting bussed into the nearest village, where they were supposed to serve as the adoring fans for a never-ending speech given by some local communist windbag. It had not occurred to me that those cheering audiences at Fidel's speeches had been bussed in, liquored up, and then shipped home, cracking jokes about their terrible government the whole way. So much for Cuban Communism.

But the Cuban people were amazing. They were hungry but would share their food. Their government couldn't have been any worse, but they were all patriots. Their world had collapsed, but they could dance all night long, whirling beacons of joy. And there I was, a stupid white boy from Jersey mangling my verb forms, watching the cruel American embargo, the Soviet implosion, and Castro's brutality drive the locals toward desperation. There were strange forces at play, almost magical in their strength and invisibility, tearing up daily life in Cuba, yet Miami, just a short plane ride north, was sinking in cocaine and air-conditioning and iced drinks and so much wretched decadence it made the head spin.

NAFTA had passed in 1994, so by now we were all becoming conversant in the forest of acronyms that were coming to rule the world—IMF, CIA, GATT, WHO, NAFTA—and so while globalization was not yet a household term, we knew it was coming. Even then, back in '94, the bars of Havana were filled with tycoons from Russia and Italy and Venezuela, everyone circling, looking for the next way to capitalize on the Cubans' misfortune. Yet at the same time, we activists and scholars were circling too, beginning to learn how to plug into international networks of solidarity.

2008: If Roosevelt had listened to John S. Service and the other members of the Dixie Mission to Yenan in the mid-1940s, he would have known that Mao wanted peace with America. But the war hawks in Washington were clueless (as it was, so it shall be!), thinking all Communists were murderous madmen, and so Roosevelt and then Truman abandoned Mao, funneled money and weapons to Chiang Kai-shek and the fascist KMT, and thus drove Mao into the arms of Stalin. In Jersey in the 1970s, we did not know any of this and so my mother—otherwise a Saint and a warrior for health justice—would say to us kids at dinner, "come on, eat your carrots. There are starving kids in China." Well, Deng decided to change all that, and so he declared that the Communists would now govern under the mantra "to get rich is noble." And so even while the Castros continued to strangle civic life in Cuba, Deng and the CPC brought "Opening and Reform" to China . . .

By the time Lisa and I landed there in May 2008, Beijing was up to 23 million inhabitants, its magnificent skyscrapers glittering in the afternoon sun, its streets teeming with unimaginable crowds, all hustling and bustling with iPhones and earbuds, stylish and hungry for more. Mao plotted the revolution from caves, but the children of Mao were now urban hipsters, albeit still toiling in the shadow of a Party that never seemed to grasp the simple fact that political legitimacy comes not from repressed speech but through flowing speech. Still, the Ministry of Education wanted to internationalize, as did the bosses at CU Denver, so there we were in Beijing, helping to administer our International College of Beijing, a thriving, joyous, and sometimes maddening affair in which Americans and Chinese learn and play and study together.

That was ten summers ago. Now, through a decade of work and travel, I have come to love the Chinese people and their laundry flapping in the breeze, their morning T'ai Chi in the park, their warm smiles and tough hearts, their cheerful questions about life in America, their constant charging ahead for a better life after generations of privation, their nighttime dinners on the street. Our students at ICB are incredible—hardest-working kids you will ever meet. And I can testify that Beijing, Shanghai, Xiamen, Qingdao, and Chengdu (among many others) all have world-class subway systems, glistening new airports, glassy-smooth roads, housing for everyone, and plentiful food for all. The ride from the airport into Beijing takes you down roads lined with walls of poplars and roses. In Denver, the drive in from the airport takes you past the Purina Dog Chow plant, belching its nauseating death smells over a concrete jungle of waste and filth. The "community park" at 20th and Lawrence is now an impromptu homeless camp. It took a while, but via the jarring power of such comparisons, I slowly came to find myself asking "Why is public transportation better in China than in America?" "Why is there no crime here?" "Why are the Chinese so patriotic, while cynicism and narcissistic foolishness reign in America?" "Must free speech come with homelessness?"

And then Lisa and I visited Hong Kong, where you get the energy and hum and rush of Beijing wrapped in the legacy of British-imposed notions of law and order and, yes, free speech. And then we made it to Taipei, once home to Chiang Kai-shek's malevolent KMT but now home to Tsai Ing-Wen—a woman president!—and her raucous DPP, where they run a city that feels like Chicago on a pulsing Saturday night. Patrick Dodge's mom lives there, so we took strolls through the famous night markets while hearing family stories. Our interviewing human rights activists and cultural memory workers took Patrick, Lisa, and me to Delhi, Dharamshala, Lhasa, Kathmandu, Taiwan's Green Island, Macau, and more, and in every one of these remarkable places, we found ourselves realizing that the American model of governance *is just one style*. We travelled in the name of doing social justice–inspired research and activism, and made friends and allies along the way, all while encountering indescribable poverty jostling next to insane wealth, mind-blowing beauty nestled amidst barbarism, and entwined despair and hope.

If nothing else, my now-obsessive commitment to international travel and research and activism had taught me that any notions I once held about universal values were silly. And so I came to believe that the world is a kaleidoscope of wonder and pain, a carnival of magic and hurt; even those of us who work for social justice are just surfers on the tidal wave of global politics—but we now all know that that ride is inescapable, there is no avoiding the pull of the forces, for good and ill, of globalization.

2018: As these vignettes indicate, globalization is the shrinking of time and space so that daily life in Asia, the Americas, Europe, Africa, and so on slowly melts together. I imagine every reader of this book has her or his own list of stories like mine, moments when the world seemed suddenly to crack open in waves of possibility and obligation. There have always been global trade routes and explorers, different waves of colonization and cultural intermingling, but now the pace of our interweaving has accelerated in speed and expanded geographically so that there are no untouched places left. And so the kids on the hard streets of post-crash Athens are wearing Yankees hats; Brazilian rap thunders along alleys in Havana; drugs grown in Pakistan are shipped through Johannesburg in route to LA; weapons made in Texas are settling rival gang scores in Nairobi; and on and on it goes, with bankers in Panama City and New York and Geneva greasing the wheels of international trade while PR shops in Tokyo and Taipei and Toronto pump out the images that define our public life; and the whole spectacular swirl of it all is now converted into harvestable data for Facebook to market, for hackers to steal, and for Russian gangsters to sell to corrupt politicians working with underground analysts to throw elections in the few remaining democracies.

It seems clear, then, that:

- As educators, if we are not revising our classes to speak to these new global realities, then we are failing our students.
- As scholars, if we are not revising our research projects to tackle these new global realities, then we are cheating ourselves and our colleagues.
- As activists, if we are not expanding our work to include partnerships with international colleagues and communities in need, then we are know-nothing yokels.
- As administrators and disciplinary leaders, if we are not trying to build partnerships that embody these international dilemmas and opportunities, then we are simply missing the boat of history and will be bypassed by those with vision and energy.

And so, based upon these experiences and beliefs, when I had the good fortune to be elected to the presidency of the National Communication Association (NCA), I launched a Task Force on Fostering International Collaborations in the Age of Globalization. Co-chaired by the brilliant and tireless Qingwen Dong (University of the Pacific) and Carolyn Calloway Thomas (Indiana University), and supported by Trevor Parry-Giles (NCA Executive Director) and the NCA's amazing team, the Task Force included 15 members representing the United States, China, Colombia, India, Kenya, New Zealand, South Korea, and Singapore and included scholars with expertise in and institutional connections with the Middle East, Africa, Latin America, Asia, and Europe. We launched a biennial conference on Communication, Media, and Governance in the Age of Globalization, which the NCA co-hosted with the Communication University of China in 2016 and 2018, with additional versions coming in 2020. We launched the Shenzhen Forum in 2019, which hosted tracks on health communication and new media, the digital journalism crisis, and communication innovation; a second version of this conference will unfold in Shanghai in 2021. In this way, we have sought to build a culture of collaboration wherein scholars from around the world convene around the day's pressing topics. We started producing so much research that we partnered with the Michigan State University Press to launch a new book series, "U.S.–China Relations in the Age of Globalization." We led panels and workshops, hosted pre-conferences, published brochures, and gave lectures everywhere, in each case working with colleagues to try to think about how our communication theories and practices could help to make sense of, and perhaps even change, the dynamics of globalization. Even after five years of work, we have just begun to scratch the surface of what is possible or of what is necessary, but we have made a good-faith effort to create venues for discussing how communication teachers, scholars, administrators, and activists can speak to, learn from, and work both in and against the currents of globalization.

Teaching is of course a key part of how we address the issues noted herein. And so our NCA Task Force's pedagogy subcommittee—led by the visionary duo of Paaige Turner and Esther Yook—edited a special issue of the *Journal of International Communication Research*, wherein the selected contributions offered readers a series of best-practices regarding working with international students, running travel study programs, and building curricula more attune to the realities of our age of globalization. Paaige and Esther's idea, working collaboratively with *JICR* editor and task force member Steven Croucher, was to create a space for sharing the experiences and insights of our colleagues on how best to rethink our pedagogical habits in light of the messy and magical realities of globalization. The book before you represents the next step in the project, as Paaige and Esther, now working with Soumia Bardhan, Tracey Quigley Holden, Eddah M. Mutua, and others have assembled a remarkable collection of essays offering fresh pedagogical insights earned via their many years of working in international venues. I hope these chapters will prove useful to fellow teachers and, perhaps, even spur a new generation of young people to find their own adventures. Stonehenge awaits. Cuban cowboys await. China's calling!

Part I

Theoretical Perspectives of Globalism, Internationalization, and the Current State of the Communication Discipline and Curriculum

1 Introduction
The Relevance of Communication in Internationalization

Paaige K. Turner and Eunkyong Lee Yook

Portions of this chapter are reprinted from an article that originally appeared in Communication Research and Practice, *a publication of Taylor & Francis. All rights reserved.*

The world was once perceived to be a vast expanse. Continents separated by miles, countries separated by cultures, individuals separated by language. With rapid advances in technology, improved communications and a heightened awareness of the interdependence of our social, political, economic and material realities, the perception has shifted. We now talk of a world that is shrinking, global citizens whose identity transcends geographic or political boundaries, global economies, global environmental impact and borderless needs. Simultaneously, we also struggle to articulate personal, cultural and national identities within a world that is increasingly interconnected. According to the International Association of Universities, an increasing interdependence among nations as well as intensified mobility of goods, ideas and people has had the effect of making internationalization more of an educational institutional imperative.[1] Responding to this mandate, universities around the world have begun expanding the recruitment of international students, study-abroad programs, dual/joint degrees and the development of international branch campuses as well as looking for ways to infuse a global perspective into the curriculum and support students as they become global citizens. Given this trend of expansion, it is past time that the communication discipline reflect upon how it can contribute and adjust to reflect a new global environment.

Despite its central role in human society, the communication discipline and its contributions to internationalization have traditionally been neglected when compared to fields of study whose titles include the term "international" (e.g., international studies, international politics) or that offer technical skills perceived as having appeal to an international market (e.g., information technology, finance or engineer). Yet higher education is tasked with teaching students not only content knowledge and technical skills but also how to analyze the meanings held by different groups or cultures and communicating that knowledge. Communication plays an integral role as subject matter while providing a framework for exploring the benefits, challenges and meanings of globalization. "While communication technologies can bring students and educators together, communication as a discipline provides our institutions and students with the theoretical and methodological ground for adjudicating the benefits, consequences and meanings of an increasingly global world" (Turner, 2019, p. 24). Communication provides the necessary theory, method and praxis for understanding how information becomes meaningful . . . and for whom . . . if we are willing to engage. Scholars within the communication field have begun to note that the communication discipline systematically lacks an explicit acknowledgement of globalization. The rest of this chapter provides a brief history of the rise and fall of internationalization and one articulation of the tensions between global and local. In doing so, it situates the need for communication as a discipline to internationalize *and* to bring its insights to the larger higher education community. It asks the question, "What is the meaning of internationalization?"

The Rise and Fall of Internationalization

"Internationalization" and "globalization" are terms used to denote a wide range of topics and foci including international studies programs, coursework, political relations, economics and colonization. In this chapter and in much of the scholarly work in international higher education, globalization refers to the movement of people, ideas, goods, capital, services, pollution and diseases across borders. Internationalization is higher education's engagement with that reality (Hill, 2013; Maringe, 2010), a reality that has radically shifted between 1980 and 2018. In 1992, the Association of International Educators published *Bridges to the Future: Strategies for Internationalizing Higher Education*, which laid out a roadmap for the field of international education. Over the next two decades, internationalization moved "from the fringe of institutional interests to the very core" (Brandenburg & DeWit, 2015, p. 15). According to the International Organisation for Economic Co-operation and Development (OECD, 2011), the number of international students worldwide rose from 0.8 million in 1975 to 3.7 million in 2009. The Institute of International Education reported that the number of international students studying at US higher education institutions grew by an impressive 8% in 2013 and 10% in 2014 (IIE, 2017). In the United States, it was projected that international students would more than double from three to more than 7 million annually from 2000 to 2025 (Banks et al., 2007; Haddad, 2006 as cited in Hudzick, 2011). In the UK, Non-EU students made up around 13% of the UK student population in 2012–13, up from 10% five years earlier (Universities UK, 2014). Universities and research articulated the benefits of internationalization to students' personal development, the needs of employers in a global economy and addressing the challenges of global warming, gender inequities, land use or the myriad of other issues identified as Sustainable Development Goals by the United Nations (United Nations, 2015). Conversations on campuses, in journals and at international conferences were shifting away from questions of, "Why should we internationalize our universities?" to "How can we engage more deeply in comprehensive internationalization?" By 2016, the overarching message was that individual nation-states could no longer address the needs of the world and that higher education had an obligation to prepare students to be not just citizens of their countries but citizens of the world. In 2016 and 2017, a resurgence of nationalism in the United States, United Kingdom and other countries created a shift in the geopolitical climate that affected the political and educational communities. Rachman (2014) projected that after years of disappointing economic growth, increased immigration, nostalgia for the eras of the great nation-states and concerns over the growth of the Islamic state would fuel a more nationalist tone in global politics. The projection turned into a prophecy.

In the United States, the 2016 elections became a contest between local interests and global affairs, with candidate Donald Trump positioning himself solidly within the discourse of nationalism. Trump's promises to build a wall, conduct extreme vetting, ban and/or track Muslims and Syrian refugees, replace free trade with fair trade and take on radical extreme terrorism carried with them the undercurrent that the US needed to focus on securing the interests of its current citizens by reinstating the borders of the nation-state. Once elected, President Trump continued to institute policies designed to "secure the US borders" including decreasing visas, reducing participation in NATO and rolling back global climate commitments. "The Trump Administration, with its lukewarm acceptance if not opposition to international agreements, seems intent on putting economic nationalism and 'America first' in the forefront of its approach to world affairs" (Newell, 2017).

The United States was not alone in its shift toward nationalism. In a referendum on June 23, 2016, 51.9% of the participating UK electorate voted to leave the EU. Individual decisions to vote for leaving the EU were strongly associated with holding socially conservative political beliefs, opposing cosmopolitanism and thinking life in Britain was getting worse rather than better (Sampson, 2017). Two of the reasons cited for the belief that life was getting worse were (1) increased immigration, which some British citizens felt put a strain on healthcare and education and increased competition for local workers for high-paying jobs, and (2) the high cost of membership in the European Union, with an emphasis upon the dollars leaving rather than entering the country (Criss, 2016). Advocates for the pro-Brexit movement and members of the VOTE LEAVE campaign group held up signs proclaiming nationalist slogans such as "We want our Country back. Vote to Leave."

The rising belief in the importance of standing up for one's own country created an environment in which transnational or international cooperation was suspect if not outright rejected. This environmental shift sent waves throughout higher education. Mayhew (2017) argued that Brexit created a risk of the "loss of research funding from EU sources; loss of students from other EU countries; the impact on the ability of the sector to hire academic staff from EU countries; and the impact on the ability of UK students to study abroad" (p. S156). Redden (2017) reported that of those responding to a national US survey, 39% of US institutions reported declining applications from international students and concern that students and their families will view the US as not providing a welcoming environment for international students. According to the IIE, the number of newly arriving international students into the US declined 3.3% in fall 2017, with 45% of campuses reporting drops in new international enrollment, according to a survey of nearly 500 campuses across the US (Redden). "We are seeing a return to nationalism in Europe and the United States because it is not clear to many that internationalism, as followed since World War II, benefits them any longer" (Friedman, 2016, para. 11). Many in international education feel "demoralized" and are looking for ways to respond and turn challenges into opportunities (Helms, 2019), including the very definition of internationalization.

In a broad sense, internationalization refers to specific policies and strategies that governments and institutions undertake to add international dimensions to their activities at home (Willis & Taylor, 2014). Historically, definitions and approaches to internationalization in higher education have appropriately focused upon how higher education institutions can bring an international or global perspective to their activities while also working to connect the global and local. For example, Knight (2004) defined internationalization as "the process of integrating an *international, intercultural or global* dimension into the purpose, functions or delivery of post-secondary education" (p. 11, emphasis added).

The term "glocal" represents an attempt by the international education community to linguistically mitigate that bifurcation and represent the relationship as both/and rather than either/or. Yet increasingly, institutions are finding themselves in situations where local, regional and even national constituents perceive that higher education has reified the global at the expense of their local concerns. While it was clearly the intent of internationalization efforts to recognize the local as part of the global rise in nationalism, challenges faced in higher education, and the concerns regarding regional relevance. In sum, global has come to mean everyone else except "us." While we can and should continue to stress the benefits of internationalization, the need to create global citizens and articulate global impact, we also need to consider how we constitute the meaning of local and global.

Doing Global

Asking the question of how we constitute the meaning of local and global invokes a constitutive view of communication. According to Nicotera (2009), "a constitutive view of communication means to presumes that communication, or interaction, is a process of meaning creation or social construction" (p. 176). Taking a meaning-centered or constitutive view of communication centers how our discussions and enactment of global may inadvertently contributing to the perception that local is not part of global, thereby fueling the resurgence of nationalism as an international ideology (Godfrey, 2008). It shifts the question from "What is global and local?" to "How are we doing global and local?"

What does it mean to define something by what is done rather than what it is or what it is said to be? In 1987, West and Zimmerman offered a perspective on gender that shifted the focus from the individual and focused upon the interactional and institutional arenas. They argue that we do gender as "an ongoing activity embedded in everyday interaction" (West & Zimmerman, p. 130). Our perspectives on what is feminine and masculine not only guide these interactions, they also define what feminine and masculine behavior mean. A decision to give a girl a doll and a boy a truck may be guided by our conceptualizations of female and male, yet that act also defines femininity and masculinity. What if we used this frame to consider how we are "doing global"? What acts are we performing that, while guided by our goals for internationalization may, inadvertently, define global as not local? Over the course of many conversations with senior international officers around the world, several heuristic questions emerged that can start us thinking in terms of how we are doing global and the possibility that we are inadvertently defining global as not local. Questions we can raise about internationalization efforts in higher education might include:

- At international or global events, is there local or regional representation? Does "Food from Around the World" include foods from the local community? Is a local flag among the international flags? At study-abroad student fairs, do inbound students present about their experiences, or is it only outbound students talking about their experiences "over there"?
- When describing the benefits of study abroad, are the benefits of learning about the local culture for both inbound and outbound students included?
- When describing the need for students to develop as global citizens, is the importance of learning about all countries included? For example, if an institution is in the US, does it discuss the benefits inbound students will accrue by

learning about the local US culture? Or does the material only focus upon what the local community will learn from inbound students?
- Does the international webpage display links to the local community? Do the banner display images from countries around the world including the host country? Does it offer links to the institution's multicultural center, the local chamber of commerce or other organizations that reflect the local community?
- When speaking with local businesses, chambers of commerce or other professional organizations, does your leadership articulate the need for local workers to understand other cultures without reciprocal recognition that other cultures need to understand local issues? Or is the need to "learn about them" in order to get jobs privileged without acknowledging what "we can offer to them"?
- When discussing the challenges facing the world today, such as the UN Sustainable Development Goals, are specific examples included of how those challenges are affecting local communities? Are global issues explicitly connected to local values *and* local values to global issues?
- When hosting visiting faculty, do they only deliver presentations and lectures as experts? Or do they attend classes and meet with individuals at the university and in the local community to learn from them?
- Does the "marked" global or diversity curriculum acknowledge that a course based upon the local perspective may or may not provide a cultural experience for individuals not from that community? For example, is "US History" listed as a diversity course for non-US students at a US campus? On a campus located in Spain, does it list "Spanish History" as a diversity course for all students including local Spanish students?

Transformational Approaches to Doing Global

There are undoubtedly many other questions that we as members of institutions of higher education might raise, but it is important to acknowledge that just as we work to create opportunities for our students to engage with individuals from differing backgrounds and perspectives, we, perhaps now more than ever, need to do the same with our scholarly and local communities. In these engagements, we can draw upon the many resources communication has generated for exploring and valuing differences of perspective. For example, the philosophical frameworks for communication articulated in Hannan (2013) offer multiple lenses. How would Martin Buber's concept of I and Thou help us frame the global and local? What would Donald Davidson's interpretational constitution of meaning lend to the explication of the relationship of global and local? There are traces of this work already being done by scholars in higher education internationalization.

Dr. Susan Buck Sutton (2010) argues for a shift from transactional to transformational partnerships. According to Dr. Sutton, in transactional international partnerships, resources are traded, instrumental, focused and product oriented. This approach is grounded in dualistic reasoning. When global and local are conceptualized and enacted as a dualism rather than duality, opposites rather than complementary, exclusionary rather than constituting of each other, we are engaging in dualistic reasoning. Moreover, when we invoke dualistic reasoning, there is a tendency to reify or focus on only one half of the duality, with a propensity to negate, demonize or obscure the other either in fact or in perception. If I discuss women's rights, a perception that I am not concerned with men's or human rights may often follow. When we engage in transactional partnerships, we are more likely to engage in activities that do global and local as a dualism rather than a duality, as opposites rather than complementary to one another and as exclusionary rather than constituting and sustaining each other. Dr. Sutton proposes that transformational partnerships pursue "what Susan Gillespie (Bard College) refers to as 'genuine reciprocity' or authentic mutual interest in which what happens to the other institution(s) is of as much concern as what happens to one's own" (Sutton, pp. 61–62). Transformational partnerships combine resources, develop common goals and projects, and are expansive, ever growing, and relationship-oriented. When we approach partnerships as transformational, we must attend to that which is both/and, us/you and global/local. We create the possibility of negating the need to argue for local over global or nationalism over internationalism because we have shifted the focus from individual locations to the relationships that exist between them. Yet there must always be an awareness of the socio-political and geo-political power differentials that exist.

The work of Sandra Harding (Steiner, 2013) could illuminate how our standpoints will always be present, creating the necessary awareness of the geo-political and socio-political power differentials. The presumption that we are engaged in the creation of meaning takes us a step closer towards a meaningful integration of academic systems, institutions, government and individuals. We answer the question "How can US higher education institutions reaffirm their regional relevance while at the same time become more globally competitive?" by posing new questions, "What is relevant? Who benefits? How do we want to engage with each other?" In this book, the authors provide illustrative examples of how the communication discipline can respond to those questions at the macro, meso and micro levels. Section one discusses the theoretical perspectives of globalism, internationalization and the current state of the communication discipline and curriculum. Section two offers a comprehensive understanding of the role, ways, and impact of internationalizing teaching, learning, and research in diverse areas of study in communication, including travel programs and initiatives to bring internationalization to the classroom. The pieces in this section include research-based articles, case studies, analytical reviews that examine key questions about the field, and themed pieces for dialogue/debate on current and future teaching and learning issues related to internationalizing the communication discipline/curriculum. Section three provides an extensive sampling of materials and resources for immediate use in internationalization in communication studies. In addition, sample syllabi, activities, examples and readings are included. In sum, our book is designed to enable communication curriculum and communication courses in other disciplines to be internationalized and to offer different approaches to enable faculty, students and administrators to incorporate and experience an internationalized curriculum regardless of time and financial limitations. We invite you to read these chapters and ask yourself, "What is relevant for the communication discipline, and how can we be relevant in today's global world?"

Note

1. International Association of Universities (April, 2012). Affirming Academic Values in Internationalization of Higher Education: A Call for Action www.iauaiu.net/sites/all/files/Affirming_Academic_Values_in_Internationalization_of_Higher_Education.pdf (Retrieved on August 20, 2012).

References

Banks, J. A., Ball, A. F., Bell, P., Gordon, E. W., Gutiérrez, K. D., Heath, S. B., . . . Zhou, M. (2007). Learning in and out of school in diverse environments. *The LIFE Center (The Learning in Informal and Formal Environments Center) and the Center for Multicultural Education*. Retrieved from www.life-slc.org/docs/Banks_etal-LIFE-Diversity-Report.pdf

Brandenburg, U., & DeWitt, H. (2015). The end of internationalization. *International Higher Education, 62*, 15–17.

Criss, D. (2016, June 20). The non-Brits guide to Brexit. *CNN*. Retrieved from www.cnn.com/2016/06/20/world/non-brits-guide-to-brexit-explainer-trnd/index.html#toc

Friedman, G. (2016, June 2). In EU and US, nationalism is rising, not fascism. *EURACTIV*. Retrieved from www.euractiv.com/section/global-europe/opinion/in-eu-and-in-us-nationalism-is-rising-not-fascism/

Godfrey, C. (2008). *The struggle between nationalism and globalization*. Retrieved from www.newrightausnz.com/2008/08/27/the-struggle-between-nationalism-globalization-part-1-by-colin-godfrey/

Haddad, G. (2006). *The importance of internationalization of higher education*. Paper presented at the International Association of Universities Conferences on the Internationalization of Higher Education: New Directions, New Challenges, Beijing, China.

Hannan, J. (Ed.). (2013). *Philosophical profiles in the theory of communication*. Bern, Switzerland: Peter Lang US.

Helms, R. (2019, April 15). Going, golden, gone? Internationalization's past, present and future. *Higher Education Today a Blog by ACE American Council on Education*. Retrieved from www.higheredtoday.org/2019/04/15/going-golden-gone-internationalizations-past-present-future/

Hill, B. (2013). *American council of education: Center for internationalization and global engagement*. Retrieved from www.acenet.edu/news-room/Pages/Center-for-Internationalization-and-Global-Engagement.aspx

Hudzick, J. (2011). *Comprehensive internationalization: From concept to action*. Washington, DC: NAFSA, Association of International Educators. Retrieved from www.nafsa.org/uploadedFiles/NAFSA_Home/Resource_Library_Assets/Publications_Library/2011_Comprehen_Internationalization.pdf

Institute of International Education. (2017). Retrieved from www.iie.org/

Knight, J. (2004). Internationalization remodeled: Definition, approaches, and rationales. *Journal of Studies in International Education, 8*, 5–31.

Maringe, F. (2010). The meanings of globalization and internationalization in HE: Findings from a world survey. In F. Maringe & N. Foskett (Eds.), *Globalisation and internationalisation of higher education: Theoretical, strategic and management perspectives* (pp. 17–34). New York: Continuum.

Mayhew, K. (2017). UK higher education and Brexit. Oxford Review of Economic Policy, 33, S155–S161.

Newell, T. (2017, March 8). With the resurgence of nationalism, the Marshall Plan is relevant now more than ever. *HuffPost*. Retrieved February 25, 2019, from www.huffpost.com/entry/the-marshall-plan-and-the-resurgence-of-nationalism_b_58bffb60e4b070e55af9e98f

Nicotera, A. (2009). Constitutive view of communication. In S. W. Littlejohn & K. A. Foss (Eds.), *Encyclopedia of communication theory* (Vol. 1, pp. 176–179). Thousand Oaks, CA: Sage Publications.

Organization for Economic Cooperation and Development. (2011). *Education at a glance*. Retrieved from www.oecd.org/edu/skills-beyond-school/48631079.pdf

Rachman, G. (2014, November 13). Nationalism is back: Bad news for the international co-operation. *The Economist*. Retrieved from www.economist.com/news/2014/11/13/nationalism-is-back

Redden, E. (2017, March 13). International applicants to US stall. *Times Higher Education*. Retrieved from www.timeshighereducation.com/news/international-applications-us-universities-stall

Sampson, T. (2017). Brexit: The economics of international disintegration. *Journal of Economic Perspectives, 31,* 163–184.

Steiner, L. (2013). Sandra harding: The less false accounts of feminist standpoint epistemology. In J. Hannan (Ed.), *Philosophical profiles in the theory of communication* (pp. 261–290). Bern, Switzerland: Peter Lang US.

Sutton, S. B. (2010, January/February). Transforming internationalization through partnerships. *International Educator,* 61–63. Retrieved from www.nafsa.org/_/File/_/janfeb10_partnering.pdf

Turner, P. K. (2019). The voice of communication in comprehensive internationalization. *Communication Research and Practice, 5,* 23–38.

United Nations. (2015). *Sustainable development goals.* Retrieved from www.un.org/sustainabledevelopment/sustainable-development-goals/

Universities UK. (2014). *International students in higher education: The UK and its competition.* Retrieved from www.universitiesuk.ac.uk/policy-and-analysis/reports/Documents/2014/international-students-in-higher-education.pdf

West, C., & Zimmerman, D. H. (1987). Doing gender. *Gender & Society, 1,* 125–151.

Willis, I., & Taylor, J. (2014). The importance of rationales for internationalization at a local level—university and individual, *European Journal of Higher Education, 2*(4), 153–166.

2 Internationalizing the Communication Curriculum
State of the Field

Soumia Bardhan

> Portions of this chapter are reprinted from an article that originally appeared in the May 2017 issue of Spectra *magazine, a publication of the National Communication Association. All rights reserved.*

A significant aspect of internationalization, in the context of higher education, is the designing of educational curricula that enable students to thrive in foreign countries and cultures and in their interactions with individuals and groups from other nations. Increasingly, internationalization is becoming an integral part of higher education, offering new opportunities for students to think globally before acting locally, interact effectively and appropriately in foreign contexts and cultures, and develop global critical-thinking skills.

The fourth report of the International Association of Universities Global Survey on internationalization of higher education, published in April 2014 (Egron-Polak & Hudson, 2014), found that when it comes to internationalization policy/strategy, the highest proportion of respondents are from Europe and Asia (56% to 61%), and North America ranging from 40% to 47%; the smallest proportion is from the Middle East (13%). "About 15% to 20% of respondents in all regions indicate that internationalization forms part of the overall policy" (p. 8). The findings show regional differences: students' increased international awareness highest in North America, Asia, and Pacific; the top-ranked benefit in Europe and the Middle East being enhanced quality of teaching and learning; strengthened knowledge production ability for African respondents; and for Latin America and the Caribbean institutions, more robust networking of faculty and researchers. This report is based on responses from 1,336 institutions of higher education located in 131 countries in every world region.

According to the National Communication Association's (NCA) Task Force on Enhancing the Internationalization of Communication, created in 2012 by then-NCA President Steve Beebe, internationalization in US higher education, specifically in the communication discipline, is often viewed as an option. Former NCA President Stephen Hartnett created the NCA Fostering International Collaborations in the Age of Globalization Task Force in 2015 to expand Beebe's task force work. Hartnett asserted (2017) that to remain intellectually engaged with scholarly developments abroad, politically attuned to international issues that will impact the United States, and culturally familiar with emerging international trends, the communication discipline must continue to expand our commitments beyond studying what is national to considering texts, images, institutions, and movements that are international. One of the most effective and cogent ways to accomplish this is through internationalization of Communication curricula/courses.

This state-of-the-field piece starts with a brief overview of the benefits of internationalization to several stakeholders, such as faculty, students, and administrators. This is followed by an exploration of the ways communication studies courses and curriculum are being/can be internationalized in US higher education, through area studies, foreign language learning, internationalizing content in individual courses, travel and exchange programs, and international research (NCA, n.d.). The piece also emphasizes the ways in which multiple stakeholders can/need to be invested for faculty to successfully include international content in their courses, design and direct travel programs, create online courses, teach using technology, and/or engage in international teaching and research experiences. Efforts through which several US universities have facilitated curriculum internationalization are also highlighted.

Stakeholders

The importance of internationalization, specifically in the field of communication, for faculty is manifold (NCA, 2017): (a) a holistic understanding and mastery of the discipline and the dynamics of communication in an age of globalization requires comprehension of its international opportunities and impasses; (b) development of scholars' international quotient, that is consciousness and knowledge of and sensitivity to international dynamics, leads to more perceptive and comprehensive communication analysis and production through focus on the interconnections between the local and the global and the context-specific yet comparative nature of communication; and (c) internationalization paves opportunities for conferences, research collaborations, and grant opportunities in the international context. For students, knowledge of diverse cultural conditions, worldviews, and perspectives is hugely beneficial (NCA, 2017): (a) it enhances understanding of and competence to live harmoniously in a wide range of settings, as well as provides opportunities for emulation of intercultural skills employers desire; (b) an eye to study and find solutions to problems from an international perspective makes students more culturally flexible; and (c) all this raises student awareness and potential to be global citizens, a benchmark of personal growth and career readiness. Finally, for campus administrators, internationalization is an important component of the mission and purpose of many higher education institutions today (NCA, 2017): (a) the ethos of internationalization creates an environment that supports diversity and inclusion among students, faculty, and staff; (b) from a finance perspective, internationalization creates opportunities for institutional collaborations abroad and generates increased tuition revenue, which can be used to support internationalization efforts in the institution; and (c) the ethos of internationalization enables administrators to support faculty's efforts at internationalization, thus leading to production of cutting-edge scholarship and teaching, in turn enhancing an institution's international reputation.

International Content in Communication Curricula/Courses

Teaching students about different countries and cultures is one of the basic approaches to internationalization. This can be incorporated in communication curricula/courses in varying degrees through (NCA, n.d.): (a) area studies, (b) teaching/encouraging learning of foreign languages, and/or (c) integrating international content into individual communication courses.

Area Studies and the Communication Curriculum

Area studies is interdisciplinary and includes courses or sequences of courses that provide in-depth knowledge of specific geographic, national/federal, or cultural regions (NCA, n.d.). The most effective and common way to incorporate area studies into communication students' course portfolios is by encouraging them (through advising and/or curricular requirements) to take a few area studies courses or major/minor in the area studies program (NCA, n.d.). One of the challenges, however, is that area studies often "require a substantial commitment of time and resources," a commitment that may not be fulfilled by all (NCA, n.d.). A more viable option is to include courses that focus on international issues and perspectives in undergraduate students' general education requirements. For example, Kansas State University's K-State 8 general education program includes global issues and perspectives as one of its important areas of general education requirements.

Foreign Language Learning

Enhancing global competence through foreign language acquisition is becoming an increasingly popular movement within US academia. Typically, "communication faculty assume this is beyond their area of expertise;" however, if students are to acknowledge the relevance of being multilingual in our globalized world, encouraging them to learn foreign languages must become a strategic goal of any communication curriculum (NCA, n.d.). Most U.S. university students lack the means to learn foreign-language skills in their academic areas; and international students rarely have opportunities to use their native language competencies during their stay in the U.S. (CLAC Consortium, n.d.).

The Cultures and Languages Across the Curriculum (CLAC) movement "emphasizes the development of effective, meaningful, content-focused language use outside traditional language classes" (Davies, n.d.); and, the movement stresses that "writing and speaking are more active language tasks than simply reading" (NCA, n.d.). Building on these, the CLAC model "establishes small study groups led by foreign students as a vehicle for reading supplementary non-English language readings relevant to a course" (NCA, n.d.), where the international and multilingual students act as language experts; the readings are summarized by each group and a discussion involving the whole class follows (NCA, n.d.). CLAC can be modified to fit any institution or curriculum; communication departments and faculty, through their institutions, can become CLAC Consortium members and work together to integrate language and cultures into their curricula/courses.

International Content in Individual Courses

An oft-pursued option is to integrate international content in individual courses (thus normalizing/naturalizing international perspectives in communication courses). For example, communication faculty can transport relevant knowledge of a specific region into the communication courses they teach, with Intercultural Communication being the course that can most substantially focus on international content (NCA, n.d.). However, "every course can potentially include at least few international examples" and non-U.S. scholarship can be used as references (NCA, n.d.).

One particularly valuable strategy for "integrating international content into a Communication course is to collaborate with faculty in another country" and/or local faculty with international experience for instructional design, team teaching, and/or guest lecturing (NCA, n.d.). Communication faculty may pursue such efforts by networking and inviting colleagues with relevant experience and expertise to help them internationalize a course. Yet another way is to assign collaborative student projects and in-class activities that include domestic and international students. New technologies can facilitate such cooperative ventures and enhance the international quotient of a course (NCA, n.d.). Specific examples include using online collaborative tools and videoconferencing through Skype, FaceTime, etc. to bring together students from disparate cultures/geographic locations to learn with and about each other, team with a classroom overseas, invite guest speakers from different parts of the world through lecture-capturing tools, and so on.

The State University of New York (SUNY) Collaborative Online International Learning (COIL) Center has pioneered a pedagogical approach for using technology to advance internationalization of teaching and learning. COIL Director Jon Rubin first piloted the COIL approach in the film courses he taught at State University College at Purchase (NY), in partnership with faculty at the European Humanities University in Belarus. Using the COIL pedagogy, "faculty members in two or more countries collaborate to design a syllabus and co-teach a course (or module), and students in each class work together online to complete assignments" (COIL Consulting, n.d.). The COIL method can be applied to courses in any academic discipline, including communication; in fact, connected classrooms can often be completely different courses even though faculty jointly develop a syllabus for the COIL portion.

Another emerging strategy for internationalization using technology is global delivery of for-credit online courses. Several communication departments in US universities offer online courses, usually administered through their global campuses. Students from various cultural and national backgrounds (and geographies) can take these courses, which advance the internationalization efforts of a department/university.

Box Item 1

Internationalization Resources:

Institute of International Education—"Scholars involved with the Institute of International Education (IIE) discuss their experiences with creating new and working with established internationalization efforts; read testimonials and watch videos" (NCA, n.d.).
www.iie.org/

NAFSA Resources for Internationalizing Teaching and Learning—"This report, published in 2012, provides a number of sources pertaining to the training of post-secondary educators on internationalization, including exemplary internationalization practices" (NCA, n.d.).
www.nafsa.org/_/File/_/2013_tls_flyer.pdf

> *The IIE Center for International Partnerships in Higher Education*—"The IIE Center for International Partnerships in Higher Education assists higher education institutions in developing and sustaining partnerships around the world" (NCA, n.d.).
> www.iie.org/Why-IIE/Centers-of-Excellence/Center-for-International-Partnerships
>
> *International Academic Partnership Program*—"This program, originally funded by the US Department of Education's Fund for the Improvement of Postsecondary Education, is a major initiative of IIE's Center for International Partnerships in Higher Education that seeks to increase the number of international partnerships between higher education institutions in the US and abroad" (NCA, n.d.).
> www.iie.org/Programs/International-Academic-Partnership-Program

Travel and Exchange Programs

The second major and popular approach to internationalize curriculum is through travel programs and exchange of students and/or faculty between US and international institutions (NCA, n.d.).

Student Programs

Study-abroad experiences can benefit students academically/intellectually, professionally, personally, and interculturally (Shulsinger, 2017). Academically, students develop skills in problem solving/foreign languages, they gain geographical and historical knowledge, and they learn to process information in ways that in-residence courses do not foster. Professionally, they network and make useful international contacts and often acquire a sense of direction and responsibility. Travel and exchange programs also allow students to appreciate and critique their own culture, enhance self-confidence, and improve their sense of personal identity and creativity. From an intercultural perspective, students develop interest in other cultures and become more culturally aware/sensitive, self-reflexive, and empathetic. Undoubtedly, the benefits of travel programs and exchanges are numerous and develop students' international competence.

There are two types of travel programs: long-term and short-term. Long-term programs last a semester to a year, and these are often most popular among students. There is a "more is better" mentality associated with long-term programs; because of the longer duration of stay/immersion in a foreign culture, these programs are considered to have more impact on student development (Kehl & Morris, 2015)). However, short-term programs, which last from two weeks to three months, are gradually growing in popularity among students in US universities. These are especially ideal for those with family/job responsibilities, those with limited financial resources, and/or those who are not ready for long-term immersion emotionally, linguistically, or otherwise (International Business Seminars, 2018). Research shows that short-term programs, if not academically rigorous, often resemble vacation study programs (Donnelly-Smith, 2009). However, if well planned, these programs can offer an intensive and focused experience.

Box Item 2

Tips to Enhance Rigor of Short-Term Travel Programs (Bardhan, 2017; Zamastil-Vondrova, 2005):

- Role as academic director
    - Know expectations
    - Be committed
    - Be hands-on
    - Have cultural competence/site knowledge
- Conduct exploratory/site visit
- Create an affordable program and a feasible program design
- Travel partner, if used, should complement the program's vision
- Have a strong academic component
    - Clear course goals and objectives
    - Detailed syllabus/itinerary
    - Relevant readings/assignments
    - Be mindful to student interests/integration into individual curriculum
- Pretravel orientation
    - Face-to-face (physical or mediated) meetings
    - Expectations/Requirements/Preparation share
    - Create a community (Facebook group)
- Use an emic model (Long et al., 2008)
    - Instill that local or native concepts, categories, and worldview are important
    - Focus on observation, reflection, dialogue/discussions, application
    - Encourage interaction with host community
- Include homestays where possible
- Encourage use of local language and participation in local rituals/customs
- Provide opportunities for guided reflection/interaction/intercultural discussions
- Include field trips with purpose/context
- Schedule regular debriefing sessions
- Schedule evening downtime to balance program activities
- Provide a safe and secure environment
- Maintain strong, healthy group dynamic
- Be mindful to and meet student expectations
- Design opportunities for debriefing, reflection, and reintegration upon return

In addition to travel programs, international exchange programs can facilitate the movement of an entire cohort of students across countries (NCA, n.d.). The Fulbright Foreign Student Program, sponsored by the US Department of State's Bureau of Educational and Cultural Affairs, "is the flagship international educational exchange program sponsored by the US government" (NCA, n.d.).

As communication departments across the United States encourage more students to participate in travel and exchange programs, support is being made available for faculty to direct travel courses that focus on cross/intercultural dynamics, intercultural dialogue, intercultural competence development, and so on. Examples include Colorado State University (Italy); University of Colorado Denver (China); Penn State (Vienna, Morocco, and India); Kansas State University (Japan, France, and Spain). Communication majors are also advised to participate in programs offered by organizations such as the Council on International Educational Exchange (CIEE), "a nonprofit, nongovernmental organization and world leader in international education and exchange" (NCA, n.d.).

Faculty Exchanges and Other Opportunities

Enhancing the international experience and global competence of faculty is vital to the success of a communication course. To that end, "university-to-university exchange agreements facilitate the movement of faculty between US and international institutions" (NCA, n.d.). The Fulbright Scholar Program sends U.S. faculty abroad for a year to teach and/or conduct research and the Fulbright Visiting Scholar Program does the same for overseas faculty (NCA, n.d.). Notable Communication scholars from the US who are also Fulbright awardees include Donal Carbaugh (Finland), Tema Milstein (New Zealand), Wendy Leeds-Hurwitz (Portugal), Paaige Turner (India). Visiting faculty appointments to international universities may be available for shorter durations, such as from few weeks to a semester (NCA, n.d.). For example, the University of Colorado Denver (CU Denver) appoints visiting faculty to its International College at Beijing, which is a joint education program between CU Denver and China Agricultural University in Beijing, China.

If full-time exchanges are too time consuming, shorter opportunities to gain international experience may be pursued, such as participating in international conferences. For example, NCA has occasionally sponsored or co-sponsored international conferences, such as the NCA Summer Conference on Intercultural Dialogue held in Istanbul in 2009. The International Communication Association, as well as the World Communication Association, sponsors a slew of international conferences. There are numerous examples of universities and educational institutes and programs from around the globe sponsoring or co-sponsoring international conferences too. A few examples are the 11th Australasian Institute of Ethnomethodology and Conversation Analysis Conference, hosted by the Department of Communication, University of Macau, Macau, China, November 27–29, 2018; the 4th International Congress on Collaborative-Dialogue Practice, co-sponsored by the Houston Galveston Institute and Taos Institute in Brno, Czech Republic, June 26–29, 2019; the 7th University of Malaya Discourse and Society International Conference in Kuala Lumpur, Malaysia, August 1–2, 2019.

> **Box Item 3**
>
> Study Abroad and Exchange Program Resources:
>
> *Council on International Educational Exchange*—"Their programs include study abroad, teach abroad, high school study, and gap-year programs; international faculty development seminars; summer work and travel exchanges; internships; professional training programs; and volunteer opportunities" (NCA, n.d.).
> www.ciee.org
>
> *Study Abroad*—"This portal provides information pertaining to several student exchange programs" (NCA, n.d.).
> www.studyabroad.com/worldwide

International Research: Faculty and Graduate Students

Faculty and (graduate) students both benefit from attending international conferences, "which result in new connections with international peers that may evolve into a wide range of research and publications" (NCA, n.d.). Funding concerns can limit student and scholar participation at international conferences; thus, international students/scholars can be invited to serve on panels at local/regional/national conferences to "bring an international voice to . . . conversations" (NCA, n.d.). During its Annual Convention, NCA hosts an International Scholars Reception to facilitate dialogue between US and non-US scholars (NCA, n.d.). Participation in workshops that have an international focus also prove beneficial; for instance, the International Rhetoric Workshop offers a platform for emerging scholars and graduate students in the global rhetoric community to connect with internationally renowned scholars and learn from each other's work (www.internationalrhetoric.com/2016-2/). The first workshop was hosted at Uppsala University (Sweden) in 2016, the second at Ghent University (Belgium) in 2018, and the forthcoming workshop is scheduled for 2020.

"The most significant impact comes from international research collaborations that usually involve faculty but can and often include graduate students" (NCA, n.d.). Such projects typically depend on connections established through one of the forms of internationalization mentioned previously. For instance, "one distinct advantage for graduate students who study abroad lies in the connections they make with locals, which can result in significantly expanded international research opportunities" (NCA, n.d.). The Center for Intercultural Dialogue is a project of the Council of Communication Associations and it "facilitates connections among communication scholars studying intercultural dialogue, as well as intercultural dialogue among communication scholars" across the discipline; it does so by promoting "international collaborative research, serving as a source for grants, and serving as a clearinghouse for information" (Center for Intercultural Dialogue, n.d.; NCA, n.d.).

> **Box Item 4**
>
> International Research Resources:
>
> *Center for Intercultural New Media Research (CINMR)*—"CINMR consists of 350 research associates in 50 countries representing 220 universities worldwide. In addition, CINMR includes student research associates. Graduate students are welcome to join CINMR. The names, university affiliations, and countries of graduate students are also listed on the CINMR public website" (NCA, n.d.).
> www.interculturalnewmedia.com
>
> *Society for Cross-Cultural Research (SCCR)*—"The SCCR is a multidisciplinary organization. Its members share a common devotion to the conduct of cross-cultural research. SCCR members are professionals and students from several social science fields" (NCA, n.d.).
> www.sccr.org
>
> *School for International Training (SIT) Graduate Institute*—"This institute of higher education focuses on internationalization studies" (NCA, n.d.).
> www.sit.edu

Concerns and Commitments

It must be reckoned that many benefits (of studying abroad, getting a second major/minoring in area studies, studying a new language/s, etc.) are accessible to students with financial resources, often leading to an unequal sharing of the profits of internationalization. There is often an overdependence on international students to produce a more internationalized institutional culture/curricula/courses, turning them into internationalization agents (Knight, 2011). While this may be the expectation of universities and faculty, it is observed that:

> Frequently, domestic undergraduate students are known to resist, or are at best neutral, about undertaking joint academic projects or engaging socially with foreign students unless specific programs are developed by the university or the instructor. International students band together and ironically often have a broader and more meaningful experience on campus than domestic students but lack a deep engagement with the host country culture.
>
> (Knight, 2011, p. 1)

It must also be remembered that for faculty to successfully include international content in their courses, design and direct travel programs, create online courses, teach using technology, and/or engage in international teaching and research experiences, multiple stakeholders must be invested (Helms, Brajkovic, & Struthers, 2017): (a) a high level of institutional commitment is needed; (b) department chairs/deans must approve changes in course schedules, authorize course releases, provide financial support, and so on; (c) faculty champions must be willing to internationalize and experiment with their courses; (d) centers for teaching innovation must be willing to share emerging practices and provide direct assistance to individual faculty; (e) instructional designers must help faculty and students use learning management systems and advise faculty in creating online collaborative assignments; (f) international education or program offices must identify partner institutions and manage the partnerships; and (g) information technology specialists must help faculty determine which technologies best suit their instructional needs and proper functioning of those technologies. The success of any effort towards internationalizing communication curricula/courses must address these concerns and seriously consider the commitments.

References

Bardhan, S. (2017). Internationalizing the communication curriculum. *Spectra*, 53(2).
Center for Intercultural Dialogue. (n.d.). *About*. Retrieved from https://centerforinterculturaldialogue.org/about/
CLAC Consortium. (n.d.). Welcome to CLAC. *Cultures and Languages across the Curriculum*. Retrieved from https://clacconsortium.org/
COIL Consulting. (n.d.). *What is COIL?* Retrieved from www.coilconsult.com/what-is-coil-.html
Davies, D. (n.d.). Principles of CLAC (a CLAC manifesto). *Cultures and Languages across the Curriculum*. Retrieved from https://clacconsortium.org/about-2/defining-clac/principles-of-clac-a-clac-manifesto/
Donnelly-Smith, L. (2009). Global learning through short-term study abroad: Tomorrow's teaching and learning. *Peer Review*, 11(4). Retrieved from https://www.aacu.org/peerreview/2009/fall/donnelly-smith
Egron-Polak, E., & Hudson, R. (2014). *Internationalization of higher education: Growing expectations, fundamental values*. IAU 4th Global Survey, International Association of Universities, Paris, France.
Hartnett, S. (2017). The enlightenment, cosmopolitanism, and decency. *Spectra*, 53(2).
Helms, R. M., Brajkovic, L., & Struthers, B. (2017). Mapping internationalization on U.S. campuses: 2017 edition. *American Council on Education*. Retrieved from www.acenet.edu/news-room/Documents/Mapping-Internationalization-2017.pdf
International Business Seminars. (2018). *Are short-term or long-term study abroad programs the best fit for you?* Retrieved from https://ibstours.com/blog/study-abroad-best-fit/
Kehl, K. & Morris, J. (2015). Differences in global-mindedness between short-term and semester-long study abroad participants at selected private universities. *The Interdisciplinary Journal of Study Abroad*, 15, 67–79.
Knight, J. (2011). Five myths about internationalization. *International Higher Education*, 62.
Long, S. O., Akande, Y. S., Purdy, R. W., & Nakano, K. (2008). Deepening learning and inspiring rigor: Bridging academic and experiential learning using a host country approach to a study tour. *Journal of Studies in International Education*, 14, 89–111.
National Communication Association. (2017). *Internationalizing the communication discipline*. Retrieved from https://www.natcom.org/sites/default/files/pages/Internationalization_Internationalizing_Communication.PDF
National Communication Association. (n.d.). *Internationalization*. Retrieved from www.natcom.org/academic-professional-resources/internationalization. I wish to acknowledge that most of the content cited from this source was written by Dr. Wendy Leeds-Hurwitz and first published by NCA in 2012.
Shulsinger, T. (2017). The unexpected ways studying abroad benefits your education and career. *Northeastern University: Graduate Program*. Retrieved from www.northeastern.edu/graduate/blog/study-abroad-benefits/
Zamastil-Vondrova, K. (2005, January–February). Good faith or hard data: Justifying short-terms programs. *International Educator*. Retrieved from www.nafsa.org/_/File/_/educationabroadjan_feb05.pdf

Part II
Internationalizing the Communication Discipline and Curriculum

3 Intercultural Communication

A 17-Year Analysis of the State of the Discipline

Soumia Bardhan, Janet Colvin, Stephen Croucher, Moira O'Keeffe, and Qingwen Dong

> The authors wish to acknowledge the contributions of Carolyn Calloway-Thomas, Myung-koo Kang, and Zhengrong Hu as members of the research sub-committee of the NCA Task Force on Fostering International Collaborations in the Age of Globalization.

Our world today, where global actions affect local dynamics and local conditions have global repercussions (Giddens, 1996; Appadurai, 1996; Beck, 1998; Bauman, 2000; Castells, 2002), provides expediencies and significant implications for internationalizing higher education. The importance of curriculum internationalization in the field of communication, as the chapters in this volume demonstrate, is manifold. In this study, we focus on the state of internationalization in "intercultural" communication research; specifically, this chapter is a review and evaluation of the state of internationalization in intercultural communication research in the last two decades and a commentary on how this benefits and/or presents challenges to internationalization of the communication curriculum.

International research endeavors have several benefits for both faculty and students (NCA, 2017). Those who undertake international research often gain a comprehensive understanding of the global dynamics of communication and the opportunities and challenges associated with scholarship dealing with international content and components. This type of research also facilitates the development of scholars' international quotient; they become more aware of and sensitive to international dynamics, and they can provide more perceptive and comprehensive communication analysis by focusing on the complex and nuanced interconnections between the local and the global and forefronting the context-specific and comparative nature of communication. Analyses and scholarly findings associated with international projects have implications for teaching and impact students, whose education, in the age of globalization, cannot be well rounded and holistic without knowledge of diverse cultural conditions, value systems and worldviews, meaning-making processes and traditions, and so on. International research, thus, presents numerous advantages for scholars, students, and higher education in general.

In this study, as stated, we focus on the state of research internationalization in the field intercultural communication. According to Stier (2006), intercultural communication is seen by some social scientific scholars as:

> One branch of communication studies, anchored in its characteristical ontological, epistemological and axiological assumptions. At the same time, intercultural

communication is a field of concern for several other academic disciplines (e.g., psychology, social psychology, sociology, education, media studies, cultural anthropology and management) . . . [and] is viewed as an object of study or a problem within the realms of these disciplines.

(p. 6)

While discussing Alexander et al.' s (2014) claim about the key issues and urgencies associated with the field of intercultural communication today, Croucher, Sommier, and Rahmani (2015) state:

An issue brought forth was the very definition of intercultural communication . . . As the field continues to diversify, a key issue is to consider the very nature of what is "intercultural communication." A glance at any intercultural communication textbooks [sic] and articles [sic] will reveal multiple definitions of intercultural communication that often share similar characteristics, with many differences.

(p. 79)

Against this backdrop, and despite the lack of an unequivocal definition of intercultural communication, according to Stier (2006), there is a "common preoccupation" (p. 6) with scholars interested in intercultural dynamics, namely, their willingness "to take on the challenge of the global, multicultural world" (p. 6), and they are often "better equipped to live up to academic internationalisation [sic] -policies" (p. 6).

With these as rationale, that is, the benefits international research holds for scholars, students, and higher education and the role intercultural communication scholars can play in academic internationalizing policies (Stier, 2006), the purpose of this chapter is to contribute to the conversation on internationalizing the communication curriculum. To that end, we begin by reviewing the origin and evolution of the field of intercultural communication to identify indicators of internationalization in the field's trajectory. Thereafter, we conduct a quantitative content analysis of keywords in articles published in 25 top-tier communication journals between 2000–2017; these keywords represent foundational concepts and diverse paradigms in intercultural communication scholarship.

Origin and Evolution of the Field of Intercultural Communication: An Overview

The roots of intercultural communication as a field of study can be traced to the Foreign Service Institute (FSI) of the US Department of State in the 1940s (Gudykunst & Kim, 1984). FSI, in its response to what was considered to be failure by US diplomats to work well and effectively with other cultures in international settings, brought together scholars from linguistics and anthropology (Leeds-Hurwitz, 1990). Leeds-Hurwitz notes that this group of scholars defined culture as "a system of patterns which must be learned . . . . [and] communication, like culture is equally patterned, learned, and analyzable" (p. 268). This definition of culture led to an approach to intercultural communication that was 'analytical' rather than 'holistic' using what are essentially uniform and stable social categories with a scientific goal of "arriving at lawlike principles and patterns in human behavior" (Kim, 2016, p. 141).

In 1960, Edward Hall and William Whyte, two of the earliest and foundational intercultural scholars, stressed that culture needs to be studied not as a general focus where it is seen as applicable to an entire group or population, as in the FSI approach, but rather, as interaction between members of different cultures. By the 1970s, communication scholars were calling for more intensive research by communication scientists (Samovar & Porter, 1972) to focus on the possibilities and challenges of specific methodologies/methods for studying intercultural communication dynamics, including survey research, controlled experiments, and ethnographic analyses (Hwang, 1973). In his discussion, Hwang (1973) outlined key difficulties of these three methods and implications for using these in intercultural communication research. He indicated that survey research has inherent problems related to sampling and fieldwork—there are logistic difficulties, low cooperation rates, and governmental issues such as incomplete or outdated data for available information, the inability to administer surveys because of varying governmental ideologies, and so on. Controlled experiments suffer from lack of comparable test environments, issues of translation associated with foreign test instruments, and/or lack of reliability and validity in testing instruments. In conducting ethnographic studies, similar issues of noncomparable test units arise as well as researcher biases in coding and observation. Essentially, Hwang suggested, each of these methods has issues with establishing equivalence and precision in translation that should be considered for intercultural work.

Gudykunst (1983) was the first to do a systematic review of intercultural communication theories. His work in 1984 titled "Communicating with strangers: An approach to intercultural communication" begins by looking at notions of cultural variation such as collectivism versus individualism and high versus low context. Throughout this decade, Gudykunst (1984) and other theorists such as Kim (1988), Ting-Toomey (1988), and Spitzberg (1988) continued theory-building work, offered further empirical support for theories about how people from different groups communicate, and research in general on all aspects of intercultural communication (Croucher et al., 2015).

Scholars such as Dreama Moon (1996), in her analysis of culture, identified trends in previous research in the way that this term is defined. She suggested that studies either focused on the nation-state or conceptualized culture "in terms of race, social class, and gender identity" (p. 72) with social debates in the 1970s influencing intercultural communication research:

> Up until about 1977, "culture" is conceptualized in a variety of ways . . . diverse analytical methods are utilized, and there is deep interest in how intersections between various nodes of cultural identity both play out in, and are constructed by, communication. Starting about 1978, "culture" comes to be conceived almost entirely in terms of "nation-state" and by 1980, "culture" is predominantly configured as a variable in positivist research projects.
>
> (p. 73)

Work also began focusing on developing specific manifestations of culture (Hofstede, 1998) such as how culture is influenced by the structure of language. The Sapir-Whorf (Sapir, 1929) hypothesis examines this linguistic idea more specifically by suggesting that the meaning of language is not fixed but ever changing, and as it changes, culture both changes language (linguistic relativity) and is changed by language (language determinism).

As work in the field of intercultural communication moved forward in the next two decades, themes of identity and acculturation (Young Yun, 2017), cultural empathy (Jackson, 2008), adaptation (Berry, 2003; Kim, 2001), and intercultural competence (Arasaratnam-Smith, 2017) became more predominant. Asante, Miike, and Yin (2014) suggested that research in this field is "increasingly confronted by more fundamental issues of identity, community, and humanity . . . intercultural communication is the only way to mitigate identity politics, social disintegration, religious conflicts, and ecological vulnerability in the global village" (p. 1).

Kim (2016), in her mapping of the domain of intercultural communication, identified four main paradigmatic/methodological perspectives focused on intercultural communication: the neo-positivist, systems, interpretive, and critical approaches. Kim (2016) called for an integration of emic and etic perspectives, longitudinal studies, and empirical data beyond historically situated and localized cases. Kim also identified (p. 142) five interrelated and often overlapping themes that have been researched and developed: "intrapersonal process in intercultural communication, intercultural communication competence, adaptation to a new culture, cultural identity in intercultural contexts, and more recently, power inequality in intercultural relations." As Kim (2017) observed, cultural discourses have become more prevalent across disciplines, and critical intercultural communication research has increased and become the focus for more and more scholars in this area. Croucher et al. (2015) identified this as a break from nation-based approaches to challenges faced by various disciplines as they explored identity and other core concepts. Particularly, they noted the need for investigating specific contexts and how power relations permeate culture.

Croucher et al. (2015), noted that the field of intercultural communication has evolved in different ways. They asserted in their overview of the field that location has been a large factor in perspectives and approaches to intercultural communication theories and research. Asante et al. suggested that the field may still not be truly intercultural and that "the topics we pursue, the theories we build, the methods we employ, and the materials we read [may not] adequately respond to the diversity of our communication experiences in a globalizing world" (2014, pp. 1–2). This overview suggests that the field of intercultural communication, since its inception, has evidenced the presence of international elements in theoretical, methodological, processual, and/or functional/applied aspects; however, this presence has been sporadic and occasional instead of consistent and holistic.

Selection of Journals and Articles: A Quantitative Analysis

Twenty-five journals were reviewed for this study: *Argumentation and Advocacy, Communication Education, Communication Monographs, Communication Quarterly, Communication Reports, Communication Research, Communication Research Reports, Communication Studies, Communication Theory, Critical Studies in (Mass) Media Communication, Howard Journal of Communication, Human Communication Research, Journal of Applied Communication Research, Journal of Broadcasting and Electronic Media, Journal of Communication, Journal of Intercultural Communication Research, Journal of International and Intercultural Communication, Journalism and Mass Communication Quarterly, Philosophy and Rhetoric, Qualitative Research Reports in Communication, Quarterly Journal of Speech, Southern Communication Journal, Text and Performance Quarterly,*

Western Journal of Communication, and *Women's Studies in Communication*. Although not an all-inclusive list, these journals with diverse aims and scope were selected because of their reputation as some of the most prominent and recognized journals in the field of communication (Griffin, Bolkan, & Dahlbach, 2018); in addition, despite the fact that most of these journals were not essentially "intercultural," due to their prominence and the interdisciplinary, multi-field, and multi-modal characteristic of both communication and intercultural work, we deemed it necessary to analyze these journals to comment on the state of internationalization of intercultural communication scholarship.

Based on the work of Croucher et al. (2015), a survey of the origin and evolution of the field of intercultural communication, and review of the *International Encyclopedia of Intercultural Communication* (Kim, 2017), 37 keywords were identified in intercultural communication research for this study. These keywords cannot be exhaustive, but they represent foundational concepts and diverse paradigmatic approaches to the study of intercultural communication. They serve as a starting point to examine the state of internationalization in intercultural communication scholarship: intercultural, cross-cultural, inter-ethnic, co-cultural, co-culture, Hofstede, individualism, collectivism, self-construal, high/low-context, uncertainty avoidance, power distance, masculinity/femininity, face negotiation theory, expectancy violations theory, anxiety uncertainty management, communication accommodation theory, linguistic relativism, cultural convergence, cultural identity, acculturation, assimilation, cultural adaptation, cultural fusion, intercultural competence, culture shock, ethnicity, diaspora, immigrant, sojourner, international student, globalization, social justice, second-language, refugee, expatriate, and glocal. All articles featuring one of these keywords published between 2000 and 2017 in the 25 journals were reviewed, excluding editorial welcomes, book reviews, and errata. Table 3.1 lists the journals and the number of times each keyword was reported in each journal between 2000 and 2017. Most articles included more than one keyword.

Table 3.1 Journal and Intercultural Communication Keywords from 2000 to 2017

Journal	Number of Articles		Number of Articles
Argumentation and Advocacy (*n* = 27)			
Intercultural	1	Diaspora	1
Globalization	3	Social Justice	10
Co-cultural	3	Co-culture	3
High/low-context	2	Masculinity/femininity	2
Expectancy violations theory	1	Cultural identity	1
Communication Education (*n* = 45)			
Intercultural	11	Cross-cultural	5
Ethnicity	2	International Student	3
Social Justice	1	Second-Language	15
Collectivism	2	Uncertainty avoidance	3
Cultural identity	2	Acculturation	1

(Continued)

Table 3.1 (Continued)

Journal	Number of Articles	Number of Articles	
Communication Monographs (n = 29)			
Intercultural	4	Cross-cultural	4
Ethnicity	1	Immigrant	2
Globalization	4	Social Justice	1
Individualism	2	Collectivism	2
Masculinity/femininity	2	Cultural identity	3
Acculturation	1	Assimilation	3
Communication Quarterly (n = 36)			
Intercultural	20	Cross-cultural	6
Ethnicity	7	Diaspora	2
International Student	1		
Communication Reports (n = 9)			
Intercultural	4	Second-Language	2
Individualism	1	Collectivism	1
Assimilation	1		
Intercultural	1	Cross-cultural	5
Ethnicity	13	Globalization	2
Hofstede	1	Individualism	4
Collectivism	5	Assimilation	3
Communication Research Reports (n = 33)			
Intercultural	6	Cross-cultural	6
Ethnicity	2	Immigrant	1
Sojourner	1	Refugee	1
Inter-ethnic	3	Hofstede	2
Individualism	1	Self-Construal	1
Uncertainty Avoidance	1	Masculinity/femininity	1
Expectancy violations theory	1	Cultural identity	4
Acculturation	1	Assimilation	1
Communication Studies (n = 32)			
Intercultural	2	Cross-cultural	1
Ethnicity	2	Immigrant	1
Globalization	2	Co-cultural	4
Co-culture	4	Hofstede	1
Individualism	1	Collectivism	1
High/low-context	2	Masculinity/femininity	3
Expectancy violations theory	3	Cultural identity	2
Assimilation	2		
Communication Theory (n = 6)			
Intercultural	2	Cross-cultural	1
Globalization	3		

Journal	Number of Articles		Number of Articles
Critical Studies in (Mass) Media Communication (n = 40)			
Intercultural	1	Cross-cultural	11
Ethnicity	2	Diaspora	1
Globalization	9	Refugee	1
Masculinity/femininity	10	Cultural identity	2
Assimilation	2	Culture Shock	1
Howard Journal of Communications (n = 138)			
Intercultural	30	Cross-cultural	2
Ethnicity	42	Diaspora	2
Immigrant	5	Sojourner	1
International Student	1	Globalization	2
Refugee	2	Expatriate	1
Co-cultural	12	Co-culture	
Individualism	3	Collectivism	
High/low context	1	Masculinity/femininity	4
Cultural identity	10	Acculturation	5
Cultural Adaptation	3		
Human Communication Research (n = 31)			
Intercultural	1	Co-cultural	1
Self-Construal	8	Uncertainty Avoidance	3
Uncertainty Avoidance	1	Linguistic Relativism	3
Cultural Convergence	1	Cultural identity	2
Acculturation	5	Assimilation	3
Cultural Adaptation	3		
Journal of Applied Communication Research (n = 28)			
Intercultural	10	Cross-cultural	2
Co-cultural	3	Co-culture	1
Hofstede	1	Individualism	1
Collectivism	5	Self-Construal	1
High/low context	2	Uncertainty Avoidance	1
Assimilation	1		
Journal of Broadcasting and Electronic Media (n = 0)			
Journal of Communication (n = 38)			
Ethnicity	1	Immigrant	1
Refugee	1	Co-cultural	5
Co-culture	5	Individualism	1
Uncertainty Avoidance	2	Power distance	8
Masculinity/femininity	10	Face Negotiation Theory	2
Cultural identity	2		

(Continued)

Table 3.1 (Continued)

Journal	Number of Articles		Number of Articles
Journal of Intercultural Communication Research (n = 256)			
Intercultural	75	Cross-cultural	31
Ethnicity	13	Co-cultural	1
Co-culture	1	Hofstede	4
Individualism	12	Collectivism	13
Immigrant	8	International Student	2
Globalization	1	Social Justice	1
Refugee	3	Expatriate	1
Self-Construal	3	High/low context	4
Uncertainty Avoidance	1	Power distance	5
Masculinity/femininity	17	Face Negotiation Theory	1
Cultural identity	16	Acculturation	12
Assimilation	6	Cultural Adaptation	11
Cultural fusion	2	Intercultural Competence	11
Culture Shock	2		
Journal of International and Intercultural Communication (n = 122)			
Intercultural	33	Cross-cultural	8
Ethnicity	5	Co-cultural	3
Co-culture	3	Diaspora	4
Immigrant	7	Globalization	8
Social Justice	2	Second-Language	2
Refugee	3	Individualism	3
Collectivism	2	Self-Construal	3
Power distance	1	Masculinity/femininity	1
Face Negotiation Theory	2	Cultural Convergence	1
Cultural identity	12	Acculturation	7
Assimilation	2	Cultural Adaptation	8
Cultural fusion	2		
Journalism and Mass Communication Quarterly (n = 6)			
Ethnicity	1	Immigrant	3
Globalization	1	Acculturation	1
Philosophy & Rhetoric (n = 16)			
Individualism	5	Collectivism	2
Refugee	1	Diaspora	1
Cultural identity	7		
Qualitative Research Reports in Communication (n = 18)			
Intercultural	1	Ethnicity	4
Social Justice	1	Hofstede	1
Individualism	1	Cultural identity	6
Acculturation	1	Assimilation	2
Cultural Adaptation	1		

Journal	Number of Articles		Number of Articles
Quarterly Journal of Speech (n = 10)			
Intercultural	1	Cross-cultural	1
Ethnicity	1	Globalization	4
Social Justice	1	Cultural identity	1
Acculturation	1		
Southern Communication Journal (n = 3)			
Refugee	1	Self-Construal	2
Text and Performance Quarterly (n = 11)			
Intercultural	2	Diaspora	1
Globalization	5	Ethnicity	1
Refugee	2		
Western Journal of Communication (n = 42)			
Intercultural	6	Cross-cultural	1
Ethnicity	2	Co-cultural	2
Immigrant	1	Globalization	1
Social Justice	3	Uncertainty Avoidance	6
Power distance	9	Refugee	2
Face Negotiation Theory	1	Expectancy Violations Theory	4
Communication Accommodation	2	Cultural identity	2
Women's Studies in Communication (n = 8)			
Ethnicity	1	Cross-cultural	1
Globalization	1	Co-cultural	1
Individualism	1	Co-culture	1
Masculinity/femininity	1	Cultural identity	1

Findings

The results reveal that from 2000 to 2017, the three journals that primarily focus on research exploring "intercultural" dynamics had articles with the most references to the keywords: *Journal of Intercultural Communication Research* ($n = 256$ keywords), *Howard Journal of Communications* ($n = 138$ keywords), and *Journal of International and Intercultural Communication* ($n = 122$ keywords). The keywords that featured in each of these journals also manifested the research paradigm/s—positivist/post-positivist, interpretive, critical—each seemed to align with most. For instance, the *Journal of Intercultural Communication Research* had keywords like masculinity/femininity, individualism, collectivism, cultural identity, appear several times; these keywords (concepts) are usually found in more positivist/post-positivist or interpretive framings of intercultural communication, thus pointing to this journal's paradigmatic leaning between 2000–2017. Similarly, the *Howard Journal of Communications* showed a more critical leaning, with frequent presence of keywords such as co-cultural and co-culture. The *Journal of International and Intercultural Communication*, based on the keyword analysis, did not exhibit an inclination for any one paradigm over the other.

Although these three journals' paradigmatic orientations could be surmised, their international quotient could not. The keywords that were most frequent across all three journals were intercultural, ethnicity, masculinity/femininity, cultural identity, cross-cultural; however, without knowledge of context, it was difficult to interpret whether these keywords were employed in research focusing on international dynamics. There was minimal presence of keywords with obvious international denotation, such as immigrant, refugee, globalization.

Aside from these three journals, none of the other journals had more than 50 keywords in the time span selected for this study. Even with that, the use of certain keywords more than others suggested these journals' paradigmatic leanings (in most cases); nevertheless, these journals rarely featured keywords that had apparent international signification. *Communication Theory* (n = 6), *Southern Communication Journal* (n = 3), and *Journal of Broadcasting and Electronic Media* (n = 0) had the lowest number of keywords referenced.

Table 3.2 lists the keywords from 2000 to 2017 from most frequently occurring to least frequently occurring across all the journals. Intercultural (n = 211), ethnicity (n =100), cross-cultural (n = 86), cultural identity (n = 73), and masculinity/femininity (n = 51) were the most frequently occurring; here too, although presence of these keywords insinuated paradigmatic leanings, it did not manifest obvious international focus. Without knowledge of context of use, their definitional approach, and the way their relationship with culture was framed, it was difficult to comprehend the keywords' (and consequently journals') international quotient. Anxiety uncertainty management (n = 0), glocal (n = 0), cultural convergence (n = 2), communication accommodation theory (n = 2), culture shock (n = 2), sojourner (n = 2), and expatriate (n = 2) were the least frequently occurring keywords across all journals. The application of these keywords, few of which have obvious international denotation (glocal, sojourner, expatriate), less than five times between 2000–2017 (and no clear indication of international application of keywords more frequent in these journals, as mentioned), pointed to a slim focus on internationalization in the last two decades in the 25 communication journals selected for this investigation.

Discussion: The State of Affairs

A review of the origin and evolution of the field of intercultural communication manifested some noteworthy moments of internationalization. For instance, a primary imperative behind the origin of the field, that is, the need for US diplomats to work effectively with other cultures in international settings, the synonymizing of culture with the idea of the nation-state, intercultural scholars' preoccupation with issues of identity, community, humanity in a global context, to name a few. Regardless of these exemplars, internationalization has failed to be a consistent and essential characteristic of the field of intercultural communication.

The content analysis of keywords pointed to robust intercultural work in the three main journals with 'intercultural' aims and scope, namely, *Journal of Intercultural Communication Research*, *Howard Journal of* Communications, and *Journal of International and Intercultural Communication*; but these journals featured

Table 3.2 Most Frequently to Least Frequently Occurring Keywords: 2000 to 2017

Keyword	n
Intercultural	211
Ethnicity	100
Cross-Cultural	86
Cultural Identity	73
Masculinity/Femininity	51
Globalization	46
Individualism	36
Acculturation	35
Collectivism	34
Co-Cultural	33
Co-Culture	30
Immigrant	29
Assimilation	26
Cultural Adaptation	26
Power Distance	23
Social Justice	20
Second-Language	19
Self-Construal	18
Refugee	16
Uncertainty Avoidance	15
Diaspora	12
Intercultural Competence	11
Hofstede	10
High/Low Context	10
Expectancy Violations Theory	9
International Student	7
Face Negotiation Theory	6
Cultural Fusion	4
Inter-ethnic	3
Linguistic Relativism	3
Expatriate	2
Sojourner	2
Culture Shock	2
Communication Accommodation Theory	2
Cultural Convergence	2
Glocal	0
Anxiety Uncertainty Management	0

sparse international scholarship. The other 22 top-tier communication journals rarely focused on either intercultural or international work. Thus, if intercultural efforts are considered indicators of the practice and/or possibility of internationalization (Stier, 2006), these journals did not exhibit strong international leanings.

Through this analysis, many of the selected journals' paradigmatic orientations could be inferred. Scholars working within certain paradigmatic frameworks, for instance positivist/post-positivist, often equate "culture" with "nation"; within that framing, all intercultural work can be characterized as international work. Therefore, journals with positivist/post-positivist leanings can be inferred to be essentially international. However, this claim risks being simplistic. Furthermore, despite awareness of paradigmatic leanings, the lack of knowledge of the context within which the keywords were used posed a challenge for inferring, with certainty, the international quotient of journals.

This, in fact, leads to a discussion of the shortcomings of this study and recommendations for more robust and nuanced evaluation of the state of internationalization in intercultural communication research. Future studies can benefit from being more systematic about choosing keywords for analysis; the list may never be exhaustive, but a simple word count of foundational concepts that represent diverse paradigms does not suffice. Foundational concepts may not always represent internationalization; manifestation of a paradigmatic leaning may not indicate internationalization. For nuanced and robust analyses, future projects should consider the following: start with a clear understanding of how important concepts such as culture and internationalization are framed for a study and choose a unit/s of analysis based on these study-specific conceptualizations; analysis of not just keywords but also words and phrases that cluster around the keywords; designate phrases, sentences, and/or article titles as units of analysis; instead of focusing only on the substantive elements of research published, examine the demographic profile of authors to assess a journal's international quotient.

In conclusion, it becomes imperative to restate that international research plays an important role in contributing to curriculum internationalization. Intercultural scholars, because of their propensity for global work (Stier, 2006) and heightened skills (NCA, 2017) such as their sensitivity to international dynamics, perceptiveness, and comprehensive communication analysis that take into consideration the complex interconnections between the local and the global, have a pivotal role (perhaps more than scholars in other fields of communication) to play in academic internationalization and in facilitating, sustaining, and strengthening internationalization of the communication curriculum. The findings of this study, albeit with its shortcomings, show that the trend for international research and scholarship in the field is feeble; but for all the reasons stated, intercultural scholars must venture beyond the local and national to embrace the global and international in their research. After all, as Stier (2006) claims, "the role of intercultural communication education [which is inherently connected to intercultural research] in attaining the goals of [curricular and academic] internationalisation [sic] is essential" (p. 6).

References

Alexander, B. K., Arasaratnam, L. A., Durham, A., Flores, L., Leeds-Hurwitz, W., & Mendoza, S. L., Halualani, R. (2014). Identifying key intercultural urgencies, issues, and challenges in today's world: Connecting our scholarship to dynamic contexts and historical moments. *Journal of International and Intercultural Communication, 7*, 38–67.

Appadurai, A. (1996). *Modernity at large: Cultural dimensions of globalization*. Minneapolis: University of Minnesota Press.

Arasaratnam-Smith, L. A. (2017). Intercultural communication competence. In K. Young Yun (Ed.), *The international encyclopedia of intercultural communication*. Hoboken, NJ: Wiley Online Library and John Wiley & Sons, Inc.

Asante, M. K., Miike, Y., & Yin, J. (2014). New directions for intercultural communication research. In M. K. Asante, Y. Miike, & J. Yin (Eds.), *The global intercultural communication reader*. New York, NY: Taylor & Francis.

Bauman, Z. (2000). *Globalisering*. Lund: Studentlitteratur.

Beck, U. (1998). *Vad Innebär Globaliseringen? Missuppfattningar och Möjliga Svar*. Göteborg: Daidalos.

Berry, J. W. (2003). Conceptual approaches to acculturation. In K. M. Chun, P. Balls Organista, & G. Marin (Eds.), *Acculturation: Advances in theory, measurement, and applied research*. Washington, DC: American Psychological Association.
Castells, M. (2002). *Internetgalaxen: Reflektioner om Internet, Ekonomi och Samhälle*. Göteborg: Daidalos.
Croucher, S. M., Sommier, M., & Rahmani, D. (2015). Intercultural communication: Where we've been, where we're going, issues we face. *Communication Research and Practice, 1*, 71–87.
Giddens, A. (1996). *Modernitetens följder*. Lund: Studentlitteratur.
Griffin, D. J., Bolkan, S., & Dahlbach, B. J. (2018). Scholarly productivity in communication studies: Five-year review 2012–2016. *Communication Education, 67*, 88–101.
Gudykunst, W. B. (1983). *Intercultural communication theory: Current perspectives*. Los Angeles, CA: Sage.
Gudykunst, W. B., & Kim, Y. Y. (1984). *Communicating with strangers: An approach to intercultural communication*. New York, NY: Random House.
Hall, E. T., & Whyte, W. F. (1960). Intercultural communication: A guide to men of action. *International Executive, 2*, 14–15.
Hofstede, G. (1998). Attitudes, values and organizational culture: Disentangling the concepts. *Organization Studies, 3*, 477.
Hwang, J. C. (1973). Problems of intercultural communication research. *Communication, 2*, 107–116.
Jackson, J. B. (2008). Globalization, internationalization, and short-term stays abroad. *International Journal of Intercultural Relations, 32*, 349–358.
Kim, Y. Y. (1988). *Communication and cross-cultural adaptation: An integrative theory*. Thousand Oaks, CA: Sage.
Kim, Y. Y. (2001). *Becoming intercultural: An integrative theory of communication and cross-cultural adaptation*. Thousand Oaks, CA: Sage Publications.
Kim, Y. Y. (2016). Mapping the domain of intercultural communication: An overview. *Annals of the International Communication Association, 24*, 139–156.
Kim, Y. Y. (Ed.). (2017). *The international encyclopedia of intercultural communication*. Hoboken, NJ: Wiley Blackwell.
Leeds-Hurwitz, W. (1990). Notes in the history of intercultural communication: The Foreign Service Institute and the mandate for intercultural training. *Quarterly Journal of Speech, 76*, 262–281.
Moon, D. G. (1996). Concepts of "culture": Implications for intercultural communication research. *Communication Quarterly, 44*, 70–84.
National Communication Association. (2017). *Internationalizing the communication discipline*. Retrieved from www.natcom.org/sites/default/files/pages/Internationalization_Internationalizi ng_Communication.PDF
Samovar, L., & Porter, R. (1972). *Intercultural communication: A reader*. Belmont, CA: Wadsworth Publishing Co.
Sapir, E. (1929). The status of linguistics as a science. *Language, 5*, 207–214.
Spitzberg, B. H. (1988). Communication competence: Measures of perceived effectiveness. In C. Tardy (Ed.), *A handbook for the study of human communication*. Norwood, NJ: Ablex.
Stier, J. (2006). Internationalisation, intercultural communication and intercultural competence. *Journal of Intercultural Communication, 11*, 1–11.
Ting-Toomey, S. (1988). Intercultural conflicts: A face-negotiation theory. In Y. Y. Kim & W. B. Gudykunst (Eds.), *Theories in intercultural communication*. Newbury Park, CA: Sage Publications.
Young Yun, K. (2017). Identity and intercultural communication. In K. Young Yun (Ed.), *The international encyclopedia of intercultural communication*. Hoboken, NJ: Wiley Online Library and John Wiley & Sons, Inc.

4 The Internationalization of a Communication Studies Major
A Global Redesign

Joseph P. Zompetti, John R. Baldwin, and Lance Lippert

Introduction

Incorporating international components into a course or completely overhauling a course can be formidable tasks. Simply adding international elements may seem daunting because some may find teaching international issues intimidating (Green, 2007), or they may lack sufficient incentives to introduce new global concepts into their courses (Lee, 2006). Recrafting an entire course can also be challenging, as it involves developing new learning outcomes, course content, exercises, assignments, and deliverables (Gilchrist, Mundy, Felten, & Shields, 2003). Despite these challenges, we embarked on internationalizing the curriculum of our major of communication studies. In this essay, we describe our experience of internationalizing the curriculum as we redesigned our major to intentionally integrate global learning in our classes. First, we discuss the background of teaching internationalization, learning outcomes, and the stages of our internationalization process. Next, we present data from a pre-test conducted on our targeted courses—courses that were a part of our redesign process and that fulfill core requirements for all of our majors. Finally, we reflect on the positive experiences and challenges, with ideas on how to move forward. Overall, we discuss how we are implementing a theory-based approach to internationalizing a communication major as an entire process—research, planning, grant requests, workshop trainings, assessment procedures—so that others interested in an internationalized communication curriculum can learn from our trials and successes.

Background

In 2017, we obtained a grant from our international studies office to internationalize the curriculum of our communication studies major. Our idea was to ask faculty to redesign their courses to be "global" in nature or to add a key component to their existing courses that would be international in nature. The grant included money to hire an expert to conduct faculty workshops, stipends for faculty to incorporate global learning in their courses, and resources to help our understanding of internationalization in a higher education context. Our efforts echoed those of Niehaus and Williams (2016), who argue that some faculty are resistant to internationalization because they lack confidence in their own teaching of international material, they do not realize professional benefits of incorporating internationalization into their courses, and they do not understand how they can grow from teaching this type of material. Many faculty fail to see how internationalization goes beyond what they "*do*" because they need to "actually transform what and how they *think*"

(2016, p. 72). We located an expert in teaching and researching intercultural and international issues and invited faculty—offering a stipend for following through with the idea of internationalization—to attend training workshops in the spring and fall of 2018, with a goal of introducing international components in the curriculum in spring 2019.

For many faculty, integrating global components can be challenging. Communication studies is a general communication major (which is common in universities although it may be called a different name) that includes interpersonal, intercultural, rhetorical, political, organizational, small-group, persuasive, and nonverbal communication, along with the basic public speaking course and communication theory course. For courses in rhetoric, political communication, and intercultural communication, introducing international concepts is rather easy. For other courses, the connection to internationalization is less obvious. Thus, we firmly believed faculty training workshops were imperative.

Given the parameters of the grant and courses under consideration, we hoped that we could—at a minimum—introduce international ideas into each course. Since faculty have academic freedom, we could not make internationalization compulsory. By providing financial incentives and by marketing this process as beneficial with a small impact on instructor workload, we anticipated that most, if not all, of our colleagues would participate.

Relevant Literature

We envisioned an intentional and integrated engagement with internationalization in our communication studies curriculum. We know internationalization is not new to higher education, nor is it a new concept for the communication discipline. In fact, we draw from previous work on internationalizing the curriculum, internationalizing course redesign, assessment of internationalizing curricula, and internationalizing higher education.

Global Learning

Global learning addresses pedagogical approaches that foster international competencies in domestic classrooms (Green & Shoenberg, 2006). Hovland (2016) defines global learning as:

> A critical analysis of and an engagement with complex, interdependent global systems and legacies (such as natural, physical, social, cultural, economic, and political) and their implications for people's lives and the earth's sustainability. Through global learning, students should (1) become informed, open-minded, and responsible people who are attentive to diversity across the spectrum of differences; (2) seek to understand how their actions affect both local and global communities; and (3) address the world's most pressing and enduring issues collaboratively and equitably.
>
> (pp. 6–7)

Doscher and Landorf (2018) stress that global learning is a pedagogical *process* that stresses skills to address "complex problems that transcend borders," since it "enables participants to discern the interconnectedness of local and global well-being" (n.p.). Global learning involves the awareness of diverse perspectives from multiple cultural vantage points so that citizens realize the interconnected relationships between different peoples (Whitehead, 2018).

For global learning to be "intentional" and "integrated," courses should be "sequenced and scaffolded" (Smith, 2015, p. 6) so that knowledge can be cumulatively cross-applied across courses (Mezirow, 1991). Rather than adding an international element in only some instances, this approach provides knowledge reinforcement. Research has demonstrated the effectiveness of this pedagogical approach (Anderson & Szabo, 2007; Blondin & Gable, 2018; Dell & Wood, 2010). Smith (2015) argues, "Students need to see issues of culture and diversity as integral to knowing and understanding any body of knowledge and their world; otherwise, those issues can be easily dismissed" (p. 8). Therefore, internationalization should be "*embedded* in module and course learning outcomes" as classes are planned and sequenced into departmental units (Jones & Killick, 2013, pp. 165–166, emphasis in original).

While learning about other cultures occurs in study-abroad experiences, many aspects of global learning can occur in a classroom. This happens out of necessity, since most students cannot afford to travel internationally. Additionally:

> Even for those students who do go abroad or attend campus events, the curriculum is still the foundation of a college education. Thus, internationalizing the curriculum—that is infusing international, global, and intercultural perspectives across courses and programs—is the key strategy to ensure that *all* students learn about other nations, languages, cultures, and histories, and global issues.
> (Green & Shoenberg, 2006, p. 1, emphasis in original)

Hence, we advocate study-abroad experiences, but we also believe that they are not the only way students can experience and learn about other cultures.

Global learning in higher education frequently occurs only as an element in one course that lacks connectivity to concepts taught in other courses, without integration into the overall curriculum (Green & Shoenberg, 2006). If we intentionally integrate internationalization into our courses, majors, units, and departments, then learning can become "transformative" for student awareness as well as for skill development (Schneider, 2016). Intentionality requires that we align our goals of teaching skills and competencies with well-articulated student learning outcomes (Green, 2012). One such set of outcomes associated with Bloom's Taxonomy comprises six dimensions of knowledge, skills, and attitudes, as defined by the Association of American Colleges and Universities (Clayton-Pedersen, Parker, Smith, Moreno, & Teraguchi, 2007): global self-awareness, perspective-taking, cultural diversity, personal and social responsibility, understanding global systems, and applying knowledge to contemporary global contexts (Anderson & Blair, 2013). Integration of global learning in intentional ways facilitates student critical thinking, reflection, perspective taking, and problem solving, especially since global learning activities foster these skills (Blondin & Gable, 2018; Dell & Wood, 2010). Furthermore, aligning the goals of global learning with student outcomes can facilitate programmatic assessment (Green & Shoenberg, 2006), vital for securing funding for internationalization initiatives and demonstrating the impact of global learning on students, especially because it is difficult to quantify how internationalization benefits students (Vainio-Mattila, 2009).

Internationalization of the Curriculum

Related to the global learning literature is the scholarship of Internationalization of the Curriculum (IoC) defined as "the incorporation of an international and intercultural dimension into the content of the curriculum as well as the teaching and learning arrangements and support services of a program of study" (Leask, 2009, p. 209). IoC has the goal of integrating global learning within a curriculum of study, not just a single course, that prepares faculty and staff with the tools necessary for its effective implementation (van der Wende, 1997). According to Leask (2013a), there are five stages in the process of IoC: review and reflect (on what is currently offered), imagine (the vision and ideal state of an internationalized curriculum), revise and plan (to see what is needed to add and delete from current offerings), act (implement the process, identifying the blockers and enablers or the attitudinal and structural helpers or constraints to the overall objective), and evaluate (assess the process in accordance with student learning objectives; see also Leask, 2015; Leask, Whitsed, & Green, 2012a, 2012b). Additionally, some scholars suggest we add reflection (critically question the process to acknowledge its strengths and weaknesses for proper amending, if necessary) to the process (Dell & Wood, 2010; Leask, 2015; Leask & Beelen, 2010).

Leask (2013b) elaborates on blockers and enablers. Key blockers include absence of financial resources, policies for tenure and promotion, skepticism among staff, staff's lack of skills or competencies, limited disciplinary ways of thinking, and "a lack of guidance in connecting institutional policy and the curriculum" (p. 114). In contrast, significant enablers include:

> International scholarships and service as criteria in tenure and promotion as well as in recruitment guidelines; The provision of small grants as springboards to promote greater involvement in internationalization . . . The opportunity for staff to share their learning and experiences with others in facilitated workshops; and The establishment of institutional disciplinary, cross-disciplinary, and cross-institutional networks of champions and leaders in IoC.
>
> (p. 114)

The process scaffolds knowledge acquisition, providing a unified framework for overlapping and meaningful instruction of global learning. Likewise, internationalizing courses and the curriculum invites diverse ways of knowing, as well as "pedagogies that promote cross-cultural understanding" and "the development of the knowledge, skills, and values" to "successfully engage with others in an increasingly interconnected and interdependent world" (Van Gyn, Schuerholz-Lehr, Caws, & Preece, 2009, pp. 26–27).

IoC is often viewed as "the most important strategy institutions can use to ensure that *all* students acquire the knowledge, skills, and attitudes they will need as citizens and workers in a rapidly changing and globalized world" (Green & Shoenberg, 2006, p. iii, emphasis in original). IoC must be intentional, carefully planned, deliberate, and flexible (Smith, 2015), as IoC is a process of change and transition, not a one-size-fits-all policy (Knight, 2012; Leask, 2015). Because each course, each department, and each university is different, the process of IoC obviously must be based on the specific contextual needs of the particular learning environment.

Because IoC involves alterations to content and the process of curriculum development, it offers students unique opportunities for learning global competencies and skills (Smith, 2015). Infusing internationalization into classes allows domestic students to learn about the world without the prohibitive cost of travel. For international students and students who have the privilege of studying abroad, internationalizing the curriculum provides opportunities to share experiences with peers and to understand what they experienced during their travel/s. At its core, IoC "provides an exposure to and an awareness of international and global issues that profoundly impact the worlds of the majority of our students" (p. 4).

Internationalization of Communication Studies

Dewine (1995) discusses how their university's interpersonal communication major integrated internationalization into the curriculum and provided expanded study abroad opportunities and faculty exchanges with a university in Thailand. Their program yielded expected and unanticipated benefits, most notably regarding the communication between two distinct cultural groups. In a similar study, Taylor (2001) examines the inclusion of internationalization assignments in public relations courses. Taylor argues that every "traditional course in the public relations curriculum can be modified to include a focus on international public relations issues" (p. 82). Taylor, like other scholars, supports the positive aspects of including international dimensions in PR courses (e.g., Chia, 2009; Fitch, 2012, 2013). Finally, Sypris (1993) explains that Communication courses in community colleges should adopt international perspectives, such as interpersonal communication, business communication, nonverbal communication, and intercultural communication. These studies tend only to identify individual courses—not a major—and they undertheorize the prospect of integrating internationalization into communication courses.

Intercultural Competence

Internationalization efforts are fundamentally concerned with interactions between different cultures (Leask & Beelen, 2010). To link global learning to communication studies, we integrated competencies and instruments from the intercultural communication literature, specifically the Intercultural Communication Competence (ICC) model. According to Spitzberg and Chagnon (2009), intercultural competence is "the appropriate and effective management of interaction between people who, to some degree or another, represent different or divergent affective, cognitive, and behavioral orientations to the world" (p. 7). Spitzberg (2000) frames ICC as including perceived effectiveness (task accomplishment) and appropriateness (cultural acceptability) of someone's behavior. ICC focuses on the "process of dyadic interaction as a function of two individuals' motivation to communicate, knowledge of communication in that context, and skills in implementing their motivation and knowledge" (p. 380).

A comprehensive test of the ICC model, the Integrated Model of Intercultural Communication Competence (IMICC), uses an "emic approach to develop a model of ICC that incorporates multiple cultural perspectives into its construction" (Arasaratnam, Banerjee, & Dembek, 2008, p. 103). The IMICC incorporates the perceiver's perspective, especially perspectives from various cultural orientations. In 2010, Arasaratnam, Banerjee, and Dembek (2010) refined the model to ultimately include attitudes toward other cultures, empathy, sensation seeking, motivation, and interaction involvement. Spitzberg (2012) explains that culture plays a role in intercultural competence through "the motivation, knowledge, and skills of the interactants involved" (p. 432). Thus, the basic model of ICC can help us understand and appreciate the cognitive (knowledge, awareness), affective (motivation, sensitivity), or behavioral (skills, adroitness) aspects of competence (Chen & Young, 2010).

Velten and Dodd (2016) report on the effect of ICC competency-based teaching, especially if such teaching yields higher levels of intercultural competency among students preparing for a study-abroad experience. Their study reinforces the validity of ICC measures but also supports that students' competencies are significantly better after ICC-related teaching in 11 of 17 different areas. The three areas with the strongest results are managing uncertainty, family accommodation, and social inclusion. Thus, this study supports that ICC measures are effective and useful. Therefore, we incorporated ICC-related measures into our own testing instrument.

Other Considerations

Finally, our efforts at internationalizing our communication studies major were informed by our previous work in course redesign. Higher education literature has discussed the course redesign process extensively (Gilchrist et al., 2003; Twigg, 2000). While the process of redesigning a course is extensive (our professional development workshops can include several weeks of instruction), it essentially involves linking course goals precisely with student learning outcomes. This relationship between goals and learning outcomes forms the skeleton of the entire course. Upon construction of the redesign, one adds specific course content, exercises, assignments, and readings. For example, our university—with facilitation by one of our authors—implemented a course redesign process for classes that adopt civic engagement initiatives. Based on that experience, we trained and encouraged communication studies faculty to integrate internationalization into their courses in a redesign fashion.

To internationalize our communication studies curriculum, we planned to engage in multiple course redesigns to carefully integrate global learning in the courses. Our goal was to scaffold global learning in cumulative ways as students move through course sequencing. We will conduct pre- and posttests in individual courses to measure student global learning in those specific courses and implement a pretest in an introductory communication studies course as students enter our program and later in their capstone course. This will allow us to measure individual student learning as well as assess programmatic success. Considering this process, we began to intentionally integrate internationalization into our major in the spring semester of 2019.

Implementation

Since one of our authors is a scholar in the area of international/intercultural training and teaching, our faculty training workshops were well prepared and implemented. However, we did not receive the attendance we had hoped. We announced our grant and our goals for this process at several faculty meetings, opened it for discussion, and encouraged colleagues to offer input or criticisms. With no objections and a general sense of excitement, we thought that once the process began, we would receive more broad-based participation. We offered one training in the spring semester (2018) and one in the fall (2018) so that integration could occur in spring of 2019. We notified everyone during the faculty meetings and sent out separate reminder emails about the training sessions. Nevertheless, about 40% of our communication studies faculty attended one or both of the workshops and participated in the integration process in 2019. While this level of participation was sufficient for us to move forward with our project, it limited the scope of internationalization and lessened its overall impact for students. Based on this experience, we now know we need to do at least three things for the future: (1) advertise the trainings and the initiative better (including the benefits of the program for both students and faculty), (2) work individually with colleagues to garner support (as opposed to broad-based announcements and emails), and (3) offer more trainings at varied times to accommodate participants' schedules.

Nevertheless, we believe that instructors who attended received valuable information regarding incorporating international content and pedagogy into their classes. We are tracking 12 undergraduate courses integrating global learning during the spring 2019 semester; participating faculty needed to demonstrate integration of global learning by submitting to us a copy of their syllabus for the designated course. Hence, we have preliminary data on pretest scores. At the time of this writing, we are in the middle of the implementation semester, so we lack finalized assessment data for our project. Our hope is that posttest data will demonstrate measurable learning associated with international issues in select courses, as well as provide pedagogical insights. If readers are interested in the survey instrument we used, they may contact us.

The classes range from lower-level to upper-level courses available as content electives and several sequence-designated courses (Introduction to Communication Theory, Communication & Social Issues, Nonverbal Communication, Communication Research Methods, Controversy & Contemporary Society, Human Communication & Aging, Political Communication, Family Communication, Organizational Communication, Intercultural Communication, Psychology of Language, and the Senior Capstone). Each course integrated some aspect of internationalization or global perspectives, either through course goals, learning outcomes, instructional activities, learning objectives, and/or course content, all of which were guided by the current literature (de Wit, 2009; Musil, 2006).

Instructional activities included readings, writing, small-group work, guest speakers, in-class structured learning experiences, debriefing, and reflection. Learning goals and outcomes from specific courses included:

1. You will become more globally aware when you learn how our communication patterns don't, in fact, dominate communication patterns around the world. You'll be a wiser tourist and a better worker in a multicultural organization, because you'll both recognize and understand the communication behaviors demonstrated by individuals from other countries and even be able to explain why others do what they do and communicate the way they communicate.
2. We will work to improve our intercultural nonverbal communication competence and explore the role of nonverbal communication in a global society.
3. Compare the aging process and views toward aging among different cultures and co-cultures.
4. Articulate different ways of being and enacting family across cultures and non-normative identities.
5. To identify global trends and tensions within the Western workplace; to increase students' global reflexivity regarding ethnocentrism and multicultural competencies; to better understand global and multicultural dimensions of everyday life and communication.

6. More specifically, we will focus on making our students more globally aware citizens. This means that globally aware students consider themselves global citizens. As such, they should:

- Be aware of how communication links nations and individuals in the global community.
- Understand the interconnectedness of the global community.
- Be aware of how the global community impacts political decision-making, including the formal and informal pacts of which nations enter
- Be aware of the social, environmental, and economic impacts of global decisions made by both national and international organizations (e.g., the UN, the IMF, etc.).

Material ranged from broad to specific in the various courses, while content had to be relevant. Faculty utilized exams, class discussions, participation, writing, and portfolios to assess learning and demonstration of specific learning objectives associated with instructional activities that connected back to learning outcomes and course goals. While the description of suggested ideas was somewhat general, we wanted instructors to have freedom to adopt material that they thought would be useful, relevant, and interesting to students. Readers interested in some of the specific approaches used may contact us, and we will be happy to provide such information.

Assessment/Evaluation

To assess our progress, we created a survey for a pre- and posttest, with student surveys matched by a unique number they enter on both tests, approved by our university's institutional review board. After clicking on the online survey and reading through the consent form, students navigated to a survey containing several sections, including elements of both internationalization and citizen engagement (since engagement can be an indicator of broader awareness and connection with one's surroundings and communities), another focus of our department. To elaborate, the 164-item survey had nine sections, starting with demographic questions and ending with three open-ended questions about students' perceptions of value of knowing about other cultures and the ways college or other experiences have helped shape their knowledge. Between these, we incorporated seven measures to gauge students' (1) cognitive approach to analysis and to other cultures; (2) intercultural competencies (behavioral); (3) perceived importance of civic/political issues; (4) awareness of self, society, and others; (5) intention to change; (6) globalization awareness, and (7) civic/political engagement intent to action. Each measure was drawn from appropriate sections of measures provided by Arasaratnam (2009); American Association of Colleges & Universities measures (Musil, 2006), AASCU (Beaumont, Colby, Ehrlich, & Torney-Purta, 2006), and Chen's measures of intercultural competence (Chen & Young, 2010; Portalla & Chen, 2010). Instructors in several classes had their students take the online survey—some in class and some as extra credit, and the survey took students approximately 30 minutes to complete.

Here, we report pretest items of our courses. Of the 290 undergraduate communication studies majors (with approximately 880 majors in the entire School of Communication), 196 (67.6%) took the preassessment. Students were instructed to take the assessment only once, even if they were in multiple courses. Of these, 64 were male (32.7%) and 130 female (66.3%), with two not reporting. There were 4 freshmen (2%), 39 sophomores (19.9%), 90 juniors (45.9%) and 62 seniors (31.6%), with one not reporting. Participants reported racial background as African American (17, 8.7%), Caucasian (151, 77.0%), Latinx (14, 7.1%), Asian/Pacific Islander (4, 2.0%), Biracial/mixed (7, 3.6%), and Other (3, 1.5%). No participant self-reported as Native American. Participants' average age was 20.88 years (sd = 2.34).

Table 4.1 reports the alpha reliabilities, number of items, and mean and standard deviation for each scale (each figured on a 5-point scale). Each of the measures that we constructed had acceptable reliabilities, with only one measure (Awareness of Self, Other, and Society) being below the suggested 8.0. The means suggest that, on all measures, students' scores are roughly neutral, between 3 and 4 on a 5-point scale. Most measures reflect no significant differences based on sex, year in school, or ethnicity (except for a small but significant difference in Civic/Political Behavior, indicating that women in the major are more likely to engage in civic behavior than men: females: $\bar{x}$ = 3.90, SD = .75; males: $\bar{x}$ = 3.65, SD = .67, t = –2.25). This suggests that, across the major, regardless of sex, ethnicity, or year in school, there is clear room for growth, both in terms of intercultural competencies, affect, and awareness (our three key dimensions) and political engagement behaviors and attitudes that might predict them.

Open-ended questions asked students about their perceived value in knowing other cultures and aspects within and beyond their degree that might help them interact with people from other cultures. Information from open-ended data help to triangulate the findings from closed-ended data and provide more nuance of understanding for future pedagogical interventions. Students indicated that there is value in learning about global communication and that gaining an international perspective is useful. Students felt that opportunities probably exist for intercultural growth throughout their college experience that can help them develop multicultural sensitivities, but such opportunities were not easily apparent or occurred through chance encounters with international students. Primarily, students encountered internationalization through study-abroad trips, living arrangements, student organizations, informal interactions on the quad or in the student center, and in-class course content or interaction with classmates and faculty. For example, one student remarked:

> In my college career I was frequently in classes with students of cultures different from my own. In many ways, these differences in culture allowed me to better understand my own culture, as well as others. My college degree

Table 4.1 Means, Standard Deviations, Reliabilities, and Number of Items of Scales

Scale	Mean	SD	Reliability	Items
Affective	3.89	.41	.86	29
Competencies	3.64	.44	.89	28
Civ/Pol Behavior	3.82	.75	.93	15
Awareness Self, Other, Society	3.42	.46	.76	22
Readiness (for Civ/Pol Action)	3.42	.64	.84	14
Global Awareness	3.52	.56	.87	16
Intent to Engage in CE/PE	3.17	.75	.95	28

N for all items is 196; reliabilities are standardized alpha signifies that I have been in a variety of classes alongside those of differing cultures, and opinions. A communication degree without courses that consider other cultures would be useless.

Co-curricular opportunities, such as study abroad, were perceived as more frequent and obvious than curricular, according to students. Communication studies students described in-class internationalization approaches to be writing, group work, oral presentations, readings, guest speakers, class discussion, and current events. Students tended to value any global discussion or element, but found such components more difficult to identify except in courses overtly directed at intercultural communication. Students reported value in learning about the ways of people from other cultures, even though as one student said, "we are all humans." In the words of different students from our open-ended survey questions:

> It is critical. If you lock yourself up in American ways exclusively, you're lame. It's interesting and fun, it's necessary in an increasingly globalizing world, you can learn so much from others who come from different backgrounds and might have some different values than you, it can help reduce discrimination, prejudice, and racism, you get to meet cool people.

> There is much value in knowing about other people's culture because it makes you a more well-rounded and open-minded person. It helps you be more understanding of people and all of our differences with each other.

> Every culture is different and matters. It is awesome to know how they do things and why. I feel there is great value in knowing about other cultures because different cultures have different viewpoints on issues that otherwise talk about.

Although the majority of students thought college helps them learn more about other cultures, one third of the respondents did not think college has prepared them; they do not see the need since they fail to see how such content helps them with job training. Some suggest that it is other experiences at the university, and not college classes, that prepare them for interacting in a diverse world: "I don't think the degree itself has helped prepare me, but the college experience may have impacted how I interact with people from other cultures."

Other students noted the lack of diversity on the campus and in the major. While there may be some students of other nations, there is little practical experience in learning how to interact with them. In addition, the teaching in their major "shifts toward one specific culture"—mainstream White culture:

> I have class with people of different cultures but we were never taught how to interact with them. In theory we have learned about interacting with people in other cultures, but there isn't (*sic*) much real-life opportunities since this campus is predominantly White.

One student stated feeling "textbook equipped" to talk with people from other cultures, but adds "I do not feel competent nor secure enough to interact with other cultures out of fear of saying something the wrong way and potentially threatening the other culture." Perhaps 30 participants (15% of the sample) feel that college has not prepared them for interacting in a global world. One participant specifically suggested, "I'm not studying to interact with anyone. I'm studying to have a successful career." Thus, open-ended responses suggest that efforts in our major have, prior to our redesign, had little perceived impact on students' global awareness. While most students see value in learning about other cultures in classes, there still seems to be some reservation regarding the notion of global learning and whether or not our campus has succeeded in living up to one of our espoused values.

In sum, these data probably surprise no one—our students are not very knowledgeable about other cultures or countries. Their overall competence and civic engagement are moderate but not strong, and although some open-ended comments are promising, others show a lack of awareness or perceived need of international diversity. This supports the need for incorporating internationalization into our curriculum. From here, future data will compare the posttest data with the pretest data of the targeted classes to see if we are teaching our students about global issues in a meaningful way. While this chapter introduces how to incorporate global learning into curricula, we also hope to provide meaningful data about our efforts in future venues.

Concluding Thoughts

In this chapter, we have outlined the need to strategize internationalization, as communication students will increasingly find themselves communicating with those from different nations whether or not they travel abroad. Further, as Baldwin (2018) has summarized, most intercultural scholars today do not think of "culture" strictly in terms of national boundaries. The attitudes, affect, and skills that apply to interacting with those from other cultures and groups should apply equally to understanding those of other cultures and groups within our country, state, or neighborhood. Further, it is possible that increased intercultural competencies may relate to other pedagogical outcomes, such as helping to develop students who are engaged civically and politically with the world that surrounds them.

While we are able to only report on the pre-test studies here, we are confident that incorporating internationalization into the classroom—and major—will yield positive learning outcomes for our students. One of the primary purposes of this chapter was to contribute to the discussion on internationalizing the communication classroom, major, and discipline as a whole. We have described a case study of a specific program for internationalization within a specific university, making this one of the few applied analyses of internationalization within an entire major, since most literature concerns specific courses or single teaching interventions. Our data suggest that, despite some encouraging aspects of students' attitudes and behaviors, there is room for growth. We realize the lack of ability to generalize from a single, midsized Midwestern university to other educational contexts, but we hope our project and data offer useful knowledge that might be transferable to other contexts. We hope that the stages of our planning, with training, design, and assessment, may help our own students to gain increased (inter)cultural competencies and that they might have implications for other classrooms and for the discipline as a whole.

References

Anderson, C., & Blair, D. (2013). Developing a global learning rubric: Strengthening teaching and improving learning. *Diversity & Democracy, 16*(3), 10–12.

Anderson, G., & Szabo, S. (2007). The "power" to change multicultural attitudes. *Academic Exchange Quarterly, 11*(2), 26–30.

Arasaratnam, L. A. (2009). The development of a new instrument of intercultural competence. *Journal of Intercultural Communication, 20*, 1–11.

Arasaratnam, L. A., Banerjee, S., & Dembek, K. (2008). The integrated model of intercultural communication competence. *Australian Journal of Communication, 35*(3), 103–116.

Arasaratnam, L. A., Banerjee, S. C., & Dembek, K. (2010). Sensation seeking and the integrated model of intercultural communication competence. *Journal of Intercultural Communication Research, 39*(2), 69–79.

Baldwin, J. R. (2018). Evolving definitions of culture and intercultural communication for emerging global realities. In W. Jia (Ed.), *Intercultural communication: Adapting to emerging global realities: A reader* (2nd ed., pp. 27–43). San Diego, CA: Cognella.

Beaumont, E., Colby, A., Ehrlich, T., & Torney-Purta, J. (2006). Promoting political competence and engagement in college students: An empirical study. *Journal of Political Science Education, 2*, 249–270.

Blondin, J. E., & Gable, R. (2018). Global learning as liberal learning for all majors. *Peer Review, 20*(1). Retrieved from www.aacu.org/peerreview/2018/Winter/VCU

Chen, G.-M., & Young, P. (2010). Intercultural communication competence. In A. Goodboy & K. Schultz (Eds.), *Introduction to communication studies: Translating scholarship into meaningful practice* (pp. 175–188). Dubuque, IA: Kendaell Hunt.

Chia, J. (2009). Intercultural interpretations: Making public relations education culturally relevant. *Journal of University Teaching & Learning Practice, 6*(1), 40–48.

Clayton-Pedersen, A. R., Parker, S., Smith, D. G., Moreno, J. F., & Teraguchi, D. H. (2007). *Making a real difference with diversity*. Washington, DC: Association of American Colleges and Universities.

Dell, C., & Wood, M. (2010). Internationalisation and the global dimension in the curriculum. *Educational Futures: e-Journal of the British Education Studies Association, 2*(2), 56–72. Retrieved from https://educationstudies.org.uk/wp-content/uploads/2013/11/dell_woodf7.pdf

Dewine, S. (1995). A new direction: Internationalizing communication programs. *Journal of the Association for Communication Administration, 3*, 204–210.

de Wit, H. (Ed.). (2009). *Measuring success in the internationalization of higher education*. European Association for International Education Occasional Paper 22. Amsterdam: EAIE.

Doscher, S., & Landorf, H. (2018). Universal global learning, inclusive excellence, and higher education's greater purpose. *Peer Review, 20*(1), Retrieved from www.aacu.org/peerreview/2018/Winter/FIU

Fitch, K. (2012). Industry perceptions of intercultural competence in Singapore and Perth. *Public Relations Review, 38*(4), 609–618.

Fitch, K. (2013). A disciplinary perspective: The internationalization of Australian public relations education. *Journal of Studies in International Education, 17*(2), 136–147.

Gilchrist, L. Z., Mundy, M. E., Felten, P., & Shields, S. L. (2003). Course transitions, midsemester assessment, and program design characteristics: A case study. *Michigan Journal of Community Service Learning, 10*(1), 51–58.

Green, M. F. (2007). Internationalizing community colleges: Barriers and strategies. *New Directions for Community Colleges, 2007*(138), 15–24.

Green, M. F. (2012). *Measuring and assessing internationalization: Association of international educators*. Retrieved from www.nafsa.org/_/File/_/downloads/measuring_assessing.pdf

Green, M. F., & Shoenberg, R. (2006). *Where faculty live: Internationalizing the disciplines*. Washington, DC: American Council on Education.

Hovland, K. (2016). What can global learners do? In D. M. Whitehead (Ed.), *Essential global learning* (pp. 5–9). Washington, DC: Association of American Colleges and Universities.

Jones, E., & Killick, D. (2013). Graduate attributes and the internationalised curriculum: Embedding a global outlook in disciplinary learning outcomes. *Journal of Studies in International Education, 17*(2), 165–182.

Knight, J. (2012). Global: Five truths about internationalization. *International Higher Education, 69*. Retrieved from https://ejournals.bc.edu/ojs/index.php/ihe/article/view/8644/7776

Leask, B. (2009). Using formal and informal curricula to improve interactions between home and international students. *Journal of Studies in International Education, 13*, 205–221.

Leask, B. (2013a). Internationalizing the curriculum and the disciplines: Current perspectives and directions for the future. *Journal of Studies in International Education, 17*(2), 99–102.

Leask, B. (2013b). Internationalizing the curriculum in the disciplines: Imagining new possibilities. *Journal of Studies in International Education, 17*(2), 103–118.

Leask, B. (2015). *Internationalizing the curriculum.* London: Routledge.

Leask, B., & Beelen, J. (2010). Enhancing the engagement of academic staff in international education. In *Proceedings of a joint IEAA-EAIE symposium* (pp. 28–40). Melbourne: International Education Association of Australia. Retrieved from www.ieaa.org.au/documents/item/41

Leask, B., Whitsed, C., & Green, W. (2012a). *Internationalisation of the Curriculum (Ioc) in action: Framework.* The University of Queensland. Retrieved from www.uq.edu.au/teach/OLT/framework.html

Leask, B., Whitsed, C., & Green, W. (2012b). *Internationalisation of the Curriculum (Ioc) in action: Process.* The University of Queensland. Retrieved from www.uq.edu.au/teach/OLT/process.html

Lee, J. J. (2006). Global citizenship: Extending students' knowledge and action to the global context. *Journal of College and Character, 7*(1), 1–5.

Mezirow, J. (1991). *Transformative dimensions of adult learning.* San Francisco, CA: Jossey-Bass Publishers.

Musil, C. M. (2006). *Assessing global learning: Matching good intentions with good practice.* Washington, DC: American Association of Colleges and Universities. Retrieved from www.aacu.org/publications-research/publications/assessing-global-learning-matching-good-intentions-good-practice

Niehaus, E., & Williams, L. (2016). Faculty transformation in curriculum transformation: The role of faculty development in campus internationalization. *Innovative Higher Education, 41*(1), 59–74.

Portalla, T., & Chen, G.-M. (2010). The development and validation of the intercultural effectiveness scale. *Intercultural Communication Studies, 19*(3), 21–37.

Schneider, C. G. (2016). Deepening the connection: Liberal education and global learning. In D. M. Whitehead (Ed.), *Essential global learning* (pp. 3–4). Washington, DC: Association of American Colleges and Universities.

Smith, S. L. (2015). A transformational learning model for designing internationalized on-campus courses. *eJournal of Public Affairs, 4*(1). Retrieved from https://ejopa.missouristate.edu/index.php/ejournal/issue/view/11/showToc

Spitzberg, B. H. (2000). A model of intercultural communication competence. In L. Samovar & R. Porter (Eds.), *Intercultural communication: A reader* (pp. 375–387). Belmont, CA: Wadsworth.

Spitzberg, B. H. (2012). Axioms for a theory of intercultural communication competence. In L. A. Samovar, R. E. Porter, & E. R. McDaniel (Eds.), *Intercultural communication: A reader* (13th ed., pp. 424–435). Boston: Wadsworth.

Spitzberg, B. H., & Chagnon, G. (2009). Conceptualizing intercultural competence. In D. K. Deardorff (Ed.), *The Sage handbook of intercultural competence* (pp. 2–52). Thousand Oaks, CA: Sage Publications.

Sypris, T. (1993). *Internationalizing the curriculum.* Washington, DC: American Association of Community Colleges. Retrieved from https://eric.ed.gov/?id=ED393496

Taylor, M. (2001). Internationalizing the public relations curriculum. *Public Relations Review, 27*(1), 73–88.

Twigg, C. (2000, May/June). Course readiness criteria: Identifying targets of opportunity for large-scale redesign. *Educause.* Retrieved from www.thencat.org/Articles/Course_Redesign.pdf

Vainio-Mattila, A. (2009). Internationalizing curriculum: A new kind of education? *New Directions for Teaching & Learning, 118*, 95–103.

van der Wende, M. (1997). Internationalising the curriculum in Dutch higher education: An international comparative perspective. *Journal of Studies in International Education*, *1*(2), 53–72.

Van Gyn, G., Schuerholz-Lehr, S., Caws, C., & Preece, A. (2009). Education for world-mindedness: Beyond superficial notions of internationalization. *New Directions for Teaching & Learning*, *118*, 25–38.

Velten, J. C., & Dodd, C. H. (2016). The effects of intercultural communication competency-based instruction on intercultural communication competence. *Intercultural Communication Studies*, *25*(3), 1–18.

Whitehead, D. (2018). Understanding and operationalizing global learning. In *Architecture for global learning*. New York: Association of International Educators. Retrieved from www.nafsa.org/_/File/_/gl_podcast_7.pdf

5 Integrating the Goals of Global Learning Into the Learning Outcomes of the Communication Curriculum

Elizabeth M. Goering

A hallmark of higher education in the 21st century around the world is the focus on learning outcomes. A "Knowledge Brief" published by the Stanford Center for Opportunity Policy in Education in 2011 advocates for colleges and universities to collectively articulate and align "a set of student outcomes that prioritize 21st century skills" (Rice, 2011, p. 1). This perspective is echoed on a more global scale in the *Assessment of Higher Education Learning Outcomes Feasibility Study Report* published in 2012 by the Organisation for Economic Co-operation and Development (OECD), a unique multinational forum with member countries from every continent except for Africa that works together to research and address the challenges of globalization. The report claims that because of globalization and changes in higher education worldwide, "learning outcomes are indeed key to a meaningful education, and focusing on learning outcomes is essential to inform diagnosis and improve teaching processes and student learning" (Tremblay, Lalancette, & Roseveare, 2012, p. 11). With increasing pressure from various stakeholder groups, including politicians, business leaders, employers, and students, to make the learning that comes through higher education relevant and transparent, considerable time and energy have been placed on defining learning outcomes and providing evidence that programs and institutions are actually providing learning opportunities that help students attain the desired outcomes.

One of the leading initiatives in the national effort to define learning outcomes for higher education is Lumina Foundation's Degree Qualifications Profile (DQP), which "provides a baseline set of reference points for what students should know and be able to do for the award of associate, bachelor's and master's degrees, regardless of their fields of study" (Lumina Foundation, 2014, p. 4). The DQP is often coupled with Tuning. While the DQP specifies general learning outcomes, regardless of degree, Tuning, a process which began in Europe in 2000 and later spread to the United States, "makes what students know, understand, and are able to do at the completion of a degree in a given discipline or professional program explicit for students, faculty, family, employers and other stakeholders" (IEBC, 2012, p. 1). Both initiatives have received widespread attention. More than 400 colleges and universities in the United States have utilized the DQP, and several disciplines in the USA, including communication, have gone through a Tuning process.

A parallel trend to the rising interest in identifying and documenting the attainment of learning outcomes in American higher education is increasing emphasis placed on global learning. The growing interest in global learning has been spurred by the awareness that:

> the big problems of the world . . . require that the graduates of tomorrow are not restricted or parochial of mind. Therefore we need to ensure that the

students of today have access to knowledge and wisdom from all parts of the world, are open to new ideas regardless of the origin of those ideas, develop the capacity to solve tricky problems and find innovative solutions and are committed to actions that benefit others as well as themselves.

(Leask, 2015, p. 23)

With the emphasis on global learning comes yet another set of learning outcomes, global or international learning outcomes (referred to as GILOs throughout this chapter). While there is no standardized set of GILOs, what global or international learning entails has been defined by several scholars (e.g., Elkin & Devjee, 2003; Kahn, 2016; Keevy & Chakroun, 2015) and articulated by individual universities as well. Departments and faculty increasingly are being challenged to internationalize the curriculum and integrate global learning experiences in the classroom to promote attainment of GILOs, adding yet another set of expectations about what should be happening in the higher education classroom.

At times the external expectations related to curriculum development and assessment can be overwhelming. Professors are asked to use VALUE rubrics to align grading with the DQPs and now to consider integrating GILOs as well. However, instead of thinking of the GILOs as another ingredient to throw into the learning outcome alphabet soup, it might be more productive to work on integrating GILOs within existing learning outcome frameworks. If the goals of global learning can be integrated into existing learning outcomes, faculty and departments may be less likely to resist efforts to internationalize curriculum because doing so will be built into what faculty already do. This chapter integrates the goals of global learning into the Learning Outcomes in Communication (LOCs) developed through a faculty-driven initiative coordinated by the National Communication Association (NCA). Additionally, it illustrates the process and potential of such an alignment through a case study of one specific communication studies department's efforts to internationalize its curriculum, a curriculum which had already been aligned with NCA's LOCs.

Learning Outcomes in Communication (LOCs)

In 2014, the National Communication Association, with the generous support of the Lumina Foundation, brought 30 communication scholars from around the country together to define Learning Outcomes for Communication. After 14 months of discussion and deliberation, the team, which consisted of faculty members from a wide variety of institutions, ranging from two-year colleges to research universities and representing all regions of the country, agreed upon a set of learning outcomes that articulate what students who complete a program of study in communication should know and be able to do.

A detailed explanation of the LOC project and the framework for learning that it offers can be found on the NCA website (www.natcom.org/learning-outcomes-communication), but to summarize, the LOCs suggest that a student graduating with a degree in communication should be able to:

- Describe the communication discipline and its central questions
- Employ communication theories, perspectives, principles, and concepts
- Engage in communication inquiry
- Create messages appropriate to the audience, purpose, and context
- Critically analyze messages

- Demonstrate the ability to accomplish communicative goals (self-efficacy)
- Apply ethical communication principles and practices
- Utilize communication to embrace difference
- Influence public discourse

(NCA, 2015)

These LOCs were never intended to serve as the foundation for a standardized curriculum for communication programs across the country; instead, they seek to provide a skeleton around which individual programs can sculpt a form that takes into account their own institutionally specific goals and missions, resources, and distinct curricular approaches.

Since the official launch of the LOCs in 2015, departments around the country have been encouraged to revisit their own curricula, using the LOCs as a framework for discussing what students graduating with communication degrees from their programs should know and be able to do. This renewed interest in curricular issues within the discipline offers a perfect opportunity for communication departments to consider ways to embed international or global learning outcomes into their curricula as well.

Global and International Learning Outcomes (GILOs)

Scholars have long agreed on the need for higher education to prepare students to thrive in an increasingly interconnected, globalized world. Hanson (2010) makes a compelling case for "the need for a radical reform to curricula to foster engaged global citizenship" (p. 70). This call was echoed in a report of the United Nations Educational, Scientific and Cultural Organization (UNESCO): "Beyond cognitive knowledge and skills, the international community is urging an education that will help resolve the existing and emerging global challenges menacing our planet, while wisely tapping into the opportunities it provides" (Keevy & Chakroun, 2015, p. 29).

In 2006, the Oxfam Development Education Program defined the characteristics of a "global citizen" as a person who:

- is aware of the wider world and has a sense of their own role as a world citizen;
- respects and values diversity;
- has an understanding of how the world works economically, politically, socially, culturally, technologically, and environmentally;
- is outraged by social injustice;
- participates in and contributes to the community at a range of levels from local to global;
- is willing to act to make the world a more sustainable place; and
- takes responsibility for their actions

(as cited by Clifford & Montgomery, 2015, p. 50)

While there is agreement on what global citizenship is, there is not a single agreed-upon set of learning outcomes that define global citizen education. Elkin and Devjee (2003) define it in terms of developing "global perspectives, international and cultural and ethical sensitivity along with useful knowledge, skills and attitudes for the globalized market place" (p. 11). The Association of American Colleges & Universities (AAC&U) has developed a Global Learning VALUE Rubric (2014) that includes the following competencies: (1) global self-awareness, (2) perspective taking, (3) cultural diversity, (4) personal and social responsibility, (5) understanding global systems, and (6) applying knowledge to contemporary global contexts. In their 2015 UNESCO report, Keevy and Chakroun identify the following "global citizen education" competencies:

- An attitude supported by an understanding of multiple levels of identity, and the potential for a collective identity that transcends individual cultural, religious, ethnic or other differences . . .;
- A deep knowledge of global issues and universal values such as justice, equality, dignity and respect . . .;
- Cognitive skills to think critically, systemically and creatively, including adopting a multi-perspective approach that recognizes different dimensions, perspectives and angles of issues . . .;
- Non-cognitive skills, including social skills such as empathy and conflict resolution, and communication skills and aptitudes for networking and interacting with people of different backgrounds, origins, cultures and perspectives . . .; and
- Behavioural capacities to act collaboratively and responsibly to find global solutions to global challenges, and to strive for the collective good.

(pp. 30–31)

Kahn (2016) offers the metaphors of "prisms, knots, and a cup of coffee" to capture the key competencies of global learning. She suggests that "students must be able to dissect knots, or complex situations, that gain meaning through multiple perspectives" (p. 52). To unravel the knots, students need to be able to "shift between various scales of understanding and practice (or see through prisms)" (p. 54). Finally, students need to be able to move from an "analytical understanding" to a "sense of commitment and responsibility to others" (p. 53).

While there are differences in these conceptualizations of the outcomes associated with global learning, there are common elements as well. Table 5.1 provides a comparative summary of these common elements, utilizing the components of Spitzberg's (1997) model of intercultural communication competence (ICC) as a framework. Global citizenship, like ICC, requires motivation, knowledge, and skills. Motivation implies a particular mind-set or attitude, and the various models of global learning are all grounded in an interculturally sensitive, ethical way of viewing the world as an interconnected system and the commitment to engage effectively and responsibly within that interconnected world. Another common thread in the different global learning frameworks is the emphasis placed on knowledge. Deep knowledge of self and of one's position within the larger global context as well as a nuanced understanding of global systems, histories, and perspectives are all essential components of global citizenship. Finally, a global citizen needs skills, useful cognitive and social competencies that are essential to putting global citizenship into action. Requisite skills include the ability to think critically and creatively, to take the perspective of others, to resolve conflicts, to communicate, to act collaboratively, and, perhaps most importantly, the ability to apply knowledge to global contexts. When combined, motivation/mindset, knowledge, and skills can prepare students to respond to global challenges and thrive in our globalized world.

While there is considerable agreement on the importance of global citizenship and the responsibility higher education has in fostering it, there is less agreement

Table 5.1 Common Elements in Global Citizen Frameworks

	Elkin and Devjee (2003)	AAC&U (2014)	Keevy and Chakroun (2015)	Kahn (2016)
Motivation/Mind-set	• "International and cultural and ethical sensitivity" • "Useful... attitudes for the globalized market place"	• "Personal and social responsibility"	• "An attitude supported by an understanding of multiple levels of identity, and the potential for a collective"	• "A sense of commitment and responsibility to others"
Knowledge	• "Global perspectives" • "Useful knowledge... for the globalized market place"	• "Global self-awareness" • "Understanding global systems"	• "Deep knowledge of global issues and universal values such as justice, equality, dignity and respect"	• "Various scales of understanding"
Skills	• "Useful... skills... for the globalized market place"	• "Perspective taking" • "Applying knowledge to contemporary global contexts"	• "Cognitive skills to think critically, systemically and creatively including adopting a multi-perspective approach" • "Non-cognitive skills" (empathy, conflict resolution, and communication skills • "Behavioral capacities to act collaboratively and responsibly to find global solutions to global challenges, and to strive for the collective good"	• Ability to "dissect knots, or complex situations, that gain meaning through multiple perspectives" • Ability to move from "analytical understanding" to a "sense of commitment and responsibility to others" • Ability to "shift between various scales of understanding and practice"

on how best to internationalize the curriculum. Increasingly, colleges and universities seem to be turning away from the "neoliberal approach" to internationalization, an approach that focuses on "producing individuals in privileged positions to travel and work across national boundaries," and embracing the "transformative approach, where citizens have an understanding of a common humanity, a shared planet and a shared future" (Shultz, 2007, p. 255). This shift is noteworthy because, as Leask (2016) points out, universities should not focus on "what some students will experience" but rather on "what all students will learn" (p. 50). All students live in a globalized world; therefore, all students should receive a global education. Consequently, global learning cannot be restricted to study-abroad experiences in which only a limited number of students can participate. Rather, the goals of global learning must be embedded in on-campus classrooms and integrated into the curriculum that all students receive so that all students leave the university with a solid understanding of themselves as global citizens.

Integrating LOCs and GILOs

Clearly there is value in embedding global learning outcomes in higher education, just as there is value in defining disciplinary-level learning outcomes to guide curriculum within communication departments. Furthermore, at most colleges and universities, global and departmental learning outcome expectations are added to university-level learning outcomes. The challenge is integrating the various learning outcomes that higher education students are expected to achieve and embedding their attainment in our curricular and co-curricular activities. If the learning outcomes are not integrated, we run the risk of prioritizing one set of outcomes over another or of treating some learning outcomes as add-ons rather than as integral to the higher education experience.

Global learning scholars emphasize the need for GILOs to be integrated at the disciplinary and course levels. Leask (2015) places disciplines and "the disciplinary teams who construct the curriculum" (p. 27) firmly in the center of her conceptual framework for internationalizing the curriculum because of the power disciplines exert over curriculum and the production of knowledge. While disciplines are the core of the university structure and, thus, serve as the locus for internationalization, Leask also highlights the need for cross-disciplinary collaboration because the complex problems facing our world cannot be addressed within disciplinary GILOs. All disciplines should be involved in the work of global learning, because, as Agnew and Kahn (2015) point out, "there are no neutral or normative fields of inquiry that do not require intercultural or global sensitivities. There is no discipline beyond internationalization" (p. 37). The communication discipline is uniquely positioned to integrate global learning into departmental curricula and to engage in cross-disciplinary collaborations that can lead to further embedding of global learning outcomes within higher education. Although the GILOs, as summarized in the previous section, and the communication discipline's LOCs seem to mesh naturally, there is value in being intentional about making those linkages explicit. As communication studies departments revisit their curricula, seeking to align them with the LOCs, I propose that we should be doing so with an eye to integrating GILOs as well.

A useful method for aligning GILOs with LOCs and integrating them into the communication studies curriculum is Backward Course Design (BCD), a framework developed by Wiggins and McTighe (2005). Wiggins and McTighe propose that instead of approaching course design by thinking first about what content you, as the instructor, want to cover in the class or what you want students to do, it is more useful to start at the end, by identifying what students should understand, know, and be able to do after they have completed the course. Once instructors know what the desired outcomes are, they can begin to identify criteria that will indicate whether those desired outcomes are being met and then design specific activities and pedagogies for encouraging that learning. Essentially Backward Course Design encourages instructors to design the course in reverse, by starting with a clear articulation of course goals (i.e., what the students should know and be able to do after completing the class that they do not already know or cannot already do). After the course goals are defined, instructors work backwards to determine how they will know that the goals have been met. Once a final assignment has been developed that can serve as a tool for assessing course goal attainment, instructors take another step backward and identify the specific knowledge and skills students need to be able to complete the final assessment successfully. Attaining that specific knowledge and skill set becomes the learning outcomes for the course. The final step in the BCD is planning class activities, readings, homework assignments, and lecture content based on the learning outcomes. Kahn and Agnew (2017) adapt the Wiggins and McTighe model specifically to internationalization of the curriculum, demonstrating how BCD can seamlessly integrate global learning goals into individual classes. Kahn and Agnew (2017) suggest that instructors, in keeping with the principles of BCD, start by embedding global learning goals in the course goals, making global learning part of what students should know and be able to do upon completion of the course. Then, working in reverse, the global learning course goals are translated into observable final assessments, learning outcomes for the course, and, finally, course content and student activities.

Internationalizing the Communication Studies Curriculum: A Case Study

So, what might a program look like that utilizes the Backward Course Design framework to align GILOs and LOCs and ensure that both sets of learning outcomes are attained within a communication studies major? This final section provides a case study of one department's efforts to accomplish this goal. The Department of Communication Studies at Indiana University Purdue University Indianapolis (IUPUI) has approximately 225 majors. The program offers a broad-based curriculum, with courses in the areas of interpersonal, group, organizational and health communication, media production, media criticism, rhetoric, and theatre/performance. The common core of the curriculum is a sequence of four required courses: a 100-level Gateway introduction to the discipline and the department; a 200-level Communication Theory class; a 300-level Communication Research Methods class; and a 400-level Capstone in Communication Studies in which students are required to reflect on and showcase their learning related to department-level learning outcomes through an ePortfolio.

One member of the IUPUI Communication faculty was on the team that developed NCA's LOCs in 2014–15, and immediately after the LOCs were launched in 2015, the department began a curriculum review that resulted in a curriculum tuned to the LOCs. Shortly thereafter, the department decided to also embed outcomes related to global learning in the curriculum. The case study that follows describes steps undertaken to accomplish this goal. Table 5.2 provides a summary of the process.

Table 5.2 Aligning Global Program Learning Outcomes with Learning Outcomes in Communication

Global Program Goals
1. Global knowledge
2. Global perspectives and understanding
3. Global citizenship skills
4. Application to global issues

Learning Outcomes in Communication (LOCs)	Potential for Alignment	Examples from Specific Classes
1. Describe the discipline and its central questions	Show how comm. is studied in other parts of the world	discuss Western bias in the discipline; assign reading on development of comm theory in China
2. Employ communication theories, perspectives, principles, and concepts	Include theories and concepts from non-U.S. scholars	include global examples in media history classes; include theories from non-U.S. scholars
3. Engage in communication inquiry	Assign research about or by scholars from other parts of the world	assign research about global issues (i.e., health crises) and by non-US scholars; share resources that empower students to include global perspectives in their own research
4. Create messages appropriate to the audience/purpose/ context	Practice creating messages for global audiences	teach intercultural comm competence models; applied projects with global focus
5. Critically analyze messages	Critically analyze messages from global sources	analyze messages related to global crises in context (i.e., Ebola outbreak); assess transferability of comm models to other cultures; show video on cultural differences in nonverbal communication
6. Demonstrate the ability to accomplish comm goals	Explore self-efficacy within a global context	study abroad program (2-week Poland experience); prepare students to adapt to new cultures (i.e., teach culture shock)
7. Apply ethical comm principles and practices	Explore communication ethics in global context	critical analysis of international case studies
8. Utilize communication to embrace difference	Most obvious link; content itself is global	utilize Global Voices; make use of global diversity on campus
9. Influence public discourse	Focus on global issues for class projects	applied intercultural comm projects; global issue focused class projects
10. Collaborate with others	Offer opportunity to collaborate in culturally diverse teams	cross-country collaborations

Defining Department-Level Global Learning Goals

The first step was to define program-level global learning goals. This was accomplished through a consensus-building decision-making process that was overseen by the director of undergraduate studies in the department. At an annual retreat focused on undergraduate curriculum, the department had agreed to globalize the curriculum, so the decision-making process typically used within the department was implemented to reach consensus about the specific global-learning goals that were most appropriate for this context. The decision-making process most commonly used within the department initially uses an online forum discussion housed in Canvas, the university's learning management system, to present information and engage faculty in conversation about topics under consideration. Then, at the monthly faculty meetings, decisions to be made are brought to the faculty as action items. In this case, information about internationalizing the curriculum was shared with the faculty. Faculty were provided with various examples of international or global learning goals, including those referenced previously in this paper (see Table 5.1) as well as IUPUI's Global Learning Goals. Then discussion threads were started in which faculty members could share their thoughts, raise concerns, discuss issues, and make recommendations about the global learning goals they perceive to be most relevant for our students. The director of undergraduate studies used the discussion forum interaction to create a proposal that spelled out departmental global learning goals, which was presented at a faculty meeting. After in-person discussion at the meeting and some modification, the faculty agreed that majors should leave with: (1) global knowledge (knowing about the world beyond our borders, knowing that there are global differences in communication, and knowing what some of those differences are); (2) global perspectives and understanding (being aware of diverse perspectives and of the value in listening to and seeking to understand others' perspectives); (3) global citizenship skills (developing a repertoire of perspective-taking, listening, and communicating skills that foster global citizenship); and (4) application to global issues (giving students opportunities to apply their learning to address global challenges in collaboration with global partners).

Aligning Departmental Global Learning Goals With LOCs

Once the programmatic global learning outcomes were agreed upon by the faculty, the next step was to align these goals with the LOCs that had been previously defined for the department. The focus of the department's annual faculty retreat in August 2016 was the undergraduate curriculum, with primary emphasis placed on revisiting the undergraduate curriculum in light of the recently released NCA LOCs. The decision-making process described in the previous section was used to lead the department to consensus on how the LOCs could best be integrated into the unique context of communication studies at IUPUI. The department agreed that graduates with a BA in communication studies from IUPUI should have at least moderate competency in all nine of the LOCs identified by NCA. In addition, a tenth learning outcome, the ability to apply skills and knowledge needed to collaborate with others, was added. This additional LOC was included because the faculty concurred that the ability to collaborate or work in teams, which is typically identified as a key competency employers are seeking in new hires (e.g., NACE, 2017), should be highlighted more than it is in NCA's original LOCs.

In this second step of the process of internationalizing the communication curriculum, aligning global learning outcomes with departmental LOCs, a discussion was undertaken about what it might mean to integrate the departmental global learning goals with the disciplinary learning outcomes previously agreed upon by the department. It soon became apparent that LOC 8, utilizing communication to embrace difference, has obvious links to global learning; however, the department did not want global learning to be an add-on that was only included in a single learning outcome. The faculty agreed that global learning needs to be embedded throughout the curriculum, so the faculty brainstormed ways in which global learning could be integrated into all of the required core courses in the major. The focus was placed initially on the required core because these are the only classes that all students are guaranteed to take. By integrating global learning into the required core, the department could ensure that all students graduating with a BA in communication studies from IUPUI would have had multiple opportunities to acquire the global learning competencies agreed upon by the faculty. After the initial brainstorming, which focused on what global learning might look like in the core classes, individual faculty members were also invited to brainstorm about how the department's global learning goals could be integrated into elective classes.

The "Potential for Alignment" column in Table 5.2 spells out some of the possibilities for integrating global learning into each of the LOCs that resulted from this brainstorming session. The faculty noted that global knowledge could be embedded into classes by assigning readings that represent global perspectives on issues; including communication scholarship (theories and research) from non-US scholars in lectures, assigned readings, or class activities; and intentionally choosing examples that offer a global perspective or that represent global experiences related to the topic being discussed. Global skills and applications could be integrated into classes by discussing and/or practicing creating messages for global audiences; discussing and/or practicing analyzing and interpreting messages generated by non-US sources; and focusing on global issues in class projects. Global perspectives could be embedded into classes by discussing what it means to be an ethical communicator in a global context. At this point in the process, these possibilities were hypothetical, but the next step was to make them a reality.

Assessing Current Global Learning Opportunities in the Department

Although the department intentionally set out to internationalize its curriculum in 2017, there were global learning activities taking place in certain classes or with individual instructors prior to the decision to address the topic programmatically. Therefore, an important step in the process of aligning global and disciplinary learning outcomes within the department was to assess current global learning activities within the department. As part of this assessment, a SWOT analysis of the strengths, weaknesses, opportunities, and threats that might impact efforts to internationalize curriculum was conducted at a faculty meeting. An important result of the SWOT analysis was identifying resources available on campus or within the department that could be used to support global learning. For the department, these local resources include the Communication Privacy Management Center, directed by Dr. Sandra Petronio, which includes scholarly articles from 44 different countries in its archives; the Global Health Communication Center, co-directed by Dr. John Parrish-Sprowl and Everold Hosein (World Health Organization), which conducts research and training designed to promote healthy behaviors around the world; and the Global Voices Speakers program that facilitates intercultural interactions by arranging for IUPUI international students to share their experiences and perspectives in classes or community events. The department was pleasantly surprised to discover the rich resources that were available locally to support globalization efforts. IUPUI's communication studies department is not unique in that regard; communication departments at different universities most likely also would discover a surprising number of resources available. Some departments may discover research centers, faculty expertise, or university support services similar to the resources at IUPUI that were identified through the SWOT analysis. Other departments will undoubtedly discover community or university resources that are unique to their specific situation. The key is to seek out available resources and make them visible.

In addition to the SWOT analysis, an assessment was conducted of what IUPUI communication studies faculty already do, strategically or unintentionally, that provides global learning opportunities to students. This assessment was carried out by the director of undergraduate studies, who emailed a survey to each full-time faculty member, asking them to describe the specific things they already do in their classes in relationship to each of the previously identified departmental global learning goals. The final column in Table 5.2 provides examples of some of the global learning activities instructors already build into their classes, as reported on these surveys. These activities range from a formal study-abroad program to activities integrated into specific on-campus classes. The department hosts a long-standing study abroad program in Wroclaw, Poland. The two-week program, intentionally designed as a short-term, intensive study-abroad experience to meet the needs of IUPUI's student body, where 60% of all undergraduates work off campus and 20% have children at home (Hansen, 2017), making longer-term study-abroad programs less feasible, culminates in a communication conference with students from several European countries. The opportunities provided through this study-abroad program to interact with students and professors from other countries, to experience living in a different cultural context for two weeks, and to visit the Auschwitz concentration camp contribute to attainment of the department's global learning goals. Students participating in the program acquire global knowledge, global perspectives, and global skills.

Study abroad is not the only way in which the department provides global learning experiences for students though. Several faculty members make a point of including global perspectives in the theories, concepts, and research they introduce in their classes. In communication theory, for example, students are assigned readings about the development of communication theory in China and de-Westernizing communication theory. In addition, instructors in several classes, including documentary film, health communication, organizational communication, and interpersonal communication, reported that they make a point of including readings/films from non-US scholars/filmmakers or research that was conducted in other parts of the world. Some faculty members identified ways in which they seek to empower students to add a global perspective to their own research. One professor makes a point of introducing students to the Communication Initiative (www.comminit.com/global/category/sites/global), which is a website that includes perspectives from around the world on topics related to communication and social change. Several instructors reported using global issues as case studies in their classes, such as examining the communication surrounding the Ebola outbreak that began in West Africa in 2013. Several respondents to the survey that was distributed to faculty, asking them to describe the global learning activities that are already a part of the classes they teach, talked about sharing their own global experiences in class, whether as a student in a study-abroad program, a researcher studying civility and discourse in Europe, or a trainer seeking to improve the quality of healthcare in Jordanian refugee camps.

Another way in which some faculty members offer global learning opportunities to students is by capitalizing on the added value that international students bring to our campus. One instructor invites a panel of international students to his Interpersonal Communication class each semester using the Global Voices Speakers program, mentioned previously. He describes the value of this interaction as follows: "It's a chance for my students to see things through the eyes of an international citizen. It really opens up their minds to consider others' perspectives from a global point of view." Another professor invited a group of students from Japan who were at IUPUI for English for specific purposes training to participate in her intercultural communication class for two weeks. The survey results demonstrated the degree to which global learning was already happening within individual classes in the department, even before the decision was made to systematically internationalize the curriculum. However, because internationalization efforts were restricted to certain professors and classes, most of which were electives, there was no guarantee that students graduating with a communication studies degree from IUPUI would be given the opportunity for global learning. The challenge, then, was to integrate global learning throughout the curriculum for the communication studies major.

Embedding Global Learning Infused LOCs Throughout the Communication Studies Major

The final step in the department's efforts to internationalize the BA in communication studies at IUPUI, a step which is still in progress, is to embed global learning infused LOCs into all of the required core classes (the gateway course, communication theory, communication research methods, and the capstone) and to reinforce them in elective courses in the major. The required 200-level communication theory class provides a good example of this process: a primary LOC for the required communication theory class is that students who complete the course are expected to be able to employ communication theories, perspectives, principles, and concepts. The global learning–infused revision of that LOC is that students should be able to employ communication theories, perspectives, principles, and concepts from a variety of cultural traditions. In moving backward from the desired outcome to specific course content as per BCD, readings on the development of communication as a discipline in China and on the value in de-Westernizing communication theory were added to the required course materials. These readings were already utilized in the sections of the theory class taught by one professor, but as part of the process of systematically integrating global learning throughout the department's curriculum, the decision was made to include them in all sections of this required class. A similar process is being followed for all of the required core classes: course goals are being revised to integrate the department's global learning goals, after which course activities are being identified that will provide students with the knowledge and skills they need to meet those global learning infused goals.

Although this final step of the process of integrating global learning throughout the communication studies curriculum is still in process, one conclusion that can be drawn from the experiences of this department is that there is value in simply starting a conversation about internationalization and global learning. Just having department-wide discussions about internationalizing the curriculum encouraged faculty to acknowledge the importance of global learning and to think more strategically about how they could globalize the learning experience of their students. In forum discussions, at faculty meetings, and on the faculty surveys, several comments were made that suggested that just asking questions about global learning raised awareness about the need to add more international elements. For example, one faculty member stated, "I don't think I do these things (although I guess I should!)," and another noted "I am not terribly global-minded in my classes—yet." The survey and the conversation also made faculty more aware of what they are doing that does add a global dimension to their teaching. Several individuals responded initially by saying things such as "I have to say that I don't do much that 'globalizes' my classes" or "Unfortunately, I can't really help with this" but then proceeded to spell out a variety of ways in which they do integrate global perspectives or issues into their classes. An important part of globalizing the classroom is making visible what is already done and then ensuring that those activities align with the desired learning outcomes for the class.

Moving Forward

In the current outcome-driven landscape of higher education, it is easy to be overwhelmed by the number of different outcomes we are expected to meet, especially since all of them seem to be essential to preparing students to thrive in our complex, interconnected, globalized world. Seeking to align the outcomes is a useful way to manage what can sometimes feel like competing demands. This chapter has attempted to highlight the logical connections between two sets of outcomes, global and international learning outcomes and NCA's LOCs, and to offer one example of how one department went about aligning them. The case study is presented not as "the" way to go but rather as one way to enhance the higher education experience of communication students by embedding a global perspective in the communication studies curriculum.

References

Agnew, M., & Kahn, H. E. (2015). Internationalization-at-home: Grounded practices to promote intercultural, international, and global learning. *Metropolitan Universities: An International Forum*, 25(3), 31–46.

Association of American Colleges and Universities. (2014). Global learning VALUE rubric. *AAC&U*. Retrieved from www.aacu.org/value/rubrics/global-learning

Clifford, V., & Montgomery, C. (2015). Transformative learning through internationalization of the curriculum in higher education. *Journal of Transformative Education*, 13(1), 46–64.

Elkin, G., & Devjee, F. (2003). *Report on internationalization*. Unpublished manuscript, Committee for the Advancement of Learning and Teaching, University of Otago, Dunedin, New Zealand.

Hansen, M. J. (2017). *Understanding IUPUI students*. Presented at IUPUI Early Career Teaching Academy Program, Indianapolis, IN. Retrieved from https://irds.iupui.edu/_documents/students/student-profiles/general/Understanding%20IUPUI%20Students%202016.pdf

Hanson, L. (2010). Global citizenship, global health, and the internationalization of curriculum: A study of transformative potential. *Journal of Studies in International Education*, 14(1), 70–88.

IEBC: Institute for Evidence-Based Change. (2012). *Tuning American higher education: The process*. Retrieved from http://degreeprofile.org/wp-content/uploads/2014/12/Tuning-American-Higher-Education-the-Process.pdf

Kahn, H. E. (2016, January/February). Scales of global learning: Prisms, knots, and a cup of coffee. *International Educator*, 25(1), 52–55.

Kahn, H. E., & Agnew, M. (2017). Global learning through difference: Considerations for teaching, learning, and the internationalization of higher education. *Journal of Studies in International Education*, 21(1), 52–64.

Keevy, J., & Chakroun, B. (2015). *Level-setting and recognition of learning outcomes: The use of level descriptors in the twenty-first century*. Paris, France: United Nations Educational, Scientific and Cultural Organization.

Leask, B. (2015). *Internationalizing the curriculum*. New York: Routledge.

Leask, B. (2016). Internationalizing curriculum and learning for all students. In E. Jones, R. Coelen, J. Beelen, & H. de Wit (Eds.), *Global and local internationalization* (pp. 191–203). Boston, MA: Sense Publishers.

Lumina Foundation. (2014). *The degree qualifications profile: A learning-centered framework for what college graduates should know and be able to do to earn the associate, bachelor's or master's degree*. Indianapolis, IN: Lumina Foundation. Retrieved from www.luminafoundation.org/files/resources/dqp.pdf

National Association of Colleges and Employers (NACE). (2017). *Job outlook 2018*. Bethlehem, PA: NACE.

National Communication Association (NCA). (2015). *What should a graduate with a communication degree know, understand, and be able to do?* Washington, DC: NCA.

Rice, E. (2011, June). *Reframing student outcomes to develop 21st century skills* (Stanford Center for Opportunity Policy in Education Knowledge Brief). Retrieved from https://edpol

icy.stanford.edu/sites/default/files/publications/reframing-student-outcomes-develop-21st-century-skills.pdf
Shultz, L. (2007). Educating for global citizenship: Conflicting agendas and understandings. *Alberta Journal of Educational Research*, 53, 248–258.
Spitzberg, B. H. (1997). A model of intercultural communication competence. In L. A. Samovar & R. E. Porter (Eds.), *Intercultural communication: A reader* (8th ed., pp. 379–391). Belmont, CA: Wadsworth Publishing.
Tremblay, K., Lalancette, D., & Roseveare, D. (2012). *Assessment of higher education learning outcomes: Feasibility study report*. OECD Publishing.
Wiggins, G., & McTighe, J. (2005). *Understanding by design*. Alexandria: Association for Supervision and Curriculum Development.

6 Internationalizing Intercultural Competence Instruction in the Community College Basic Course

Wei Sun, Donna Oti, Andrew Jared Critchfield, and Taryn K. Myers

Introduction

Globalization and internationalized campuses have brought tremendous changes to the higher education system in the United States. International students, defined as those who have crossed an international or territorial boundary and are enrolled outside of their country of origin (UNESCO), also greatly impact higher education in the U.S.; worldwide, U.S. colleges and universities receive 21% of international students (Butler, 2016). Between 2001 and 2014, 160,000 international students attended community colleges in the U.S., and 40,000 students earned associate degrees (Bhandari & Blumenthal, 2011; Ruiz, 2014). By 2016, nearly half of the undergraduate students attending community colleges were classified as international students. Community colleges can begin to internationalize their curriculum and meet the needs of their diverse student populations by adopting intercultural competence training within the communication Basic Course.

Literature Review

International perspectives should be integrated at multiple points in the higher educational system using various strategies to effectively prepare students for a globalized world (Butler, 2016). Students need access to a curriculum that helps them develop intercultural competencies. Equally important, the learning community should model a commitment to diversity by actively seeking opportunities to support diversity and inclusion. This need has led some campuses to develop independent offices to coordinate efforts to internationalize the curricula as well as to ensure the wider learning community of students, faculty, and staff values diversity and reflects intercultural sensitivities in teaching, research, and service.

Internationalization of Campuses

As microcosms of an increasingly globalized world, higher education campuses provide a unique opportunity to shape emerging views about diversity and inclusion. English-speaking universities and colleges have long recognized the importance of internationalization of campuses (Back, Davis, & Olsen, 1996; Subtirelu, 2017). The primary aims of internationalization efforts have been to foster cross-cultural cooperation and increase diversity (Bennett, & Salonen, 2007; Grabove, 2009; Subtirelu, 2017). Jin and Cortazzi (2017) suggest that to promote and sustain internationalization in U.S. higher education, universities must take a systematic approach, embedding cultural learning into policies and practices. In addition, intercultural competence training should extend beyond the classroom to include all students, administrators, faculty, and staff (Kudo, 2016). The curriculum and learning environment should motivate the entire community of learners to engage in internationalized content and intercultural learning contexts (Yook & Turner, 2018).

Knight (2001) echoes the importance of an integrated approach that encompasses the entire learning community, defining internationalization as a "process of integrating an international perspective into teaching/learning, research and service functions of a higher education institution" (p. 229). Knight (1997, 2001, 2004, 2015) reviews the growth and development of policies, programs, and initiatives that bolster the internationalization of universities and notes the six major phases of the internationalization process: awareness, commitment, planning, operationalize, review, and reinforce. This circular model underscores the long-term commitment needed for successful internationalization initiatives, stressing the need for corrective actions and continuous improvements throughout the lifecycle of the initiative.

Intercultural Communication Competence Pedagogy

Lantz-Deaton (2016) asserts intercultural competence should be an outcome of the internalization of college-level curriculum and policies. Developing a diversity-focused pedagogy that supports intercultural competence is crucial to internationalizing universities and colleges. However, early development of an internationalized pedagogy focused on merely incorporating globalization into the content of the curriculum. This focus primarily centered on disciplines within the arts and humanities while dismissing the potential to infuse such disciplines as the biological sciences with intercultural curriculum (Lee, Shaw, Williams, & Wambach, 2012). Content-focused pedagogy allows students to learn a wider array of information, multiple perspectives, and different discourses; however, this approach to pedagogy does not allow the student to develop skills needed to apply the information and awareness learned. Scholars acknowledge that the content-focused model of pedagogy is problematic; instead, effective models should offer a critical perspective rather than simply relying on learning content without the benefit of actively engaging with the information (Lee et al., 2012). In the U.S., learning is primarily centered on cognitive content or abstract conceptualization; however, reflection on the experience and active experimentation are shown to be the most important elements of the learning process. Students are more likely to learn when they are encouraged to reflect, interact with their peers, and discuss diversity (Lee et al., 2012), which is the focus of intercultural competence training.

Community College Internationalization and Intercultural Competence

Raby and Valeau (2007) identify four significant historical phases in the internationalization of community college curriculum and campuses wherein the impetus was more about providing an internationalized experience for US students and less to welcome international students to US campuses. The first is the recognition phase (1967–1984), wherein policymakers began to recognize the potential for community colleges to embrace international education, and a few colleges initiated international programs. The second is the expansion and publication phase (1980–1990), which saw an increase in the adoption and documentation of international education in community college settings. During this phase, community colleges received increased funding to internationalize the curriculum in order to prepare students to be competitive in an increasingly global workforce. The third is the augmentation phase (1990–2000). Community colleges enhanced their internationalization efforts by infusing more disciplines with international curriculum and developing study-abroad programs. The fourth stage is the institutionalization phase (2000–2007). During this phase, internationalization was inserted into the mission statements of many community colleges through both state and national education policies, and many international programs were funded by state and federal governments.

Ross (2016) cites three factors for international students increasingly enrolling at community colleges: relatively easy admission, affordable tuition compared to higher university rates, and academic programs for English learners. Between the academic years of 2014–2015 and 2015–2016, community colleges that offer baccalaureate and associate degrees recorded a 12% increase in international students (Institute of International Education, 2016). While there are measurements to track the number of students enrolled, revenue generated, and international projects completed, there are no real metrics to measure how well internationalization has been integrated into the curriculum (Grabove, 2009). On community campuses, there are a variety of programs with high enrollment rates, especially in programs dedicated to international, global, or diversity education. However, a lack of interest from institutions and faculty prevents the curriculum from being fully internationalized on many campuses (Grabove, 2009; Prieto-Flore, Feu, & Casademont, 2016). In Canada, 80% of universities suggest they support internationalization, but 87% have no formal guidelines on how to reward internationalization efforts (Charbonneau, 2014). Of US colleges that offer solely associate degrees, only 7% reward their faculty for international work, and 5% consider international work and experiences in tenure and promotion decisions (American Council on Education, 2017).

In sum, it is critical for community colleges, which are on average more diverse than other educational institutions, to develop integrated, systematic strategies for internationalization. Proposed strategies should take into consideration needs at various levels, including the individual student who can grow personally and professionally (Chen & Starosta, 1996), faculty that will be better able to develop curricula that encourage curiosity about and understanding of international ideas and practices administrators who can deliver programs that prepare students adequately to address global issues with local implications, the learning community that benefits from a wealth of diverse perspectives and creativity, and the national level that enjoys innovations inspired by a global mindset. Individually, students need to develop intercultural competence to communicate effectively in an increasingly globalized world.

Theories on Intercultural Communication Competence

For five decades, scholars have studied intercultural communication competence. Intercultural communication competence is derived from communication competence theory. Krauss and Glucksberg (1969) researched children's communication skills, finding that to make a message understood, the speaker must adjust the knowledge level to the capability of the listener. McCroskey (1982) and McCroskey and McCroskey (1988) developed a Self-Perceived Communication Competence Skills Measurement, defining communication competence as an "adequate ability"

(p. 109) to speak and to write effectively. They distinguished the difference between the ability to perform and actual performing in situated contexts. Spitzberg (1983) added knowledge, skill, and motivation to the definition of communication competence and states competence is contextual, judged by a continuum of appropriateness and effectiveness, functional, and creates an interpersonal impression to observers. Rubin and Martin (1994) developed ten dimensions of interpersonal communication competence, including self-disclosure, empathy, social relaxation, assertiveness, interaction management, altercentrism, expressiveness, supportiveness, immediacy, and environmental control. Since the late 1980s, intercultural communication scholars have conducted intensive and exhaustive research in intercultural communication competence (Arasaratnam & Doerfel, 2005; Chen & Starosta, 1996; Cupach & Imahori, 1993; Deardorff, 2004, 2006; Hammer, 2012; Kim, 1991; Lustig & Koester, 2012; Wiseman, Hammer, & Nishida, 1989; Zimmerman, 1995).

Based on McCroskey's (1988) Communication Competence Model, Moeller and Nugent (2014) added willingness to communicate as an important part in building intercultural communication competence in language classrooms. Perceived communication competence and level of communication comprehension determine whether a student will initiate talking to another person.

Deardorff (2006) introduced the intercultural communication competence model and its components: "world knowledge, foreign language proficiency, cultural empathy, approval of foreign people and cultures, ability to practice one's profession in an international setting" (Deardorff, 2006, p. 247). Understanding cultural differences, self-awareness of one's own culture, and experiencing other cultures have been key components in some institutions' cultural competence definition.

Deardorff (2006) developed a Pyramid Model of Intercultural Competence, from a personal level moving upward to an interpersonal level. The first level consists of requisite attitudes of respect and openness and curiosity. The second level consists of knowledge and comprehension and skills. Knowledge and comprehension include cultural self-awareness, deep understanding of culture, culturally specific information, and sociolinguistic awareness. Skills include the ability to listen, observe and interpret, analyze, evaluate, and relate. The third level is desired internal outcome and includes adaptability, flexibility, an ethno-relative view, and empathy. The fourth level is desired external outcome, which includes the ability to behave and communicate effectively to achieve goals (Deardorff, 2006, p. 254).

Internationalization of Communication Basic Course

The communication Basic Course is part of the general education curriculum in 95.2% of two-year colleges, compared to 37.9% in 2010 (Morreale, Myers, Backlund, & Simonds, 2016). The communication Basic Course in both two-year and four-year institutions often includes the following topics: the communication process, ethical communication, public speaking, critical thinking, listening, communication confidence, information literacy, culture and diversity, technology and communication, self-evaluation, peer evaluation, argumentation, and group work. Few pedagogical support services outside the classroom are available for instructors at two-year colleges, such as graduate and assistant tutors or online services, except the publisher's website associated with the textbook (Morreale et al., 2016). The communication Basic Course fulfills a General Education requirement on many campuses and is taught commonly as principles or foundations of oral communication, public speaking, interpersonal communication, or business communication.

The Basic Course at some schools is a hybrid, combining public speaking and interpersonal communication; the combination of online teaching and the face-to-face classroom may also be referred to as a hybrid course.

The National Communication Association recognizes "adapting to others" as one of seven core communication competencies for introductory communication courses, as well as monitoring and presenting yourself, practicing communication ethics, practicing effective listening, expressing messages, identifying and explaining fundamental communication processes, and creating and analyzing message strategies (Engleberg, Ward, Disbrow, Katt, Myers, & O'Keefe, 2017). The competency is stated as "the ability to understand, respect, and adapt messages to a diversity of human characteristics and attitudes in order to accomplish communication goals within and across a variety of communication contexts" (Engleberg et al., 2017, p. 14). The rationale for this competency mentions the variety of communication contexts wherein adaptation is required, "beyond the personal and professional environments into both civic and cultural arenas. Also, as the world becomes 'smaller' through technological integration, the ability to adapt to others becomes a distinguishing feature of all introductory communication courses" (Engleberg et al., 2017, p. 14).

Intercultural Communication Competence Training in Community Colleges

The National Communication Association (NCA) established an "Internationalizing the Communication Discipline" Task Force (2017) which identified five levels of internationalized curricular development. Descriptions of the five levels, from highest to lowest, follow. Level 5 (moving from course design to the department's curricular scaffolding) is reached when students are encouraged to study abroad as a capstone course experience, international courses are required, and certificates for international competencies are offered, such as an International Studies Certificate that includes communication courses. For a discussion of Level 4 (the course involves immersion in international settings), Orbe and Orbe (2018) offer a template for study abroad experiences enhanced by intercultural theories from faculty and student perspectives. Walker, Cardon, and Artiz (2018) provide an example of Level 3 (the entire course has an international orientation), collaborative coursework between teams in seven countries. A semester-long project on intercultural friendship (Gareis, Goldman, & Merkin, 2019) demonstrates Level 2 (the course dedicates a complete unit to international questions). Provided below are suggestions for internationalizing the Basic Course at Level 1 (the course contains some international elements).

Metro Community College

The anonymized Metro Community College (Metro) is a public, accredited, and open admission junior college located less than 20 miles from a major metropolitan city. Founded as a nighttime high school with a few dozen students, today the Metro has three campuses, serving 60,000 students with more than 170 academic programs. Metro students recently were 11% Asian, 28% Black, 27% Hispanic, 24% White, and 10% international. Of Metro's 1,300 full-time and part-time faculty members, 922 are White, 199 Black, 51 Hispanic, 118 Asian, and 3 internationals. The mission statement for Metro suggests striving to become a "national model" institution but does not include words indicating internationalization is a priority, such as "international" or "global."

The required speech course in the General Education requirements was recently made optional, despite communication faculty advocating for its continued inclusion. Students still have the option of choosing an introductory communication course or professional communication course—from among 50-plus other courses—which counts as a required "global and cultural perspective" course. Fewer communication Basic Course sections are offered each semester due to declining enrollment, attributed to issues such as communication apprehension and competing course titles and subjects that may seem more interesting or less demanding to students. Some instructors internationalized their communication Basic Course for many years at Metro prior to the requirements change; it is now imperative that all instructors at Metro and other campuses internationalize their Basic Course to interest students seeking engagement in a global world.

The Basic Course at Metro utilizes pedagogical activities that were developed by the first author, across four levels following Deardorff's Model of Intercultural Competence (2006). Intercultural communication competence training focusing on motivation, knowledge, skills, sensitivity, awareness, and appropriateness is emphasized.

Respect, Openness, and Curiosity

This level of competence is established at the beginning of the semester to set the tone for the class. The first day of class consists of the instructor welcoming each student to the class, introducing herself, and reviewing the syllabus. Then the first activity, "Introducing Your Classmate," serves as an icebreaker to get all students involved in a nonthreatening way. The instructor presents a series of interview questions for each student to ask another, such as: What is the meaning of your name? Where are you from? How many languages do you speak? How far have you traveled? Did you experience culture shock while traveling? Students pair up and discuss the questions for a few minutes. At the conclusion of the activity, students take turns introducing their partners in front of the class. Because of the diversity of the student population at Metro, most students have diverse backgrounds and experiences. The instructor engages students in a conversation designed to help them identify commonalities across cultures. This exercise serves to build connections and a sense of community among the students, which can last through the semester and subsequent terms. By the end of the first class, each student will at least know one partner whom he or she interviewed and introduced. Throughout the semester, this episode will be brought up several times to illustrate various intercultural contexts. For example, during discussions about high and low contexts, culture shock, and anticipated communication apprehension, students can reflect on the icebreaker and their peers' experiences. If students are initially hesitant to share their experiences in the Basic Course, Knifong (2017) provides experiences of students of different cultural backgrounds that could be shared in the Basic Course to encourage participation.

Critchfield (2006) suggests using proverbs as pedagogy to internationalize the curriculum. At the beginning of each class period (or for online courses, it could be each module or discussion boards), a proverb is shared to focus students on the study of communication and to provide insights for just a few minutes. The proverbs, such as "the shoe knows if the stocking has holes," which is said in The Bahamas, are listed on the syllabus so students know what will be discussed at the beginning of each class period and can ruminate on the proverbial meaning prior to class.

Knowledge, Comprehension, and Skills

To meet the requirements of the Basic Course at Metro, students must demonstrate proficiency based on communication competencies (Ellingboe, 1998; Engleberg et al., 2017). They learn principles of communication as well as an understanding of the self and its relationship to others in real communication settings through assignments and assessments, including presentations and a group project that have an intercultural focus. Students are encouraged to share with the class their experiences practicing what they learned. For example, several students shared their experiences of overcoming communication apprehension while speaking in meetings or in other communication contexts. Munz and Colvin (2018) provide an important reminder for Basic Course instructors, to be mindful of how student backgrounds, including religious practices, influence communication apprehension.

As the semester proceeds, students experience measurable improvements in communication competence and are ready to further reflect on their personal communication competencies. A self-concept paper addressing components of communication, perceptions, culture, and self is written and then presented to peers while sitting in a circle. On several occasions, students of different backgrounds overcome apprehension to share with the class their thoughts and discuss critical moments which led to "what makes you who are you today." The session sometimes serves as a catharsis, which gives students the opportunity to learn more about themselves as well as their classmates. Usually after this assignment, students find more common ground and begin to value differences; this establishes a deep sense of closeness among the students. It helps to eliminate further apprehension as students gain the opportunity to reduce uncertainty about others.

Anderson-Lain (2017) offers a similar assignment but, in addition to the essay, requires a multimedia representation of personal identity. Students review the representations individually at a forum and then complete journal entries about what they observed in their peers' representations. In hybrid face-to-face and online courses, the journal assignment can be adapted to a discussion board topic.

Teaching this Basic Course at Metro for many years, the instructor still often feels touched by the students' experiences and their willingness to freely share their learning. In one instance, an immigrant student recalled how her mother came to the United States, overcoming difficulties to acclimate to a new culture. The student wishes her mother could have benefited from the Basic Course at Metro! A benefit of developing intercultural competencies throughout the Basic Course is that students and the instructor experience deeper empathy for each other based on shared narratives. In certain cases, students might not be willing to share intimate details of their lives. The instructor respects boundaries set by the students and reminds all students of the importance of boundaries. The classroom context, rich with diverse cultures, sets a stage for insightful discussions that enable students to explore how people from cultures different from their own think, behave, and react.

Internal Outcomes: Adaptability, Flexibility, Ethno-Relative Views, and Empathy

Students' personal experiences are always solicited to add examples of communication interactions and contexts to analyze concepts from lectures. In the discussion of culture shock and adaptation, the best examples come from students who have traveled to a country with a very different culture compared to their own. If few students have traveled abroad, the instructor asks students about their initial experiences at Metro: what surprised them and how the student adapted. Through these examples, everyone understands that culture shock is a normal psychological reaction for new contexts and situations (Sun & Chen, 1999). To teach ethnorelativism, the instructor first introduces ethnocentrism and its consequences. Life experiences of the instructor and the students are exchanged and discussed. For example, tipping at restaurants is expected in the U.S. But in many countries, tipping is not expected and may insult. If an international guest does not tip one of the many Metro students who work in the dining industry, it would be easy to form stereotypes about the guests from an ethnocentric view. Additionally, an instructor can find international examples in open educational resources such as Dhanesh (2014).

External Outcomes: Communicate Effectively to Achieve Goals

The primary learning outcome of the Basic Course is to make students competent communicators in speaking and writing in interpersonal and professional settings. In discussing nonverbal communication, such as body movement and eye contact, students learn about cultural differences. Instructional episodes using cultural scenarios such as "when stopped by a police officer, what do you do and not do" are enlightening and prompt discussion. Students will offer different appropriate and inappropriate actions based on their culture and experiences. In the US, a driver is expected to stay inside the car unless advised otherwise. Drivers are expected to keep their hands on the wheel, roll down the car window, and await the officer's approach. Conversely, in some countries, a driver would be expected to demonstrate compliance and respect by opening the car door and taking documents to the waiting police officer. Doing the opposite of what is expected in varied cultural contexts could be costly. Police brutality and racial profiling in domestic and international scenarios are also discussed. These situations produce rich conversations and debates about appropriate communication behavior and consequences of perceived inappropriate actions, especially if students are currently law enforcement personnel or seeking careers in that field.

Once the instructor had a student from an Asian culture in which younger women are prohibited from engaging in eye contact with men and seniors to show respect. The student received many complaints at her US salon job because customers perceived her avoidance of eye contact as indifference, not following the cultural expectation in the US that good customer service includes sustained eye contact and interest (even if feigned). She made tremendous progress at work and increased her tips after understanding how her lack of eye contact was perceived and practicing the expected eye contact in the Basic Course at Metro. Her peers offered eye contact help and practice; suggestions included focusing on the person's nose or forehead instead of their eyes initially to get more comfortable with direct eye contact.

Identification of language biases and their contribution to gender stereotypes is an important area of study in the Basic Course. Because there are many second language learner students at Metro, they may be less familiar with how their new language use can divide and exclude. Common phrases such as "all men are created equal" are highlighted so students understand how sexist language is subconsciously embedded in daily interactions. Another example is that students working in the hospitality industry are invited to think about how greeting every group with a "hi, guys" may exclude. The instructor devised a "collecting gender stereotypes" activity to address this. In groups, students are asked to list ten negative and ten positive characteristics for each gender. Then the lists are exchanged and critiqued. This generates fierce debate on gender roles and stereotypes and how they are formed and further enacted by family, society, and mass media. Antony (2016) suggests a similar opportunity wherein students make posters that embrace or reject stereotypical identities.

Conclusion

This study offers suggestions for internationalizing the community college communication Basic Course through teaching students intercultural competence. As community colleges become more internationalized—especially through their enrolled students—Basic Course instructors can ensure their classes appropriately prepare students to be global citizens who comfortably and competently interact interculturally. The first section of this study reviewed the history of internationalization on US and community college campuses, intercultural communication pedagogy, and intercultural competence. The second section provides instructor experiences in teaching the communication Basic Course and how pedagogical activities helped diverse students develop intercultural communication competencies utilizing Deardorff's (2006) Intercultural Competence Model. First, the model includes teaching students to respect others, display openness, and remain curious. Second, the importance of gaining knowledge, mastering comprehension, and gaining skills are explained. Third, adaptability, flexibility, ethno-relative views, and empathy are emphasized. Fourth, communicating effectively to achieve goals is offered as an ongoing aim.

Communication educators can internationalize their Basic Course classrooms, even if they personally do not have international experience or institutional support and resources to internationalize the curricula. Included in this essay are specific pedagogical activities—and citations for additional international curricula ideas—which can be adapted to any communication Basic Course and student population. The Basic Course is an opportunity to demonstrate to students the importance of adopting internationalized perspectives and intercultural communication competence to be effective global citizens and leaders.

References

American Council on Education. (2017). *Mapping internationalization on U.S. campuses: 2017 edition*. Retrieved from www.acenet.edu/news-room/Documents/Mapping-Internationalization-2017.pdf

Anderson-Lain, K. (2017). Cultural identity forum: Enacting the self-awareness imperative in intercultural communication. *Communication Teacher, 31*(3), 131–136.

Antony, M. G. (2016). Exploring diversity through dialogue: Avowed and ascribed identities. *Communication Teacher, 30*(3), 125–130.

Arasaratnam, L., & Doerfel, M. (2005). Intercultural communication competence: Identifying key components from multicultural perspectives. *International Journal of Intercultural Relations, 29*(2), 137–163.

Back, K., Davis, D., & Olsen, A. (1996). *Internationalization of higher education: Goals and strategies*. Canberra, Australia: IDP Education.

Bennett, J. M., & Salonen, R. (2007). Intercultural communication and the new American campus. *Change, 39*(2), 46–50.

Bhandari, R., & Blumenthal, P. (2011). Global student mobility and the twenty-first century Silk Road: National trends and new directions. In R. Bhandari & P. Blumenthal (Eds.),

International students and global mobility in higher education: National trends and new directions (pp. 1–25). New York, NY: Palgrave Macmillan.

Butler, D.-A. C. (2016). *Comprehensive internationalization: Examining the what, why, and how at community colleges* (Unpublished doctoral dissertation), College of William and Mary, Williamsburg, VA.

Charbonneau, L. (2014, December 9). Why students aren't buying into universities' internationalization efforts?: The benefits of studying abroad just aren't getting through to them. *University Affairs*. Retrieved from www.universityaffairs.ca/opinion/margin-notes/arent-students-buying-universities-internationalization-efforts/

Chen, G. M., & Starosta, W. J. (1996). Intercultural communication competence: A synthesis. *Communication Yearbook, 19,* 353–383.

Critchfield, A. J. (2006). Proverbs as pedagogy. In B. Hugenberg & L. Hugenberg (Eds.), *Teaching ideas for the basic communication course* (Vol. 10, pp. 109–112). Dubuque, IA: Kendall Hunt Publishing.

Cupach, W. R., & Imahori, T. T. (1993). International and intercultural episodes and relationships. In R. L. Wiseman & K. Koester (Eds.), *Intercultural communication competence* (pp. 112–131). Thousand Oaks, CA: Sage Publications.

Deardorff, D. K. (2004). Internationalization: In search of intercultural competence. *International Educator, 13*(2), 13–15.

Deardorff, D. K. (2006). Identification and assessment of intercultural competence as a student outcome of internationalization. *Journal of Studies in International Education, 10*(3), 241–266.

Dhanesh, G. (2014). Speaking to a global audience. [chapter 14] *Public Speaking: The Virtual Text.* Retrieved from http://publicspeakingproject.org/psvirtualtext.html

Ellingboe, B. J. (1998). Divisional strategies to internationalize a campus portrait: Results, resistance, and recommendations from a case study at a US university. In J. A. Mestenhauser & B. J. Ellingboe (Eds.), *Reforming the higher education curriculum: Internationalizing the campus* (pp. 198–228). Phoenix, AZ: Oryx.

Engleberg, I. N., Ward, S. M., Disbrow, L. M., Katt, J. A., Myers, S. A., & O'Keefe, P. (2017). The development of a set of core communication competencies for introductory communication courses. *Communication Education, 66*(1), 1–18.

Gareis, E., Goldman, J., & Merkin, R. (2019). Promoting intercultural friendship among college students. *Journal of International and Intercultural Communication, 12*(1), 1–22.

Grabove, V. L. (2009). Reflections on trends and challenges in internationalizing an Ontario community college. *New Directions for Teaching & Learning, 118,* 15–23.

Hammer, M. R. (2012). The intercultural development inventory: A new frontier in assessment and development of intercultural competence. In M. Vande Berg, R. M. Paige, & K. H. Lou (Eds.). *Student learning abroad* (pp. 115–136). Sterling, VA: Stylus Publishing.

Institute of International Education. (2016). Retrieved from www.iie.org/

Jin, L., & Cortazzi, M. (2017). Practising cultures of learning in internationalizing universities. *Journal of Multilingual & Multicultural Development, 38*(3), 237–250.

Kim, Y. Y. (1991). Intercultural communication competence: A systems-theoretic view. In S. Ting-Toomey & F. Korzenny (Eds.), *Cross-cultural interpersonal communication: International and intercultural communication annual* (pp. 259–275). Newbury Park, CA: Sage Publications.

Knifong, D. (2017). Listening to students of different cultural backgrounds. *Listening to Students.* Retrieved from www.csus.edu/saseep/ListeningSurvey/Students%20of%20Different%20 Cultural%20Backgrounds.2.pdf

Knight, J. (1997). A shared vision? Stakeholders' perspectives on the internationalization of higher education in Canada. *Journal of Studies in International Education, 1*(1), 27–44.

Knight, J. (2001). Monitoring the quality and progress of internationalization. *Journal of Studies in International Education, 5*(3), 228–243.

Knight, J. (2004). Internationalization remodeled: Definition, approaches, and rationales. *Journal of Studies in International Education, 8*(1), 5–31.

Knight, J. (2015). International universities: Misunderstandings and emerging models? *Journal of Studies in International Education, 19*(2), 107–121.

Krauss, R. M., & Glucksberg, S. (1969). The development of communication: Competence as a function of age. *Child Development, 40*(1), 255–266.

Kudo, K. (2016). Social representation of intercultural exchange in an international university. *Discourse: Studies in the Cultural Politics of Education, 37*(2), 256–268.

Lantz-Deaton, C. (2016). Internationalization and the development of students' intercultural competence. *Teaching in Higher Education, 22*(5), 532–550.

Lee, A., Shaw, M., Williams, R., & Wambach, C. (2012). Developing a pedagogy that supports intercultural competence. *ASHE Higher Education Report, 38*(2), 45–63.

Lustig, M. W., & Koester, J. (2012). *Intercultural competence: Interpersonal communication across cultures* (7th ed.). Upper Saddle River, NJ: Prentice Hall.

McCroskey, J. C. (1982). Communication competence and performance: A research and pedagogical perspective. *Communication Education, 31*, 1–8.

McCroskey, J. C., & McCroskey, L. L. (1988). Self-report as an approach to measure communication competence. *Communication Research Reports, 5*, 108–113.

Moeller, A. J., & Nugent, K. (2014). Building intercultural competence in the language classroom. In S. Dhonau (Ed.), *Unlock the gateway to communication* (pp. 1–18). Eau Clarie, WI: Crown Prints.

Morreale, S., Myers, S. A., Backlund, P. M., & Simonds, C. J. (2016). Study IX of the basic communication course at two- and four-year U.S. colleges and universities: A re-examination of our discipline's "front porch". *Communication Education, 65*(3), 338–355. doi:10.1080/03634523.2015.1073339

Munz, S. M., & Colvin, J. (2018). Communication apprehension: Understanding communication skills and cultural identity in the basic communication course. *Basic Communication Course Annual, 30*, Article 10. Retrieved from https://ecommons.udayton.edu/bcca/vol30/iss1/10/

National Communication Association. (2017). *Internationalizing the communication curriculum brochure*. Retrieved from www.natcom.org/sites/default/files/pages/Internationalization_Internationalizing_Communication.PDF

Orbe, M. P., & Orbe, I. P. (2018). Intercultural theorizing for a global communication curriculum: A short-term study abroad pedagogical template. *Journal of Intercultural Communication Research, 47*(5), 1–7.

Prieto-Flores, O., Feu, J., & Casademont, X. (2016). Assessing intercultural competence as a result of internationalization at home efforts. *Journal of Studies in International Education, 20*(5), 437–453.

Raby, R. L., & Valeau, E. J. (2007). Community college international education: Looking back to forecast the future. *New Directions for Community Colleges, 138*, 5–14.

Ross, K. M. (2016, June 16). Community colleges with the most international students. *US News*.

Rubin, R. B., & Martin, M. M. (1994). Development of interpersonal communication competence. *Communication Research Reports, 11*(1), 33–44.

Ruiz, N. G. (2014). *The geography of foreign students in US higher education: Origins and destinations*. Washington, DC: Brookings Institution. Retrieved from www.immigrationresearch-info.org/system/files/geography_of_foreign_students.pdf

Spitzberg, B. H. (1983). Communication competence as knowledge, skill and impression. *Communication Education, 32*(3), 323–329.

Subtirelu, N. C. (2017). Students' orientations to communication across linguistic difference with international teaching assistants at an internationalizing university in the United States. *Multilingua, 36*(2), 247–280.

Sun, W., & Chen, G. M. (1999). Dimensions of difficulties Mainland Chinese students encountered in the United States. *Intercultural Communication Studies, 9*(1), 19–30.

UNESCO. (n.d.). *Definition: International (or internationally mobile) students*. Retrieved from http://uis.unesco.org/en/glossary-term/international-or-internationally-mobile-students

Walker, R. C., Cardon, P. W., & Artiz, J. (2018). Enhancing global virtual small group communication skills. *Journal of Intercultural Communication Research, 47*(5), 421–433.

Wiseman, R. L., Hammer, M. R., & Nishida, H. (1989). Predictors of intercultural communication competence. *International Journal of Intercultural Relations*, *13*(3), 349–370.

Yook, E. L., & Turner, P. K. (2018). Bringing international perspectives to the communication curriculum in the age of globalization. *Journal of Intercultural Communication Research*, *47*(5), 375–381.

Zimmerman, S. (1995). Perceptions of intercultural communication competence and international student adaptation to an American campus. *Communication Education*, *44*(4), 321–335.

7 Internationalizing the Communication Center
Rhetorical and Multilingual Frameworks

Laura A. Stengrim

> For you may bring me someone as learned, as sharp-witted and intelligent, and as ready in delivery as you like: if, for all that, he is a stranger to the customs of his community, its precedents and models, its traditions, and the character and inclinations of his fellow citizens, then those commonplaces from which arguments are produced, will not be of much benefit to him.
>
> Cicero, *De Oratore*, Book 2, 131

Two weeks into the fall semester, a first-year student wanders into the library, looking for assistance with a research project. The circulation desk directs the student to the writing center. The writing center directs the student to the reference librarian. A draft of the paper yields comments from the instructor, which the student struggles to interpret. Mid-semester, the student is shepherded into the communication center for purposes of developing a class presentation. The student does not know where to begin and is afraid to talk in front of classmates . . .

The above scenario is a daily, sometimes hourly occurrence in communication centers that serve as interdisciplinary hubs supporting the rhetorical practices of speaking and writing across the curriculum. Often, familiar aspects of a student's background and identity, including but not limited to their status as a first-generation college student, their language background, or their cultural dispositions, comprise the "stranger to the community" status that Cicero described, unfamiliar with the customs, traditions, and discursive machinations of US higher education. Operating outside of the classroom and thereby outside of the realm of evaluation, communication centers offer an important space and source of support for students to navigate the institution. Indeed, as Paul Kei Matsuda (2012) suggests, the process of developing a "discursive repertoire in particular rhetorical situations" is not all that different for first- and second-language speakers (p. 40). Through peer- and near-peer interaction in one-to-one and small-group settings, students develop rhetorical competencies that inform their social and academic communication practices and overall progress throughout their time at the institution.

This chapter argues that in observing the relationships between changing current student demographics, and, specifically, by shifting toward a translingual paradigm, communication centers have the potential to play a vital role in the discipline of communication as it maneuvers what some have called the "global turn" (Wang, 2016). The number of international students in the United States rose in 2016, for example, to an all-time high of 1,043,839, for the first time comprising more than 5% of higher education enrollment (Institute of International Education, 2016).

Although that number decreased in certain regions and institutions in subsequent years, many colleges and universities continue to rely on the recruitment of international students to their campuses (Redden, 2018). Internationalization, as it has unfolded in the past two decades, is "about equipping people to understand and adapt to a more tightly interdependent world" (Fischer, 2019). Even though the international student population has dramatically waxed and then waned in recent years, as a long-term trend, college campuses in the United States have become ethnically and linguistically diverse. In 1976, nearly 85% of American undergraduate students in the US were white and presumably spoke English as their primary language; by 2015, according to the National Center for Education Statistics, the number dropped to 58% (2018).

Meanwhile, economic diversity among the student body has become a goal and institutional measure, with a rapidly growing number of Pell Grant-eligible, low-income, and first-generation domestic students attending colleges and universities. In a 30-year period, the number of low-income students enrolling in college has grown from 37% to 67%, a trend that challenges a perceived tradition that higher education is reserved for the elite and middle classes (Cooper, 2018). Indeed, the 2008 recession and 2011 Occupy Wall Street movement brought into question the idea of the "neoliberal university," or, in other words, an institutional complicity of U.S. higher education within a system of globalization that is "a source of economic dislocation, scattering winners and losers in its wake" (Seal, 2018; Fischer, 2019). Under public scrutiny, and given a trend of decline in the overall population of prototypical college-ready freshmen, many institutions began to explicitly address and include economically diverse students in their strategic plans for recruitment and enrollment. Communication centers, as key sources of support for student retention, thus find themselves at a crossroads between education's socio-cultural and socio-economic imperatives.

Offering an analytical review of research in communication center studies as it intersects with a growing literature on multi/pluri/translingualism and transliteracy pedagogies in rhetorical studies, I argue that our current moment of internationalization in US higher education requires a paradigm shift that moves toward transliteracy while recognizing and interrogating the neoliberal economic moment in which it finds itself. The following sections revolve around the idea and potential of communication centers in adopting a translingual paradigm, put into conversation in a historically situated era of globalization that is riddled with both opportunity and inequity. As the discipline internationalizes its curriculum and grapples with the demographic and ethical complexities of higher education's role in the global economy, communication centers are well equipped to lead the way.

The Idea of a Communication Center

In a significant and often-cited article, North (1984) forwarded the maxim that the mission of a writing center is to "make better writers, not necessarily—or immediately—better texts" (p. 441). While writing centers have long histories on college campuses, communication centers are a relatively new but increasingly drawn-upon resource and model for supporting a continuum of rhetorical practices, including oral communication and multimodal literacies. They nevertheless share the adage that "the goal isn't better speeches, but better speakers" by focusing on a process orientation (Turner & Sheckels, 2015, p. xiv). At some institutions, communication centers work in tandem with the basic introductory or public speaking course, where at others they fulfill a campuswide effort to facilitate communication in and across the disciplines, working with students as well as faculty and instructors. Communication centers are informed by the discipline's classical roots and ongoing developments, and they are usually staffed by student peer consultants who work with speakers in one-to-one and small-group settings.

With underpinnings in rhetorical history and theory, communication center consultants assist speakers with gaining an understanding of those elusive "customs of the community" that Cicero recognized, thus supporting the institution's mission. Indeed, as Hobgood (2014) notes, "a speech center may be the very setting in which an understanding of rhetoric as disciplinary, interdisciplinary, and extra-disciplinary abides" (p. 67). That is, communication centers not only bring expertise about oral communication and presentation skills to bear on their work with students or speakers who attend sessions, but they also promote the discipline throughout campus, contributing to a larger dialogue about how we articulate the discursive norms and expectations of our various communities of research and practice.

Operating outside of the formal classroom and curriculum, communication centers provide low-stakes environments for students to develop and practice communication skills and competencies, usually in one-to-one or small-group, peer-to peer settings (Yook & Atkins-Sayre, 2012). Communication scholars have shown that such settings, with highly trained students acting as peer consultants, tutors, or mentors, are effective in attaining higher GPA and retention rates, especially for first-generation and underrepresented students who lack social support (Gist-Mackey, Wiley, & Erba, 2018; see also Smith, 2013). When students encounter cognitive or learning thresholds, peer-to-peer interaction can prove a key source and strategy for their success, development, and capacity to apply skills and concepts to new situations. Communication centers thus teach for transfer—which is especially important in explicating the discursive practices with which students are previously unfamiliar for the purpose of future recontextualizing (Nowacek, 2011).

Recent years have seen an increasing number of scholarly publications related to or about communication centers in general, yet only a small portion of that literature has focused on their work with students who grew up speaking languages other than English (Turner & Sheckels, 2015). Much of the scholarship on international students and multilingual speakers comes from disciplines related to education and literacy, though it confirms the suggestion that communication centers are poised to be crucial sites in the internationalization of US higher education and its relationship to the global economy's vicissitudes. For example, students can begin to develop an awareness of the complexities of cultural and linguistic diversity outside of the formal, traditional classroom, observing that "where peer exchange and other collaborative approaches were emphasized, attitudes to working in cross-cultural groups at university appeared more positive" (Montgomery, 2010, p. 127). The discipline of communication studies also brings a distinct expertise on intercultural communication (e.g., Palmerton, 2015) as well as interpersonal and organizational communication that can inform how institutions approach multilingual and otherwise diverse student populations.

However, in developing a nuanced vision and approach to communication center theory and practice that understands internationalization as a "multitude of aspects that aim to promote an environment that actually integrates a global perspective into the whole university" (Montgomery, 2010, p. 5), communication centers might do more to attend to and problematize English itself. A critical and rhetorical approach to language questions, for instance, the usefulness and consequences of marketization discourse in education that equates students with consumers and that treats the English language as a commodity (Lu, 2004, p. 27) or "piece of property or hot stock" (Prendergast, 2008, p. 1). Rather, as seen in the following sections, describing and discussing language as a mobile and dynamic resource informs how communication centers can most ethically serve the diverse domestic and international students who wander through our doors.

Translingual Paradigm

Communication centers can facilitate the discipline's internationalization by starting with an understanding that regardless of citizenship status, nation of origin, regional dialect, or economic circumstances, humans communicate by learning to mobilize discursive resources within various and varying contexts. A rhetorical perspective infuses how peer consultants are trained, how they interact with speakers, and how the discipline informs the campus and community's attitudes, beliefs, and values around language; it opens a conversation about the act of disciplining itself, leading to rich examination of norms, genres, and audience expectations in distinct circumstances. A rhetorical perspective also questions the language used to describe the work of the communication center. For instance, labels such as ESL (English as a second language) and ELL (English language learner) fail to capture the complexity of language backgrounds of domestic and international students alike.

Indeed, the experiences of English and other language study can vary greatly in terms of reading, writing, and speaking practices and pedagogies, and for many students English is a third or fourth area of language study. Moreover, as Canagarajah (2013) observes, "those who are considered monolingual are typically proficient in multiple registers, dialects, and discourses of a given language. Even when they speak or write in a single 'language,' they still have to communicate in relation to diverse other codes in the environment" (p. 8). The word *multilingual* might better encompass a range of language experience, yet it implies an adding onto, as well as the possibility of mastery. For Canagarajah (2013), multilingual does not capture the dynamic interactions between languages and communities that *translingual* does; translingualism allows for a portable and varied approach to the rhetorical acts of reading, writing, and speaking. It sees English as a "heterogenous, bustling, complicated, shifting, fluid mix of languages, dialects, and creoles" (Horner, NeCamp, & Donahue, 2011, p. 288; see also Horner, Lu, Royster, & Trimbur, 2011).

You (2016) makes a further distinction between *translingualism* and *transliteracy*, the latter indicating a reflexive capacity to code-switch, code-mesh, and code-swap in a variety of cultural encounters and situations. This self-reflexive and evolving capacity to adapt to new discursive environments is a powerful outcome for any student as they navigate the academic and extracurricular straits of colleges and universities. In the communication center, a guiding philosophy of both translingualism and transliteracy can lead to conversations not only about linguistic similarities and differences but also, explicitly, acts of transfer, "not mastery but open-ended development of more semiotic resources" (Canagarajah, 2013, p. 176). In other words, transliteracy provides a vocabulary that rejects a deficiency model and recognizes that, in fact, the many subject and language positions that we occupy serve not as limitations but as sources of knowledge, experience, and growth.

In this way, translingualism and transliteracy also work, and not subtly, to critique monolingual nativism as experienced in 21st-century globalization. It is imperative that scholars and educators in communication and rhetorical studies adopt an internationalist perspective that questions nationalist assumptions as well as the privileging of Western rhetorical traditions (Hurlbert, 2012). Further, it is imperative that we "look outside language and link language explicitly to the socioeconomic order" (Piller & Cho, 2013, p. 24; see also Phillipson, 2008). In opening up a space for conversation about nonstandard Englishes through a translingual paradigm, communication centers can provide a way of thinking that both supports the educational goals of institutions of higher education and, at the same time, counters neoliberal ideology through what David Harvey calls "revolutionary humanism," or "the belief that we can through conscious thought and action change both the world we live in and ourselves for the better" (2014, p. 282).

Internationalization's Local Histories

International students have a long history of studying in US colleges and universities, their presence often tied to the needs of local economies as well as to the nation's foreign policy objectives. In the early 20th century, particularly during the economic boom that followed World War I, international houses for elite youth were established in major cities such as New York and Chicago by donors and philanthropists aiming to build a generation of world leaders. The post–World War II era saw more American students studying abroad, as well as more international students studying in the United States. Wendy Leeds-Hurwitz (1990) has argued, in fact, that the field of intercultural communication stems from the interdisciplinary work of linguists and anthropologists in the State Department and Foreign Service Institute's postwar programs in diplomacy training (see also Leeds-Hurwitz, 2010). The post–World War II era indeed "was set apart by a widespread, sharpened sense of foreign students as critical actors in the global politics of the Cold War and decolonization" (Kramer, 2012, p. 17). Strategic partnerships and programs such as Fulbright raised America's role in the postwar world, and the presence of international students also served in parallel to cultural and economic dynamics.

At many institutions, intensive English programs served both the national interest and local industry. At the University of Southern Mississippi, for example, a 1957 advisory council speech boasted that the university's Latin American Institute had the "rare and golden opportunity of being the 'firstest with the mostest' in the implementation of the Golden Rule and the Good Neighbor policy" (Reindorp, n.p). Tied intimately to the opening of the port of Mississippi following World War II, the Latin American Institute's very foundations responded to hemispheric economic, cultural, and strategic alliances. In 1948, Melvin Nydegger, the Institute's first director, wrote, "The future trade and industrial hopes of this section of the United States lie to the South with its great and relatively undeveloped market in the Caribbean" (p. 185). The Chiquita brand, notably, had been trademarked in 1947 as the port of Mississippi opened to a flood of Latin American goods and commodities. The institute would continue to evolve along with shifting the regional, national, and global landscape, and the countries from which students would come to study would vary according to the times; for example, the 1978 oil boom brought an influx of Saudi students and necessitated a "survival English course for Saudi Arabian wives," and in the 1980s, the highest number of students at the Institute was from Japan (*History of the English Language Institute*, n.d.).

The internationalization of US higher education is therefore not new, nor are the pressures for institutions to adapt to local and global economic forces. Kramer (2012) argues that "international education has reflected neoliberal economic and political trends of privatization and a globalized business world," especially from the 1970s onward (Garlitz & Jarvinen, p. 7). Twenty-first-century globalization has seen these trends accelerate, along with increased economic inequality and at the same time greater diversity in student demographics. The history and growth of communication centers, in particular, aligns with the technological shifts that have, on the one hand, opened the way for creativity and innovation in how we think about rhetorical pedagogies in higher education's current landscape and, on the other, amped up the pressure to prepare students to become competitive participants in a global economy that runs on commodified English.

A translingual perspective in the communication center engages the discipline in systemic critique by reckoning with our history while carefully supporting the needs of diverse students in our current moment of internationalization. In explicitly recognizing and talking about linguistic differences, literacies, and rhetorical adaptability, it is a dynamic "practice that is politically savvy and socially conscious, and sensitive to power, social norms, and audience" (You, 2016, p. ix). However, as Ryoko Kubota (2016) and others (Matsuda, 2014; Gilyard, 2016; Nguyen, 2017) have observed, translingual and transliteracy approaches are not a panacea; without critical reflection, they risk complicity in the very same neoliberal logics of cosmopolitan elitism that they seek to disrupt while eliding important cultural and linguistic distinctions. Communication center consultants must be trained, therefore, to honor the needs and goals of each unique speaker and to empower one another through conversation and ongoing reflexive practice.

Institutionally, communication centers must continually redefine themselves as radically welcoming spaces and defy misconceptions that we are in the problematic business of 'accent reduction' that upholds Standard American English (SAE) as preeminent. As You (2016) writes, "by marginalizing certain styles of English and other languages," educators run the risk "of occluding other ways of knowing and meaning making, ending up crippling their students' education" (p. 231; see also Hyland, 2016). By serving as a counterweight to educational models and programs that take English for granted and thereby take for granted the economic forces that both drive the need for recruitment of international students and at the same time cause deepening class divisions, communication centers can help pave a more careful and ethical path forward.

While it is important to prepare students to be successful in job interviews and to speak in ways that are comprehensible and effective for the given context, it is also important to encourage them to think critically about the ways in which human beings are capable of mobilizing discursive resources in many different settings. A translingual and transliterate perspective allows for the recognition that the more Englishes that are brought to the table, the more delightful the conversation will be.

Conclusion

As the discipline of communication continues to respond to shifts in student demographics and to grow in relevance, and as technologies allow for easier and faster methods of communication throughout the globe, communication centers are becoming integral in thinking about rhetorical pedagogies within higher education's changing economic and cultural landscape. Because communication centers exist outside of the formal curriculum, they pose an opportunity for students to converse about language, culture, and diversity in a low-stakes environment that is mutually beneficial; at the same time, communication centers bring visibility to the discipline across campus, thus benefitting the institution as a whole and becoming a resource for decisions about programming, particularly in the areas of student success and retention of international and otherwise at-risk students. In short, to borrow from Cicero again, communication centers can introduce the "customs of the community" so that no student is made to feel as though they are a stranger to it.

References

Canagarajah, S. (2013). *Translingual practice: Global Englishes and cosmopolitan relations*. New York: Routledge.
Cooper, P. (2018). College enrollment surges among low-income students. *Forbes*. Retrieved from www.forbes.com/sites/prestoncooper2/2018/02/26/college-enrollment-surges-among-low-income-students
Fischer, K. (2019). How international education's golden age lost its sheen. *The Chronicle of Higher Education*. Retrieved from www.chronicle.com/interactives/2019-03-28-golden-age
Garlitz, R., & Jarvinen, L. (Eds.). (2012). *Teaching America to the world and the world to America: Education and foreign relations since 1870*. London: Palgrave Macmillan.
Gilyard, K. (2016). The rhetoric of translingualism. *College English*, 78(3), 284–289.
Gist-Mackey, A. N., Wiley, M. L., & Erba, J. (2018). You're doing great: Keep doing what you're doing: Socially supportive communication during first-generation college students' socialization. *Communication Education*, 67(1), 52–72.
Harvey, D. (2014). *Seventeen contradictions and the end of capitalism*. New York: Oxford University Press.
History of the English Language Institute. (n.d.). USM—Latin American Institute. Mississippiana vertical file indexes, special collections, The University of Southern Mississippi Libraries, Hattiesburg, MS.
Hobgood, L. (2014). Training speech center consultants: Moving forward with a backward glance. *Southern Discourse in the Center: A Journal of Multiliteracy and Innovation*, 19(1), 60–69.
Horner, B., Lu, M., Royster, J., & Trimbur, J. (2011). Language difference in writing: Toward a translingual approach. *College English*, 73(3), 303–321.
Horner, B., NeCamp, S., & Donahue, C. (2011). Toward a multilingual composition scholarship: From English only to a translingual norm. *College Composition and Communication*, 62(2), 269–300.
Hurlbert, C. (2012). *National healing: Race, state, and the teaching of composition*. Boulder: University of Colorado Press.
Hyland, K. (2016). Academic publishing and the myth of linguistic injustice. *Journal of Second Language Writing*, 31, 58–69.
Institute of International Education. (2016). International student enrollment trends, 1948/49–2015/16. *Open Doors Report on International Educational Exchange*. Retrieved from www.iie.org/opendoors
Kramer, P. A. (2012). Is the world our campus? International students and U.S. global power in the long twentieth century. In R. Garlitz & L. Jarvinen (Eds.), *Teaching America to the world and the world to America: Education and foreign relations since 1870* (pp. 11–50). London: Palgrave Macmillan.
Kubota, R. (2016). The multi/plural turn, postcolonial theory, and neoliberal multiculturalism: Complicities and implications for applied linguistics. *Applied Linguistics*, 37(4), 474–494.
Leeds-Hurwitz, W. (1990). Notes in the history of intercultural communication: The foreign service institute and the mandate for intercultural training. *Quarterly Journal of Speech*, 76, 262–281.
Leeds-Hurwitz, W. (Ed.). (2010). *The social history of language and social interaction research*. Cresskill, NJ: Hampton Press.
Lu, M. (2004). An essay on the work of composition: Composing English against the order of fast capitalism. *College Communication and Composition*, 56(1), 16–50.

Matsuda, P. K. (2012). Teaching composition in the multilingual world: Second language writing in composition studies. In K. Ritter & P. K. Matsuda (Eds.), *Exploring composition studies: Sites, issues and perspectives* (pp. 36–51). Boulder: University of Colorado Press.

Matsuda, P. K. (2014). The lure of translingual writing. *PMLA, 129*(3), 478–483.

Montgomery, C. (2010). *Understanding the international student experience*. New York: Palgrave Macmillan.

National Center for Education Statistics. (2018). *Digest of education statistics, 2016*. Retrieved from https://nces.ed.gov/fastfacts/display.asp?id=98

Nguyen, K. H. (Ed.). (2017). *Rhetoric in neoliberalism*. London: Palgrave Macmillan.

North, S. (1984). The idea of a writing center. *College English, 46*(5), 433–446.

Nowacek, R. (2011). *Agents of integration: Understanding transfer as a rhetorical act*. Carbondale: Southern Illinois University Press.

Nydegger, M. (1948). Better international relationships through student-teacher exchanges. *The Modern Language Journal, 32*(3), 184–189.

Palmerton, P. (2015). Working with diverse clientele. In W. Atkins-Sayre & E. L. Yook (Eds.), *Communicating advice: Peer tutoring and communication practice* (pp. 107–122). New York: Peter Lang.

Phillipson, R. (2008). The linguistic imperialism of neoliberal empire. *Critical Inquiry in Language Studies, 5*(1), 1–43.

Piller, I., & Cho, J. (2013). Neoliberalism as language policy. *Language in Society, 42*(1), 23–44.

Prendergast, C. (2008). *Buying into English: Language and investment in the new capitalist world*. Pittsburgh, PA: University of Pittsburgh Press.

Redden, E. (2018). New international enrollments decline again. *Inside Higher Ed*. Retrieved from www.insidehighered.com/news/2018/11/13/new-international-student-enrollments-continue-decline-us-universities

Reindorp, R. (1957). *You and the Institute*. USM—Latin American Institute. Mississippiana Vertical File Indexes, Special Collections, The University of Southern Mississippi Libraries.

Seal, A. (2018). How the university became neoliberal. *The Chronicle of Higher Education*. Retrieved from www.chronicle.com/article/How-the-University-Became/243622

Smith, B. (2013). *Mentoring at-risk students through the hidden curriculum of higher education*. New York: Lexington.

Turner, K. J., & Sheckels, T. F. (Eds.). (2015). *Communication centers: A theory-based guide to training and management*. New York: Lexington.

Wang, B. (2016). The global turn and the question of "speaking from". *Composition Studies, 44*(1), 134–137.

Yook, E. L., & Atkins-Sayre, W. (Eds.). (2012). *Communication centers and oral communication programs in higher education: Advantages, challenges, and new directions*. New York: Lexington.

You, X. (2016). *Cosmopolitan English and transliteracy*. Carbondale: Southern Illinois University Press.

8 Internationalizing Rhetorical Studies

Alberto González and Amy N. Heuman

Beginning with Plato and extending through neo-Aristotelian approaches to rhetorical communication in the mid-20th century, speakers and audiences were largely considered *known subjects*. While they may have varied across a few demographic categories (such as age), and they certainly had personal interests and ambitions at stake, rhetors and their hearers were assumed to share the same worldview. Additionally, audiences involved in deliberative, epideictic, or forensic occasions were sufficiently narrowed by the hegemonies of their time such that the underlying logic of persuasive appeals would be commonly understood.

The "New Rhetoric" of the latter 20th century expanded the scope of rhetorical topics and methods and began to complicate notions of rhetor and audience. But these approaches still largely presumed rhetoric in monocultural and monolinguistic settings. Kenneth Burke famously stated that persuading another is possible "insofar as you can talk his language by speech, gesture, tonality, order, image, attitude, idea, *identifying* your way with his" (Burke, 1962/1969, p. 55). Burke does not go on to recommend second- and third-language acquisition in anticipation of a non-English-speaking listener and thus does not encourage critics to expand understandings of rhetors to diverse, polycultural, and multilingual contexts.

Rhetorical studies, whether in the undergraduate or graduate curriculum, have focused most specifically on US political (that is, governmental) discourses. Since the 1990s, theory-building and critique have expanded beyond political oratory to include mediated contexts and a variety of critical perspectives including postcolonial, feminist, and whiteness studies as well as vernacular rhetoric, among others. In light of this expansion, our central question in this chapter is: *How does rhetoric look beyond the US context?* The short answer is, it depends. As we reply to this question, we draw from published rhetorical scholarship that implicates global perspectives and topics in a variety of ways to provide directions for internationalizing courses and resources on rhetorical theory and criticism. Though they are describing communication studies generally, what Rodriguez and Chawla (2008) argue applies perhaps more urgently to rhetorical studies. They conclude that there is "a disciplinary unwillingness to allow Other understandings of Communication Studies that reflect Other worldviews to flourish, as such understandings inherently challenge the status quo" (p. 33). Examples of "Other worldviews" are to be found in primary communication publications but not in abundance. Writing ten years after Rodriguez and Chawla, Law and Corrigan (2018) point to "whitespeak" in graduate education. They argue that "white-speak functions through an often unstated modality of silencing, disciplining, disrupting, and regulating nonwhite and/or non-normative bodies, practices, and forms of knowledge, preventing critical inquiry and alternative ontological and epistemological frameworks, and stifling the performance of critics of color" (p. 326). Critical rhetoric invites alternative international perspectives and viewpoints that have been excluded by the structural privileging mechanisms of the academy. However, according to Law and Corrigan, critical rhetoric "has not succeeded" in this regard (p. 326). Such hegemonic patterns continue within our journals even with McKerrow's (1989) calls for critical rhetoric, which invites international and co-cultural perspectives. For McKerrow, "Rhetoric requires relationality—it must have the ability to 'construct' a reality from diverse fragments in order to provide a commensurable world in which communication can occur" (McKerrow, 2000, p. 43). These "diverse fragments" imply international and intercultural contexts and epistemologies, thus pointing to a need for a more reflexive broadening and deepening of our 'internationalizing' rhetorical sensibilities.

This chapter begins by describing what we mean by "internationalizing" rhetorical studies. Next, we explore how the notion of "rhetorical legacy" (Hammerback & Jensen, 1994), or what others call "rhetorical tradition" (Garrett & Xiao, 1994; Garrett, 2000), gains access to rhetorical activity beyond the US. Rhetorical tradition acknowledges that rhetorical action is culture-based and that awareness of rhetorical traditions (i.e., Chinese and/or Mexican traditions) allow a better understanding of culturally grounded advocacy. Third, we examine the contributions to rhetoric from the three perspectives of transnational feminism, postcolonial studies, and Africanist ways of knowing to demonstrate how such lenses serve to internationalize rhetorical studies. Finally, we review instances in which scholars examine speeches delivered outside the US to international audiences by US speakers.

Working Against National Rhetorics

Our goal within this chapter is to call for an "internationalizing," or diversifying, of rhetorical understandings while simultaneously pointing to the problematic tendency to equate internationalizing with a rhetoric of nations. What do we mean when we say that our goal is to "internationalize" rhetorical studies? We turn to a purview of rhetorical studies that elucidates efforts to expand rhetorical standards. Second, we describe the various ways that the term "international" can apply to analyses of rhetorical communication.

In the West, the study of rhetoric is as old as the Greeks. Platonic and Aristotelian approaches to rhetoric are summarized in books such as *The Rhetoric of Western Thought: From the Mediterranean World to the Global Setting* (Golden, Berquist, Coleman, & Sproule, 2011). Bitzer (1968) notes that scholars of rhetoric, influenced by the Greeks, study "types of speeches [and] types of proof, lines of argument, strategies of ethical and emotional persuasion, the parts of a discourse and the functions of these parts, qualities of styles, [and] figures of speech" (p. 2). What gets left out of this scope is the cultural nature of rhetoric. Eventually, as rhetorical studies expanded, the links to culture became explicit. As early as 1990, Asante observes that "The effectiveness of each rhetorical act is based on the communication patterns and strategies employed by a particular society" (p. 250). This realization was the impetus for Asante's Afrocentric approach to rhetoric. Analysis of rhetoric expanded from the examination of a specific speaker to social movements (Griffin, 1952), ideology (Wander, 1983), feminist rhetoric (Campbell, 1973, 1980), and postmodern rhetorics (McKerrow, 1989; Jablonski 1998). At their core, rhetorical studies seek to examine how meanings are symbolically created, organized, and expressed to others to accomplish or move toward goals that will implicate the "sacred" objects of societies such as identity, community, motive, value, and power.

While the limitations of US-centric theories and topics were less apparent when studying US political discourses of the 19th and 20th centuries, with globalization came the need to acknowledge the interdependence between various US rhetorics and the discourses of other nations and cultures. Additionally, new attention was drawn to the applicability of prevailing definitions and critical methods. As early as 1993, Lu and Frank note that searching for the equivalent of "rhetoric" across nations will limit what is found. In the case of Chinese discourse, they state, "Western rhetorical scholars will miss the depths and nuances embedded within ancient Chinese texts if they use 'rhetoric' as the English equivalent for the Chinese senses of *bian*" (p. 451). Did the prevailing US-centric frameworks remain insightful across national contexts? Was it even ethical to apply US-centric critical values and assumptions when examining the rhetorical efforts of non-Western nations and sensibilities? These questions reveal why rhetorical studies have increasingly become more self-conscious of the cultural and political values that were reproduced in studies that involved nondominant or international discourses. Rhetorical studies had to confront the charge that "working from the terms of Western Rhetoric merely re-colonizes the Other" (McKerrow, 2002, p. 291). Shome (2013) identifies the challenge presented to academic journal editorial boards when examining submissions with "a global trajectory" given that paper reviewers are "firmly placed in a straight rhetorical tradition" (p. 515). Although drawing primarily from the Western tradition, Goldzwig (1998) forecasts that rhetorical criticism "will require an openness to new theories, critical practices, skills acquisition, and commitments" (p. 285).

As we show in this chapter, critics of rhetoric have responded in various ways to the challenges of internationalism and globalism. But before we continue, we need to address a notable topic within international and intercultural communication scholarship. The topic concerns the application of the term "nation" (and often "nation-state" or "nationstate") to describe communication, or in this case, rhetoric. Often, we might use the expression "American rhetoric" or "Japanese rhetoric." But what does this describe? Many scholars have pointed out the problematic use of these ways of naming a nation's discourse. Ono (2011) argues that "As constructs, nationstates necessarily have limited explanatory power, especially when attempting to represent the diversity of ideas, opinions, lifestyles, and behaviors of people" (p. 88). Following this argument, Collier (2014) "rejects the validity of predicting or generalizing about the . . . preferences of groups of people whose upbringing or citizenship aligns with a nation-state" (p. 9). From a critical perspective, a homogenous treatment of nation normalizes the dominant political way of speaking and advocating and mutes the advocacy and epistemologies of co-cultural and indigenous groups. Also, such a treatment assumes that discourses work in isolation and are not influenced by the discourses of other co-cultural groups. For example, the preacherly vernacular rhetoric of the US Civil Rights Movement has influenced much of the "dominant" political communication for decades. Finally, the notion of a singular national rhetoric reduces the opportunities to explore the variety of rhetorical values and strategies within nations thereby, reducing the growth of theory development.

While we acknowledge the problematic application of "nation" in communication studies and in rhetorical studies in particular, the fact remains that nations exist and rhetors speak from and about those nations and others, and they claim citizenship to particular nation-states. As a result, rhetorical scholars have written about cross-national rhetoric in a variety of ways, and we want to distinguish those ways. However, we also want to suggest how those ways can inform one another in higher education curricula and in research with an international sensibility. Hence, by "internationalizing rhetorical studies," we include three types of studies. First, we include rhetorical studies that are informed by and deepen our understanding of native or indigenous discursive values and practices. These values and practices would be considered external to the US. Second, we include studies such as transnational feminism, postcolonial criticism, and Africanist approaches to rhetoric that are premised on cross-national histories and influence. Finally, we include studies that focus on US speakers abroad, and we also include studies that examine speakers from other nations whose rhetoric is examined using US-based rhetorical concepts. The next section describes criticism that draws from indigenous forms of advocacy that are not US based.

Rhetorical Traditions

Rhetorical critics writing in the US have found it useful to base analysis of rhetoric upon the distinctive ways of communicating within a culture. This is what Garrett and Xiao (1994) call a culture's "discourse tradition" (p. 31) or "discourse community and tradition" (p. 38). In their analysis of Chinese 19th-century political rhetoric, they note that "most treatments of the rhetorical situation ignore the role of the discourse tradition," and this tradition shapes audience expectations for appropriate argument (p. 38). Hence, in the case of Chinese rhetoric, depictions of Westerners as "little barbarians" who could be kept at bay with a "loose rein" trade policy were persuasive to audiences in whose worldview these depictions were taken-for-granted truths. Theoretically, Garrett and Xiao complicate notions of "audience" by linking listener cultural knowledge and assumptions to the analysis of rhetoric. Similarly, in their examination of the rhetorical movement for California farmworker rights, Hammerback and Jensen (1994) reviewed movement speeches and plans for protest. "The rhetorical dimensions of these Mexican-American documents become clear only within the context of their own rhetorical tradition, a tradition anchored in Mexican history and developed from the Mexican-American's culture and experiences" (p. 54).

In her analysis of the letters written by Dolores Huerta, co-founder of the United Farm Workers, to César Chávez, Sowards (2012) notes that their interactions are not adequately explained by the dominant US values of individualism and competition but instead "by cultural norms and forces rooted in collectivism and collaboration" (p. 304) that derive from their Mexican heritage. Huerta's letters are not simply expressions of her thoughts and concerns for the labor movement and its strategies. Her letters also enact a Latinx preference toward interdependence and familialism.

Finally, though he does not use the term "rhetorical tradition," Lake (1991) explains that in Native American activist rhetoric "the circle is the root metaphor of existence" (p. 134) that emerges from traditional rituals that venerate cyclical patterns observed in nature. The indigenous epistemology that centers natural rhythms is heard in Native American advocacy for self-determination.

How can critics make use of rhetorical traditions? Lu and Frank (1993) urge "authentic" interpretations of rhetoric that require knowledge of a culture's discourse tradition and an awareness of the limitations of Western criteria for rhetorical discourses. For example, an examination of the *Tao Te Ching* that applies

Western expectations for practical reasoning might conclude that Chinese author Lao Tzu was against argument and critical thinking (p. 450). Yet a culturally attuned reading would take an integrative or holistic approach that focused on "identification of paradoxical as opposed to literal meanings" (p. 450). In this case, a reading grounded in cultural sensibilities sets aside Western criteria for reasoning and persuasion and instead applies expectations premised in Chinese culture and preferences.

An additional way to acknowledge a rhetorical tradition is to focus on indigenous terms used by rhetors that have deep meaning within a cultural community. For example, in their analysis of Jomo Kenyatta's Independence Day address in 1963, Mutua-Kombo and González (2013) focus on Kenyatta's use of the Swahili terms *harambee* (pulling together) and *uhuru* (freedom; p. 14). Kenyatta was the first elected president following the end of British colonization. The address was delivered in Nairobi, Kenya, and Kenyatta's rhetorical challenge was to reassure the British that independence would unite a fractured Kenya and to motivate Kenyans to support the new government. *Harambe* and *uhuru* carried "deep ideological meaning" (p. 15) among Kenyans, and these terms were familiar elements within the Swahili speech tradition. Drawing from indigenous languages of nations (while not defining nations by a dominant language) helps rhetorical studies escape the charge of being monolingual and global languages averse.

A third way to involve rhetorical traditions is to utilize critical approaches that are relatively adaptable to different international contexts. For example, Lee and Campbell (1994) employ generic criticism to critique the unique aspects of a speech delivered by South Korean President Roh Tae-woo. In the genre of presidential rhetoric, his 1988 inaugural address emerges from "a tradition . . . that is a mixture of Western-style of rhetorical practice with Confucian principles" (p. 38). Roh was elected after a period of intense political turmoil, and to gain support for his government, he appealed to his audience(s) "in a uniquely Korean way" (p. 44). Roh drew upon a very common national belief—that Koreans are one people—when he addressed his audience as "my sixty million compatriots," a number that included North Koreans (p. 44). Roh tapped into knowledge that only Koreans would fully understand. Without naming events directly, he alluded to the Japanese colonization of Korea and to the Confucian value of focused communal labor. This study by Lee and Campbell illustrates how an approach to criticism can accommodate the distinct histories and expectations of audiences.

The major benefit to learning about a particular discourse tradition is that it makes for a richer analysis. Rhetorical critics are very good at focusing on an artifact and describing its circumstances and explaining how it functions as a social force. Critics are hesitant to describe how the artifact operates as *cultural discourse*. Neglecting relevant cultural features to a speech or other artifact can result in flattening the discourse or reducing its distinctiveness such that it might as well have been produced in the US. The study of this speech or rhetorical artifact then succumbs (through the author's design or through the editorial process) to what Shome calls "the politics of recognition" (2013, p. 515). At best, it limits what we understand about the discourse, and at worst, it implicates the critic in a practice of cultural imperialism. On the other hand, placing discourse within a cultural framework provides a more nuanced interpretation of the rhetor's effort. There will be additional examples of studies that draw from rhetorical traditions in a later section of this chapter on Africanist epistemologies. In the next section, we provide an overview of three areas of study that are available for internationalizing rhetorical studies.

Three Cross-National Perspectives for Rhetorical Studies

In this section, we describe three areas of research that are inherently international. Transnational feminism views the critique of gendered structures and the struggles for equity as a global project. Postcolonial rhetorical studies decenter colonizer representations and include indigenous perspectives and resistance. Africanist epistemologies are animated regionally, often crossing arbitrarily drawn national borders. We include studies to illustrate international topics in rhetorical studies and realize that many additional scholars are doing important work.

Transnational Feminism. Meyer (2007) defines feminist rhetoric as "*a commitment to reflexive analysis and critique of any kind of symbol use that orients people in relation to other people, places, and practices on the basis of gendered realities or gendered cultural assumptions*" (p. 3). She argues that the introduction of feminist rhetoric into rhetorical studies, beginning with Campbell's (1973) essay on women's liberation, is important because such analyses work to illuminate women as communicators and essentially work against a monolithic rhetoric. Such moves, then, open up spaces for writing women into our histories and knowledge bases while also challenging standards for evaluating rhetoric. However, that is not to say that feminist lenses have always been wholly inclusive. In fact, the beginning works within feminist rhetoric, as with feminist activism and praxis, have been questioned and critiqued for being White and US women centered and not attending to intersectional difference in specific places and contexts. Further, as Meyer notes, the field of rhetorical studies, when including women, tends to be driven by White women with advanced educations. As such, the inclusion of women within rhetorical studies also prompts attention to the imperative of considering diverse gendered subjectivities and positionalities within feminist rhetoric.

As a response to such critiques, transnational feminisms emerged turning a keen eye toward patriarchal systems of governance in the global sphere as well as to the problematic ways difference has been addressed within feminist praxis (Dempsey, Parker, & Krone, 2011). Transnational feminism, as asserted by Shome (2006), avows that "gender is, and always has been, global—whether recognized or not" and therefore calls for an interrogation of "how unequal global relations (of culture and economy) continually articulate the politics of gender in any local context, and how local relations are always at work in macro global processes" (p. 255). Perhaps one of the most prominent transnational feminists is Chandra Mohanty (2003), who has encouraged interrogations of how difference is accounted for in feminist praxis and also has called for feminist alliances across difference. Attention to intersectional difference and coalition/alliance building illuminates the detriments of supposing a universalized woman in complex matrices of domination (Hill Collins, 1995; hooks, 1984; Ong, 2006). Drawing attention to the interlocking nature of oppressive systems through attention to culture, race, ethnicity, class, nationality, gender, sexuality, and religion allows for an understanding of how ideologies such as patriarchy, heteronormativity, racial superiority, upward mobility, nationalism, and other such culturally specific ideologies might intersect and play off of one another, albeit in different ways, in specific places and contexts. And, these examinations also reveal how such interplay might impact women differently according to their positionalities within hegemonic systems.

Within communication studies, scholars have explored the implications of their own efforts pertaining to transnational and intersectional feminist praxis (Carrillo-Rowe, 2008, 2009, 2010; Collier, Lawless, & Ringera, 2016; Lee, 1998b; Linabary &

Hamel, 2017). As a response to the cultural and economic inequities of global forces, Collier, Lawless & Ringera (2016) outline the need for "critical reflexivity" in transnational feminist praxis as well as the importance of "situated feminism" to understand Kenyan women's articulations and practices of feminism within the local power structures and cultural contexts. Moreover, Linabary and Hamel (2017) promote postcolonial reflexivity as a transnational feminist practice within their analysis of the World Pulse, an organization aimed at raising transnational women's voices for social transformation.

Specific to rhetorical studies, Lee (1998a) calls for "inter-rhetorical reflexivity" as a means of working against scholarly tendencies to frame reflexivity as a self-analytic practice. Through her analysis of Chinese naming practices of women, Lee argues that interrhetorical reflexivity encourages scholars to rhetorically question their "process of rebuilding, knowledge construction, and teaching performance" (p. 307). Given this, she asserts that rhetorical critics ought to embrace a process of interrhetorical reflexivity focused on contextualizing both the author and the audience. Such forms of reflexivity, whether rhetorical or grounded in feminist praxis, call for scholars to "confront how histories, geographies, nations, cultures, and economies remain simultaneously *connected* and *disconnected* in complex and unpredictable ways in the continual making and unmaking of gender" (Shome, 2006, pp. 255–256) and also highlight how particular rhetorical lenses shape subsequent analyses of culture.

Similarly, Coplean and Dingo (2018) note that transnational feminist scholarship emphasizes the ways that "colonial and neocolonial legacies shape the current racial, gendered, political, and economic oppression of people across the world, and that global capitalism continues to create relations of inequality and exploitation" (p. 307–308). In their critique of scholarship attending to differences, they stress that rhetorical scholars must be cognizant of how such dynamics are connected to "race and racialization" because "such inequalities and exploitations largely impact people of color" in the global sphere. As a result, Coplean and Dingo call for the enactment of change within rhetorical studies and transnational feminist work in particular—from the content of our research to scholarly ethics within our research and to our active efforts for disciplinary and institutional change. They issue this imperative, mindful of the tendency for rhetorical studies to center White vantage points and consequentially "flatten out racial difference and power," what they call drive-by scholarship, "by not placing communication practices within structures of violence" such as through trade agreements, embargos, and local and national policies that have real impacts on people and their communities (p. 306). Drive-by scholarship, then, does not attend to complex economic and geopolitical processes of racialization and therefore renders an irresponsible and skewed analysis. Due to this propensity within rhetorical analyses, they urge scholars to engage in a more thoughtful discussion of race, gender, and geopolitical context as a means of attending to ethical transnational feminist practices. As these scholars demonstrate, utilizing a transnational feminist rhetorical lens is imperative within rhetorical studies and clearly provides a framework for internationalizing rhetorical studies.

Postcolonial Studies

Another way that pedagogues and scholars might work to internationalize rhetorical studies is through postcolonial rhetorical criticism. Shome and Hegde (2002) assert that "the politics of postcoloniality is centrally imbricated in the politics of communication"(p. 249) and therefore promote analyses that explore how communication is interwoven within the dynamics, problematics, and contexts of de/colonization. Much like transnational feminism, postcolonial criticism prompts rhetors to consider multiple forms, subjectivities, positionings, and histories and to critique Euro-centered hegemonic, master narratives of knowledge production.

Postcolonial studies place emphasis on centering postcolonial histories, subjects, and experiences—both past and present (Chawla & Atay, 2018)—that "emanate from the history of colonialism" (Madison, 2012, p. 55). Schwartz-Dupre (2018) notes that postcolonial analyses attend to the ways that "certain forms of knowledge are privileged while others—often indigenous knowledges and viewpoints—are often exploited, subjugated, and commodified" (p. 1694). As such, postcolonial critics turn a critical lens to examinations of the dialectical relationship between the colonizer and colonized as notably first described through the Occident/West and the Orient/Middle East in Edward Said's *Orientalism* (1978).

An early example of such attention to the dialectical relationship between colonizers and colonized can be found in Lee's (1998b) postcolonial feminist approach to Chinese footbinding discourses. Mindful of the nuanced and complex subjectivities and positionalities of colonizers and colonized, she employs a processual epistemology aimed at treating differentiation and identification as a simultaneous process. Processual epistemology concurrently attends to content orientation as a means of engaging in an intersectional analysis cognizant of differences connected to race, class, gender, and nationality. In doing so, Lee points to the multiple and distinctive discourses at work surrounding the practice of footbinding. In this sense, Lee's approach offers an example of how scholars might address transnational, postcolonial, and feminist concerns regarding rhetorical analyses of culture in complex, thoughtful ways.

Hasian and Wood (2010) provide an example of the role of rhetoric in mediating postcolonial histories. Their analysis of the Belgian Royal Museum for Central Africa argues that the museum is an "evolving site in the rhetorical struggle over how to remember Belgian and Congolese histories" (p. 129). Belgians, who had been taught that the colonization of the Congo was "relatively benign," had to confront a new version of their presence in Africa that revealed that millions of Congolese perished as resources were looted "to pay for Belgium's magnificent buildings" (p. 130). Their analysis charts how the museum changed or "evolved" its exhibits in the face of increasing pressure to represent the devastating consequences of Belgian colonization. Hasian and Wood urge critics to attend to both what is inside the museum *and outside*, to include "how various communities renegotiate the past as they craft new visualities and textual rhetorics" (p. 132). This study and others (see Na'puti, 2019) issue challenges to rhetorical critics to engage a decolonizing method that places epistemic value on the communities, places, and practices erased by imperialism.

Africanist Epistemologies

We also highlight studies that are based on the communication terms and practices found in various African perspectives to point to yet other ways that scholars internationalize rhetorical studies. We use the term "Africanist" rather than "Afrocentric" for two reasons. First, Africanist refers to a general African sensibility in the same way we might refer to a North American sensibility or a Latin American sensibility. Cultures and communities are vastly diverse across continents, but we wish to direct attention to a loose orientation toward discourse rather than to denote a center. Second, we want to acknowledge the multidisciplinary quality of these studies since they reject the disciplinary constraints often found in US scholarship.

Asante (1990) conducted research in Yoruba to describe "what constitutes effective advocacy oratory in the Yoruba tradition" (p. 251). To identify the practices of that rhetorical tradition as found in the courts, he drew from Yoruba novelists and direct observation. Not being a native to Yoruba, Asante also confirmed his sketch of cultural values with cultural insiders. Asante found that gendered hierarchies, quick resolution, keeping the "trouble-making" spirit away, and direct and simple explanations were prescribed by tradition (p. 252). Asante's study was an early example of US scholars exploring non-Western rhetorical practices.

In his analysis of Wangari Maathai's Green Belt Movement, Yartey (2018) explains that Maathai's approach to environmental activism had its origins in the beliefs of the Kikuyu in Kenya (p. 50). The Kikuyu believed that humans and the earth were interdependent, and each had to take care of the other. This interdependence led Maathai to her philosophy of "linkages" among economic self-determination, environmental preservation, social equity and government accountability (p. 48). She then illustrated this notion of linkages in her speeches by describing a wooden three-legged stool whose components worked together to function as a seat. What is noteworthy here is that Yartey moves from the local beliefs of the Kikuyu through the representation of these beliefs in symbolic forms (image of a stool, the famous hummingbird story, etc.), to Maathai's argument about the linkages that hold together people, politics, and nature.

Hagan (2010) writes from an Africanist and feminist perspective in her analysis of the rhetoric of *pagne* (a cloth wrap) among the women of Cote d'Ivoire. Hagan notes that communication across African nations "eludes definitional equivalents found in classical Western rhetorical theory" (p. 143). In Cote d'Ivoire, "Proverbial communication gives insight into an African epistemology that determines what is culturally known among people in a community" (p. 144). The *pagne*, then, is often named from or associated with a proverb or element of community wisdom that, when worn by a woman, communicates her opinion about social and political manners. The *pagne* allows women a rhetorical presence that is prohibited in other social domains. As feminist activism, the *pagne* reclaims a traditional public voice for women that was virtually wiped out by French colonialism (p. 148).

While an Africanist perspective can show how traditional knowledge is maintained and reproduced in public discourse, this perspective can also show how the opposite happens. Muneri (2016) examines the activity of civil society organizations (CSOs) in Zimbabwe. After Zimbabwe's independence in 1980, the CSOs were arguing against the repression of a violent ruling party and created a democratic discourse that advanced "individual rights, free and fair elections, and the participation of the people in the country's political, social, and economic affairs" (p. 10). At the same time, within the discourse of the CSOs, democracy was seen as a "universal" (p. 9) struggle whose terms and strategies drew from the West. Further, CSOs were introducing notions of "limited government" and expectations that democracy was an externally funded enterprise (p. 10), hallmarks of neoliberalism. As the CSOs competed with the ruling party over what kind of government to implement, "The overall hegemonic effect was to centralize Western democratic norms as the standards to which Zimbabwe should hold itself" (p. 14). In the case of Zimbabwe, postcolonial tensions arose over how quickly international rules would replace native norms.

For Wangari Maathai, people come to know and understand their social environments by interacting with the earth and natural cycles. Persuasion is based on narratives drawn from nature. In Cote D'Ivoire, knowing is premised on communal and collaborative relations even in the face of the individualism imposed from Europe. Here, persuasion is largely nonverbal and drawn from well-known proverbs. The inclusion of Africanist epistemologies into the study of rhetoric is important in order to show how traditional and colonialist ways of knowing and advocating course through one another in postcolonial Africa. This way of internationalizing rhetorical studies potentially broadens our capacity to examine the rhetoric of co-cultural groups in the US and elsewhere.

Rhetoric and International Contexts

Scholars have examined global topics using US-based perspectives and critical frameworks (Murray, 2018; Stec, 2016; Stuckey, 1995). Typically, the goal of these studies is more to illuminate the discourse of a US leader speaking abroad or speaking about a global issue than to explore the differences that such activities might generate. But these studies are not to be dismissed. According to Garrett (2000), "There is nothing inherently wrong with such a step, if it is used provisionally, with awareness of the dangers of forcing a fit, of overlooking significant aspects of the material, of misinterpretation, and so on" (p. 54). Depending on the case, it is even possible that cross-national applications might generate unique insights. For Garrett (2000), "a foreign framework may allow the researcher to notice aspects of a phenomenon that she would not see otherwise, and she may even conclude that in some instances the foreign term or category is more illuminating than misleading" (p. 54). This is the largest category of study, and we highlight two prominent threads here. By including these two threads, our goal is to remind readers (both students and researchers) that there has been an ongoing direct and indirect interest by rhetorical critics in topics of international import.

One thread is the examination of leaders of other nations (Fay, I., & Kuypers, J. A. 2012; Kelley, C. E. 1988) and events in other nations through film (Hasian, Anderson, & Wood, 2011) using rhetorical methods currently in use in the US. For example, Sheckels (2010) draws concepts from Kenneth Burke (consubstantiality), Walter Fisher (narrativity), and Mikhail Bakhtin (polyphony) to explain the rhetorical strategies of Thabo Mbeki's "I am an African" speech. While the author offers a convincing argument for the "theoretical pluralism" (p. 324) employed in the article, it is not clear how this combination of perspectives is more appropriate to a South African speaker than a South African discourse tradition. Sheckels observes that Mbeki bases his speech on epic Biblical narratives, stylizes his voice in the manner of US President John F. Kennedy to evoke an association with a "Camelot vision" and acknowledge Kennedy's enduring popularity across Africa (p. 323), and shifts from "I" to "we" to suggest the common substance shared by Africans.

Hasian, Anderson, and Wood (2011) use critical race theory to show how the film *Blood Diamond* "rendered invisible" the voices and experiences of the people of Sierra Leone, the very people whose plight the film seeks to reveal (p. 233). To provide a check on their interpretation of the film, the authors conducted personal interviews "with presidents and paupers" (p. 234) in Sierra Leone. They conclude that while the consciousness-raising rhetoric of the film is well intended in calling attention to the horrors of the international diamond trade, ultimately it falls short in representing the people of Sierra Leone and their experiences.

A second fascinating thread in this literature pertains to US characterizations of international actors and events as savage. Ivie (1984) provides a critique of President Reagan's attempt to build support for increased military spending and various peace initiatives in the face of an increasing Soviet threat. Reagan's language casts the Soviets as "animals," "machines," "criminals," "mentally disturbed," "fanatics" and "Satanic" (p. 42). Butler (2002) describes President Clinton's use of the "savage other" to justify military action in Somalia in the early 1990s. It was necessary for Clinton to depict Somalia as "a primitive society that does not appreciate its problems or the benevolent intentions of those who wish to help" (p. 13). Though primitive, Somalis are "modern savages" who are more dangerous than past eras of US imperialism because warlords and clans can purchase dangerous weapons and create regional chaos. Finally, Cloud (2004) reveals the same dehumanizing technique applied by news media and other information sources toward Afghan women after the September 11, 2001, terrorist attacks on the US and the subsequent invasion of Afghanistan. By depicting Afghan women as "backward and pre-modern" (p. 286), the US maintains its sense of exceptionalism to justify war. Ivie employs metaphoric criticism (Soviet as savage) and Cloud employs ideographic criticism (clash of civilizations). Both the root metaphor and the ideograph are critical tools that access important (if not core) beliefs in the dominant US society. Utilizing these studies provides an opportunity to reflect on the meanings to which US audiences respond regarding the African, Russian, and Afghan other and to also explore the important contrasting interests and histories of other cultures and nations.

Other rhetorical studies offer fascinating and timely critiques of cross-national topics. For example, McCloskey (2019) examines how Russian President Vladimir Putin attempts to subvert US "exceptionalism" by advancing a "discourse of internationalism" in a *New York Times* editorial and in his nomination for a Nobel Prize in 2013. Hunt (2014) combines ecofeminism and critical rhetoric to reveal the feminist and anticolonial praxis in Wangari Maathai's Green Belt Movement. Edwards (2010) explores the rhetoric of *apologia* to suggest how the concept of "collective apology" (p. 58) is expressed by national leaders for past injustice and repression. Apologies expressed by the US, Australia, and Canada (and others) are examined for their potential to "lead to improved communal bonds and possible reconciliation amongst various communities within and between nation states" (p. 58). These studies point to an evident interest by critics to explore international contexts.

We encourage further interest in rhetoric in international contexts. At the same time, following Garrett, critics must be highly reflexive all along the writing process. The critic might ask: Am I understanding the rhetor's language, persuasion, and symbolic action *from the point of origin*? What might I be missing? What additional sources of insight into this activity should I consult? What are the limitations of my critical concepts and assumptions? Consideration of these questions can lead to an authentic critique of cross-national rhetoric.

Conclusion

In December 2018, a special issue of the *Journal of Intercultural Communication Research* was devoted to charting pedagogical and research exigencies provoked by globalization. Stephen Hartnett makes several closing assertions within this special issue, one of which deals with communication research. "As scholars," he states, "if we are not revising our research projects to tackle these new global realities, then we are cheating ourselves and our colleagues" (p. 437). This is a strong claim but one that must be taken seriously in rhetorical studies. Scholars should follow their passions and expertise, but they ignore or otherwise omit global influences at their peril.

In this chapter, we have directed attention to topics and research agendas that can serve as resources or models for internationalizing rhetorical studies. We encourage scholars to explore across the continents and not equate culture and nation-state. To enrich their analyses of rhetorical artifacts, critics should research the discourse traditions that inform ways of speaking, arguing, and advocating. We also directed attention to three areas of study that overlap with rhetorical studies: transnational feminism, postcolonial studies, and Africanist epistemologies. These areas continue to break new critical ground and must be consulted when the project is to internationalize rhetorical studies. Finally, we highlighted examples of rhetorical studies that treated international speakers and issues in ways that might be instructive for future research and/or pedagogy.

Where might this lead? The future is already appearing in our journals. In February 2015, the *Journal of International and Intercultural Research* published an article that described the vernacular rhetoric of Latino/a and South Asian bloggers as they reacted to Arizona's enactment of broader local police powers to enforce federal immigration law. The article offers a critique of "how bloggers, while contesting and challenging this legislation, use vernacular rhetorics to respond to and rearticulate its construction of brownness" (Mudambi, 2015, p. 46). While a rhetorical analysis of vernacular expressions, it is difficult to imagine this study being published in the *Quarterly Journal of Speech* or *Rhetoric & Society Quarterly*, the dominant US venues for research on rhetorical communication. This article converges the very elements that lie beyond the comfort zone of much of current rhetorical studies: interdisciplinary citations, multiethnic/international perspectives, social media artifacts, disrupted binaries, activist questioning of larger racial structures in the US, *and being an author of color* (Chakravartty, Kuo, Grubbs, & McIlwain, 2018). Future studies will continue to reveal and question the colonizing practices of nation-states, studies will adopt intersectional approaches to identity and express skepticism toward "citizenship" as a useful identity marker, and studies will more explicitly urge resistance to repressive cross-national policies and agreements. Whatever our positionality to rhetorical studies, we are obligated to not "cheat ourselves and our colleagues" by ignoring or omitting the new round of research that is emerging.

References

Asante, M. K. (1990). The tradition of advocacy in the Yoruba courts. *Southern Journal of Communication*, 55(3), 250–259. doi:10.1080/10417949009372793

Bitzer, L. F. (1968). The rhetorical situation. *Philosophy and Rhetoric*, 1(1), 1–14.

Burke, K. (1969/1962). *A rhetoric of motives*. Berkeley, CA: University of California Press.

Butler, J. R. (2002). Somalia and the imperial savage: Continuities in the rhetoric of war. *Western Journal of Communication*, 66(1), 1–24. doi:10.1080/10570310209374723

Campbell, K. K. (1973). The rhetoric of women's liberation: An oxymoron. *Quarterly Journal of Speech*, 59, 74–86.

Campbell, K. K. (1980). Stanton's "solitude of self": A rationale for feminism. *Quarterly Journal of Speech*, 66(3), 304–312. doi:10.1080/00335638009383528

Carrillo-Rowe, A. (2008). *Power lines: On the subject of feminist alliances*. Durham, NC: Duke University Press.

Carrillo-Rowe, A. (2009). Subject to power: Feminism without victims. *Women's Studies in Communication*, 32(1), 12–35.

Carillo-Rowe, A. (2010). Entering the inter: Power lines in intercultural communication. In T. K. Nakayama & R. T. Halualani (Eds.), *The handbook of critical intercultural communication* (pp. 216–226). Malden, MA: Blackwell.

Chakravartty, P., Kuo, R., Grubbs, V., & McIlwain, C. (2018). #CommunicationSoWhite. *Journal of Communication, 68*(2), 254–266. doi:10.1093/joc/jqy003

Chawla, D., & Atay, A. (2018). Introduction: Decolonizing autoethnography. *Cultural Studies ↔ Critical Methodologies, 18*(1), 3–8. doi:10.1177/15327086177289

Cloud, D. L. (2004). "To veil the threat of terror": Afghan women and the <clash of civilizations> in the imagery of the U.S. war on terrorism. *Quarterly Journal of Speech, 90*(3), 285–306.

Collier, M. J. (2014). *Community engagement and intercultural praxis: Dancing with difference across diverse contexts.* New York, NY: Peter Lang.

Collier, M. J., Lawless, B., & Ringera, K. (2016). Negotiating contextually contingent agency: Situated feminist peacebuilding strategies in Kenya. *Women's Studies in Communication, 39*(4), 399–421. https://doi-org.lib-e2.lib.ttu.edu/10.1080/07491409.2016.1225272

Coplean, M., & Dingo, R. (2018). Beyond drive-by race scholarship: The importance of engaging geopolitical contexts. *Communication and Critical/Cultural Studies, 15*(4), 306–311.

Dempsey, S. E., Parker, P. S., & Krone, K. J. (2011). Navigating socio-spatial difference, constructing counter-space: Insights from transnational feminist praxis. *Journal of International and Intercultural Communication, 4*(3), 201–220. doi: 10.1080/17513057.2011.569973

Edwards, J. A. (2010). Apologizing for the past for a better future: Collective apologies in the United States, Australia, and Canada. *Southern Communication Journal, 75*(1), 57–75. doi:10.1080/10417940902802605

Fay, I., & Kuypers, J. A. (2012). Transcending mysticism and building identification through empowerment of the rhetorical agent: John F. Kennedy's Berlin speeches on June 26, 1963. *Southern Communication Journal, 77*(3), 198–215. doi:10.1080/1041794X.2011.637601

Garrett, M. M. (2000). Some elementary methodological reflections on the study of the Chinese rhetorical tradition. In A. González & D. V. Tanno (Eds.), *Rhetoric in intercultural contexts* (pp. 53–63). Thousand Oaks, CA: Sage Publications.

Garrett, M. M., & Xiao, X. (1994). The rhetorical situation revisited. *Rhetoric and Society Quarterly, 23*, 30–40.

Golden, J. L., Berquist, G. F., Coleman, W. E., & Sproule, J. M. (Eds.). (2011). *The rhetoric of Western thought: From the Mediterranean world to the global setting* (10th ed.). Dubuque, IA: Kendall and Hunt.

Goldzwig, S. R. (1998). Multiculturalism, rhetoric and the twenty-first century. *Southern Journal of Communication, 63*(4), 273–290. doi:10.1080/10417949809373102

Griffin, L. M. (1952). The rhetoric of historical movements. *Quarterly Journal of Speech, 38*(2), 184–188. doi:10.1080/00335635209381762

Hagan, M. A. (2010). Speaking out: Women, pagne, and politics in the Cote D'Ivoire. *Howard Journal of Communications, 21*(2), 141–163. doi:10.1080/10646171003727433

Hammerback, J. C., & Jensen, R. J. (1994). Ethnic heritage as rhetorical legacy: The plan of Delano. *Quarterly Journal of Speech, 80*(1), 53–70.

Hartnett, S. J. (2018). Notes on, confessions about, and hopes for globalization. *Journal of Intercultural Communication Research, 47*(5), 434–438. doi:10.1080/17475759.2018.1480518

Hasian, M., Anderson, C. W., & Wood, R. (2011). Cinematic representation and cultural critique: The deracialization and denationalization of the African conflict diamond crises in Zwick's *Blood Diamond*. In M. G. Lacy & K. A. Ono (Eds.), *Critical rhetorics of race* (pp. 233–246). New York, NY: New York University Press.

Hasian, M., & Wood, R. (2010). Critical museology, (post)colonial communication, and the gradual mastering of traumatic pasts at the Royal Museum for Central Africa (RMCA). *Western Journal of Communication, 74*(2), 128–149. doi:10.1080/10570311003614484

Hill Collins, P. (1995). Toward a new vision: Reconceptualizing categories of race, class, and gender. In P. H. Collins & M. L. Anderson (Eds.), *Race, class, and gender* (pp. 35–45). Belmont, CA: Wadsworth Press.

hooks, b. (1984). *Feminist theory from margin to center.* Boston: South End Press.

Hunt, K. P. (2014). "It's more than planting trees, it's planting ideas": Ecofeminist praxis in the Green Belt Movement. *Southern Communication Journal, 79*(3), 235–249.

Ivie, R. L. (1984). Speaking "common sense"; about the Soviet threat: Reagan's rhetorical stance. *Western Journal of Communication, 48*(1), 39–50. doi:10.1080/10570318409374140

Jablonski, C. J. (1998). A reflection on curricular reform: A challenge and a role for rhetorical studies. *Southern Journal of Communication, 63*(4), 337–345. doi:10.1080/10417949809373108

Kelley, C. E. (1988). The public rhetoric of Mikhail Gorbachev and the promise of peace. *Western Journal of Speech Communication, 52*(4), 321–334. doi:10.1080/10570318809389645

Lake, R. A. (1991). Between myth and history: Enacting time in Native American protest rhetoric. *Quarterly Journal of Speech, 77*(2), 123–151.

Law, M., & Corrigan, L. M. (2018). On white-speak and gatekeeping: Or, what good are the Greeks? *Communication and Critical/Cultural Studies, 15*(4), 326–330.

Lee, S. C. & Campbell. K. K. (1994). Korean President Roh Tae-Woo's 1988 inaugural address: Campaigning for investiture. *Quarterly Journal of Speech, 80*(1), 37–52.

Lee, W. S. (1998a). In the names of Chinese women. *Quarterly Journal of Speech, 84*, 283–302.

Lee, W. S. (1998b). Patriotic breeder or colonized convert: A postcolonial feminist approach to footbinding discourses in China. In D. V. Tanno & A. González (Eds.), *Communication across cultures* (pp. 11–33). Thousand Oaks, CA: Sage Publications.

Linabary, J. R., & Hamel, S. A. (2015). At the heart of feminist transnational organizing: Exploring postcolonial reflexivity in organizational practice at world pulse, *Journal of International and Intercultural Communication, 8*(3), 237–248, doi:10.1080/17513057.2015.1057909

Lu, X., & Frank, D. A. (1993). On the study of ancient Chinese rhetoric/Bian. *Western Journal of Communication, 57*(4), 445–463. doi:10.1080/10570319309374467

Madison, D. S. (2012). *Critical ethnography: Methods, ethics, and performance* (2nd ed.). Thousand Oaks, CA: Sage Publications.

McCloskey, T. (2019). "We must not forget that God created us equal": Putin and American exceptionalism. *Southern Communication Journal, 84*(1), 44–56. doi:10.1080/1041794X.2018.1540016

McKerrow, R. E. (1989). Critical rhetoric: Theory and praxis. *Communication Monographs, 56*(2), 91–111. doi:10.1080/03637758909390253

McKerrow, R. E. (2000). Opening the future: Rhetoric in a multicultural world. In A. González & D. V. Tanno (Eds.), *Rhetoric in intercultural contexts* (pp. 41–46). Thousand Oaks, CA: Sage Publications.

McKerrow, R. E. (2002). Coloring outside the lines. *Southern Communication Journal, 67*(3), 290–294. doi:10.1080/10417940209373237

Meyer, M. D. E. (2007). Women speak(ing): Forty years of feminist contributions to rhetoric and an agenda for feminist rhetorical studies. *Communication Quarterly, 55*(1), 1–17.

Mohanty, C. T. (2003). *Feminism without borders: Decolonizing theory, practicing solidarity*. Durham, NC: Duke University Press.

Mudambi, A. (2015). The construction of brownness: Latino/a and South Asian bloggers' responses to SB 1070. *Journal of International and Intercultural Communication, 1*(8), 44–62.

Muneri, C. T. (2016). Challenging the co-opting of democracy: Discourse from civil society organizations in Zimbabwe. *Howard Journal of Communications, 27*(1), 1–15.

Murray, B. (2018). Who are we, where are we, and what can we do? The "place" of localized activism in the Global Extraordinary Rendition and Torture Program. *Western Journal of Communication, 82*(4), 493–512. doi:10.1080/10570314.2017.1320808

Mutua-Kombo, E., & González, A. (2013). Ideographs of suppression: Jomo Kenyatta's independence day speech. *African Yearbook of Rhetoric, 4*(1), 12–19.

Na'puti, T. R. (2019). Archipelagic rhetoric: Remapping the Marianas and challenging militarization from "A Stirring Place". *Communication and Critical/Cultural Studies, 16*(1), 1–22. doi:10.1080/14791420.2019.1572905

Ong, A. (2006). *Neoliberalism as exception*. Durham, NC: Duke University Press.

Ono, K. A. (2011). Reflections on "Problematizing 'nation' in intercultural communication research". In R. Halualani & T. Nakayama (Eds.). *Blackwell handbook of critical intercultural studies* (pp. 84–97). Oxford, England: Blackwell.

Rodriguez, A., & Chawla, D. (2008). Locating diversity in communication studies. In L. A. Flores, M. Orbe, & B. J. Allen (Eds.), *International and intercultural communication annual* (Vol. 31, pp. 33–57). Washington, DC: National Communication Association.

Said, E. (1978). *Orientalism*. New York, NY: Random House.

Schwartz-Dupre, R. L. (2018). Postcolonial approaches to intercultural communication. In Y. Y. Kim & K. L. McKay-Semmler (Eds.), *The international encyclopedia of intercultural communication* (Vol. 3, pp. 1694–1698). Medford, MA: Wiley-Blackwell.

Sheckels, T. F. (2010). The rhetorical success of Thabo Mbeki's 1996 "I Am an African" address. *Communication Quarterly, 57*(3), 319–333.

Shome, R. (2006). Transnational feminism and communication studies. *The Communication Review, 9*, 255–267.

Shome, R. (2013). The obligation of critical (rhetorical) studies to build theory. *Western Journal of Communication, 77*(5), 514–517.

Shome, R., & Hegde, R. S. (2002). Postcolonial approaches to communication: Charting the terrain, engaging the intersections. *Communication Theory, 12*(3), 249–270.

Sowards, S. K. (2012). Rhetorical functions of letter writing: Dialogic collaboration, affirmation, and catharsis in Doleres Huerta's letters. *Communication Quarterly, 60*(2), 295–315.

Stec, F. J. (2016). Bringing attention to the human costs of war: Grievability, deliberation, and anti-war numbers. *Southern Communication Journal, 81*(5), 271–288. doi:10.1080/1041794X.2016.1216159

Stuckey, M. E. (1995). Competing foreign policy visions: Rhetorical hybrids after the Cold War. *Western Journal of Communication, 59*(3), 214–227. doi:10.1080/10570319509374518

Wander, P. (1983). The ideological turn in modern criticism. *Central States Speech Journal, 34*(1), 1–18. doi:10.1080/10510978309368110

Yartey, F. N. A. (2018). The rhetorical potency of storytelling: The narrative role of the hummingbird in the Green Belt Movement. In E. M. Mutua, A. González, & A. Wolbert (Eds.), *The rhetorical legacy of Wangari Maathai: Planting the future*. Lanham, MD: Lexington Books.

9 The Internationalization of Scientists' Communication
An Essential Literature Review

*Helena Torres-Purroy and
Sònia Mas-Alcolea*

Introduction: The Globalization of Science and Scientists' Communication in the Context of the Internationalization of Higher Education (IoHE)

The effects of globalization and higher education (HE) institutions' "internationalization policies" on science have long been documented: the consolidation of an international labor market for scientists, the predominance of English as the "language of science," the formation of multinational research teams and of joint cross-national projects, and the cross-border communication through international conferences and international publications, among others. These have, as a result, new scenarios with inevitable implications for scientists' communication, understood as interactions among scientists and between scientists and other interlocutors around their scientific practice, which is however an underresearched topic in the IoHE literature. Some implications of the influence of globalization and internationalization for scientists' communication are (a) less dependence on the spoken and printed word, (b) a quicker dissemination of ideas and consequently more opportunities for their questioning, (c) the concern for open-access publications, the possibility of more powerful means for representation (down to molecular level) and calculation, and (d) the evolution in writing practices of scientists—from publishing in a local language that used to be translated into an international lingua franca "in order to be accessible for a greater scientific community" (Karlsson, 2015, p. 63) to publishing directly in English (Karlsson, 2015).

Accordingly, new needs for innovation in the communication curriculum of pre- and pos-doctoral researchers, in this case, arise. It ought to accommodate to the new trends imposed by the IoHE. Any innovation proposal in this line should rely on a well-informed review of the literature. As regards the communication curriculum for scientists, a significant feature of it is the fact that scientists' training from the doctoral level and beyond is unstructured and consists in the execution of tasks in autonomous and proactive ways. Much of scientists' learning takes place through their interaction with other scientists, and hence scientific communication appears as a *de facto* element that is "acquired" in practice, rather than learned or taught. This might explain, at least partially, why the internationalization of scientific communication curriculum is not yet in itself an established research field. This chapter constitutes a preliminary step in this direction.

With the aim of contributing to this endeavor, this chapter will review works from diverse areas of study but with the common ground of revolving around scientists' communication and communication within the IoHE. These areas of study include the multimodal communication of science, the sociology of science, science communication, academic literacies, the internationalization of higher education, and the globalization of science, addressing issues like the construction of scientific facts, scientific representation, scientists' interpersonal interactions in the workplace, and their publishing practices, among others. It will thus be an attempt to frame the multiple forms that scientists' communication may take and identify how it interacts with the IoHE in order to inspire works in and innovative proposals for the internationalization of scientists' communication curriculum.

In what follows, main works addressing internationalization aspects of scientists' communication will be referenced and key implications for the internationalization of scientists' communication curriculum suggested. The four forthcoming sections will be devoted to works in multimodal communication and science communication, the scientific construction of facts and scientific representation in the sociology of science, global socio-political aspects of scientists' communication, also in the sociology of science, and academic literacies, respectively.

Scientists' Multimodal Communication and Science Communication

An insightful work exploring interpersonal communication among scientists from a multimodal perspective is Mondada (2005), whereby the author analyzes several interactions among scientists working in Europe, in multiple circumstances—e.g., in the same research group, as part of the same interuniversity networks, in interdisciplinary projects, or in international workshops—with diverse purposes and from different fields, like cartography, ecology, culture studies, surgery, and history. Regarding multilingual exchanges and contrasting with the general view in the literature on the IoHE, Mondada asserts that *English as a lingua franca* is neither the only strategy adopted by scientists in their interactions nor the most widespread one. Instead, multiple languages are diversely used by scientists even within the same communication session, responding to their local accommodation to the contingencies of a particular interaction.

There is also a line of research on communication in the science classroom from a multimodal social semiotics perspective (Lemke, 1990, 2000; Kress, Jewitt, Ogborn, & Tsatsarelis, 2001). Lemke (1990, 2000) offers a critical analysis of this phenomenon. Following Lemke, the science of the 20th century is ruled by a (selected) "technocratic elite," and discourses of objectivity and value-neutrality of scientific facts—which contribute to the "mystification" of science—rely on interests of technocrats and serve to legitimize them. With reference to the international dimension of science, Lemke (1990, p. 138) claims that "[s]cience is not limited to one culture, one dialect of English, or one style of communication," alerting of the primacy of Western culture in science. In Lemke (2000), the scholar remarks the importance for the science curriculum of considering the integration skills of multiple literacies that science requires, like "specialized verbal, visual, and mathematical literacies" (Lemke, 2000, p. 247). This is what Lemke calls "complex multiliteracy practices." In this sense, scientific literacies entail not only understanding scientific phenomena and using scientific concepts but also using representational resources in a specific way. A main implication of this for science education, and for scientists' communication curriculum in this case, is that it should emphasize and make explicit such generic, multidimensional and multimodal requirements and thus train and assess students in a more targeted way.

Regarding the curriculum of communication in education (and scientific discourse), Kress (1996) underscores the impact on it of the two processes of globalization and internationalization, which imply the introduction of "the generic/social structures of one place to another, whether that place has the means to cope with them or not" (Kress, 1996, p. 190). This indicates a "specialization of modes of communication," which the scholar deems a "fundamental change" in education. According to Kress (1996), the new requirements of internationalization and globalization of communication may imply the action of creative individuals that are allowed to manage and transform the semiotic resources they have available to produce innovative designs. Besides this, the increasing use of electronic technologies and the generalization of the information-based economy, the author argues, may entail greater importance of visual modes of communication in the future and in more areas of a globalizing world.

Apart from studies addressing one-to-one communication and the communication of science in the classroom—micro-level communication—there is another line of literature exploring meso- and macro-level communication in science: science communication studies. As a field of research, also called "the science of science communication," it is concerned with the systematic evaluation (of the social and political aspects) of the communication of scientific information by scientists to the public and with the ways in which the public interprets it. It thus takes a more generalizing approach to scientists' communication than the literature previously referred to in this section. That is, it makes reference to groups of actors, such as "scientists," "the public," "the audience," "stakeholders," "policymakers," etc., in a generalizing way and hence with a generalizing intention.

Great concern in the related literature has been the ideation of communication models that aid the explanation of science communication, by identifying and defining its elements and their behavior—e.g. linear models (sender-medium-receiver information transfer), diffusion models (widespread information transmission), the Garvey-Griffith model (cf. Garvey & Griffith, 1972), etc. As a reaction against the traditional, "hierarchical," "top-down" (Bucchi & Trench, 2016) "knowledge deficit model," whereby a well-informed public may be more receptive to and supportive of science, in the last two decades, many researchers have centered on highlighting the convenience of two-way- and multiway-dialogue models, where scientists, communicators, policymakers and publics interact (Akin & Scheufele, 2017). They claim for "more recent models" that "recognize the importance of context and social negotiation of meaning" (Burns, Connor, & Stocklmayer, 2003: 186) and that hence reflect the complexities of science communication. With reference to communication models in science communication, there is also the belief that contemporary trends in science may require new models that integrate it with society (Bucchi & Trench, 2016), and these should be developed considering also internationalization trends of science and of HE.

Considering political aspects of science, science has been argued to be a political instrument, imbued with a tenor of "unrealism," "insensitivity to uncertainty and variability," and "incapability of admitting its own limits" (Wynne, 1992, p. 294) [addressing the politics of science see Epstein (1996), Latour (2004) and Pielke (2007)]. And this rhetorical stance, also analyzed in the field of science communication, may often be found in scientists' discourse. Characteristics of it, as suggested by Wynne (1992), may be the standardization of processes, formal and inflexible methods and procedures, ethos of prediction and control, and exaggerated sense of certainty. Nonetheless, despite this rhetoric of certainty and absoluteness, scientists' communication is not devoid of interferences. Scientists adopting a communicator role may face difficulties, especially due to their detachment from novice and/or nonexpert status, like lacking accurate intuitions about people's beliefs and information requirements, composing complex messages with excessive information, or using specialist jargon (Bruine de Bruin & Bostrom, 2013). These and other related issues have been explored by a discipline that has traditionally evolved in parallel to science communication (Bucchi, 2008), that is, the sociology of science. Chief works of this field related to scientists' communication will be summarized in the next section.

Internationalized Communication in the Scientific Construction of Facts and in Scientific Representation

The sociology of science, or otherwise the "sociology of scientific knowledge," especially after its theoretical and epistemological turn in the 1970s (the "practice turn"), whereby it became "the new sociology of scientific knowledge" (Pinch, 1985), is based on the observation of scientific practice *in situ*. Through this perspective, science was seen as "immanently practical, locally organized, and infused with interpersonal trust and tacit knowledge" (Coopmans, Vertesi, Lynch, & Woolgar, 2014, p. 3), and this gave place to several ethnographies in laboratories in the late 1970s and early 1980s, known as "laboratory studies" (Woolgar, 1982). Although communication was not their central focus, these works have given important insights into aspects of communication among scientists in the laboratory as well as into scientific representation more generally, such as the consensus-like validation of scientific knowledge, the importance of communication within the scientific community, the organization of scientific work, the political strength of collaborations, the units and institutions that take part in scientific practice (e.g., the experiment, the laboratory), and identity construction of individual scientists, among others.

A relevant exponent of these "laboratory studies" is Latour and Woolgar's (1986 [1979]) two-year anthropological research in a scientific laboratory, observing the daily practices of its members. An important implication of this work for communication in science is the constructionist view of scientific knowledge and of "reality," also present in other works of the aforementioned authors, like Latour (1993) and Woolgar (1988). In it, "out-there-ness" "is the *consequence* of scientific work rather than its *cause*" (Latour & Woolgar, 1986 [1979]: 182; original emphasis), and it is thus the result of a negotiation. In a similar vein, Knorr-Cetina (1981) conceives science as a process of consensus achievement, dependent on the scientists' perception and anticipation of the opinion of other members of the community, and on the positioning of the potential publishing journal. It is thus the result of a strategy. Also, Law and Williams (1982) argue that scientific knowledge may very plausibly be determined by market commands. The scholars conclude that the array of elements that writing a paper consists in is at the same time the activity of positioning them in a network of value. In his laboratory study, Lynch (1985) intends to show how the so-claimed-for "scientific objectivity" takes the shape of agreement among colleagues in particular instances of scientific "shop talk."

Following these studies, scientific knowledge might be seen as a discourse rather than as a "reality," as a negotiation rather than as an object, and as a process of standardization and thus of simplification. In terms of scientists' communication curriculum, these findings imply that scientists should be trained in the "rhetoric of persuasion" "in order to draw attention to and legitimate their findings" (Zenzen & Restivo, 1982, p. 459) and that the communication curriculum should highlight the importance of environmental elements in the construction and validation of scientific facts.

Parallel to these "laboratory studies," there was a concurrent strand of studies more centered on "textual" documents or otherwise "presentations" and "inscriptions," such as published articles, prize acceptances, scientific reports, graphs, diagrams, equations, models, photographs, etc., which in the last 30 years has become "an established topic" and "a rich field of inquiry" (Coopmans et al., 2014, p. 1). These works attempted to demonstrate the constructionist and relativistic facet of scientific reports by emphasizing the rhetorical strategies they followed. Examples of these are Bazerman (1981), Lynch (1988) and Mody (2014).

Coopmans et al. (2014) give a brief overview of the evolution of this topic. Developments in this area have been: (a) the increasing emphasis on circumstantial factors in the process of knowledge production, (b) the changes in representational practice triggered by the technological innovations that have been adopted in science (so as to cause the renaming of the field as "science and technology studies," STS), like computers, color digital screens, simulators, diverse software for representation and representation processing, mobile digital devices, etc., besides the traditional means for representation, such as whiteboards, markers, notebooks, pens, books, Post-it notes and labels, (c) the increasingly blurry distinction between laboratory and field, (d) the "reframing" of representation from comprising linguistic representation only to encompassing image as well, and (e) the different kinds of relations between visual traces and numerical measurements on the one hand and objects on the other.

Two interrelated topics that have attracted much attention in the related literature are the development and use of new technologies and techniques (e.g., modeling, simulation) for scientific representation and the trustworthiness of such presentations.

On the one hand, new technologies bring about both new affordances and constraints for visual representation (Rijcke & Beaulieu, 2014) and complex "perceptual configurations" (Carusi & Hoel, 2014), which has been claimed to require a new "approach" (Alač, 2014). Yet on the other hand, the democratization of image processing technologies has sharpen the discussion about the "transparency" of images, which appears to be now especially threatened (Frow, 2014) so as to produce a "crisis of trust" (Kemp, 2014). Latour (2014) also claims for the abandonment of the mimetic paradigm of scientific representations and the uptake of a new perspective that considers its purposeful referential rationale.

The digital era has thus brought about greater concerns around trustworthiness of scientific presentations, especially image. As Frow (2014) explains, in the last years, many journals have dictated guidelines for good practices regarding image presentation and manipulation due to a general belief among journal editors that trustworthiness is higher for unprocessed images. Frow suggests that digital imaging and new technologies should be approached as an opportunity for enhanced scientific representation and higher trustworthiness, while trust in images should be secured by means of adequate formal training on image-crafting techniques; and common norms of image creation, manipulation, description, and documentation should be negotiated and established within each specialized area.

These studies again highlight the constructionist (cf. Myers, 1988) and often politically influenced (cf. Yearley, 1988) facet of science; they suggest the relevance of contingencies and contextual elements in the construction of scientific accounts and point to the partiality of scientific presentations (cf. Bazerman, 1981), which requires recovery skills from the part of their interpreters (cf. Amerine & Bilmes, 1988). Inscriptions are hence produced in relevant social environments, whose traces are often removed from them, and within authority frameworks of which scientists are aware and take part by adopting an active role in the persuasion game of science.

Finally, the intersection between scientists' local communication practices and their global dimension is present in multiple aspects within the sociology of science, like (a) reified scientific objects—that are internationalized when they are "black-boxed" and consequently "mass produced and distributed" (Pinch, 1985, p. 30); (b) standardization processes—e.g., of scientific representations, of experiment protocols, etc., which entail their long-reach distribution and the generalization of their use (also addressed by Knorr-Cetina, 1981; Latour & Woolgar, 1986 [1979]; Star & Griesemer, 1989); (c) mobility of artifacts, individuals, "texts" and discourses; and (d) scientists' identity and discourse style.

The mobility of artifacts, individuals, "texts," and discourses has been approached diversely, in its multiple facets: (a) studies on the mobility of scientists between industry and university (Kleinman & Vallas, 2006); (b) on boundary objects and their mobility across "social worlds" in science (Star & Griesemer, 1989); as well as (c) on "standardized packages"—of tools, concepts, theories, and methods—and the "translation" of interests between diverse social realms—e.g., between scientific disciplines, between science and nonscience, etc.—(Fujimura, 1992); (d) on (learning) trajectories of scientists and (developmental) trajectories of lab artifacts and their common relational trajectories (Nersessian, Kurz-Milcke, Newstetter, & Davies, 2003); (e) on trajectories of scientific debates (Shwed & Bearman, 2010); and (f) on trajectories of scientific discourses between performance in the laboratory and the writing of a scientific paper for publication (Knorr-Cetina, 1981; Latour, 1987).

Concerning scientists' "identity" and "discourse style," internationalization may be found in the "neutral" style of their scientific discourse, be it due to scientists' caution not to impose the personal discourse onto the collective, which has the legitimate authority (Fleck, 1935) or to scientists' commitment to universalism, their belief in objectivity, and their will to highlight the phenomena over their agency (Hyland, 2012). The internationalization of science may imply the increasing complexity of scientists' roles related to the emergence of new organizations mediating among former delimited fields—e.g., university, industry, and science—(Hess, 2006).

Global Socio-Political Issues in Scientists' Communication

The turn of the century has brought about a new turn in the sociology of science, coinciding with the new attention drawn by anthropologists and feminists "to macrosociological categories of analysis, social problems, culture and power, and interactions with lay groups and social movements" (Hess, 2006, p. 124). It has consisted in a renewed attention to structural and institutional factors, often by means of monographs, like those on democracy and politics (Kleinman, 2000; Latour, 2004; Brown, 2009; Gauchat, 2012; Bolsen & Druckman, 2015), on the impact of science on culture (Erickson, 2005), on industry–university relations (Croissant & Restivo, 2001), and on the role of feminism in science (Creager, Lunbeck, & Schiebinger, 2001). These advocate for a renewed focus on the contextual elements of science (Kleinman, 2003). This approach inquiries about issues like profit-driven research, the conventions that guide decision making concerning research, access to knowledge, and the reasons certain knowledge is constructed while other is not.

In terms of communication, two opposing tendencies have been noticed: on the one hand, there has been in recent years an increase in the number of scientific articles and journals, but on the other hand, only a small group of them attract most of the attention and interest (Young, Ioannidis, & Al-Ubaydli, 2008, p. 1420). This is the so-called communication function of the Matthew effect—the tendency for the accumulation of resources by those who already owned them—which appears to be "increasing in frequency and intensity with the exponential increase in the volume of scientific publications" (Merton, 1973, p. 449). Such hierarchical relations among journals are the result of the "citation game" (Biagioli, 2016). This consists in considering citation among scientists as an "objective" measure of scientific quality and success. This is the case of the "impact factor" of scientific journals (cf. Chew, Villanueva, & Van Der Weyden, 2007; Stock, 2009). Moreover, there seems to be a motivation to restrict access to journals, and this triggers their behavior as "luxury items" (cf. Ireland, 1994), which gives rise to an "artificial scarcity" (Young et al., 2008). As these latter authors suggest, low acceptance rates trigger exclusivity based on merit and more hectic competition.

The existence of a "scientific star system" has also been suggested, for which few scientists are "visible" and recognized even by mass media, raising interest for both their professional and personal achievements (Claessens, 2008; Bucchi, 2015). This results in the "personalization" of science (Bucchi, 2015) and a new "power mechanism" "whereby the weight of positions and institutions depends on the visibility of the scientists with whom they are able to associate themselves" (Bucchi, 2015, p. 243), which has been named "communitarian reputation" (Pizzorno, 2007; Bucchi, 2015). In addition to this, there is a tendency for the increasing mediatization of science (cf. Clay, 2010; Schäfer, 2014).

Also remarkable is the existence of "gatekeepers"—individuals acting as a "quality- and information-control filter" (Nosek & Bar-Anan, 2012, p. 226)— who hold positions of power so that they can decide about the allocation of resources, the distribution of information, an organization's structure, etc. As Frow (2014) suggests, journal editors are key gatekeepers in science, who establish norms that constrain authors' creativity within a framework of accepted conventions.

Informal communication—through unpublished, private means—has been also found to be very determining in science (cf. Collins, 1974; Garvey & Griffith, 1971). Garvey and Griffith (1971) explore "informal communication" in a specific domain (psychology) and elaborate a list of functional distinctions between "informal" and "formal" scientific communications. Some relevant points the authors make are: (a) the existence of an oligarchy or elite of a few scientists that are most active paper producers, communicating with and meeting one another, etc., (b) the high reliance of scientists on informal networks, (c) the essential importance of informal information flows for critical feedback and encouragement, and (d) the existence of a hierarchy of journals and conference-organizing societies. The authors are clearly in favor of the "long judicious procedure" of scientific knowledge production and communication, which they deem core in quality assurance. For this, they argue, the boundary between the informal and formal domains is essential.

The increasing competition in science and its growing commercialization may also affect communication among scientists, especially concerning the sharing of core information (Walsh & Maloney, 2007). The effective communication of science over centuries has brought about the "cultural authority of science," a very powerful resource for communication, and even for political communication (Blank & Shaw, 2015; Akin & Scheufele, 2017). However, the traditional cornerstone of such authority, that is, the "scientific objectivity" ideal, is nowadays in crisis, coinciding with the onset of the scientific postacademic era (Ziman, 2000)—whereby the industry exerts great influence on higher education. And this may signify one of the greatest challenges for the communication of science. The next section will deal with key sites of communication for scientists: publications, addressed by literature in the field of academic literacies.

The Internationalization of Scientists' Publishing Practices (Academic Literacies)

A chief means whereby scientists seek the "effective communication" of science is through the production of texts for publication, in journals, books, and conferences (Casanave & Vandrick, 2003). This significant aspect of their communicative practices and also of their research career is addressed in the "academic literacies" field (Lillis & Scott, 2007). The related literature addresses aspects like university students' and scholars' writing practices, academic genres, publishing processes, and gatekeeping in academia, among others. Some latest trends in academic literacies that may affect the communication curriculum for scientists are: (a) the study of the impact on literacies of new information and communication technologies, (b) the increasing adoption of the multimodal perspective to approach scientists' academic literacies, and (c) the evolution of gatekeeping practices in academia as a consequence of the IoHE.

Regarding the first issue, the adoption of new communication technologies is widening the meaning of the term "literacies" itself, which in the digital age may not only refer to reading and writing but also to the presentation and perception of information in many other forms (Lanham, 1995). There is concern among scholars in this area about the mismatch between the use of these technologies by young people and the flawed related formal training available (Tusting, 2008). Other aspects of interest are the crossing of boundaries, in terms of genres, on the one hand, giving place to hybrid genres, and in terms of disciplines, on the other, as well as the combination of multiple languages, of different rhetoric resources and of other communicative resources.

As regards the increasing adoption of multimodality, it is deemed a fruitful approach to transcend the traditional focus on logocentric "academic literacies" and extend it to the wide range of resources and practices comprised in the notion of "multimodal communication"—encompassing all types of semiotic resources and not only language—(Archer, 2006; Prince & Archer, 2014). This is not unfamiliar to the field of academic literacies, which has adopted multimodality in the analysis of "genre modes" (Lea & Street, 2006); in the exploration of the use of online technologies for teaching and learning in a globalized world (Snyder & Beavis, 2004); and in the reflection on new developments in communication and literacy practices that give place to "multiliteracies" (Cope & Kalantzis, 2000), among others.

Another line of research is the one dealing with gatekeeping in academia, as well as with the politics of academic knowledge production more broadly, including the politics behind the use of English as the global lingua franca for academic texts. Following this strand and based on Wallerstein's (2004) "world systems theory," Bennett (2014) distinguishes between three zones of behavior in academia: center, semiperiphery, and periphery (cf. Santos, 1985). These vary in the amount and quality of available resources, in prestige, in the strength of the meritocratic or "publish or perish" (cf. Nygaard, 2015) culture, and in the hegemony of English, among other aspects. While central institutions are "endowed with ample resources and characterized by a rigorous meritocratic culture" (Bennett, 2014, p. 1) and peripheral ones are humble and "disadvantaged," semiperipheral institutions act as mediators, filtering knowledge, models, and techniques from center institutions and making them available for peripheral ones. In terms of language, semiperipheral nodes are also usually language brokers between English and other languages. The tendency is for the semiperiphery to approach the "necessary" center—which is a source of funding and partnerships—and to enrich it with new inputs, possible only in other positions, whenever the "scorn" for peripheral elements is overcome.

In order to deal with this hierarchization of academic positions, brokering practices from professionals in central positions have become usual. The influencing positions of these "literacy brokers" (Lillis & Curry, 2006, 2010) in academic journals, especially in English-medium ones, favors the supremacy of an English-center literacy orientation, also named "Western Anglo academic literacy practices" (Lillis & Curry, 2006, p. 30), and this might also trigger the dependency on such brokering practices and thus on such professionals by periphery non-Anglophone authors.

Still related to power and politics, Hyland (2015) explains the state of academic publishing influenced by the economic marketplace and the academic prestige marketplace. The author cautions about existing top-down pressures on academics for publishing. These may apparently influence their chosen research topics, which may follow publishers' interests rather than disciplinary interests. As Hyland contends, English is increasingly the chosen language for publication despite initiatives to publish in other languages for reasons like developing a scientific register in those. The increasing pressure on scholars to publish in English has been also noticed by Lillis, Magyar, and Robinson-Pant (2010). This is led by Anglophone journals, positioned in center zones, which impose center-based evaluation systems, privileging material and linguistic resources not easily available to peripheral authors (see also Canagarajah, 2002). Also Uzuner's (2008) review of the literature on multilingual scholars' publishing practices reveals the existence of manifold reasons for the use of English for publication, among which aspirations to reach a wide audience or to participate in the global scientific arena (motivated by intrinsic or extrinsic reasons, like the need to publish in international journals), institutional requirements, and learning aspirations. Some obstacles they encounter are difficulties in accommodating to the discursive conventions, incapability of transcending the local research context, greater time investment for publishing in a second language, and lack of core networks.

Concluding Remarks

Against the apparent coincidence nowadays of the process of the IoHE and the introduction of EMI in higher education institutions (Altbach, Reisberg, & Rumbley, 2009), this chapter has shown the multiple aspects and processes that the internationalization of communication, of scientists in this case, entails. Besides the increasing use of English as the lingua franca, scientists' communication is present in their daily informal and formal, interpersonal communicative practices in the workplace, in their collective construction of scientific facts, in the rhetoric of scientific discourse—that fosters its mystification, authority, and imposition—in scientists' design of (multimodal) scientific presentations, in their simplification of their activity and observations, in the standardized processes they follow, as well as in the artifacts they use, in their struggle to position themselves in the scientific world, in their publishing practices, and in their use of *linguae francae* (not only English), among many other sites.

We have also made an effort to identify *loci* of interaction between scientists' communication and the IoHE, though this is a rather unexplored issue. Examples of these are the generalization of protocols and objects, the imposition of standards and evaluation systems, the international circulation of scientific objects, lab artifacts, scientific discourses and debates, the imposition from center to periphery scientists of discourse styles, the rise of "literacy brokers" in intermediate positions, the imposition from center to periphery stakeholders of research topics, the emergence of a ruling elite of scientists and institutions and the increasing dependence of others in them, the generalization of scientific communication genres, the increasing importance of image in science worldwide, and the growing intent to counterbalance the democratization of image-processing technologies through image-processing guidelines.

Accordingly, the internationalization of scientists' communication curriculum, despite not corresponding to a "formal" curriculum, should not be neglected. It should imply the targeted training of the scientists of the future also in communication; the creation of discourses that raise scientists' awareness of their communication practices; the explicit acknowledgment that language is neither the only communicative resource of science nor even the most important one; the implication of stakeholders and institutions in constructing a "fair" "market of value" that transcends the center–periphery divide and that accepts as legitimate all possible discourses of "scientificness" regardless of their provenance. In this attempt, the IoHE literature should recognize scientific communication as a key aspect of this process and integrate all the perspectives comprised in this chapter into a holistic picture of the internationalization of scientists' communication.

In forthcoming years, the internationalization of scientists' communication should consolidate as a steady research field, inasmuch as many core questions remain unanswered while HE institutions and individual actors are already fully involved in the IoHE. Some of these questions in the individuals' plane are how scientists can position their work in a "market of value" in a globalized science through communication; how this market can be "fair" and fruitful for all agents; in the institutional plane, how an internationalization curriculum of the unstructured communication of scientists can be designed and handled; to what extent and in what ways HE institutions' internationalization strategies could suit it; and more generally, how can a "locally contextualized" science be reconciled with veracity and credibility against the decontextualizing forces of internationalization and globalization.

References

Akin, H., & Scheufele, D. A. (2017). Overview of the science of science communication. In K. H. Jamieson, D. M. Kahan, & D. A. Scheufele (Eds.), *The Oxford handbook of the science of science communication* (pp. 25–33). Oxford: Oxford University Press.

Alač, M. (2014). Digital scientific visuals as fields for interaction. In C. Coopmans, J. Vertesi, M. Lynch, & S. Woolgar (Eds.), *Representation in scientific practice revisited* (pp. 61–87). Cambridge, MA: MIT Press.

Altbach, P., Reisberg, L., & Rumbley, L. (2009). *Trends in global higher education: Tracking an academic revolution: A report prepared for the UNESCO 2009 world conference on higher education*. Paris: UNESCO.

Amerine, R., & Bilmes, J. (1988). Following instructions. *Human Studies, 11*(2/3, Representation in Scientific Practice), 327–339.

Archer, A. (2006). A multimodal approach to academic "literacies": Problematising the visual/verbal divide. *Language and Education, 20*(6), 449–462.

Bazerman, C. (1981). What written knowledge does: Three examples of academic discourse. *Philosophy of the Social Sciences, 11*(3), 361–387.

Bennett, K. (Ed.). (2014). *The semiperiphery of academic writing: Discourses, communities and practices*. New York: Palgrave Macmillan.

Biagioli, M. (2016). Watch out for cheats in citation game. *Nature, 535*(7611), 201.

Blank, J. M., & Shaw, D. (2015). Does partisanship shape attitudes toward science and public policy? The case for ideology and religion. *Annals of the American Academy of Political and Social Science, 658*(1), 18–35.

Bolsen, T., & Druckman, J. N. (2015). Counteracting the politicization of science. *Journal of Communication, 65*(5), 745–769.

Brown, M. B. (2009). *Science in democracy*. Cambridge, MA: MIT Press.

Bruine de Bruin, W., & Bostrom, A. (2013). Assessing what to address in science communication. *Proceedings of the National Academy of Sciences, 110*(Supplement_3), 14062–14068.

Bucchi, M. (2008). Of deficits, deviations and dialogues: Theories of public communication of science. In *Handbook of public communication of science and technology* (pp. 57–76). Abingdon, UK: Routledge.

Bucchi, M. (2015). Norms, competition and visibility in contemporary science: The legacy of Robert K. Merton. *Journal of Classical Sociology, 15*(3), 233–252.

Bucchi, M., & Trench, B. (2016). Science communication and science in society: A conceptual review in ten keywords. *Tecnoscienza, 7*(2), 151–168.

Burns, T. W., Connor, D., & Stocklmayer, S. M. (2003). Science communication: A contemporary definition. *Public Understanding of Science, 12*(2), 183–202.

Canagarajah, A. S. (2002). *A geopolitics of academic writing*. Pittsburgh, PA: University of Pittsburgh Press.

Carusi, A., & Hoel, A. S. (2014). Toward a new ontology of scientific vision. In C. Coopmans, J. Vertesi, M. Lynch, & S. Woolgar (Eds.), *Representation in scientific practice revisited* (pp. 201–221). Cambridge, MA: MIT Press.

Casanave, C. P., & Vandrick, S. (Eds.). (2003). *Writing for scholarly publication: Behind the scenes in language education*. Mahwah, NJ: Lawrence Erlbaum Associates.

Chew, M., Villanueva, E. V., & Van Der Weyden, M. B. (2007). Life and times of the impact factor: Retrospective analysis of trends for seven medical journals (1994–2005) and their Editors' views. *Journal of the Royal Society of Medicine, 100*(3), 142–150.

Claessens, M. (2008). European trends in science communication. In D. Cheng, M. Claessens, T. Gascoigne, J. Metcalfe, B. Schiele, & S. Shi (Eds.), *Communicating science in social contexts: new models, new practices* (pp. 27–38). Berlin: Springer.

Clay, E. (2010). Mediated science, genetics and identity in the US African diaspora. In S. M. Hoover & M. Emerich (Eds.), *Media, spiritualities and social change* (pp. 25–36). London: Bloomsbury Publishing.

Collins, H. M. (1974). The TEA set: Tacit knowledge and scientific networks. *Social Studies of Science, 4*(2), 165–185.

Coopmans, C., Vertesi, J., Lynch, M., & Woolgar, S. (2014). Introduction: Representation in scientific practice revisited. In C. Coopmans, J. Vertesi, M. Lynch, & S. Woolgar (Eds.) *Representation in scientific practice revisited* (pp. 1–12). Cambridge, MA: Massachusetts Institute of Technology Press.

Cope, B., & Kalantzis, M. (2000). *Multiliteracies: Literacy learning and the design of social futures*. London and New York: Routledge.

Creager, A. N. H., Lunbeck, E., & Schiebinger, L. L. (2001). *Feminism in twentieth-century science, technology, and medicine*. Chicago: University of Chicago Press.

Croissant, J., & Restivo, S. P. (Eds.). (2001). *Degrees of compromise: Industrial interests and academic values*. New York: State University of New York Press.

Epstein, S. (1996). *Impure science: AIDS, activism, and the politics of knowledge*. Berkeley: University of California Press.

Erickson, M. (2005). *Science, culture and society: Understanding science in the twenty-first century*. Cambridge: Century Polity Press.
Fleck, L. (1935). *Entstehung und Entwicklung einer wissenschaftliche Tatsache* (Eng. tr. Genesis and Development of a Scientific Fact; 1979) (T. J. Trenn & R. K. Merton, Eds.). Chicago: University of Chicago Press.
Frow, E. K. (2014). In images we trust? Representation and objectivity in the digital age. In C. Coopmans, J. Vertesi, M. Lynch, & S. Woolgar (Eds.), *Representation in scientific practice revisited* (pp. 249–267). Cambridge, MA: MIT Press.
Fujimura, J. H. (1992). Crafting science: Standardized packages, boundary objects, and "translation". In A. Pickering (Ed.), *Science as practice and culture* (pp. 168–211). Chicago: University of Chicago Press.
Garvey, W. D., & Griffith, B. C. (1971). Scientific communication: Its role in the conduct of research and creation of knowledge. *American Psychologist, 26*, 349–362.
Garvey, W. D., & Griffith, B. C. (1972). Communication and information processing within scientific disciplines: Empirical findings for psychology. *Information Storage and Retrieval, 8*, 123–126.
Gauchat, G. (2012). Politicization of science in the public sphere. *American Sociological Review, 77*(2), 167–187.
Hess, D. J. (2006). Antiangiogenesis research and the dynamics of scientific fields: Historical and institutional perspectives in the sociology of science. In S. Frickel & K. Moore (Eds.), *The new political sociology of science: Institutions, networks, and power* (pp. 122–147). Madison: University Wisconsin Press.
Hyland, K. (2012). *Disciplinary identities: Individuality and community in academic discourse*. Cambridge: Cambridge University Press.
Hyland, K. (2015). *Academic publishing: Issues and challenges in the construction of knowledge*. Oxford: Oxford University Press.
Ireland, N. J. (1994). On limiting the market for status signals. *Journal of Public Economics, 53*(1), 91–110.
Karlsson, T. (2015). Progress and milestones in scientific communication: A 150 years' perspective. *Upsala Journal of Medical Sciences, 120*(2), 63–64.
Kemp, M. (2014). A question of trust: Old issues and new technologies. In C. Coopmans, J. Vertesi, M. Lynch, & S. Woolgar (Eds.), *Representation in scientific practice revisited* (pp. 343–346). Cambridge, MA: MIT Press.
Kleinman, D. L. (Ed.). (2000). *Science, technology, and democracy*. New York: State University of New York Press.
Kleinman, D. L. (2003). *Impure cultures: University biology and the world of commerce*. Madison: University of Wisconsin Press.
Kleinman, D. L., & Vallas, S. P. (2006). Contradiction in convergence: Universities and industry in the biotechnology field. In S. Frickel & K. Moore (Eds.), *The new political sociology of science: Institutions, networks, and power new political sociology of science* (pp. 35–62). Madison: University of Wisconsin Press.
Knight, J. (1997). Internationalization of higher education: A conceptual framework. In J. Knight & H. de Wit (Eds.), *Internationalization of higher education in Asia Pacific countries*. Amsterdam: European Association for International Education.
Knorr-Cetina, K. (1981). *The manufacture of knowledge: An essay on the constructivist and contextual nature of science*. Oxford: Pergamon Press.
Kress, G. (1996). Internationalisation and globalisation: Rethinking a curriculum of communication. *Comparative Education, 32*(2), 185–196.
Kress, G., Jewitt, C., Ogborn, J., & Tsatsarelis, C. (2001). *Multimodal teaching and learning: The rhetorics of the science classroom*. London, NY: Continuum.
Lanham, R. (1995). Digital literacy. *Scientific American, 273*(3), 253–255.
Latour, B. (1987). *Science in action: How to follow scientists and engineers through society*. Cambridge, MA: Harvard University Press.
Latour, B. (1993). Le " pédofil " de Boa Vista: Montage photo-philosophique. *Petites leçons de sociologie des sciences*, 171–225.

Latour, B. (2004). *Politics of nature: How to bring the sciences into democracy.* Cambridge, MA: Harvard University Press.
Latour, B. (2014). The more manipulations, the better. In C. Coopmans, J. Vertesi, M. Lynch, & S. Woolgar (Eds.), *Representation in scientific practice revisited* (pp. 347–350). Cambridge, MA: MIT Press.
Latour, B., & Woolgar, S. (1986 [1979]). *Laboratory life: The construction of scientific facts.* Princeton, NJ: Princeton University Press.
Law, J., & Williams, R. J. (1982). Putting facts together: A study of scientific persuasion. *Social Studies of Science, 12,* 535–558.
Lea, M. R., & Street, B. V. (2006). The "academic literacies" model: Theory and applications. *Theory into Practice, 45*(4), 368–377.
Lemke, J. L. (1990). *Talking science: Language, learning and values.* Norwood, NJ: Ablex Publishing Corporation.
Lemke, J. L. (2000). Multimedia demands of the scientific curriculum. *Linguistics and Education, 10*(3), 247–271.
Lillis, T., & Curry, M. J. (2006). Professional academic writing by multilingual scholars. *Written Communication, 23*(1), 3–35.
Lillis, T., & Curry, M. J. (2010). *Academic writing in a global context: The politics and practices of publishing in English.* London: Routledge.
Lillis, T., Magyar, A., & Robinson-Pant, A. (2010). An international journal's attempts to address inequalities in academic publishing: Developing a writing for publication programme. *Compare: A Journal of Comparative and International Education, 40*(6), 781–800.
Lillis, T., & Scott, M. (2007). Defining academic literacies research: Issues of epistemology, ideology and strategy. *Journal of Applied Linguistics, 4*(1), 5–32.
Lynch, M. (1985). *Art and artifact in laboratory science: A study of shop work and shop talk in a research laboratory.* Abingdon, UK: Routledge & Kegan Paul.
Lynch, M. (1988). The externalized retina: Selection and mathematization in the visual documentation of objects in the life sciences. *Human Studies, 11*(2/3, Representation in Scientific Practice), 201–234.
Merton, R. K. (1973). *The sociology of science: Theoretical and empirical investigations.* Chicago: University of Chicago Press.
Mody, C. C. M. (2014). Essential tensions and representational strategies. In C. Coopmans, J. Vertesi, M. Lynch, & S. Woolgar (Eds.), *Representation in scientific practice revisited* (pp. 223–248). Cambridge, MA: MIT Press.
Mondada, L. (2005). *Chercheurs en interaction: comment émergent les savoirs.* Lausanne: Presses Polytechniques et Universitaires Romandes.
Myers, G. (1988). Every picture tells a story: Illustrations in E.O. Wilson's sociobiology. *Human Studies, 11*(2/3, Representation in Scientific Practice), 235–269.
Nersessian, N. J., Kurz-Milcke, E., Newstetter, W. C., & Davies, J. (2003). Research laboratories as evolving distributed cognitive systems. In Alterman, R., & Hirsh, D. (Eds.), *Proceedings of the Twenty-Fifth Annual Conference of the Cognitive Science Society* (pp. 857–862). Mahwah, NJ: Lawrence Erlbaum Associates.
Nosek, B. A., & Bar-Anan, Y. (2012). Scientific utopia: I. Opening scientific communication. *Psychological Inquiry, 23*(3), 217–243.
Nygaard, L. P. (2015, September). Publishing and perishing: An academic literacies framework for investigating research productivity. *Studies in Higher Education, 5079,* 1–14.
Pielke, R. (2007). *The honest broker: Making sense of science in policy and politics.* Cambridge, England: Cambridge University Press.
Pinch, T. (1985). Towards an analysis of scientific observation: The externality and evidential significance of observational reports in Physics. *Social Studies of Science, 15*(1), 3–36.
Pizzorno, A. (2007). Dalla reputazione alla visibilità. In *Il velo della diversità: studi su razionalità e riconoscimento* (pp. 220–247). Milano: Feltrinelli.
Prince, R., & Archer, A. (2014). Exploring academic voice in multimodal quantitative texts. *Literacy and Numeracy Studies, 22*(1), 39–58.

Rijcke, S. de, & Beaulieu, A. (2014). Networked neuroscience: Brain scans and visual knowing at the intersection of atlases and databases. In C. Coopmans, J. Vertesi, M. Lynch, & S. Woolgar (Eds.), *Representation in scientific practice revisited* (pp. 131–152). Cambridge, MA: MIT Press.

Santos, B. D. S. (1985). Estado e sociedade na semiperiferia do sistema mundial: o caso português. *Análise Social*, 21, 869–901.

Schäfer, M. S. (2014). The media in the labs, and the labs in the media: What we know about the mediatization of science. In K. Lundby (Ed.), *Mediatization of communication* (pp. 571–593). Berlin: De Gruyter.

Shwed, U., & Bearman, P. S. (2010). The temporal structure of scientific consensus formation. *American Sociological Review*, 75(6), 817–840.

Snyder, I., & Beavis, C. (Eds.). (2004). *Doing literacy online: Teaching, learning and playing in an electronic world*. Cresskill, NJ: Hampton Press, Inc.

Star, S. L., & Griesemer, J. R. (1989). Institutional ecology, "translations" and boundary objects: Amateurs and professionals in Berkeley's museum of Vertebrate Zoology, 1907–39. *Social Studies of Science*, 19(3), 387–420.

Stock, W. G. (2009). The inflation of impact factors of scientific journals. *ChemPhysChem*, 10(13), 2193–2196.

Tusting, K. (2008). Ecologies of new literacies: Implications for education. In A. Creese, P. Martin, & N. H. Hornberger (Eds.), *Encyclopedia of language and education* (2nd ed., pp. 317–329). New York: Springer US.

Uzuner, S. (2008). Multilingual scholars' participation in core/global academic communities: A literature review. *Journal of English for Academic Purposes*. Elsevier Ltd, 7(4), 250–263.

Wallerstein, I. M. (2004). *World-systems analysis: An introduction*. Durham and London: Duke University Press.

Walsh, J. P., & Maloney, N. G. (2007). Collaboration structure, communication media, and problems in scientific work teams. *Journal of Computer-Mediated Communication*, 12(2), 712–732.

Woolgar, S. (1982). Laboratory studies: A comment on the state of the art. *Social Studies of Science*, 12(4), 481–498.

Woolgar, S. (1988). Time and documents in researcher interaction: Some ways of making out what is happening in experimental. *Human Studies*, 11(2/3, Representation in Scientific Practice), 171–200.

Wynne, B. (1992). Misunderstood misunderstanding: Social identities and public uptake of science. *Public Understanding of Science*, 1(3), 281–304.

Yearley, S. (1988). The dictates of method and policy: Interpretational structures in the representation of scientific work. *Human Studies*, 11(2/3, Representation in Scientific Practice), 341–359.

Young, N. S., Ioannidis, J. P. A., & Al-Ubaydli, O. (2008). Why current publication practices may distort science. *PLoS Medicine*, 5(10), 1418–1422.

Zenzen, M., & Restivo, S. (1982). The mysterious morphology of immiscible liquids: A study of scientific practice. *Social Science Information*, 21(3), 447–473.

Ziman, J. (2000). *Real science: What it is, and what it means*. Cambridge: Cambridge University Press.

10 Internationalizing Public Relations Education

Maureen Taylor

Globalization and technology allow organizations to communicate with publics across cultures, countries, and mediated platforms. Organizational messages created in one country that are based on local cultural, organizational media systems and social values often become disseminated globally. Yet social and cultural values differ across nations and messages; slogans and logos created for local publics may not resonate with people in other cultures. Worse yet, culturally narrow messages, slogans, and logos may create misunderstandings that threaten organizational brands and reputations. Examples of "missed" opportunities in global communication include Nike's sneakers marked with what looked like the phrase "Allah" written on the shoes (Amatulli, 2019) and Pepsi's Chinese translation disaster of "Come alive with Pepsi," which could be interpreted as "raise your ancestors from the dead" (Zakkour, 2014).

Communication has become more complex over the last two decades because of globalization and technology. Organizational strategies and tactics created for building relationships with publics in Chicago may not be appropriate for those who live in Shanghai. Likewise, a company's response to a crisis in one country may need to feature different responses in another country. Some crisis responses may only satisfy some publics. For example, in 2016 IKEA announced a US recall of the MALM series furniture due to the U.S. Consumer Product Safety Commission's investigation results. The MALM series was sold across the world, with the largest sales in the US and China. Dressers were tipping over and killing/harming small children. IKEA delayed the product recall in the Chinese market, and when it finally made the recall, it treated Chinse consumers differently and unequally. For American consumers, IKEA offered a full refund for the furniture, a free "anchor kit," and, if requested, an IKEA representative would come to a person's home to anchor the dresser to the wall. In China, initially consumers were told that they needed to buy their own kit at the store or online. IKEA treated consumers in two countries very differently (Feng, 2016). IKEA's justification was that China had different product standards and that it was following national guidelines in each country. Chinese consumers did not want to be treated differently than American consumers. Eventually, IKEA provided the same level of support for Chinese consumers after the Chinese government intervened.

How can organizations better understand and communicate with publics across the world? Many organizations use public relations strategies and tactics to formulate objectives and campaigns for relationship building. At its core, public relations is about using communication to negotiate relationships among groups (Botan, 1997). Public relations serves as the eyes, ears, voice, and conscience of the organization. For example, the public relations function in organizations serves as the "eyes" of an organization when it conducts environmental scanning through research to understand the culture and context in which the organization operates. The public relations function in organizations serves as the "ears" of an organization when it listens to what the public, government, marketplace, and employees want. The public relations function in organizations serves as the "voice" of an organization when it formulates and disseminates messages to publics. Finally, the public relations function in organizations serves as the "conscience" of an organization when public relations professionals counsel their organization on how to behave and, sometimes, counsel organizational leaders how not to behave. The next section outlines some of the conceptual foundations that underpin the study, practice, and pedagogy of international public relations.

The Conceptual Foundations of International Public Relations

There are several conceptual areas that provide the foundation for preparing students for communicating with international publics. Students need to learn about culture, media, regulation, ethics, and the diverse roles of public relations in society. Each foundational area will be discussed in what follows.

The Impact of Culture on Relationships

Communication with publics is one of the most common topics in international public relations courses (Peterson & Mak, 2006; Mak, 2017). Culture is a learned, shared phenomenon that affects the way people think, communicate, behave, and express their emotions. Hall observed that "culture is communication and communication is culture" (p. 168). Hall (1976) noted that "there is not one aspect of human life that is not touched and altered by culture" (p. 16). Culture is learned, shared by certain groups of people, and it influences the way people think and behave in certain situations and contexts. Culture consists largely of the different beliefs, attitudes, and behaviors that groups consider to be societal norms.

Contemporary approaches understand culture as "mental programming" that guides people's behavior and beliefs. According to Geert Hofstede (1984), a Dutch psychologist, a portion of mental programming is inherited at birth, while others parts are learned and developed during childhood and reinforced through adulthood by schools and organizations. Hofstede's research originally developed four cultural dimensions, through which countries enact differing values in the workplace. Hofstede's original four dimensions include power distance, individualism versus collectivism, masculinity versus femininity, and uncertainty avoidance. Later in his career, he added two more dimensions: long-term orientation versus short-term orientation (previously known as Confucian Work Dynamism) and indulgence versus restraint (Hofstede, 2001; Minkov & Hofstede, 2010, 2011). The six cultural dimensions form a framework for analyzing the similarities and differences of how people and organizations operate within the context of their national culture.

Hofstede's dimensions provide useful insights into public relations practice and relationships and have become core conceptual areas included in international public relations courses. Students learn about power distance and the way that power and social status are unequally distributed across societies (Hofstede, 1984). Public relations students learn that in high-power-distance societies, an emphasis is placed on social status, referent power, legitimacy, and authority. In low-power-distance societies, there is more egalitarianism, equal rights, and less on hierarchical power. People living in countries that are high in power distance, such as China, Saudi Arabia, and Malaysia, tend to respect authority figures and accept that power is unequally distributed among members of the society. Those living in lower-power-distance countries, such as Ireland and Germany, are more egalitarian and respect equal rights. From a public relations perspective, power distance will influence how people view organizations that have experienced a crisis. Taylor (2000) found that publics with high uncertainty avoidance and high power distance demand more from organizations during a crisis.

Hofstede also provided discussions about how individualism and collectivism help us understand how individuals are integrated into groups and the value that is associated with being part of groups. In individualistic societies, individual expression and decision making is valued and desirable. In collectivist societies, the group is perceived to be more valuable and desirable. The family and community unit are given the highest importance in collectivist cultures such as Russia, Mexico, and Brazil. Countries such as the United States, Australia, Canada, Denmark, and the UK are more individualistic.

Understanding how individualism and collectivism shape relationships in a society matters a great deal in international public relations. For example, in Chinese culture, collectivist goals are put ahead of personal goals, and individuals and organizations try to present themselves as positively as possible to others. Face and facework are valuable lens to look at interpersonal relationships in societies. In a China, a high fac--saving culture, Chinese organizations seek to save both their "face" and other groups' "face," and achieve a harmonious environment in crisis situation. "Face" is a traditional Chinese value mentioned in most literatures about Chinese cultures. Saving face is the act of protecting one's own or other people's self-image (Goffman, 1955; Hu, 1944; Yu & Wen, 2003). Social "face" means the individual has obtained a position of honor in society (Chan, 2006). When Chinese organizations experience a crisis, the leaders of the organization normally try to maintain both their company and the competitor's "face."

Taking the "upper-level line" is also a feature of Chinese organizations' approach to crisis communication. The "upper-level line" refers to the reliance on government by organizations to solve crises and problems (Ye & Pang, 2011). In China, the government is regarded as one of the most important stakeholders of organizations (cf. Taylor & Kent, 1999). Handling the "upper-level line" properly will ultimately help Chinese organizations to get a beneficial position in the larger Chinese society, including gaining and maintaining access to powerful government officials.

Hofstede also conceptualized masculinity versus femininity to explain gender roles of a society, the types of products and services a society produces, and even how achievement is defined (Hofstede, 2001). Cultures leaning more toward the masculine end of this dimension tend to value ambition, assertiveness, and success. Masculine societies also set strict, clearly defined gender roles, indicating what is and is not appropriate behavior for men and women. Feminine societies, on the other hand, tend to value nature, beauty, fantasy, and nurturing. Feminine societies also have less clear-cut gender roles, creating less restrictions on how men and women behave. Japan, Switzerland, and Venezuela are considered to be masculine countries, while Chile, Honduras, and the Netherlands are feminine countries. The implications of masculinity and femininity for public relations practice across the world are important for several reasons. First, in many cultures, public relations is treated as a feminized career, with women mainly filling public relations positions (Aldoory & Toth, 2002). The professionalization of public relations is inevitably influenced by major social trends such as international professionalization, globalization, and the confrontation and convergence of local cultures. In China, for instance, public relations has been viewed as young and beautiful ladies who lack professional training and ability. These PR ladies have traditionally worked in public relations agencies for maintaining "guest relations," arranging activities, and taking care of clients and guests (Culbertson & Chen, 1996). The feminized function of public relations is not unique in China—we see it in India (Sriramesh, 1992), Japan, South Korea (Sriramesh, Kim, & Takasaki, 1999), and Singapore (Yeo & Sriramesh, 2009). Kim and Kim (2010) found that masculinity affected perceptions of corporate social responsibility (CSR) in Korea.

Another dimension of interest is Hofstede's uncertainty avoidance, which addresses a society's tolerance for ambiguity and uncertain situations. Public relations communication seeks the reduction of ambiguity and uncertainty. Organizations communicate with publics to reduce uncertainty. Societies such as Greece, Mexico, and Japan seek to avoid uncertain situations. These high-uncertainty-avoidance cultures tend to value commonplace circumstances, security, and low-risk situations. Public relations messages in these locations will seek to clarify information. Countries like the Philippines, Canada, and Colombia score lower on uncertainty avoidance, meaning people living in these countries in general can tolerate new situations, ambiguity, and uncertainty. Public relations in these countries may not need to reduce uncertainty as much.

Hofstede and other scholars put forward two additional dimensions: long-term orientation versus short-term orientation (previously known as Confucian Work Dynamism) and indulgence versus restraint (Hofstede, 2001; Minkov & Hofstede, 2010), which have implications for local and global practices of public relations. Long-term orientation versus short-term orientation refers to whether members of a society live in a way that considers the future or in a way that considers the present (Hofstede, 2001). Long-term orientation, generally seen as more positive, reflects a dynamic and future-oriented mentality, whereas short-term orientation can be viewed as short-sighted. Both have implications for public relations practice. Organizations use public relations to communicate about change, and the orientation of the target publics will influence how publics understand messages. Short-term-oriented societies show a more static and tradition-oriented mentality. Hofstede (1997) characterized the long-term orientation by "persistence, ordering relationships by status, thrift and having a sense of shame" and the short-term orientation by "personal steadiness, protecting face, respect for tradition, reciprocation of greetings, favors and gifts" (p. 31). Public relations messages in a long-term-orientation society will focus on the organization's history, long-term planning, and traditions. For example, in public relations materials, many brands list their start date in their promotional materials in acknowledgment that longevity matters. Consider the American bourbon brand Jim Beam. Look at its label and you will see "Jim Beam since 1795" as part of its branding.

Indulgence versus restraint reflects how well members of a society can delay gratification of material needs, impulses, and desires (Minkov & Hofstede, 2011). Maleki and de Jong (2014) defined indulgence as the "tendency to allow relatively free gratification of some desires and feelings (leisure, casual sex, spending, and consumption)" (p. 134). Restraint stands for the tendency to delay the fulfillment of desires and feelings due to strict social norms preventing indulgent behavior (Maleki & de Jong, 2014). Australia and Chile are classified as indulgent countries, while Thailand and China are more restrained, for example.

Each of Hofstede's dimensions of culture is important for internationalization because they provide an explanation for how national culture accounts for behavioral and attitudinal differences between people across nationalities. Further, academic studies by Chen (2018), Kim and Kim (2010), Taylor (2000), and Zaharna (2018) have extended Hofstede's work by applying the dimensions to organizational culture and public relations. By applying the dimensions of culture to businesses, nonprofits, public diplomacy, and other forms of international relationship building, it is easier to understand how national culture may affect the public relations activities of organizations. Today, communication can transcend national boundaries even faster than ever before. Media and social media present both opportunities and challenges to international public relations.

The public relations function is dynamic and complex and, in a globalized world, the quality of the educational background and professionalism of people who practice public relations matters a great deal (Sriramesh, 2009). There are other conceptual frameworks to consider when thinking about international public relations, but the previous section outlined the most relevant ones for communication educators. The next section provides a brief review of public relations education.

Public Relations as a Global Academic Subject

Public relations' undergraduate classes, majors, and minors have grown over the last three decades as the need for specialized communication experts has increased. Public relations curricula vary widely across the world (Peterson & Mak, 2006). This makes sense because the practice of public relations varies across the world. Mak (2017) recently noted that international public relations courses have doubled from 2005 to 2016. Today, more universities offer more units or courses about international public relations than in 2005. Additionally, there are more professors from international backgrounds teaching in public relations programs. There are four major academic approaches to public relations education: mass communication, communication, business, and technical writing. Each approach teaches public relations a bit differently.

In the mass communication and journalism approach, public relations is taught as an extension of the news and media business. Students take journalism courses first and learn how to write for media audiences. Classes such as reporting, magazine writing, multimedia design, and ethics serve both journalism and public relations students. As students progress through the curriculum, they learn more specific organizational writing skills such as news releases, backgrounders, position papers, and brochures. Students who complete a public relations degree in a school of journalism or mass communication often study in accredited departments that put technical skills ahead of conceptual skills. Students leave well versed in writing but have little academic preparation in understanding how organizations work and how meaning is socially constructed.

In the communication approach, public relations is taught as an organizational communication function. Students take communication courses first and learn about public speaking, rhetoric, interpersonal and group communication, and ethics. As they progress through the curriculum, they learn writing skills. Students who complete a public relations degree in a communication program graduate knowing more about communication processes and the social construction of reality, but they may not have had extensive writing or journalism training.

In the business approach, public relations is taught as part of business strategy and management. Public relations is rarely a free-standing major within a business school but rather is part of general business curriculum. Students in this approach take a business curriculum such as accounting, management, marketing, and finance. As they progress through the curriculum, they may take courses in business, advertising, and professional writing and participate in marketing internships or classes that touch on public relations. Students who complete a public relations focus within a business program graduate knowing how the business world works but often lack a communication or media orientation.

In the technical communication approach, public relations is taught as writing. Students take writing courses such as English (or local language) and learn about the technical aspects of writing. This type of curriculum is not journalism because they are not learning how to do investigative reports. As students progress through the curriculum, they learn writing skills such as long-form and short-form writing, news releases, backgrounders, position papers, and brochures. Students who complete a public relations degree in a technical communication program graduate knowing more about writing, design, and production of communication processes. They may not have had exposure to business, media, or communication theories such as interpersonal, organizational, small group, or culture.

The disciplinary approach will influence how a public relations student understands the practice of public relations. Each approach creates student expectations about careers after graduation. There are larger forces shaping the academic preparation of public relations students. For instance, today, university journalism and mass communication enrollments are heavily weighted toward public relations (and advertising) majors with fewer and fewer students seeking careers in journalism. Likewise, communication programs that once trained students in debate, rhetoric, and interpersonal communication find that most of their students want applied courses in public relations. Business school curriculum changes have also influenced how public relations is taught. As business schools increase their course offerings in marketing, they tend to draw more students with an interest in public relations. Parents are especially interested in having clear career pathways for their children, and marketing and public relations fulfill parental desires for a clear job trajectory after graduation.

There are many approaches to public relations education, but one thing is certain for the next generation of public relations professionals: they will need to operate in a global and technologically complex environment. The best way to prepare students for this awesome responsibility is to internationalize public relations education.

Initiatives to Internationalize Public Relations Education

The first international public relations courses emerged in the United States in the mid-1990s as globalization and new communication technologies such as the Internet made it clear that students needed to learn more the world outside their home country (Taylor, 2001). Professional associations also played a role in expanding the public relations curriculum to include internationalization. Sriramesh (2009) credited the discussion of international public relations

> for moving the public relations body of knowledge toward greater cultural relativism in order to make it more relevant to practitioners who are faced with the challenge of communicating effectively with the diverse publics of the emerging markets of Asia, Eastern Europe, Latin America, and Africa.
>
> (p. 1)

There is no one blueprint for an undergraduate course in international public relations or topics that can globalize existing class content. For universities with a public relations major, there are two ways to best prepare students for working in a globalized world: create specific courses in international public relations or embed units of internationalization in existing public relations courses. Each approach is explored in what follows.

Creating a dedicated international public relations course: A three-credit required international public relations course or elective is an easy way to teach students about the issues facing international public relations. A review of syllabi suggests that most international public relations courses include some discussion of the foundational topics mentioned in this chapter. Students learn about culture, media, economic, and political systems. They often learn through the case study method how public relations contexts change public relations actions. The most common books used in courses dedicated to international public relations include *Global Public Relations: Spanning Borders, Spanning Cultures* by Alan R. Freitag and Ashli Quesinberry Stokes (2009). Another book that is often used in international public relations classes is *International Public Relations: Negotiating Culture, Identity, and Power* by Patricia A. Curtin and Kenn Gaither (2007). *Cultures and Organizations: Software of the Mind* by Geert Hofstede (1997) provides a broader organizational and societal approach to understanding the role of culture in organizations. Many professors do not limit their class readings to one textbook and instead draw upon book chapters and articles that provide insights into the different dimensions affecting international public relations. Book chapters from Hofstede et al.'s *Cultures and Organizations: Software of the Mind* (2007) or Katerina Tsetsura and Dean Kruckeberg's *Transparency, Public Relations and the Mass Media: Combating the Hidden Influences in News Coverage Worldwide* (2017) are useful supplements.

When there is a full class dedicated to international public relations, students can complete multiple assignments exploring public relations in different cultures and contexts. Case studies, research papers, group projects, and campaigns can be useful pedagogical activities. Learning outcomes may include but are not limited to:

1. Understand how context (social, cultural, political, historical) influences public relations practice.
2. Interpret intercultural theories and practices informing international public relations.
3. Apply public relations theories to international public relations tactics, strategies, or campaigns.
4. Examine case studies addressing international communication problems and opportunities.
5. Communicate and work effectively in culturally diverse environments.
6. Understand and explain the relationships between public relations, marketing, and advertising, the media, international actors (state, NGOs, and international business), and international publics.
7. Critically evaluate international public relations campaigns.

Having a dedicated class in international public relations provides an important educational experience to students. There are, however, other ways to give students a global perspective.

120 *Maureen Taylor*

Embedding the Discussion of Culture and Context in Existing Public Relations Courses

For many universities, there is not enough space in the curriculum for a dedicated course focusing exclusively on international public relations. In these cases, units can make the decision to embed the discussion of culture and international contexts in the regular public relations course sequence. Following are suggestions for internationalizing traditional public relations courses:

Table 10.1 PR Courses, Objectives, and Ways to Internationalize Content in Existing Courses

Course	General Content Overview	Ways to Internationalize the Course
Introduction to PR	Broad survey of the history, theories, functions, profession and ethics	Focus on early, non-Western forms of public relations practice Study how different cultures enact public relations Use case studies of PR campaigns in different nations, cultures
PR Writing	Introduction to writing PR materials including news releases, backgrounders, newsletters, and promotional materials	Draft materials for different national and cultural audiences Learn about different media systems and the relationships between media and PR
PR Research	Developing, analyzing, and using qualitative and quantitative research methods for understanding public's attitudes, values, and lifestyles	Include cultural components in research tools Understand how culture impacts research participation
PR Cases/PR Management	Applying the case study and strategic planning method to gain insights from past public relations campaigns	Integrate multicultural case studies Track transnational case studies Examine failed international campaigns
PR Design	Mastering design concepts and developing PR materials for various publics and media outlets	Gain familiarity with how culture affects color, design choices Discuss cultural sensitivity in designing promotional materials or products
Advanced PR Writing	Strengthening writing skills and enacting organizational voice	Write for other countries' media Learn how to target diverse or diasporic media outlets in US
Social Media	Understanding how to use social media in public relations	Introduce non-Western social media tools Trace social media messages and user input across countries
PR Campaigns	Planning, executing, and evaluating a real-time campaign for a client	Add diversity publics to campaign targets Select an international client

Course	General Content Overview	Ways to Internationalize the Course
Foundations of PR Legal and Ethics	Gaining familiarity with the legal and ethical guidelines shaping public relations communication	Discuss other nations' legal systems Learn about other cultures' ethical norms

Regardless of whether a university can create a dedicated class to the topic of international public relations or embed internationalization in existing curricula, there are conceptual foundations that appear regularly throughout courses dedicated to the topic. Each of these topics will be discussed.

Media and Social Media

Another consideration for internationalizing public relations education is to teach students about different media systems. It is through media, both traditional and now social media, that organizations build relationships with publics.

Media Ownership or Government Control Over Media Content May Negatively Influence Public Relations

Siebert, Peterson, and Schramm (1956) identified four models of media ownership (and control) across the world. Who owns media will influence the ways public relations works with media. For Seibert et al., media can be viewed as a tool of government power (authoritarian model) rather than a tool of citizen empowerment (libertarian model). Sometimes, government-controlled media becomes the only acceptable media channel when dissonant perspectives or outlets are outlawed or marginalized (Stockmann & Gallagher, 2011). In countries like China, the media organizations and institutions are controlled by the state and disseminate propaganda on behalf of the state (Stockmann & Gallagher, 2011).

Repucci (2019) describes a downward spiral of case studies from the former Soviet Union, Africa, the Middle, Asia, and Latin America suggested that many nations have treated media channels and content as tools of the state. Government control over media is not a new phenomenon. For example, Taylor (2018) noted that

> the control over Russian media started before the birth of the Soviet Union. Every group from the Czars, to the Bolsheviks, to the Communists and Vladimir Putin have sought to limit freedom of speech and press. Newspapers such as *Pravda* and *Izvestia* and television stations like Channel One have been controlled by whoever is in power. In this model, editors and journalists follow the "party line" and the dominance of the state has been ensured. Journalism education was essentially training in pro-government propaganda. (p. 459)

In societies with freer or more open media ownership, public relations provides an information subsidy (Gandy, 1982) to media organizations such as newspapers, magazines, broadcast outlets, and now digital outlets such as blogs, online news, and websites. The term "information subsidy" is important to understand media and marketing communications, because the public relations function "packages" information into easy to use units for media thus "subsidizing" the cost of news production for the media. Today, with shrinking newsrooms across the world, public relations provides more and more of the content for media. Public relations also helps media by providing earned media activities such as events, fundraising dinners, educational displays, product launches, interviews with organizational leaders, site visits, and other events that attract media attention. Earned media events vary across the world, and public relations students need to understand that what counts for news in one nation might not count for news in another context. The relationship between public relations and the news media also affects the professionalization of the field. Across the world, public relations provides information subsidies to media (Gandy, 1982). Yet in some countries, public relations provides more than just an information subsidy, it provides an "economic subsidy" that buys positive news coverage or silences criticism. This practice is known by many names including black PR, media transparency, cash for news, and media bribery. Media transparency has been extensively study by Tsetsura and colleagues (Kruckeberg &Tsetsura, 2003, 2004; Tsetsura & Luoma-aho, 2010). Yang (2012) noted that "the cash-for-news phenomenon should be studied not only as a journalism ethical issue but also as a social problem with potential sociological, economic, and cultural causes" (p. 203). The lack of media transparency undermines both sides of the information subsidy and diminishes the credibility of messages that are carried by the media.

Traditional Media and the Public Relations Function

Traditional media include print and broadcast outlets such as newspapers, magazines, television, and radio and online web-based media. Public relations creates information subsidies for traditional media and in some cases actually develops the content. In some countries, public relations professionals send out news releases and media advisories to traditional media. Public relations professionals compete with other organizations for media attention. The news media decide which news is most relevant to their audiences. Public relations messages carried by credible media outlets have more value than messages carried by less respected outlets. Napoli's (2018) edited volume, *Mediated Communication*, reminds us that the value a society places on a media outlet is based on a combination of its history, performance, perceptions of impartiality, and usefulness to audiences. There has been a worldwide crisis for many traditional media outlets over the last decade as mergers and acquisitions of media by corporations have reduced the number of journalists and made media outlets more dependent on public relations materials. While greater reliance on public relations publicity materials may initially seem like a boon for the public relations function, it is actually a problem. A weak media system that is reliant on free news and content no longer performs its role in society as a watchdog. When no one trusts the media, no one trusts the messages that media carry. Public relations loses a way to communicate to its publics.

Social Media and Public Relations

For many public relations professionals, social media are "must-have" communication tools. Kent defined social media as "any interactive communication channel that allows for two-way interaction and feedback" (2010, p. 645). The two major features of social media are that they are relational and involve some kind of feedback or interaction.

Internationalizing Public Relations Education 123

Social media, social networking platforms, and apps now number in the millions, and new ones emerge regularly linking people to others who share the same interests or views. Many organizations use social networking platforms like Instagram, Snapchat, Facebook, YouTube, and Twitter to communicate with stakeholders and publics. Many other tools, apps, and networking sites exist for smaller niche or cultural groups to interact. Social media such as QQ, Wechat, Viber, and Line are popular outside of the US. Figure 10.1 shows social media users across different countries.

Public relations as a communication function has capitalized on the relational and feedback features of social media. Local social media apps allow local organizations to interact with publics in their own countries. For instance, Chinese use Sina Weibo, Russians use Vkontakte, and people living in Middle Eastern countries seem to prefer What's App. Culturally appropriate messaging from organizations to publics is now possible. Relationships can be created, maintained, and changed through social media. Organizations can also learn valuable insights into their publics' attitudes and behaviors from social media monitoring.

Most of the world's social media messages are not written in English. Having the ability to read a second language comes in handy for social media monitoring. For those who don't speak multiple languages, there are now social media analytics services that help aggregate, translate, and analyze foreign-language social media posts. What content, images, and messages can and cannot be communicated by organizations varies across the world. The next section addresses different approaches to regulating the public relations profession.

Licensing of Public Relations

Public relations operates in most countries with little to no regulation. Public relations communication is treated as free speech because organizations have a role

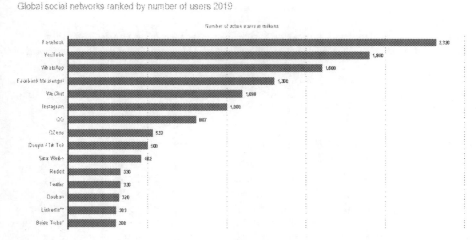

Figure 10.1 Social Media Platform Users (per million)

Source: https://www.statista.com/statistics/272014/global-social-networks-ranked-by-number-of-users/

to play in political and social conversations. However, there are some contexts in which public relations messages and actions are regulated. Several countries such as Brazil, Nigeria, and most recently Puerto Rico have adopted licensing for public relations practitioners (Sha, 2011).

Public relations plays a major role for corporations, nonprofits, and activist organizations around the world, and valid arguments for regulation have emerged. Proregulation advocates claim that without proper licensing, anyone can practice in the field of public relations whether they have any knowledge on the subject or not (Bernays, 1992; Brody, 1984). Their arguments go like this: It is neither unacceptable nor smart to hire a doctor or a lawyer who is not licensed. So why is it acceptable for a communication profession that has an equally significant impact on society to not be put under some sort of testing? Society understands that licensing for these fields helps improve skill level and stakeholder trust. Trust is a major requirement for successful public relations because that is what relationships are based on. Licensing would assure publics that someone has completed studies in an area at an accredited university and has passed rigorous examinations. With so much at stake, it must be ensured that trusted professionals follow ethical and industry standards. The call for licensing would help ensure a steady and bright future for the field of public relations. Improvements would be made in a plethora of areas from teaching ethics in the classroom to practicing ethics in the real world. The media has negatively portrayed public relations for decades, providing images that may become part of public perceptions (White & Park, 2010). Licensing would play a major role in refuting the public's image of unethical practices by public relations practitioners. With better-educated and -trained students, relationships will be stronger, and crises would be managed better. It would also improve the skill level of practitioners as well as increase competition. Edward Bernays, the father of American public relations, argued that licensing would assure the public that the professional has competency in the values, ethics, and standards of public relations (1992). It is unmistakable that licensing through testing would assist in the credibility of public relations for years to come.

A slightly less restrictive approach to ensuring high-quality, ethical public relations is accreditation. Accreditation, such as that offered by the Public Relations Society of America, is a type of self-regulation. Accreditation by a professional body ensures professional development, sets standards of excellence, and upholds codes of ethics. However, accreditation of public relations is usually not mandatory and has little enforcement power. Instead, many advocate for strong professional associations to ensure ethical practice.

Professional Associations Ensure Ethical Practice Across Nations

The past two decades have witnessed an unprecedented growth worldwide in the number of practitioners and organizations dedicated to public relations across the world. According to a 2006 report from Institute for Public Relations, it is estimated that there are about 2.3 million to 4.5 million public relations professionals around the world (Falconi, 2006). Studies have documented the evolution of public relations as a profession that has evolved from image building and publicity to different models of professionalization and sophistication around the world (Sriramesh & Verčič, 2009). Public relations wants to be viewed as a valued societal profession with standards and ethics.

Professional Associations

In addition to tertiary education in public relations, professionalization in public relations is fostered by national and regional professional associations. Associations such as the Public Relations Society of America (founded in 1948), the International Public Relations Association (founded in 1955), and the International Association of Business Communicators (founded in 1970) represent some of the largest professional associations. There are professional associations in more than 60 nations, with several countries having more than one association dedicated to furthering professionalism in public relations. Table 10.2 shows some of the details of public relations professional associations across the world including the general aggregated annual revenue associated with public relations practice, number of education programs (including undergraduate and graduate degrees), number of firms that are members of national associations, and the number of codes of ethics suggested by national associations.

PR associations support the development of professionalism by holding trainings, offering accreditation, providing mentoring opportunities, interfacing with the academic community, sponsoring research, and mentoring entrants to the field. Hence, it is reasonable to expect that professional associations also shape public relations practices that build social capital.

Codes of Ethics and Systems of Accreditation

The development of codes of ethics is a natural step for any field as it seeks to gain legitimacy in a society (Nessmann, 1995). Physicians, accountants, engineers, lawyers, journalists, and other professions have developed codes of ethics delineating acceptable behaviors from unacceptable behaviors. Public relations codes of ethics are necessary, though not sufficient, criteria if public relations is granted status as a bona-fide profession. Huang (2001) suggested that code enforcement rather than the existence of the code is the key to professionalization in public relations.

Accreditation is also a step toward greater professional and ethical standards. The process of accreditation creates another level to professionalization that takes the code of ethics even further. Accredited professionals, those who extend their professional education and pass a series of knowledge-based, practice-based, and ethical tests are considered highly qualified leaders and mentors in the field (https://www.prsa.org/professional-development/accreditation-in-public-relations-(apr).

Answering the Question: What Is Public Relations' Role in Society?

By now, it should be clear that there are different ways to internationalize public relations education. Units can take the dedicated class approach or embed discussions of internationalization in existing classes. The two approaches are not mutually exclusive, as competencies built in a stand-alone international public relations course could be reinforced across other classes. The content of this chapter has provided a fairly standard discussion of international public relations, and many educators will see their unit's approach represented in this chapter. There is, however, one more topic that should be added to an initiatives to internationalize public relations. This topic is asking the big question: What is public relations' role in society?

As noted in the earlier part of the chapter, the disciplinary approach within which public relations is taught will influence how that student views and eventually

126 *Maureen Taylor*

Table 10.2 Characteristics of Global PR Professional Organizations

Countrya	PR Annual Revenue (Million)	Number of PR Education Programs	Number of National Association Member Firms	PR Codes of Ethics
Argentina	–	30	30	1
Australia	304.00	33	175	2
Austria	34.50	12	15	1
Belgium	30.00	13	25	1
Brazil	283.00	51	341	3
Canada	49.30	68	–	2
Chile	–	18	–	1
China	2400.00	104	40	1
Croatia	9.50	8	15	1
Czech Republic	27.00	4	18	1
Denmark	40.00	12	31	1
Finland	45.00	7	31	1
France	172.00	47	38	1
Germany	180.00	51	35	1
India	110.00	93	18	1
Ireland	40.00	5	31	2
Italy	136.00	5	44	1
Japan	–	32	525	1
Mexico	193.29	76	–	1
Netherland	400.00	14	105	1
Norway	64.00	9	25	2
Poland	61.00	7	33	1
Portugal	52.00	–	31	2
Russia	74.50	62	32	1
Saudi Arabia	–	12	–	–
Singapore	2.20	5	–	2
Slovakia	5.50	7	12	2
Slovenia	73.00	–	14	1
South Africa	204.00	16	–	2
South Korea	–	–	–	1
Sweden	140.00	10	35	1
Switzerland	53.00	–	22	3
Turkey	16.00	14	19	1
UAE	19.33	15	–	2
United Kingdom	872.00	93	300	2
United States	2,500.00	484	360	2
Mean	277.09	40.49	85.71	–
SD	559.31	82.60	131.27	–

Reprinted from Yang and Taylor (2013)

practices public relations. Students who learn about public relations in a journalism school will have a good understanding of how public relations works with the media. Students who learn about public relations in a communication department or school will have a good understanding of how meaning is constructed by organizational messages. There is a higher-level question about the role of public relations in society that needs to be asked and answered for students to truly understand the value and potential of public relations in any context.

Taylor (2018) identified three possible answers to explain public relations' role in society. The first role is a functional role. A public relations practitioner or scholar who follows a functional approach might answer the question about public relations' role in society as "public relations creates and disseminates information that helps the organization to accomplish its goals" (Taylor, 2018, p. 106). This societal role of public relations would most likely be accepted without question by many professionals in business, government agencies, and the nonprofit community. The second role is a co-creational role in which "public relations uses communication to help groups to negotiate meaning and build relationships." A defining value of the co-creational perspective is that publics are not treated as "economic variables" that merely buy, sell, or respond to organizational outputs. The co-creational perspective avoids segmenting publics into demographic or even psychographic categories to predict their behaviors. Rather, a co-creational perspective treats individuals or groups who share interpretations as partners that are necessary for decision making at different levels of society. The third possible role emerges from the potential of public relations "to create (and recreate) the conditions that enact civil society" (Taylor, 2018, p. 107). A public relations approach to civil society allows us to understand how cooperative relationships help shape, change, and sustain communities ranging from small collectives all the way up to the nation-state.

If we want students to become ethical public relations practitioners capable of working with individuals and groups across the world, we need to instill in them an understanding of public relations that goes beyond functional approaches. Public relations educators need to imbue students with the excitement and possibility that public relations is not just a corporate, nonprofit, or government function. PR goes beyond helping organizations communicate to publics. Public relations is that which creates the conditions for civil society, because public relations is about using communication to negotiate relationships among groups. Public relations professionals serve as the eyes, ears, voice, and conscience of organizations and help their organizations adapt to the expectations of society.

References

Aldoory, L., & Toth, E. (2002). Gender discrepancies in a gendered profession: A developing theory for public relations. *Journal of Public Relations Research, 14*, 103–126.

Amatulli, J. (2019). *Thousands say Nike Air Max sneaker "offensive" to Muslims: Petition for recall*. Retrieved from www.huffingtonpost.com.au/2019/01/30/thousands-say-nike-air-max-sneaker-offensive-to-muslims-petition-for-recall_a_23657126/

Bernays, E. (1992). An introduction to Bill #374. *Prmuseum.com*. Retrieved March 24, 2013, from www.prmuseum.com/bernays_1990.html

Botan, C. H. (1997). Ethics in strategic communication campaigns: The case for a new approach to public relations. *Journal of Business Communication, 34*(2), 188–202.

Brody, E. W. (1984). The credentials of public relations: Licensing? Certification? Accreditation? An overview. *Public Relations Quarterly, 29*(2), 6–9.

Chan, K. L. (2006). The Chinese concept of face and violence against women. *International Social Work, 49*, 65–73.

Chen, R. (2018). Consumer engagement in social media in China. In K. A. Johnston & M. Taylor (Eds.), *The handbook of communication engagement* (pp. 475–489). London: Wiley Blackwell.

Culbertson, H. M., & Chen, N. (1996). *International public relations: A comparative analysis*. Mahwah, NJ: Lawrence Erlbaum Association.

Curtin, P. A., & Gaither, T. K. (2007). *International public relations: Negotiating culture, identity, and power*. Thousand Oaks, CA: Sage Publications.

Falconi, T. M. (2006). *How big is public relations?* Gainesville, FL: Institute for Public Relations.

Feng, E. (206). *Ikea under fire in China after limiting dresser recall to North America*. Retrieved from www.nytimes.com/2016/07/06/world/asia/china-ikea-dresser-recall.html

Freitag, A. R., & Stokes, A. Q. (2009). *Global public relations: Spanning borders, spanning cultures*. Abingdon, UK: Routledge.

Gandy, O. (1982). *Beyond agenda setting: Information subsidies and public policy*. Norwood, NJ: Ablex.

Goffman, E. (1955). On face-work: An analysis of ritual elements in social interaction. *Psychiatry: Interpersonal and Biological Processes, 18*, 213–231.

Hall, E. T. (1976). *Beyond culture*. New York: Anchor Books.

Hofstede, G. H. (1984). *Culture's consequences: International differences in work- related values*. Newbury Park, CA: Sage Publications.

Hofstede, G. H. (1997). *Cultures and organizations: Software of the mind*. New York, NY: McGraw Hill.

Hofstede, G. H. (2001). *Culture's consequences: Comparing values, behaviors, institutions, and organizations across nations* (2nd ed.). Thousand Oaks, CA: Sage Publications.

Hu, H. C. (1944). The Chinese concepts of "face". *American Anthropologist, 46*(1), 45–64.

Huang, Y.-H. (2001). Should a public relations code of ethics be enforced? *Journal of Business Ethics, 31*, 259–270.

Kent, M. L. (2010). Directions in social media for practitioners and scholars. In R. L. Heath (Ed.), *Handbook of public relations* (2nd ed., pp. 645–656). Thousand Oaks, CA: Sage Publications.

Kim, Y., & Kim, S. Y. (2010). The influence of cultural values on perceptions of corporate social responsibility: Application of Hofstede's dimensions to Korean public relations practitioners. *Journal of Business Ethics, 91*(4), 485–500.

Kruckeberg, D., & Tsetsura, K. (2003). *International index of bribery for news coverage* (Institute for Public Relations). Retrieved September 3, 2009, from www.instituteforpr.org/files/uploads/Bribery_Index_2003.pdf

Kruckeberg, D., & Tsetsura, K. (2004). International journalism ethics. In A. S. de Beer & J. C. Merrill (Eds.), *Global journalism* (4th ed., pp. 84–92). Boston: Pearson Allyn & Bacon.

Mak, S. (2017). Teaching international public relations: An update report among educators. *Journalism and Mass Communication Educator, 72*(2), 168–182.

Maleki, A., & de Jong, M. (2014). A proposal for clustering the dimensions of national culture. *Cross-Cultural Research, 48*, 107–143.

Minkov, M., & Hofstede, G. (2010). Hofstede's fifth dimension: New evidence from the world values survey. *Journal of Cross-Cultural Psychology, 43*, 3–14.

Minkov, M., & Hofstede, G. (2011). The evolution of Hofstede's doctrine. *Cross Cultural Management: An International Journal, 18*(1), 10–20.

Napoli, P. M. (Ed.). (2018). *Mediated communication* (Vol. 7). Berlin: Walter de Gruyter GmbH & Co KG.

Nessmann, K. (1995). Public relations in Europe: A comparison with the United State. *Public Relations Review, 21*(2), 151–160.

Peterson, J., & Mak, A. K. Y. (2006). Teaching international public relations: An examination of individual and institutional attributes of public relations educators in the U.S. *Public Relations Review, 32*, 416–419.

PRSA. (n.d.). *Accreditation in public relations*. Retrieved from https://www.prsa.org/professional-development/accreditation-in-public-relations-(apr).

Repucci, S. (2019). *Freedom and the media: A downward spiral*. Washington, DC: Freedom House.

Sha, B. L. (2011). Accredited vs. non-accredited: The polarization of practitioners in the public relations profession. *Public Relations Review, 37*, 121–128.

Siebert, F. S., Peterson, T., & Schramm, W. (1956). *Four theories of the press: The authoritarian, libertarian, social responsibility, and Soviet communist concepts of what the press should be and do*. Urbana: University of Illinois Press.
Sriramesh, K. (1992). Societal culture and public relations: Ethnographic evidence from India. *Public Relations Review, 18*, 201–211.
Sriramesh, K. (2009). Globalisation and public relations: The past, present, and the future. *Prism, 6*(2). Retrieved from http://praxis.massey.ac.nz/prism_on-line_journ.html
Sriramesh, K., Kim, Y., & Takasaki, M. (1999). Public relations in three Asian cultures: An analysis. *Journal of Public Relations Research, 11*, 271–292.
Sriramesh, K., & Verčič, D. (2009). *The global public relations handbook: Theory, research, and practice* (2nd ed.). Florence, KY: Routledge.
Stockmann, D., & Gallagher, M. E. (2011). Remote control: How the media sustain authoritarian rule in China. *Comparative Political Studies, 44*(4), 436–467.
Taylor, M. (2000). Cultural variance as a challenge to global public relations: A case study of the Coca-Cola scare in Europe. *Public Relations Review, 26*(3), 277–293.
Taylor, M. (2001). Internationalizing the public relations curriculum. *Public Relations Review, 27*(1), 73–88.
Taylor, M. (2018). Reconceptualizing public relations in an engaged society. In K. A. Johnston & M. Taylor (Eds.), *The handbook of communication engagement* (pp. 103–114). London: Wiley Blackwell.
Taylor, M., & Kent, M. L. (1999). Challenging assumptions in international public relations: When government is the most important public. *Public Relations Review, 25*(2), 131–144.
Tsetsura, K., & Kruckeberg, D. (2017). *Transparency, public relations and the mass media: Combating the hidden influences in news coverage worldwide*. New York: Routledge.
Tsetsura, K., & Luoma-aho, V. (2010). Innovative thinking or distortion of journalistic values? How the lack of trust creates non-transparency in the Russian media. *Ethical Space: The International Journal of Communication Ethics, 7*, 30–38.
White, C., & Park, J. (2010). Public perceptions of public relations. *Public Relations Review, 36*(4), 319–324.
Yang, A. (2012). Assessing global inequality of bribery for news coverage: A cross-national study. *Mass Communication and Society, 15*, 201–224.
Yang, A., & Taylor, M. (2013). The relationship between the professionalization of public relations, societal social capital and democracy: Evidence from a cross-national study. *Public Relations Review, 39*, 257–270.
Ye, L., & Pang, A. (2011). Examining the Chinese approach to crisis management: Cover-ups, saving face, and taking the "Upper Level Line." *Journal of Marketing Channels, 18*, 247–278.
Yeo, S. L., & Sriramesh, K. (2009). Adding value to organizations: An examination of the role of senior public relations practitioners in Singapore. *Public Relations Review, 35*, 422–425.
Yu, T. H., & Wen, W. C. (2003). Crisis communication in Chinese culture: A case study in Taiwan. *Asian Journal of Communication, 13*, 50–64.
Zaharna, R. S. (2018). Global engagement: Culture and communication insights from public diplomacy. In K. A. Johnston & M. Taylor (Eds.), *The handbook of communication engagement* (pp. 313–330). London: Wiley Blackwell.
Zakkour, M. (2014). *China's golden week: A good time to make sure you don't 'bite the wax tadpole*. Retrieved from www.forbes.com/sites/michaelzakkour/2014/10/02/chinas-national-day-golden-week-a-good-time-to-make-sure-you-dont-bite-the-wax-tadpole/#29d4d463560f

11 Internationalization Opportunities for Strategic Communication

Engaging With Latin America and the Latino Communities in Public Relations and Advertising Courses

Juan Mundel, Esther Quintero, and Maria De Moya

> Unlike many of the physical goods and resources that formed the basis of industrial production, knowledge is a largely public good in the sense that its value depends less on scarcity, but more on sharing and collaboration.
> (Starke-Meyerring & Wilson, 2008, p. 6)

"Internationalization" is one of those buzz words that faculty, administrators, international programs centers, and others in higher education seem to encounter on a regular basis (Starke-Meyerring & Wilson, 2008). Yet the internationalization of campuses, curricula, and classrooms responds less to trends and more to a more global society, where learning and knowledge are the result of collaborations across cultures (Kapitzke & Peters, 2007; Peters & Besley, 2006).

Education plays a significant role in preparing global citizens, which includes helping individuals develop the skills, knowledge, and experience necessary to communicate effectively across multiple boundaries. At the same time, globalization provides higher education institutions with the opportunity to expose their students to people from other countries and cultures. Internationalization of higher institutions has gained such relevance that the World Trade Organization (WTO) actively promotes policies that facilitate conditions for global education (Green, 2016; Stiglitz, 2006).

While no discipline is free of the effects of globalization in higher education, globalization has influenced strategic communication significantly. Strategic communication is defined as "the purposeful use of communication by an organization to fulfill its mission" (Hallahan, Holtzhausen, Van Ruler, Verčič, & Sriramesh, 2007, p. 3). As a discipline, it can incorporate public relations, marketing communication, advertising, political communication, and social media strategies, among other communication functions used by organizations of all sizes (Hallahan et al., 2007).

The trend of consolidation within the global advertising and public relations landscape (Springer, 2018) requires students to be prepared to operate within a challenging global market. Big media groups (e.g., WPP, Publicis) have acquired a number of smaller agencies to allow for the creation of full-service ad agencies that include an array of services (e.g., strategic planning, digital buying, among others) all over the world (Chu, Yang, Yang, & Mundel, 2019). For future strategic communication professionals, the Latinx market in particular is becoming an important market to understand.

In fact, in the US alone, this market is estimated at 1.7 trillion dollars (eMarketer 2019). Latinx consumers have become a large market that companies are increasingly trying to reach as they have become aware of the size and attractiveness of Latin America's population, and the increasing buying power of countries like Brazil, Mexico, and Argentina (Fastoso & Whitelock, 2010; Fastoso & Whitelock, 2011; Kantar MillwardBrown, 2017) is changing the strategic communication landscape. However, only a handful of programs across the country prepare undergraduate students to understand these consumers. At DePaul University, communication students engage with these publics in a variety of ways, including the Latino Media and Communication program, international public relations and advertising courses, and real-world clients and study-away opportunities.

In this chapter, we describe the creation and implementation of the Latino Media and Communication Program, programs led by the Office of Global Engagement at DePaul University, and faculty-led programs to introduce students to not only the Latinx community but also the Latin American markets. These initiatives prepare students to create communication plans for Latinx consumers through a mix of courses, a faculty-led study abroad and away programs, scholarly research, and expert speakers. Through this focus on the Latinx/Latin American community, this chapter provides (1) an overview of the strategies and factors that contribute to the success of the internationalization of undergraduate programs, (2) an analysis of the benefits and challenges of preparing students to understand complex cultural factors, and (3) a "roadmap" of practical advice and best practices for faculty interested in developing similar efforts.

Internationalization at DePaul

Located in Chicago, DePaul University is the largest Catholic (Vincentian) university in the United States (DePaul, 2019). With more than 22,000 students, the student body includes people from all 50 states and more than 100 nations (DePaul, 2019). Internationalization has long been a priority for the university. For example, its 2012–2018 strategic plan included a goal to connect the university to the global city of Chicago, and it calls for infusing "international and comparative perspectives throughout teaching, research and service missions of the university" (DePaul Academic Affairs, 2019, para. 2). To do so, the university has been focusing on recruiting international students, offering opportunities for student and faculty mobility (e.g., study abroad and courses including online global learning experiences[1]), international partnerships, and the internationalization of the curriculum (DePaul Academic Affairs, 2019).

The university's 2019–2024 strategic plan (DePaul Office of the President, 2019), identifies as one of the six priorities to "excel in preparing all students for global citizenship and success" (p. 5). This priority specifies a need to "reflect the complexity of cultural and social issues, the diversity of opinions and ways of thinking, and appreciation of difference" (p. 10). Additionally, the academic and professional success for graduates is defined in terms of developing critical-thinking skills and intercultural and multilingual competences, among other related skills and experiences. Developing "cultural agility" and "effective communication" as well as increasing students' "global perspectives" (p. 11) are also identified as important. Internationalization is also included in the other strategic areas through activities such as international outreach, attention to global issues (e.g., homelessness), opportunities for interconnectedness through partnerships and technology, and global learning projects.

Although these priorities are pursued in a variety of ways through the university's colleges and programs, the Office of Global Engagement has a leadership role by providing opportunities for leadership and collaboration for students, faculty, and staff (DePaul Global Engagement, 2019a). The office's associate directors lead strategy and develop programs at the regional level, with a special focus on India, China, and Latin America. The role of these associate directors is to find partnerships regionally, promote mutual visits and study-abroad programs to their assigned region, and connect with the communities of the countries associated with their task (e.g., cultural centers and consulates). These areas were identified as strategic locations based on aspects such as demographics of the state and city, student population, and trends in academic mobility. Latin America and Mexico in particular were defined as a priority due to the demographic profile of Hispanic population in Illinois.[2]

DePaul's Engagement With Latinx and Latin American Communities

Working with partners in Latin America as well as the Latinx community in Chicago, DePaul offers students an opportunity to interact with international perspectives through study-abroad opportunities, bringing guest speakers to campus, and supporting the inclusion of Latinx issues and voices in the curricula. Using a glocal approach, we introduce students to global knowledge and the way to connect it with their city reality. This strategy is responsive to trends in globalization and international trade, which make it necessary for the development of educational programs based on multidisciplinary curriculum, teaching students to think globally and act locally. This curriculum is particularly important in multicultural urban areas where the internationalization and multiculturalism are critical concepts (Caraballo, 2017). Moreover, the development of global skills serves not exclusively to maintain a cordial and peaceful professional environment but also to create working inclusive environments prone to creativity and inclusion (Paletz, Miron-Spektor, & Lin, 2014).

Nonetheless, providing students in higher education with global learning opportunities is not a goal that is easily accomplished. More often than not, participating in an international program is perceived as another economic burden instead of a benefit or academic advantage (Alghamdi & Otte, 2016). Creating a strategic plan to tackle this challenge must include the participation of faculty, staff, administrators, and, importantly, external academic partners (Klahr, 2011). At DePaul, including this priority in the strategic plan (DePaul Office of the President, 2019) signals the importance of internationalization to students, faculty, staff, and the extended community. A comprehensive strategy can create affordable, meaningful, and sustainable experiences that achieve the goals of an internationalized educational model.

Although the identification of champions (i.e., university faculty or staff with a motivation to accomplish goals related to internationalization) has been recommended as an essential stratagem (Klahr, 2011), it is important for a university to have a comprehensive support system for those involved in the internationalization of the curricula and to eliminate hurdles that impede reaching strategic goals.

Global Engagement at DePaul is to support faculty in their international endeavors, guiding the planning and implementation of study-abroad programs, establishing a strategic network of the international community and organizations in Chicago,[3] bringing the internationalization to the campus with conferences, special speakers, international art festivals, or exhibits, and most recently, facilitating the inclusion of technology in class to connect with partners abroad (DePaul Teaching Commons, 2019). This support is essential, given that many faculty do not explore internationalization opportunities because of the significant investment of time and resources required for successful experiences. Lack of logistical support, the dedication of time to the development of international programs and networks, may result in the neglect of one's regular academic duties of teaching, research, and service. However, leaving the responsibility of internationalization in the hands of just a few entrepreneurial faculty with initiative could be ineffective considering the overwhelming duty in the already hectic academic schedule. Therefore, the role of DePaul's Office of Global Engagement has been to facilitate these connections and ensure shared responsibility and ownership of internationalization programs.

Creating the financial and logistical conditions, including adequate support staff and partnerships with universities and institutions that contribute to the global strategy, is critical for developing strong partnerships. Strong support behind a global strategy results in the inclusion of international components in the curriculum, internationalization to the campus, implementing international community service, or increasing affordable and safe study-abroad destinations to our students. DePaul has established partnerships and signed agreements with a variety of institutions in Latin America. This network includes public and private institutions, such as Universidad Panamericana and Universidad Nacional Autónoma in Mexico, the Brazilian Federal Agency for the Support and Evaluation of Graduate Education, the Pontifical Catholic University of Peru, Universidad Blas Pascal in Argentina, and Pontifical Catholic University of Chile, to mention only some of them (DePaul Global Engagement, 2019b). Together, DePaul and its partners collaborate in student exchanges, global learning engagement programs, faculty development, and interdisciplinary academic visits.

Internationalization in the Strategic Communication Curricula

Universities in the United States offering public relations and advertising education have adopted a strategic communication focus, integrating strategies from a variety of disciplines (Hallahan et al., 2007). At DePaul, the Public Relations and Advertising program offers a bachelor's, master's and minor (DePaul College of Communication, 2019b). At every level, students have the option to take classes with a clear international and/or Latinx focus, as well as to participate in study-abroad courses in the region.

Additionally, the Latino Media and Communication program provides students another opportunity to gain the skills and experiences heralded as benefits of internationalization of curricula, including cultural competence and cross-cultural and international experiences. Since its inception in 2011, the program has offered "focused courses based on an awareness and appreciation of Latino cultures in the U.S." (DePaul College of Communication, 2019a. para.1). Despite its US-centric focus, the program has always included Latin American perspectives, since the US Latinx experience is still tied to the Latin American heritage and immigrant experiences (Hernandez, 2017; Lynch, 2018; Sweet, 2016). From a strategic communication perspective, media coverage of topics related to immigrants can lead to a mixing in the identities of two distinct populations, Latin Americans and the Latinx community in the United States. Media coverage can also shape the perceptions of Latin Americans and Latinos held by other social and ethnic groups (Bleich et al., 2018; Rodríguez, 2017; Vargas, Sanchez, & Valdez, 2017). The program thus prepares students to understand the diverse and evolving nature of Latino communities at the local, national, and global levels while gaining intercultural communication skills and developing cross-cultural competences (DePaul College of Communication, 2019a). Additionally, the program helps students gain insights into behaviors of Latino consumers (e.g., product decisions, purchase process, and information search), employees (e.g., relationship development, social harmony, personal contact, and respect for authority) and media (e.g., community development and dealing with less saturated media).

Undergraduate students declaring a minor or concentration in LM&C are required to take one introductory course about the Latinx community's sociocultural and economic realities (DePaul College of Communication, 2019a). For this introductory course, students have the option of taking a broader view in Constructing Latino Communities,[4] which has an interdisciplinary focus and explores the socio-historical foundations of major Latinx groups in the United States, as well as the factors that shape Latinx identity, including immigration, economic factors and media representation. Conversely, they can choose a communication course titled *Latino Communication Culture and Community*,[5] which focuses on the relationship between Latinx cultures, communication, institutions, and public and private life while incorporating a service-learning component. This service component is conducted with Latinx communities in the city, which in Chicago always involves immigrant populations as well as US-born Latinx individuals. Once they have met this requirement, students complete the program by taking three to five electives[6] with a Latinx focus, the majority of which are taught in the College of Communication, with others which are part of the University's Latin American and Latino Studies program (DePaul College of Liberal Arts and Social Sciences, 2019).

For the strategic communication classes, cultural competencies are taught alongside practical skills. Some of the cultural and global competencies identified in scholarly research are substantive knowledge, intercultural communication skills (Olsen & Kroeger, 2001), openness, fluency in a different language, tolerance of ambiguity, awareness of issues facing the community, cross-cultural empathy, and knowledge of the in-group and the out-group (Donatelli, Yngve, Miller, & Ellis, 2005), as well as creating and analyzing messaging strategies (Engleberg et al., 2017).

Each LM&C class addresses several of the competencies detailed above. For example, Engaging Latinx Communities is a course that takes a public relations and advertising lens to understanding culture and identity as they relate to communication practices and preferences. Working with a class client,[7] students identify and study Latinx publics to understand the most effective way to communicate with them and engage them around the client's goods and/or services. Students begin by exploring the subcultures in the U.S. Latinx communities, by national heritage as well as race and ethnicity issues (which involves the knowledge and cross-cultural empathy competencies). Based on secondary data, students analyze research on consumer behavior, media consumption, and communication preferences of these groups (e.g., Nielsen, 2017, 2018; Sanderson, 2018). These analyses also contribute to the knowledge and awareness of issues such as stereotyping in the media, tokenization, and racism. Students conduct their own research and design communication strategies appropriate for the Latinx community, which requires them to apply their messaging strategies and cross-cultural communication competencies. This pedagogical approach to learning enables students to examine the subject with openness and tolerance for ambiguity as they learn and appreciate the fluidity and subjectivity of culture. Depending on the focus of each course (e.g., advertising, journalism, performance studies), students gain a deeper knowledge and understanding of culture, needs of the community, and the organizations that serve them. For example, students learn about advocacy and activism in the Latinx community; political participation and health disparities;[8] purchasing behaviors;[9] international business and marketing;[10] and media representation of the community.[11]

Through the extended network of Latin American Academic partnerships, students have the opportunity to experience the diversity of the regional culture and, consequently, understand the nuances of the local Latinx community. Our experience at DePaul has shown that students are more attracted to participate in faculty-led programs. For some of our students, this is their first experience in another country, and they feel more confident in the faculty guidance. Traveling with faculty allows students to understand the context and connect it to their academic interests in the United States.

In the following section, we will discuss the procedures used by the authors when designing, implementing, and leading short-term study-abroad programs that support the internationalization of the curricula.

Developing Faculty-Led Study-Abroad Programs

Given the growing pressures from higher education institutions and the globalized economy for faculty and administrators to internationalize their curricula, educators are faced with questions pertaining to how to help "students and ourselves navigate, participate in, and shape these changes as we build rich shared learning" in a globally networked world (Starke-Meyerring & Wilson, 2008, p. 7). Professional motivations, such as understanding the complex cultural waters in the fields of strategic communication, prompt students to pursue opportunities to study abroad (Urban & Palmer, 2014).

Study-abroad programs foster international competitiveness and help produce graduates capable of being active in a globalized society (Take & Shoraku, 2018). However, while the number of US Americans studying abroad continues to increase,[12] the nature of the programs seems to have shifted in design. Conversely, an *Inside Higher Ed* report shows that participation in short-term programs is booming, while the number of students studying abroad for a full year is decreasing (Redden, 2017). While historically study-abroad programs were tied to language-learning objectives (e.g., Hispanic language and culture programs), efforts to make study abroad appealing to a broader array of students from different disciplines (e.g., engineering, public relations, and business administration) have resulted in the creation of several short, faculty-led study-abroad programs (e.g., Michigan State University's Public Relations a-la-Mediterranean, Richmond University's MBA six-week program in Argentina).

At DePaul University, it has become a priority for the university and the program to internationalize our curricula to serve advertising and public relations students. We have developed three short-term faculty-led study-abroad programs for students in public relations and advertising (PRAD): Argentina: International Social Marketing; France, Netherlands, and Spain: Creativity and Portfolio Building

Abroad; Taiwan and Japan: International Branding; and an additional study away (i.e., a program similar to study abroad in which students travel to another city in the same country) four-day program to New York City. Below we will focus on the development of programs and offer recommendations based on the authors' experience in designing Argentina: International Social Marketing.[13]

Program Overview: Argentina, International Social Marketing

Location Rationale

A focus on emerging markets for strategic communications programs is important, because most existing theories and generalizations derived from data gathered in the developed countries are not always applicable to developing countries (Steenkamp, 2005). Exposing students to a new market is particularly important, taking into account that approximately 86% of all marketing research is conducted on Europe, Japan, and the US (Craig & Douglas, 2005). Large emerging countries in Latin America, such as Brazil, Argentina, and Mexico, are particularly active in marketing communications. The region has a population of more than 550 million and a GDP of approximately US$4 trillion. Among the Latin American countries, Argentina is a particularly fertile ground for examining communicational practices aimed at promoting products and services (Ahn & Mundel, 2015).

With 15% of all US students choosing Latin America for study abroad, only behind Europe (54.4%; Redden, 2017), Argentina has been gaining momentum among students and faculty. In 2017, more than 50,000 foreign students chose Argentine universities for their undergraduate or graduate studies (Costa & Lacroze, 2017). Furthermore, Buenos Aires ranked first in the QS Best Students Cities Ranking 2017, which measures the best cities for students to live in. Students choose Argentina because of its affordability (the Argentine peso has been in a downhill battle with the American dollar, losing 40% of its value in 2018 alone), landscapes and tourism opportunities, and the quality of its higher education institutions.

Academics/Curriculum/Teaching Style/Methodology

The Argentina: International Social Marketing course is open to all DPU students but is geared towards students in the College of Communication, and a previous background in marketing communications is preferred. During the program, students have the opportunity to visit major global and local advertising and marketing agencies as well as media companies (i.e., newspapers and television stations, among others) to learn about practices and challenges associated with the development of global campaigns. Except for several guest speakers in Buenos Aires and Córdoba, the faculty leader is responsible for teaching the course while abroad. In two weeks, students work with a local nonprofit to develop a social marketing campaign to help them connect with their publics, raise awareness about their organizations, and/or raise funds.

The course load is distributed so that there are classes on Monday through Friday in the morning, with free time to travel and discover the country during the weekends. During their free time, students have participated in walking tours, explored local markets, and discovered new foods in local restaurants. During the evenings, students engage in cultural activities such as city tours, museum visits, tango and horseback riding lessons, and even trips to neighboring countries such as Uruguay.

Travel Details

The daily itinerary is planned so that the students maximize their time in each of the host cities. This allows students free time during some afternoons to take advantage of the many cultural opportunities these cities have to offer. We strongly recommend working with either a travel agency to help you set up tourism activities and excursions or with a local university that can act as your host partner. When developing the Argentina: International Social Marketing program, the author worked with Universidad Blas Pascal (with locations in Buenos Aires and Córdoba), a private university with extensive experience in incoming programs. Travel agencies providing support have included STA Travel and Seminars International.

The group travel between cities is booked by the faculty, along with a travel agency, and the cost is included within the program fee. Students are responsible for their airfare to Argentina.[14] Given the size of the group, traditionally this program rents a full hotel in Palermo (Buenos Aires) and stays at the UBP residence dorms in Córdoba. The mix of different housing opportunities allows for an affordable program fee. Efforts are made to book students in double/triple rooms to keep housing costs down. According to budget needs, arrangements can be made to offer group meals in selected local restaurants. Students should, however, be provided with an estimate of out-of-pocket costs before departing.

Foreign Languages and Minimum Qualifications of Students

Because of the short duration of the overseas experience, and because there will be faculty members fluent in Spanish traveling with them, students do not need an additional foreign language requirement. However, it is recommended that students interested in enrolling in the class would benefit from taking introductory courses in Spanish to help them navigate the cities more confidently. Arrangements are made with our partner university to give students a "Spanish for survival" class, as well as some Argentine culture activities.

Recruitment

The authors have adopted a comprehensive promotional and recruitment process, which starts about a year before the program runs. Faculty leaders visit every in-person course at least once for about 5 to 10 minutes to speak directly to students about the program. The Study Abroad office designs and prints flyers that are distributed to the students in each visit and also posted around campus. Several emails are sent by the college's advisors to the students enrolled in majors and minors that are relevant to the program's objectives. Further, we hold at least one but often more than one informational session where students interested in the program can meet with the faculty leaders to discuss concerns. We recommend recruiting at least ten more students than the minimum since a number of factors (e.g., students' unexpected financial limitations, internship openings, family situations) might impact the enrollment of those who accept a place in the program.

On-Site Arrival and Orientation

Upon arrival, students are invited to settle in their rooms. With the assistance of the local partners' staff, we hold an on-site orientation, repeating program rules, information about health insurance, distribute safety cards, pick-pocketing in public transit, and expectations. We follow the orientation with a series of team building activities based on improvisation. Students are separated into groups and invited to complete each other sentences, make up ideal personas, and communicate without words, which allow students to get to know each other and the faculty leaders better.

Program Evaluation and Results

The structure implemented at DePaul University requires that upon return from a study-abroad program, the faculty leader submits a program report to the college's Internationalization Committee within four weeks. The report includes a list of key positives, major challenges, and recommendations for future iterations. In addition, the faculty leader is to discuss a summary of each stage of the program (i.e., predeparture preparation, abroad time, and postprogram classes and objectives), paying special attention to successes and concerns. We recommend that faculty keep a daily journal as soon as they start designing their programs and take notes that can help solve issues associated with student recruitment (i.e., whether the applicant pool was appropriate for the course content and level), the time frame (i.e., the time abroad was sufficient for supporting learning goals), on-site facilities and logistics (i.e., safe and clean accommodations, use of local partners, budget and affordability), and university support (i.e., whether the study-abroad office provided the faculty leader with the necessary help for identifying partners, travel agencies, and/or help with resolving issues with conflictive students).

Positives, Major Challenges, and Students' Comments

Next we discuss excerpts from our journals documented during the last iteration (December 2018) of DePaul University's Argentina: International Social Marketing.

Key Positives

The Argentine peso has greatly devalued, hence making the program affordable for students (e.g., food was cheaper than expected, which allowed for more meals paid for by the program). Students did not perceive a language barrier in Buenos Aires, which allows participants to feel more comfortable in the destination location. The accommodations in Cordoba were evaluated positively by the group (Universidad Blas Pascal's student dorms). Students enjoyed being in a closed campus with a pool to enjoy the warm summer days. The service learning component of the class helped students gain stronger cultural insights about the struggles of South American countries. We raised almost $1,200 to help the local non-profit the class used as a client, called Merendero Mis Pimpollos.[15] With the money raised, we bought school supplies, food for the afternoon, and many gallons of milk and drinks for the nonprofit.

Major Challenges

We found that pickpocketing was an issue in Buenos Aires (two students got cell phones stolen in two weeks). Students should be encouraged to be more cautious. Further, cultural shock was experienced by the group, which was associated with Argentina's economic struggles (e.g., the number of homeless children, the lack of access to basic resources such as electricity, water, or plumbing).

Recommendations for Future Iterations

We believe students would benefit from a longer course (e.g., 6-credit class), with a 2-credit class taught in the quarter previous to travel. Before departure the class could examine the history of the country, the foundations of social marketing, and prepare students for culture shock. Upon arrival, students would complete the work as planned in the original syllabus and close with a reflection on their experiences.

Student Evaluation of the Program

In general, the majority of students felt that as a result of the program, they developed a stronger comfort in interacting with people from different backgrounds (78.5%), adaptability (i.e., tolerating change, handling uncertainty, accepting risks; 94.73%), and gained skills for problem solving (87.5%). The qualitative evaluation ("What were the three most valuable things gained through study abroad?") showed that short-term study can have a positive impact on the students. Consider the following extracts: "Exposure to social marketing concepts and the impact on cultures outside of my own. Historical knowledge of Argentina and its beautiful people. Understanding on how to implement my learnings into a future career within social responsibilities." Or "1. A renewed interest in Marketing as a career choice 2. A level of comfort in traveling alone (even though I was with a group) 3. A time to reflect upon my life, not only in regards to academic and career pursuits but also on a personal behavior level."

Conclusions

Education must respond to changes in the real world. Global education has been described as an indispensable component of any educational system worldwide, with a goal of providing students with skills needed for being globally competent and civically engaged. Although many educators believe international education is restricted to specific disciplines and limited to study-abroad programs in liberal arts and language acquisition (Bellamy & Weinberg, 2006), global education must go beyond this definition and provide students in different disciplines with the skills to face a competitive professional environment through a variety of cost-efficient initiatives. In this chapter, we reviewed the different levels of support implemented by DePaul University in support of initiatives related to Latin American and Latino communities. In sum, we show that there can be a symbiosis between the goals of faculty, colleges, and administration.

Strong internal and external support is the foundation upon which a productive and healthy internationalization strategy must be built. The need for staff that works coordinately with faculty to execute all internationalization efforts across the institution becomes increasingly patent and can be the avenue to develop more programs aimed to allow students to develop the necessary skills to face a professional environment, every time more competitive and demanding.

Additionally, flexibility and creativity are deemed important for the success of internationalization initiatives. The varied offering of programs, including short-term outbound faculty-led, semester- and academic-year-long, study away, along with local initiatives ensures that students can take advantage of the environment around them.

Notes

1. This is a virtual exchange program, in which faculty members connect with an international partner who teaches in a similar discipline and, through a DePaul-supported-program, develops a GLE project to implement in one of their courses (Global Teaching Commons, 2019).
2. An estimated 17% of the state population is Hispanic/Latino, 80% of which are of Mexican origin (Pew Hispanic, 2015).
3. For example, engaging the consuls of Latin American nations (DePaul Newsline, 2018).
4. LST-202, offered through the Latin American and Latino Studies program, which is part of the College of Liberal Arts and Sciences.
5. CMNS-335, offered through the communication studies program, which is part of the College of Communication.
6. Undergraduate students must take four Latinx-focuses classes for a concentration and six courses for a minor. Graduate students only have the option of a concentration, which requires taking three classes.
7. A local organization, which agrees to serve as a client (pro bono) to brief students on their work and communication needs and, following research conducted by the students, receive strategic planning recommendations from the class.
8. PRAD 594—Communication Campaigns for Social Change.
9. PRAD-511 Consumer Insights.
10. CMN-398 International Social Marketing in Argentina, PRAD-384 International PR.
11. JOUR-377 Special Topics in Journalism.
12. Participation in study-abroad programs grew by 2.3% in academic year 2016–17 compared to the previous year (Open Doors, 2018).
13. A sample syllabus can be found online at: www.dropbox.com/s/r5abjopr7jla2kf/SAMPLEINTLSOCMKT.pdf?dl=0
14. This is a cost-effective alternative for students not in the departure city during break. Other students take advantage of mileage for saving.
15. For linguistic context, *merienda* is a light afternoon meal, similar to breakfast, because Argentinians eat late dinners. *Pimpollos* is the Spanish word for rosebud, referencing a young flower, much like the children that go to the *merendero*.

References

Ahn, H., & Mundel, J. (2015). Luxury brand advertising in Argentina: Changes following import restrictions. *Journal of Marketing Communications, 24*(3), 291–303.

Alghamdi, H., & Otte, S. (2016). The challenges and benefits of study abroad. *International Journal of Humanities and Social Science, 6*(5), 16–22.

Bellamy, C., & Weinberg, A. (2006). Creating global citizens through study abroad. *Connection: The Journal of the New England Board of Higher Education, 21*(2), 20–21.

Bleich, E., Callison, J. P., Edwards, G. G., Fichman, M., Hoynes, E., Jabari, R., & van der Veen, A. M. (2018). The good, the bad, and the ugly: A corpus linguistics analysis of US newspaper coverage of Latinx, 1996–2016. Journalism, 1464884918818252.

Caraballo, L. (2017). Students' critical meta-awareness in a figured world of achievement: Toward a culturally sustaining stance in curriculum, pedagogy, and research. *Urban Education, 52*(5), 585–609.

Chu, S. C., Yang, C., Yang, J., & Mundel, J. (2019). *Understanding advertising client-agency relationships in China: The impact of relationship quality and Guanxi on agency performance.* American Academy of Advertising Annual Conference, Dallas.

Costa, J. M., & Lacroze, L. (2017). *Cuántos extranjeros estudian en universidades argentinas y de qué países vienen.* Retrieved from www.lanacion.com.ar/2071328-cuantos-extranjeros-estudian-en-universidades-argentinas-y-de-que-paises-vienen

Craig, C. S., & Douglas, S. P. (2005). *International marketing research*. Chichester: John Wiley & Sons.
DePaul. (2019). *About DePaul*. Retrieved from www.depaul.edu/about/Pages/default.aspx
DePaul Academic Affairs. (2019). *Globalization*. Retrieved from https://offices.depaul.edu/academic-affairs/initiatives/Pages/globalization.aspx
DePaul College of Communication. (2019a). *Latino media and communication*. Retrieved from https://communication.depaul.edu/academics/minors-concentrations/Pages/latino-media-and-communication-minor.aspx
DePaul College of Communication. (2019b). *Public relations and advertising*. Retrieved from https://communication.depaul.edu/academics/public-relations-and-advertising/Pages/default.aspx
DePaul College of Liberal Arts and Social Sciences. (2019). *Latin American and Latino studies*. Retrieved from https://las.depaul.edu/academics/latin-american-and-latino-studies/Pages/default.aspx
DePaul Global Engagement. (2019a). *About global engagement*. Retrieved from https://offices.depaul.edu/global-engagement/about/Pages/default.aspx
DePaul Global Engagement. (2019b). *International partnerships*. Retrieved from https://offices.depaul.edu/global-engagement/partnerships/international-partnerships/Pages/default.aspx
DePaul Newsline. (2018, March 15). *Consuls general meet with Dr. Esteban*. Retrieved from https://resources.depaul.edu/newsline/multimedia/Pages/Consuls-General-meet-with-Dr.-Esteban.aspx
DePaul Office of the President. (2019). *Grounded in the mission: The plan for DePaul 2024*. Retrieved from https://offices.depaul.edu/president/strategic-directions/grounded-in-mission/Documents/Grounded_in_MissionPlan%20Booklet%2011%20pgs%20FINAL.pdf
DePaul Teaching Commons. (2019). *Global learning experience*. Retrieved from https://resources.depaul.edu/teaching-commons/programs/global-learning/Pages/default.aspx
Donatelli, L., Yngve, K., Miller, M., & Ellis, J. (2005). Technology and education abroad. In J. L. Brockington, W. W. Hoffa, & P. C. Martin (Eds.), *NAFSA's guide to education abroad for advisors and administrators* (pp. 129–150). Washington, DC: NAFSA: Association of International Educators.
eMarketer (2019). *$1.5 Trillion spending power of US Hispanics sas a caveat*. Retrieved from https://www.emarketer.com/content/1-5-trillion-spending-power-of-us-hispanics-has-a-caveat
Engleberg, I. N., Ward, S. M., Disbrow, L. M., Katt, J. A., Myers, S. A., & O'Keefe, P. (2017). The development of a set of core communication competencies for introductory communication courses. *Communication Education*, 66(1), 1–18.
Fastoso, F., & Whitelock, J. (2010). Regionalization vs. globalization in advertising research: Insights from five decades of academic study. *Journal of International Management*, 16(1), 32–42.
Fastoso, F., & Whitelock, J. (2011). Why is so little marketing research on Latin America published in high quality journals and what can we do about it? Lessons from a Delphi study of authors who have succeeded. *International Marketing Review*, 28(4), 435–449.
Global Teaching Commons. (2019). Retrieved from: https://resources.depaul.edu/teaching-commons/Pages/default.aspx
Green, A. (2016). *Handbook of global education policy*. Hoboken, NJ: John Wiley & Sons.
Hallahan, K., Holtzhausen, D., Van Ruler, B., Verčič, D., & Sriramesh, K. (2007). Defining strategic communication. *International Journal of Strategic Communication*, 1(1), 3–35.
Hernandez, D. P. (2017). Race, ethnicity and the production of Latin/o popular music. In *Global repertoires* (pp. 57–72). New York, NY: Routledge.
Kantar MillwardBrown. (2017). *2017 Top 50 Latin American brands*. Retrieved from www.millwardbrown.com/brandz/top-latin-american-brands/2017
Kapitzke, C., & Peters, M. A. (2007). *Global knowledge cultures* (Vol. 14). AW Rotterdam, The Netherlands: Sense Publishers.

Klahr, S. C. (2011). Identifying and selecting appropriate partner institutions. In S. Sutton & D. Obst (Eds.), *Developing strategic international partnerships: Models for initiating and sustaining innovative institutional linkages* (pp. 29–32). New York: The Institute of International Education.

Lynch, A. (2018). A historical view of US Latinidad and Spanish as a heritage language. In *The Routledge handbook of Spanish as a heritage language* (pp. 31–49). New York, NY: Routledge.

Nielsen. (2017). *Latina 2.0: Fiscally conscious, culturally influential and familia forward.* Retrieved from www.nielsen.com/us/en/insights/reports/2017/latina-2-0.html

Nielsen. (2018). *Descubrimiento digital: The online lives of Latinx consumers.* Retrieved from www.nielsen.com/us/en/insights/reports/2018/descubrimiento-digital-the-online-lives-of-latinx-consumers.html

Olsen, C. L., & Kroeger, K. R. (2001). Global competency and intercultural sensitivity. *Journal of Studies in International Education, 5*(2), 116–137.

Open Doors. (2018). *Number of international students in United States reaches new high of 1.09 million.* Retrieved from www.iie.org/Research-and-Insights/Open-Doors

Paletz, S. B., Miron-Spektor, E., & Lin, C. C. (2014). A cultural lens on interpersonal conflict and creativity in multicultural environments. *Psychology of Aesthetics, Creativity, and the Arts, 8*(2), 237.

Peters, M. (2007). Higher education, globalization, and the knowledge economy: Reclaiming the cultural mission. *Ubiquity, 8*(18), 1–27.

Peters, M., & Besley, T. (2006). *Building knowledge cultures: Education and development in the age of knowledge capitalism.* Lanham and Oxford: Rowman & Littlefield.

Pew Hispanic. (2015). *Demographic profile of Hispanics in Illinois, 2014.* Retrieved from www.pewhispanic.org/states/state/il/

Redden. (2017). *Trends in U.S. study abroad.* Retrieved from www.nafsa.org/Policy_and_Advocacy/Policy_Resources/Policy_Trends_and_Data/Trends_in_U_S__Study_Abroad/

Rodríguez, C. E. (2018). *Latin looks: Images of Latinas and Latinos in the US media.* New York, NY: Routledge.

Sanderson, L. (2018). *Hispanic trends series: Technology.* Retrieved from https://corporate.univision.com/technology-social/2018/09/14/hispanic-trends-series-technology/

Springer, P. (2018). Advertising, agencies and globalisation. In J. Hardy, H. Powell, & I. Macrury (Eds.), *The advertising handbook* (pp. 200–215). New York, NY: Routledge.

Starke-Meyerring, D., & Wilson, M. (2008). Learning environments for a globally networked world: Emerging visions. *Designing Globally Networked Learning Environments: Visionary Partnerships, Policies and Pedagogies*, 1–17.

Steenkamp, J. (2005). Moving out of the U.S. Silo: A Call to Arms for Conducting International Marketing Research. *Journal of Marketing, 69*(4), 6–8.

Stiglitz, J. E. (2006). *Making globalisation work.* Economic and Social Research Institute. Retrieved from www.esri.ie/system/files/media/file-uploads/2015-07/GLS35.pdf

Sweet, E. L. (2016). Locating migrant Latinas in a diverse economies framework: Evidence from Chicago. *Gender, Place & Culture, 23*(1), 55–71.

Take, H., & Shoraku, A. (2018). Universities' expectations for study-abroad programs fostering internationalization: Educational policies. *Journal of Studies in International Education, 22*(1), 37–52.

Urban, E. L., & Palmer, L. B. (2014). International students as a resource for internationalization of higher education. *Journal of Studies in International Education, 18*(4), 305–324.

Vargas, E. D., Sanchez, G. R., & Valdez, J. A. (2017). Immigration policies and group identity: How immigrant laws affect linked fate among US Latino populations. *Journal of Race, Ethnicity and Politics, 2*(1), 35–62.

12 Internationalizing Public Relations From the Global South
"Thinking Globally, Acting Locally"

B. Sibango and M. Tabane

Introduction

A globalized and hierarchical world is the context within which public relations (PR) and other organizational communication activities are practiced today. For various communication (sub)disciplines, this has meant internationalizing courses to suit the current globalized context (Fitch, 2013). Consequently, public relations has seen an increased growth in studies focusing on the influence of globalization on its practice and theory (e.g., Curtin & Gaither, 2007; Sriramesh, 2009; Servaes, 2016). This scholarly attention has led to the development of a body of work referred to as international or global public relations. Internationalization can be briefly defined as "the process of integrating an international, intercultural and/or global dimension into the purpose, functions (teaching, research and service) and delivery of higher education" (Knight, 2006, as cited in Leask & Bridge, 2013 p. 80). Our focus is on internationalization of the PR curriculum in South Africa.

Studies on international PR foreground the influence of the sociopolitical environment on PR practice and theory (Sriramesh, 2009; Gregory & Halff, 2013). These studies have identified several environmental variables that influence PR such as political context, media systems, economic system, and culture, which usually differ from country to country (Grunig, Grunig, Sriramesh, Huang, & Lyra, 1995; Sriramesh, 2009). However, other variables such as power and colonial history that influence PR have received minimal attention (see Bardhan & Patwardhan, 2004; Edwards, 2013). Furthermore, although the majority of studies acknowledge the influence of culture on public relations, they tend to use old theories and/or essentialist approaches to culture (Rittenhofer & Valentini, 2015). This tendency to use the essentialist approach, with its overemphasis on "cultural differences," tends to mask "power differences" born out of histories of colonialism and subordination of some cultural (or national) groups (Reygan & Steyn, 2017). Accordingly, we argue that PR scholarship and practice would benefit from a nuanced and interdisciplinary approach to culture. In communication studies, interdisciplinary approaches to culture borrow from various social science disciplines and draw attention to power imbalances among cultural groups, social and discursive construction of culture (e.g., race or ethnicity), intracultural differences, the fluid nature of culture, and stable features of culture that are resistant to change (Wodak, 2008; Kim, 2013; Anthias, 2013). Furthermore, we acknowledge the role of power and colonial history in influencing public relations theory and practice in the global context.

This chapter explores ways that an interdisciplinary approach to culture can be integrated into international public relations theory and practice. Second, the chapter highlights the need to focus on power imbalances between global North and South and colonial history as some of the environmental variables that influence international public relations practice. The chapter is organized in three parts; first, we begin by providing a brief description of international public relations; second, we discuss culture and public relations, followed by a suggestion for an interdisciplinary definition of culture in Public relations. Lastly, we discuss power and public relations in relation to the PR curriculum in South Africa and conclude by proposing how an interdisciplinary approach to culture and the concept of power can be incorporated in international public relations theorizing.

International Public Relations

International public relations is mainly defined as the "strategic communications and actions carried out by private, government or non-profit organizations to build and maintain relationships with various publics in socio-economic and political environments outside their home location" (Molleda, 2009). Similar to other international communication (sub)disciplines such as international marketing, international PR has been stimulated by expansion of corporations to foreign markets, multinational organizations such as international non-governmental organizations (NGOs) or intergovernmental organizations as well as growth of information communication technologies (ICTs; Mukhudwana, 2014). Since multinational organizations communicate with multicultural and multinational publics, international public relations theory and practice considers the influence cultural and/or international differences as well as the broader sociopolitical environment on public relations (Sriramesh, 2009).

It is also worth noting that many African states have long been working with organizations or corporations from the European countries since the colonial eras in the 1600s, and South Africa is one of the countries with this long history (see Moore et al., 2011). Globalization, according to some (global South) scholars thus resembles colonialism, due to its tendency to reproduce some of the inequalities inherited from the colonial era (e.g., Ndlovu-Gatsheni, 2014). In fact, they claim that colonialism has been replaced by coloniality (see Quijano, 2000; Maldonado-Torres, 2007). Coloniality refers to "long-standing patterns of power that emerged as a result of colonialism, but that define culture, labor, intersubjective relations, and knowledge production well beyond the strict limits of colonial administrations" (Maldonado-Torres, 2007, p. 244). Colonial history influences how multinational corporations originating from Europe are perceived in countries that were once colonized by European nations (see Bardhan & Patwardhan, 2004). As previously noted, international public relations scholarship has substantially explored the influence of environmental variables such as political, media, legal, and economic systems and extent of activism as well as culture of a nation on public relations (Grunig et al., 1995; Sriramesh, 2009). Our focus is to draw attention to the proper contextualization of culture in PR scholarship (e.g., Jang & Kim, 2013; Sison, 2009) as well as the influence of power (an underexplored variable) on public relations theory and practice.

Culture and Public Relations

International public relations studies emphasize the importance of understanding cultural values of host countries in which multinational corporations (MNCs) and other global organizations operate (Sha, 2006; Kiambi & Nadler, 2012). Several studies have shown that public relations tends to be influenced by culture and sociopolitical context in which it is practiced, thereby implying that a "one-size-fits-all" approach to public relations may not be appropriate (Gregory & Halff, 2013; Servaes, 2016). Sriramesh (2009) points out that since public relations is fundamentally a communication activity, it is logical to conclude that culture affects communication (and therefore public relations). Similar to other communication activities (e.g., journalism), public relations may in turn influence culture through stereotypic portrayal of certain cultural groups in communication campaigns and other organizational communication materials such as websites or brochures (Khan, 2014).

Accordingly, several PR scholars have used intercultural communication theories, in particular, the value frameworks such as Hofstede's (1993/2010) work on cultural dimensions to classify certain countries or cultural groups in terms of their cultural values (Kiambi & Nadler, 2012; Servaes, 2016). For example, the majority of Western nations tend to be described as individualistic, while the majority of non-Western nations are classified as collectivist nations. The aim of these taxonomies is to help organizations plan their communication strategies in accordance with a country's cultural values. It is also assumed that cultural values can also be used to predict communication behavior of diverse publics (Sha, 2006; Servaes, 2016). Another theory of culture that tends to be used is Hall's classifications of cultures into high- and low-context cultures (e.g., Taylor, 2001). Both these theories focus on differences in cultural values which also influence communication styles of various cultural groups. This heavy focus on cultural differences is however problematic, as it assumes that publics will behave according to the presumably stable traits or values associated with their cultural group, and it also ignores intracultural differences and similarities between groups (see Jang &Kim, 2013).

This overreliance by public relations practitioners and scholars on these "value frameworks" has been subject to criticism (Rittenhofer & Valentini, 2015; Sison, 2009). First, studies tend to focus on international or intercultural differences, ignoring intracultural differences as well as intercultural similarities (Tsetsura, 2011). In other words, scholarship in PR tends to treat cultural groups as "separate (rather than interconnected) and static units of analysis" (Bardhan & Weaver, 2011, p. 5). Second, power differences between cultural groups have also received little attention in international public relations theorizing (Sejrup, 2014; Edwards, 2013). The tendency to overlook inequalities between cultural groups is usually referred to as depoliticized multiculturalism or "culturalization of politics" (Soudien, 2012; Žižek, 2008). Culturalization of politics refers to a process whereby "political differences, differences conditioned by political inequality, economic exploitation, etc., are naturalized/neutralized into 'cultural' differences, different 'ways of life,' which are something given, something that cannot be overcome, but merely 'tolerated'" (Žižek, 2008, p. 660).

The majority of public relations studies thus tend to use old theories of culture and intercultural communication, ignoring other approaches to theorizing as reflected in recent studies on culture and/or intercultural communication (Rittenhofer & Valentini, 2015; Sison, 2009). Recent studies in intercultural communication, for example, use various paradigms such as social constructivism and critical theory to define culture (Martin, Nakayama, Schutte, & Van Rheede Van Oudtshoorn, 2013). These approaches highlight the role of the sociopolitical context in understanding culture and intercultural communication. Critical scholars stress the fact that intercultural communication takes place in a hierarchical society marked by power difference between dominant and subordinate cultural (or national) groups, which has implication for how action or communication by the dominant national or cultural group is decoded (e.g., Steyn, 2011). Other approaches such as the intersectional and interpretivist approaches also draw attention to intranational differences as well as the fluid nature of cultural identities, which may help practitioners avoid treating cultural groups as stable or unchanging entities (Kim, 2013; Anthias, 2013). Curtin and Gaither (2007) argue that miscalculating the values of a cultural group can doom any public relations initiative. Generally, international public relations may benefit from an interdisciplinary definition of culture that incorporates issues of power and the role of the sociopolitical context in understanding culture (Reygan & Steyn, 2017).

Towards an Interdisciplinary Definition of Culture in Public Relations

The idea of culture as fixed or coherent has long been contested in intercultural communication (Wetherell, 2010; Martin et al., 2013). Studies on culture and communication or intercultural communication use various theoretical paradigms such as critical theory and social constructivism to theorize culture. In recent years, there has been a focus on how cultural groups (e.g., racial groups) are constructed. Rather than studying cultural differences, there has been attention on the processes of differentiation or how differences are socially constructed (e.g., social constructivism or discursive approach; Kim, 2013; Reygan & Steyn, 2017). Other studies have focused on the critical approach that interrogates power imbalance among cultural groups based on discrimination or oppression of less powerful groups and unflattering (or dehumanizing) representation of these groups by the media (Lentin, 2014; Mastro, 2015). Similarly, the intersectional approach draws attention to intracultural power imbalances or 3differences based on the fact that individuals have multiple identities such as gender, class, ethnicity, sexuality, race, nationality (Anthias, 2013; Vardeman-Winter, Jiang, & Tindall, 2013).

Critical theory and intersectionality are useful approaches to situating culture in international public relations scholarship in a globalized world. These approaches allow for a deeper understanding of culture as well as the sociopolitical context in which international and/or intercultural public relations occurs. Thus, paying attention to how culture is evolving as well as intracultural differences may be a good starting point in studying and classifying various cultural groups (Tsetsura, 2011; Vardeman-Winter et al., 2013). While culture evolves, individuals may also cling to certain cultural values or rituals in order to maintain a sense of a coherent identity (Kanemasu, 2013). In sum, it is fruitful to pay attention to changes and continuities within a given society and at the same time acknowledge intracultural differences. Hughey and Byrd (2013) observe that members of a cultural group are neither homogenous nor a disconnected mass of actors—they share some similarities as well as intragroup differences.

Second, paying attention to power imbalances between cultural groups remains crucial, in particular, due to experiences of colonialism in Africa. For example, European and African cultural groups not only have cultural differences, but there are power differences as well (Steyn, 2011). More importantly, such power differences and the resultant intercultural hostilities remain a concern in most parts of the world. For example, European-headquartered corporations (and recently China) are viewed skeptically in most parts of Africa (Koper, Babaleye, & Jahansoozi, 2009). More specifically, they are commonly perceived as recolonizing or exploiting Africa or its resources and labor.

Thus, the historical context of intercultural communication and to some extent international/intercultural public relations now seem important factors to take into consideration in efforts to internationalize PR curriculum. In this regard, there is a need to side-step "culturalizing" politics—using a cultural frame instead of socio-economic frames such as exploitation, inequality and injustices to argue, analyze, or theorize culture (Lentin, 2014). Steyn's (2011) concept of "critical diversity" or critical multiculturalism highlights inequalities and cultural differences in ways that enhance current conceptualization of culture in international public relations.

Third, another prominent approach to culture is the discursive approach, which views cultural identities as products of discourses that "speak them" into being (Kannen, 2008; Wodak, 2008). The discursive approach posits that racial or national identities and attendant stereotypes are products of (e.g., political/media) discourses that are internalized and/or performed by individuals (Reay, 2010). Organizational discourses or communication materials (e.g., magazines or websites) also contribute to constructing or reinforcing stereotypes associated with groups (Khan, 2014). Employing this approach in public relations or organizational communication in general stands to sensitize organizations to possible interpretations of their communication. For example, some renowned organizations have found themselves in conflict with consumers over advertising materials considered to promote racial epithets. In 2018, the H&M store headquartered in Sweden received a global outcry for an advertisement considered racist in the manner it reinforced stereotypes associated with blacks. The advertisement had a black child with a jacket written "coolest monkey in the jungle," while a white child in the same advertisement had a coat written "survival expert" (Snowdon, 2018). In South Africa, H&M stores were vandalized. Many blacks used social media to communicate messages vowing to boycott the stores. International public relations studies show that cultural sensitivity is one of the skills required for public relations professionals in a globalizing world. However, in view of the H&M ad, it is evident that the understanding and practice of international public relations has to be expanded to include sensibilities associated with diverse cultural groups. These sensibilities are to be embedded in an understanding of a multifaceted definition of culture, history between diverse groups, power dynamics resulting from histories of colonialism, and internal conflicts.

Another variable that requires more attention in international public relations is power.

Power and Public

Historically, fields such as public relations, advertising and marketing developed out of the need for companies and governments to push products, ideologies, and services on consumers (Miller & Dinan, 2007). Recently, business models of companies have come under scrutiny for their lack of responsible practices in terms of their consideration of the people and the planet (e.g., Manby, 2000; Munshi & Kurian, 2005). Moreover, there is an emerging criticism of Eurocentric and North American business and management education, which raises questions about relevant theoretical and pedagogical approaches to public relations studies in a globalized world (Moyo, 2016; Mersham, Skinner, & Rensburg, 2011). For a long time, South African public relations education drew heavily from Euro-American models (Mersham et al., 2011; Moyo, 2016) due to its colonization by European and British powers. Presently, the South African education system is grappling with the legacy of the "Westernisation and colonisation of its curricular" (Moyo, 2016,

p. 4). Due to portrayal of Africa as a "dark continent" and Africans as savages, pre-colonial African PR practices and their epistemologies in general were squashed by European theories—a form of cultural violence known as "epistemicides" (Mueller, 2017; Rensburg, 2003). Rensburg (2003) notes that in the pre-colonial era, Ancient Egyptian Pharaohs used to publicize their achievements using word art on monuments. Similarly, chiefs in many South African villages used spokespersons to channel all communication with the community or outsiders. These individuals had to be well versed in African customs and traditions. These examples attest to Rensburg's (2003) view that PR in Africa has been around before colonialism and commercialization but in a different format. However, as noted earlier, African PR practices and knowledge were rendered primitive and backwards when Europeans arrived on the continent. During the colonial period, Eurocentric models of public relations were mainstreamed while those from Africa were on the margins (Asante, 2019).

Africanisation of PR Curriculum in South Africa

To address some of the epistemic injustices brought about by colonization in the public relations education, the curriculum in South Africa is being transformed to incorporate African indigenous knowledge underpinnings with those that originate from the global North (Matthews, 2018). This curriculum transformation stems from the need to Africanize what students are learning in South Africa and other parts of the continent. The purpose is to make the curriculum relevant to African lived realities (Mersham et al., 2011; Mersham, Rensburg, & Skinner, 1995). Some of the PR scholars note that PR in South Africa should address the legacies of colonialism, apartheid, and the developmental needs of the country (e.g., Rensburg, 2004). For instance, shortly after South Africa became a democratic country in 1994, the government called on corporations to play a role in national development, and thus PR had to emphasize corporate social responsibility (Naidoo, 2009). Consequently, South African PR scholars emphasize the need for corporate social responsibility in engaging with the publics. Debates on what an Africanized PR should look like are still ongoing. So far, there are efforts for collaboration among African scholars to address the dominance of the Euro-American models in higher education at the present moment (Moyo, 2016). For example, the University of South Africa, which is the largest open distance education university in Africa is currently leading the Africanization of the curriculum with what it calls the, African Intellectuals project (Asante, 2019). This project highlights the need to develop a curriculum that draws attention to injustices of the past and present. For example, Moyo, notes that in the postcolonial moment, "critical theory and pedagogy are recast as a necessary political and moral project that not only re-awakens the academic public sphere, but also creates agency to confront all forms of power and coloniality in the agora" (2016. p. 2). Apart from this, communication and public relations departments in various universities in South Africa and outside hold conferences and seminars with the Africanization and decolonization themes. For example, the Unisa (University of South Africa) hosts yearly decolonial summer school and a decolonial conference since 2014. The aim of these engagements is to develop ways in which South African universities can decenter Euro-American models and recenter PR theories from the South (Moyo, 2016). In this respect, South African scholars also attempt "to build an African body of knowledge of public relations and theory based on an African world view so that Africa may effectively engage in . . . discussions on how public relations is practised in various countries and on different continents"

(Mersham et al., 2011. p. 3). In essence, knowledge produced in South Africa aims to be relevant for the continent and at the same time attempts to challenge the hegemony of Euro-American models in global public relations Gregory & Halff, 2013).

So far, South African scholars have begun developing models of public relations based on African values such as Ubuntu. This philosophy of humanism—which stresses mutual beneficial relationships and acknowledges interdependence of different stakeholders and communalism, is captured in the phrase *isandla sigeza esinye*, which basically means members of communities and organizations can truly thrive by helping one another. Put simply, "Ubuntuism" and communalism place the importance on reciprocity, negotiation, inclusiveness, transparency, respect and generally genuine care for the other in relationship building and maintenance (Mersham et al., 2011; Van Heerden, 2004). Although these values are similar to those used in Euro-American models of public relations such as the two-way symmetry and the dialogic approach, models based on the African values highlight (collectivism as opposed to individualism) and building relationships for the benefit of all stakeholders and not just organizations, as was the case in the systems theory (Kent & Taylor, 2011). Mainstream public relations scholarship has also ignored the hierarchy of publics or "powerless" publics in general, which African models of PR seek to recenter (Mersham, 2011). For instance, African indigenous communities have been placed in powerless positions for some time due to the oppression they suffered under apartheid. During apartheid, African indigenous publics were oppressed and too poor to matter to corporations (Edwards, 2013; Holtzhausen, 2005) . Generally, what African PR scholars highlight is the need to consider the historical context of international and/or intercultural public relations. PR models based on African values are, however, still at an embryonic stage. More research is needed that shows how PR models rooted in African values look like in practice (Van Heerden, 2004), as well as how they are similar to and/or differ from dominant PR models from the global North.

Conclusion and Future Direction for Research

Internationalizing public relations opens up the field of public relations to multiple perspectives that interrogate culture and power in globalized contexts previously ignored in public relations theory and practice. The aim of this chapter was to argue for an approach to PR theory and practice that is embedded in realities of the African cultural, historical, economic, and political contexts.

Rather than focus solely on "cultural differences", we argued for an approach that challenges various ways in which culture has been theorized in the majority of social sciences including communication (sub)disciplines such as intercultural communication. We highlighted factors vital in the theorization of culture in international public relations, specifically power imbalances between cultural groups resulting from colonization of Africa by European countries. While international public relations scholarship has made some progress in showing how public relations could be expanded by taking into consideration other mitigating factors such as culture, it runs the risk of stereotyping cultural groups by relying on the individualist/collectivist dichotomy that ignores intracultural differences as well as the fluid nature of culture.

The role of power imbalances has also received minimal attention in mainstream public relations scholarship. Globally, power imbalances have resulted in ethnocentric (Euro-American centric) public relations curriculum that has ignored the practice of public relations in other parts of the world until recently (Gregory &

Halff, 2013). Additionally, although international public relations scholarship has made headway in showing how public relations is practiced in other parts of the world, research from the African context has been rather sparse (Van Heerden, 2004; Sriramesh, 2009). This chapter contributes to the growing body of work on PR practice geared towards developing models of public relations rooted in the African cultural values (see Mersham et al., 2011; Mbeke, 2009).

Generally, we argue that PR would benefit from incorporating an interdisciplinary approach to culture. This can be done by drawing from theories of culture in other disciplines such as intercultural communication or sociology that address power imbalances between and within cultural groups as well as the fluid nature of culture. Similarly, African models of public relations have to pay attention to cultural differences as well as intra-African differences based on ethnicity and power imbalances within the continent.

International public relations theory can also add power resulting from history of Euro-American domination of the world as one of the variables that influence public relations in the global context. Specifically, this can be done by highlighting power imbalances between global North and South and among publics. Also, the role played by PR in reinforcing or disrupting global and local hierarchies needs to be placed at the center of PR theorizing. A few scholars have already grappled with this question (e.g., Berger, 2005). Overall, the historical context of public relations needs to be brought to the center of international public relations theorizing.

References

Anthias, F. (2013). Intersectional what? Social divisions, intersectionality and levels of analysis. *Ethnicities*, *13*(1), 3–19.

Asante, M. K. (2019, April). *The Rubric for Afrocentric curriculum at the university level*. Paper presented at the Principal and Vice Chancellor's African Intellectuals Project seminar at the College of Human Sciences at Unisa, Pretoria, South Africa.

Bardhan, N., & Patwardhan, P. (2004). Multinational corporations and public relations in a historically resistant host culture. *Journal of Communication Management*, *8*(3), 246–263.

Bardhan, N., & Weaver, C. K. (2011). Introduction: Public relations in global cultural contexts. In N. Bardhan & C. K Weaver (Eds.), *Public relations in global cultural contexts: Multi-paradigmatic perspectives* (pp. 1–28). New York: Routledge.

Berger, B. (2005). Power over, power with, and power to relations: Critical reflections on public relations, the Dominant Coalition, and Activism. *Journal of Public Relations Research*, *17*(1), 5–28.

Curtin, P. A., & Kenn Gaither, T. (2007). *International public relations: Negotiating culture, identity, and power*. Thousand Oaks, CA: Sage Publications.

Edwards, L. (2013). Institutional racism in cultural production: The case of public relations. *Popular Communication*, *11*(3), 242–256.

Fitch, K. (2013). A disciplinary perspective. *Journal of Studies in International Education*, *17*(2), 136–147.

Garcia, C. (2016). De-Westernizing public relations : A comparative analysis of culture and economics structure in China and Mexico, *Asia Pacific Journal*, *17*(2), 9–27.

Gregory, A., & Halff, G. (2013). Divided we stand: Defying hegemony in global public relations theory and practice? *Public Relations Review*, *39*(5), 417–425.

Grunig, J. E., Grunig, L. A., Sriramesh, K., Huang, Y., & Lyra, A. (1995). Models of public relations in an international setting. *Journal of Public Relations Research*, *7*(3), 163–186.

Hofstede, G. (1993). Cultural constraints in management theories. *Academy of Management Perspectives*, *7*(1), 81–94.

Holtzhausen, D. R. (2005). Public relations practice and political change in South Africa. *Public Relations Review*, *31*(3), 407–416.

Hughey, M. W., & Byrd, W. C. (2013). The souls of white folk beyond formation and structure: bound to identity. *Ethnic and Racial Studies*, 36(6), 974–981.

Jang, A., & Kim, H. (2013). Cultural identity, social capital, and social control of young Korean Americans: Extending the theory of intercultural public relations. *Journal of Public Relations Research*, 25(3), 225–245.

Kanemasu, Y. (2013). A national pride or a colonial construct? Touristic representation and the politics of Fijian identity construction. *Social Identities*, 19(1), 71–89.

Kannen, V. (2008). Identity treason: Race, disability, queerness, and the ethics of (post) identity practices. *Culture, Theory & Critique*, 49(2), 149–163.

Kent, M., & Taylor, M. (2011). How intercultural communication theory informs public relations practice in global settings. In N. Bardhan & C. K Weaver (Eds.), *Public relations in global cultural contexts: Multi-paradigmatic perspectives* (pp. 50–76). New York: Routledge.

Khan, S. (2014). Manufacturing consent? Media messages in the mobilization against HIV/AIDS in India and lessons for health communication. *Health Communication*, 29(3), 288–298.

Kiambi, D. M., & Nadler, M. K. (2012). Public relations in Kenya: An exploration of models and cultural influences. *Public Relations Review*, 38(3), 505–507.

Kim, Y. Y. (2013). The identity factor in intercultural conflict. In J. G. Oetzel & S. Ting-Toomey (Eds.), *The SAGE handbook of conflict communication: Integrating theory, research, and practice* (pp. 639–660). Thousand Oaks, CA: Sage Publications.

Koper, E., Babaleye, T., & Jahansoozi, J. (2009). Public relations practice in Nigeria. In K. Sriramesh & D. Verčič (Eds.), *The global public relations handbook: Theory, research and practice* (pp. 312–330). New York, NY: Routledge.

Leask, B., & Bridge, C. (2013). Comparing internationalisation of the curriculum in action across disciplines: Theoretical and practical perspectives. *Compare*, 43(1), 79–101.

Lentin, A. (2014). Post-race, post politics: The paradoxical rise of culture after multiculturalism. *Ethnic and Racial Studies*, 37(8), 1268–1285.

Maldonado-Torres, N. (2007). On the coloniality of being: Contributions to the development of a concept. *Cultural Studies*, 21(2–3), 240–270.

Manby, B. (2000). *Shell in Nigeria: Corporate social responsibility and the Ogoni crisis.* Retrieved from http://data.georgetown.edu/sfs/programs/isd/%5Cnhttp://docs.google.com/a/usc.edu/fileview?id=F.f66d68d6-87ca-46dd-aa39-8116d0f30f16

Martin, J. N., Nakayama, T. K., Schutte, P., & Van Rheede Van Oudtshoorn, G. P. (2013). *Experiencing intercultural communication: South African edition.*

Mastro, D. (2015). Why the media's role in issues of race and ethnicity should be in the spotlight. *Journal of Social Issues*, 71(1), 1–16.

Matthews, S. (2018). Confronting the colonial library: Teaching political studies amidst calls for a decolonised curriculum. *Politikon*, 1–18.

Mbeke, P. O. (2009). Status of public relations in Kenya. In *The global public relations handbook* (Revised and Expanded ed., pp. 370–393). Abingdon, UK: Routledge.

Mersham, G., Skinner, C., & Rensburg, R. (2011). Approaches to African communication management and public relations: A case for theory-building on the continent. *Journal of Public Affairs*, 11(4), 195–207.

Mersham, G. M., Rensburg, R. S., & Skinner, J. C. (1995). Public relations, development and social investment: A Southern African perspective. *Pretoria: Van Schaik*, 44.

Miller, D., & Dinan, W. (2007). *Thinker, Faker, Spinner, Spy: Corporate PR and the assault on democracy.* London: Pluto.

Molleda, J. C. (2009). *Global public relations.* Retrieved from https://instituteforpr.org/global-public-relations/

Moore, K., Kleinman, D. L., Hess, D., & Frickel, S. (2011). Science and neoliberal globalization: A political sociological approach. *Theory and Society*, 40(5), 505–532.

Moyo, L. (2016). *The post-apartheid moment: Rethinking theory and pedagogy in Communication studies in South Africa.* Retrieved from www.academia.edu/29275311/Last_Moyo_2016_The_post-apartheid_moment_Rethinking_theory_and_pedagogy_in_Communication_studies_in_South_Africa_Sacomm_Conference_University_of_Freestate_Blomfontein_3-5_October_2_016

Mueller, J. C. (2017). Producing colorblindness: Everyday mechanisms of White ignorance. *Social problems, 64*(2), 219–238.

Mukhudwana, R.F. (2014). Agency, continuity and discontinuity in international communication scholarship. In N. C. Lesame (Ed.), *International Communication* (pp. 39–54). Pretoria: Unisa Press.

Munshi, D., & Kurian, P. (2005). Imperializing spin cycles: A postcolonial look at public relations, greenwashing, and the separation of publics. *Public Relations Review, 31*(4), 513–520.

Naidoo, R. (2009). *Corporate governance: An essential guide for South African companies.* Pretoria, South Africa: Juta and Company Ltd.

Ndlovu-Gatsheni, S. J. (2014). Global coloniality and the challenges of creating African futures. *Strategic Review for Southern Africa, 36*(2), 181–202.

Quijano, A. (2000). Coloniality of power and Eurocentrism in Latin America. *International Sociology, 15*(2), 215–232.

Reay, D. (2010). Identity making in schools and classrooms. In M. Wetherell & C. T. Mohanty (Eds.), *The Sage handbook of identities* (pp. 277–294). London: Sage.

Rensburg, R. (2003). Public relations in South Africa: From rhetoric to reality. In K. Sriramesh & D. Vercic (Eds.), *The global public relations handbook* (pp. 145–178). Mahwah, NJ: Lawrence Erlbaum Associates, Inc.

Reygan, F., & Steyn, M. (2017). Diversity in basic education in South Africa: Intersectionality and critical diversity literacy. *Africa Education Review, 14*(2), 68–81.

Rittenhofer, I., & Valentini, C. (2015). A "practice turn" for global public relations: An alternative approach. *Journal of Communication Management, 19*(1), 2–19.

Sejrup, J. (2014). Awakening the sufferers: Reflections on public relations, activism, and subalternity in postcolonial controversies between Taiwan and Japan. *Public Relations Inquiry, 3*(1), 51–68.

Servaes, J. (2016). Guanxi in intercultural communication and public relations. *Public Relations Review, 42*(3), 459–464.

Sha, B. L. (2006). Cultural identity in the segmentation of publics: An emerging theory of intercultural public relations. *Journal of Public Relations Research, 18*(1), 45–65.

Sison, M. D. (2009). Whose cultural values? Exploring public relations' approaches to understanding audiences. *PRism, 6,* 1–13.

Snowdon, K. (2018, 13 January). South Africa H&M Stores targeted by Economic Freedom Fighters protesters over 'Racist' Ad. *HuffPost.* Retrieved from https://www.huffingtonpost.co.uk/entry/south-africa-hm-stores-economic-freedom-fighters-protestors_uk_5a5a7605e4b04f3c55a31aaf

Soudien, C. (2012). *Realising the dream: Unlearning the logic of race in the South African School.* Pretoria: HSRC Press.

Sriramesh, K. (2009). The relationship between culture and public relations. In K. Sriramesh & D. Verčič (Eds.), *The global public relations handbook: Theory, research and practice* (pp. 52–67). New York, NY: Routledge.

Steyn, M. (E.d.). (2011). *Being different together: Case studies on diversity interventions in some South African organisations.* Cape Town: iNCUDISA.

Taylor, M. (2001). Internationalizing the public relations curriculum. *Public Relations Review, 27*(1), 73–88.

Tsetsura, K. (2011). How understanding multidimensional diversity can benefit global public relations education. *Public Relations Review, 37*(5), 530–535.

Van Heerden, G. (2004). *The practice of public relations in Africa: A descriptive study* (Doctoral dissertation), University of Pretoria, South Africa.

Vardeman-Winter, J., Jiang, H., & Tindall, N. T. J. (2013). Information-seeking outcomes of representational, structural, and political intersectionality among health media consumers. *Journal of Applied Communication Research, 41*(4), 389–411.

Wetherell, M. (2010). The field of identity studies. In M. Wetherell & C. T. Mohanty (Eds.), *The Sage handbook of identities* (pp. 3–26). London: Sage.

Wodak, R. (2008). Us' and "them": Inclusion/exclusion-discrimination via discourse. In G. Delanty, P. Jones, & R. Wodak (Eds.), *Migration, identity, and belonging* (pp. 54–78). Liverpool: Liverpool University Press.

Žižek, S. (2008). Tolerance as an ideological category. *Critical Inquiry, 34*(4), 660–682.

13 Adapting to Students From Different Family Backgrounds on Campus

Seokhoon Ahn

There has been a growing trend toward diversity and internationalization in higher education across the US, recruiting students from diverse backgrounds. The increasing number of international students enrolled in the US evidences universities' effort in internationalizing their campuses. The statistical improvement of diversity in higher education, with more than 1 million students of international backgrounds studying in the US since 2015 (Institute of International Education, 2018), has offered various benefits including different cultural insights (Luo & Jamieson-Drake, 2013; Soria & Troisi, 2014), intellectual knowledge (Chellaraj, Maskus, & Matto, 2008), and economic resources (NAFSA, 2018). In view of the diverse student body in many US universities, there are efforts that warrant institutional and pedagogical support to address a variety of emerging needs that students from different backgrounds face. Although some campuses have started to develop campus resources to support this growing population (Perez-Encinas & Ammigan, 2016), there is still a lack of instructional support that is customized to serve the various needs (Forbes-Mewett & Nyland, 2012).

Recognizing the substantial impact of families on students' academic performances (Castro et al., 2015), this chapter examines diverse familial experiences of diverse students and offers pedagogical strategies and on-campus resources needed to effectively facilitate student success in a globalized academic environment. The first part of the chapter will discuss (i) various immigration statuses of students' families in a host country, such as refugee families (Kanu, 2008; McBrien, 2005; Taylor & Sidhu, 2012) or undocumented families (López, Mojtahedi, Ren, & Turrent-Hegewisch, 2015), and (ii) diverse educational experiences due to separation from their family back home while interacting with a host family in a host country (McMeekin, 2017; Ward & Masgoret, 2004). The second part of the chapter will discuss scholarly models that can help instructors to develop an effective pedagogy to manage classrooms with students from various familial backgrounds. The last segment will introduce some existing on-campus diversity policies and support programs for higher education instructors to consider implementing, with a discussion of future improvements.

Diverse Familial Backgrounds of Students

Among different challenges that students face in college, family is one of the most important factors that impact the pursuit of their academic goals. Internationalized campus environments across the world have invited students from different forms of family, which in turn inevitably leads to different educational challenges. For example, some first-generational students may not have an immediate family that can offer college advice because their family members have never gone to school and thus do not have firsthand college experiences (Dennis, Phinney, & Chuateco, 2005). Other students may struggle due to lack of financial support from their family (Payne-Sturges, Tjaden, Caldeira, Vincent, & Arria, 2018) and give up on their education out of the fear of accruing a significant amount of debt (Houle, 2014). The unique challenges stemming from familial experiences necessitate the importance of understanding the various forms of families among students. In this regard, it is imperative for educators and college administrators to develop effective pedagogical strategies and college resources to serve what the diverse student population needs to succeed. Specifically, some of the diverse familial experiences include refugee families, undocumented families, and transnational families.

Students From Refugee Families

The United States has historically been a new home for approximately 3.4 million refugees from all over the world including Vietnam, Hong Kong, Afghanistan, Iraq, Somalia, and more (US Department of State, 2019). In the 1951 Geneva Convention, the United Nations defined refugees as individuals with a well-founded fear of being persecuted for reasons of race, religion, nationality, membership of a particular social group or political opinion, is outside the country of his nationality and is unable or, owing to such fear, is unwilling to avail himself of the protection of that country; or who, not having a nationality and being outside the country of his former habitual residence as a result of such events, is unable or, owing to such fear, is unwilling to return to it.

Refugee families' adaptation to host countries has been the focus of much scholarly attention, particularly with regard to adequate education for refugee students (Kanno & Varghese, 2010; Matthews, 2008; McBrien, 2005; Taylor & Sidhu, 2012). The educational attainment rates among refugee families are extremely low, and statistics show that only 1% of refugee students are enrolled in college, in comparison to 36% of nonrefugee students across the world (UNHCR, 2018). Even if refugee students wish to pursue higher education to improve life in the destination country, they often experience hindrances to continuing their learning due to financial pressures (Wilson, Murtaza, & Shakya, 2010). Refugee families are exposed to high risks of poverty and face challenges in obtaining employment and housing (Weine et al., 2011). Refugee families are forced to work low-status and less-profitable jobs because their prior educational achievement and professional experiences are often not recognized in the destination country (Kanu, 2008). In addition to financial obstacles, students from some refugee families suffer from fears and anxieties of war and terrorism experienced in the past (MacDermid & Wadsworth, 2010). Not only do the refugee families experience anxiety or depression, but some also have a great risk of developing posttraumatic stress disorder from their traumatic experiences of escaping their home country (Robjant, Hassan, & Katona, 2009; Silove, Sinnerbrink, Field, Manicavasagar, & Steel, 1997; Silove, Steel, McGorry, & Mohan, 1998; Silove et al., 2007).

Due to the many challenges that refugee families face upon arrival in a foreign country, refugee parents are less likely to involve themselves in their refugee children's education. Refugee parents often struggle with employment issues such as seeking a job or adjusting to cultural differences in business relationships (Newman, Bimrose, Nielsen, & Zacher, 2018) while facing language barriers (Sossou & Adedoyin, 2012). The lack of parental involvement and support, as a result, causes refugee students to develop identity issues, especially lacking a sense of belonging at school, and this becomes a substantial barrier to education attainment (McBrien, 2005). Some refugee students also experience acculturation gaps with their parents in terms of identity, behavior, and language, which often becomes a source of intergenerational conflicts in the family (Birman, 2006).

Students From Undocumented Families

Undocumented immigration has been a focal point of political agendas since the 2016 presidential election. Undocumented immigrants are defined as "immigrants who do not possess a regular residence permit and are therefore not entitled to legally reside and work in the host country" (Dustmann, Fasani, & Speciale, 2017, p. 3). Statistics show that only 5% to 10% of 65,000 undocumented students who obtain their high school diploma pursue their college degree every year, with even fewer completing the college program (US Department of Education, 2015). As of July 31, 2018, there are 703,890 recipients of the Deferred Action for Childhood Arrivals (DACA) program, which was established by the Obama administration in 2012. DACA allows undocumented students to stay in the US until they complete their education. The students can renew their permission and obtain a work permit in the US after graduation (US Department of Homeland Security, 2018).

However, a number of students from undocumented family backgrounds are affected by recent political circumstances (e.g., strict immigration enforcement, elimination of support programs for undocumented immigrants, and temporary pause of DACA program as identified by Pierce, Bolter, & Selee, 2018). Particularly, the legal status of DACA recipients was suspended in 2017 when President Trump repealed the program through executive authority, and the situation has remained unpredictable ever since. The uncertainty about current and future residency status has caused undocumented students much stress and anxiety and loss of motivation to continue their education (Andrade, 2019).

Suárez-Orozco and her colleagues (2015) identified challenges that undocumented students encounter in their journey to college and found that family plays a key factor in their educational success. Undocumented immigrant families are exposed to radical and permanent changes in their familial configuration. Due to deportation, undocumented students are sometimes forcefully separated from one or both of their parents or other family members, which results in students' negative emotional state (Derby, 2012). Undocumented students are often the first generation in their families to attend college and, as a result, they are often unfamiliar with campus resources or unable to access or navigate them (Suárez-Orozco et al., 2015). Students from undocumented families are also likely to carry family financial burdens (Terriquez, 2015), in addition to supporting themselves financially and covering increasing tuition and/or expensive housing costs (Bjorklund, 2018; Manley, 2016)

International Students From Transnational Families

Many parents in non–English-speaking countries who can afford high education costs prefer their children to attain education in English-speaking countries for better socioeconomic opportunities (Lee & Johnstone, 2017). Some students arrive in the destination country and finish their college degree alone (Bahna, 2018; Harvey, Robinson, & Welch, 2017). In other instances, some students travel to a foreign destination with one parent while the other parent remains in the country of origin to provide financial support to family members overseas.

An example of the latter has been increasingly occurring in South Korea, creating a new configuration of transnational families, the so-called "wild-geese families" (Lee & Koo, 2006). The notion of "wild-geese families" illustrates how the separated family members (usually a wife and child) fly back and forth across the Pacific Ocean to reunite with the other family members (usually a father) who provide financial support from the home country. Because of the substantial sacrifices that parents have made, students from wild-geese families experience stress and extreme pressure to succeed academically and to meet their parents' high expectations (Lee & Johnston, 2017). Some wild-geese family members are prone to emotional difficulties and acculturation gaps, and the paternal relationship becomes somewhat distant after a lack of in-person interactions over a long period of time (Jung & Wang, 2018).

Some international students who leave their home and family and arrive in a destination country alone choose homestay for their accommodations. Their homestay experiences are often determined by the linguistic competence of the international students and the intercultural competence of students and host families. For example, in comparison to high school international students who come to a host country at a younger age, college international students find it more challenging to build close bonds with host families because of a lack of the legal responsibility that host families have for the adult international students (Kinginger, 2015). Ironically, although international students choose homestay for improving their linguistic proficiency and cultural knowledge, poor language skills and cultural misunderstandings can hinder satisfactory homestay experiences. Students may experience stressful adjustment processes if they feel unable to express themselves or understand the host family due to limited language proficiency or if they are from countries that restrict male–female interactions but are assigned to a mixed-gender homestay (Shackleford, 2011).

Theoretical Models to Address the Challenges of Students From Diverse Familial Backgrounds

Intercultural Sensitivity

The Intercultural Sensitivity Model enables instructors to develop a pedagogy that effectively adapts and supports students from diverse familial backgrounds. Intercultural sensitivity is defined as "the ability to discriminate and experience relevant cultural differences" (as cited in Hammer, Bennett, & Wiseman, 2003, p. 422) and "how people construe cultural differences" (p. 423), which is the foundation of *Bennett's* Developmental Model of Intercultural Sensitivity (1993). Bennett and Bennett (2004) suggests six levels of developing intercultural sensitivity including denial, defense, minimization, acceptance, adaptation, and integration. The first three developmental levels in the continuum of intercultural sensitivity development belong to the *ethnocentric* orientation (i.e., individuals' cultures are used as the core of assessing the reality by assuming that there exists only one universal way to do things), and the second three levels occur in the *ethnorelativistic* orientation (i.e., individuals are open to possibilities of interpreting others' beliefs and behaviors).

Bennett and Bennett (2004) point out that the integration stage does not necessarily exceed the adaptation stage because integrating two cultures may not necessarily produce the best outcomes, depending on the contexts. Recognizing the diverse backgrounds of numerous students in each class, it may be almost infeasible for an instructor to integrate his/her own culture with each student's various familial backgrounds and to create an entirely new pedagogy that works for every student. Rather, adapting to different students' needs seems more adequate and realistic for instructors to adopt. Bennett and Bennett (2004) emphasize that empathy is essential for adapting to others, understanding students' familial contexts, and embracing differences in cultural views and practices. It is important to distinguish between adjusting one's own beliefs about best approaches to teaching students from different familial backgrounds and abandoning one's teaching philosophy to assimilate or integrate, but successful teaching may require tailoring pedagogies to adapt to different needs.

Intercultural Competence

Theoretical discussions about intercultural competence have only offered generic definitions and models (Deardorff, 2009) with interchangeable usage of other terminologies such as intercultural sensitivity, cross-cultural adaptation, and interculturality (as cited in Dervin, 2010). An early study of intercultural competence from the communication perspectives defines the construct as "the ability of an interactant to choose among available communicative behaviors in order that he may successfully accomplish his own interpersonal goals during an encounter while maintaining the face and line of his fellow interactants within the constraints of situation" (Wiemann, 1977, p. 198). The subsequent definitions refined by later scholars also emphasized "other-orientedness" (p. 15) by highlighting *appropriateness* to effectively accomplish interpersonal communication goals in intercultural contexts (Chen, 2014).

Intercultural competence consists of multiple components, including knowledge, attitudes, and skills (Deardorff, 2006). Deardorff's pyramid model of intercultural competence emphasizes positive attitudes such as respect for differences, openness to learning from others, and tolerance of ambiguity as a first step to becoming interculturally competent. With a positive mind-set, individuals should develop cross-cultural knowledge (e.g., awareness of their own and other cultures) and various communication skills, such as listening, interpreting, analyzing, evaluating, and relating in interactions.

In the context of internationalized higher education, instructors should develop "student-oriented" pedagogies that appropriately accommodate and support the diverse needs of minority students. Universities should support and train their instructors to have open-minded approaches to engage students from diverse familial backgrounds, respect different learning styles, yet strive to identify what learning styles will successfully lead each student to accomplish their desired learning outcomes. In light of intercultural competence, Deardorff (2004) proposes the Process Model that can promote positive attitudes, better knowledge of students of diverse familial backgrounds, and effective interactions with the students.

Training programs on the basis of the Process Model may start with developing positive attitudes toward minority students' different educational experiences due to their family backgrounds. Positive attitudes may entail respecting different cultural values, holding off on judgment, and embracing ambiguous situations. Since instructors may not be able to know every circumstance that minority students face, training programs should focus on how to help instructors hold positive attitudes. Followed by the affective component of training, the Process Model suggests development of knowledge and comprehension. The cognitive component of training mainly deals with cultivating self-knowledge and other-knowledge. To enhance cognitive competence, the model suggests developing practical skills such as analyzing, interpreting, and relating. Training programs may introduce various real-life cases that demonstrate minority students' challenges due to familial circumstances and help instructors analyze each case, identify possible ways to be interpreted differently, and appropriately relate the interpretations to students' various academic experiences. The last component of training programs aims to develop behavioral competence, which focuses on instructors' actual interactions with minority students. The behavioral component assesses two outcomes including internal and external outcomes. The internal outcome of interactions focuses on instructors' adaptability, flexibility, and empathy while the external outcome of interactions promotes effective and appropriate communication with minority students.

The three aforementioned components of training, including affective, cognitive, and behavioral components, should be able to help instructors in higher education to effectively develop accommodative pedagogies for students from various familial backgrounds. The following sections, then, will overview what practical programs have been implemented on campus to serve minority students and meet their diverse needs.

Practical Programs for Students From Different Familial Background

Diversity Committee for Inclusive Academic Environment

In the US, colleges and universities have embraced efforts to promote diversity and inclusion in the era of globalization. Attention has been placed on advancing efforts to promote diversity mission statements. Diversity councils, committees, or leadership boards are examples of the pursuit to create harmonious co-existence in face of differences on university campuses. Furthermore, diversity committees play an important role in setting the formal tone for diversity by establishing strategic plans for university policies and procedures. However, their success may be compromised by the fact that many universities have not come to consensus as to how diversity is defined in higher education. The ambiguous definition of diversity may result in a failure to serve voiceless minority students.

For instance, Leon and Williams (2016) identified three themes of campus strategic diversity plans in ten colleges, including creating welcoming campus atmosphere, addressing and preventing discrimination issues, and ensuring minority student well-being. Of the three themes, international students or undocumented students are less engaged than other underserved student populations in the institutional effort to enhance missions of diversity and inclusion on campus (Leon & Williams, 2016). In the wake of this finding, diversity leadership boards should intentionally and actively seek to build support for the marginalized students who have been underserved, even among other minority groups whose needs have not been met, to ensure their successful pursuit of learning.

University of California-Berkeley's Support Program for Undocumented Students

Recognizing the aforementioned limitations, some schools have created a separate program to address the challenges that the voiceless students from disadvantaged families face. University of California-Berkeley (UC-Berkeley thereafter), for example, has established a support program specifically for undocumented students (Undocumented Student Program, or USP), and the program offers academic counseling services, mental health services, legal services, financial and emergency assistance, and housing and food security services (Five-year Strategic Plan, n.d.). While financial and housing services mainly provide undocumented students with assistance and guides to help them explore financial aid and housing options rather than providing financial subsidies, USP developed a strategy that has been customized for the particular needs of undocumented students due to their immigration status (Sanchez & So, 2015). The strategy identifies three categories of university support programs for undocumented students. It uses three colors of lights (i.e., green, yellow, and red) to indicate the requirements of immigration status to receive campus resources and assistance.

Programs assigned green lights indicate that support does not require any particular immigration status. Yellow lights are assigned to programs that do not have particular wording for immigration status requirements, in which case USP would directly contact relevant staff in charge to clarify. Programs that specifically require applicants' immigration status are identified as red lights. By coding university support programs and procedures in the system, USP examines and determines what support and information should be provided at individual, departmental, and institutional levels and how the procedures and policies can be changed to improve their support for undocumented students within the legal boundaries. For example, one of the federal programs for students' work-study support was labeled as a red light. In response, the leadership board at UC-Berkeley was able to reallocate the budget to expand the program to eligible undocumented students.

Peer-Support Programs for Students From Different Family Backgrounds

Scholars have found that peer-mentoring programs have a strong influence on academic and cultural adaptation of students from international backgrounds (Thomson & Esses, 2016). College students are influenced by their peers more than by their family back home, who may not have in-depth understanding of the educational system of another country, and the support that minority college students receive from their friends carries greater influence in students' lives than does the support that they receive from their family members (Rodriguez, Mira, Myers, Morris, & Cardoza, 2003).

Matching mentees of diverse familial backgrounds with domestic mentors has been found to have mixed results in improving the success of mentoring programs. Differences within a mentor–mentee dyad can offer a learning opportunity, but similar backgrounds between mentor and mentee can help the mentee to relate and build confidence. Scholars have emphasized that participants' attitudes and mind-sets may matter more than their backgrounds (Kochan & Pascarelli, 2012; Lee, 1999).

In view of this, it is important to consider ways to sustain successful mentoring programs. We suggest that after matching mentors and mentees, it is important to train both participants to ensure successful outcomes of mentoring programs. While there are various ways to conduct training programs based on the circumstances of each collegiate organization, building a trusting relationship between a mentor and mentee is the key to help mentees adjust to challenging academic environments due to their different backgrounds (Kochan, 2012). Cross-cultural mentoring programs should help mentors to (1) increase knowledge about mentees' experiences, (2) build common ground, and (3) hold discussions on challenging and uncomfortable issues that their mentees may face (Bellon-Harn & Weinbaum, 2017).

New London Group's Guidelines for Inclusive Pedagogies

In 1994, a number of scholars in the United Kingdom formed the New London Group to address the inequalities in higher education by acknowledging and adapting to different learning patterns arising from students' divergent experiences within the context of an increase in the number of minority students and limitations of traditional pedagogy, which assumes mainstream education as a norm (Cope & Kalantzis, 2015). Montgomery's review of the New London Group (2012) offers two important principles of successful internationalized pedagogies to meet the needs of students with different familial backgrounds.

First, pedagogies need to offer a sense of belonging for students in the learning processes. A sense of belonging is important for students from international familial backgrounds and helps them to persist and obtain their educational degrees (Curtin, Stewart, & Ostrove, 2013; Thomas, 2016). Inclusive pedagogical strategies for fostering international students' sense of belonging can start with implementing simple actions such as interpersonal attention through one-on-one interactions, expressions of concern about students' well-being, and appreciation for students' contributions (Glass, Kociolek, Wongtrirat, Lynch, & Cong, 2015).

The second principle highlights facilitation of *transformative* learning, in which students actively engage to work with differences. This is important because it helps schools to create an open-minded academic culture where students from different backgrounds feel safe and comfortable with their cultural identities and to overcome struggles arising from their familial backgrounds. Transformative learning also offers opportunities for other students to recognize different ways of living and learning, to foster the capacity of adapting themselves to cultural differences, and to help themselves to be more accepting of others in a world of complex intercultural dynamics. The New London Group emphasized the importance of students' engagement with communities outside the classroom. Having a growing population of international students can offer easier access for domestic students at an earlier age to expose themselves to different world experiences by connecting themselves to other students from different backgrounds on campus.

Conclusion

This chapter has explored challenges facing students from diverse familial backgrounds in changing academic environments in the US. These familial experiences include students' families' immigration statuses (i.e., refugees and undocumented families), family separations for better education attainment among some international students (i.e., South Korea's transnational families in English-speaking countries, known as wild-geese families), or international students' challenges within homestay families. Two scholarly models, intercultural sensitivity and intercultural competence, highlight instructors' ability to adjust their pedagogies and teaching environments to students' needs stemming from different familial backgrounds and experiences. While there has been initial effort for schools to create support and diversity programs and policies, schools need to expand their programs to provide customized services to various student groups, especially students from certain familial and cultural backgrounds who still remain marginalized due to the political situation and bureaucratic academic environments.

References

Andrade, L. M. (2019). "The war still continues," part II: The importance of positive validation for undocumented students one year after Trump's presidential victory. *Journal of Hispanic Higher Education*, [Online], 1–14.

Bahna, M. (2018). Study choices and returns of international students: On the role of cultural and economic capital of the family. *Population, Space and Place*, 24(2), e2082.

Bellon-Harn, M. L., & Weinbaum, R. K. (2017). Cross-cultural peer-mentoring: Mentor outcomes and perspectives. *Teaching and Learning in Communication Sciences & Disorders*, 1, 1–30.

Bennett, J. M., & Bennett, M. J. (2004). Developing intercultural sensitivity: An integrative approach to global and domestic diversity. In D. Landis, J. M. Bennett, & M. J. Bennett (Eds). *Handbook of intercultural training* (pp. 147–165). Thousand Oaks, CA: Sage Publications.

Bennett, M. J. (1993). Towards ethnorelativism: A developmental model of intercultural sensitivity. *Education for the Intercultural Experience*, 2, 21–71.

Birman, D. (2006). Acculturation gap and family adjustment: Findings with Soviet Jewish refugees in the United States and implications for measurement. *Journal of Cross-Cultural Psychology*, 37, 568–589.

Bjorklund, P., Jr. (2018). Undocumented students in higher education: A review of the literature, 2001 to 2016. *Review of Educational Research*, 88, 631–670.

Castro, M., Expósito-Casas, E., López-Martín, E., Lizasoain, L., Navarro-Asencio, E., & Gaviria, J. L. (2015). Parental involvement on student academic achievement: A meta-analysis. *Educational Research Review*, 14, 33–46.

Chellaraj, G., Maskus, K. E., & Mattoo, A. (2008). The contribution of international graduate students to US innovation. *Review of International Economics*, 16, 444–462.

Chen, G. M. (2014). Intercultural communication competence: Summary of 30-year research and directions for future study. In X. Dai & G.-M. Chen (Eds.), *Intercultural communication competence: Conceptualization and its development in cultural contexts and interactions* (pp. 14–40). Tyne, UK: Cambridge Scholars Publishing.

Cope, B., & Kalantzis, M. (2015). The things you do to know: An introduction to the pedagogy of multiliteracies. In B. Cope & M. Kalantzis (Eds.), *A pedagogy of multiliteracies* (pp. 1–36). London, UK: Palgrave Macmillan.

Curtin, N., Stewart, A. J., & Ostrove, J. M. (2013). Fostering academic self-concept: Advisor support and sense of belonging among international and domestic graduate students. *American Educational Research Journal*, 50, 108–137.

Deardorff, D. K. (2004). *The identification and assessment of intercultural competence as a student outcome of internationalization at institutions of higher education in the United States* (Unpublished doctoral dissertation), North Carolina State University, Raleigh, NC.

Deardorff, D. K. (2006). Identification and assessment of intercultural competence as a student outcome of internationalization. *Journal of Studies in International Education*, 10, 241–266.

Deardorff, D. K. (2009). Implementing intercultural competence assessment. In D. K. Deardorff (Ed.), *The SAGE handbook of intercultural competence* (pp. 477–491). Thousand Oaks, CA: Sage Publications.

Dennis, J. M., Phinney, J. S., & Chuateco, L. I. (2005). The role of motivation, parental support, and peer support in the academic success of ethnic minority first-generation college students. *Journal of College Student Development*, 46, 223–236.

Derby, J. (2012). The burden of deportation on children in Mexican immigrant families. *Journal of Marriage and Family*, 74, 829–845.

Dervin, F. (2010). Assessing intercultural competence in language learning and teaching: A critical review of current efforts. *New Approaches to Assessment in Higher Education*, 5, 155–172.

Dustmann, C., Fasani, F., & Speciale, B. (2017). Illegal migration and consumption behavior of immigrant households. *Journal of the European Economic Association*, 15, 654–691.

Forbes-Mewett, H., & Nyland, C. (2012). Funding international student support services: Tension and power in the university. *Higher Education*, 65, 181–192.

Glass, C. R., Kociolek, E., Wongtrirat, R., Lynch, R. J., & Cong, S. (2015). Uneven experiences: The impact of student-faculty interactions on international students' sense of belonging. *Journal of International Students, 5*, 353–367.

Hammer, M. R., Bennett, M. J., & Wiseman, R. (2003). Measuring intercultural sensitivity: The intercultural development inventory. *International Journal of Intercultural Relations, 27*, 421–443.

Harvey, T., Robinson, C., & Welch, A. (2017). The lived experiences of international students who's family remains at home. *Journal of International Students, 7*, 748–763.

Houle, J. N. (2014). Disparities in debt: Parents' socioeconomic resources and young adult student loan debt. *Sociology of Education, 87*, 53–69.

Institute of International Education. (2018). *Open doors*. Retrieved from www.iie.org/Research-and-Insights/Open-Doors/Data/International-Students/Enrollment

Jung, G., & Wang, H. (2018). The identity strategy of "Wild-Geese" fathers: The craft of Confucian fathers. *Religions, 9*, 208–221.

Kanno, Y., & Varghese, M. M. (2010). Immigrant and refugee ESL students' challenges to accessing four-year college education: From language policy to educational policy. *Journal of Language, Identity, and Education, 9*, 310–328.

Kanu, Y. (2008). Educational needs and barriers for African refugee students in Manitoba. *Canadian Journal of Education, 31*, 915–940.

Kinginger, C. (2015). Language socialization in the homestay: American high school students in China. In R. Mitchell, N. Tracy-Ventura, & K. McManus (Eds.), *Social interaction, identity and language learning during residence abroad* (pp. 53–74). Amsterdam, Netherland: Eurosla Monographs.

Kochan, F. (2012). Comprehensive view of mentoring programs for diversity. In D. Clutterbuck, F. Kochan, & K. M. Poulsen (Eds.), *Developing successful diversity mentoring programmes: An international casebook* (pp. 213–221). New York, NY: Open University Press.

Kochan, F., & Pascarelli, J. T. (2012). Perspectives on culture and mentoring in the global age. In S. Fletcher & C. A. Mullen (Eds.), *Sage handbook of mentoring and coaching in education* (pp. 184–198). Thousand Oaks, CA: Sage Publications.

Lee, E., & Johnstone, M. (2017). A production of education migrants: A case study of South Korean transnational families in Canada. *International Social Work, 60*, 307–320.

Lee, W. (1999). Striving toward effective retention: The effect of race on mentoring African American students. *Peabody Journal of Education, 74*, 27–43.

Lee, Y. J., & Koo, H. (2006). "Wild geese fathers" and a globalised family strategy for education in Korea. *International Development Planning Review, 28*, 533–553.

Leon, R. A., & Williams, D. A. (2016). Contingencies for success: Examining diversity committees in higher education. *Innovative Higher Education, 41*, 395–410.

López, M. N., Mojtahedi, Z., Ren, W., & Turrent-Hegewisch, R. (2015). Removing barriers to postsecondary success for undocumented students in Southern New Mexico. *University of California, Los Angeles, Institute for Research on Labor and Employment, 29*, 1–14.

Luo, J., & Jamieson-Drake, D. (2013). Examining the educational benefits of interacting with international students. *Journal of International Students, 3*, 85–101.

MacDermid Wadsworth, S. M. (2010). Family risk and resilience in the context of war and terrorism. *Journal of Marriage and Family, 72*, 537–556.

Manley, M. (2016). More money, more problems: The impact of tuition increases on undocumented student achievement. *Chicago Policy Review (Online)*.

Matthews, J. (2008). Schooling and settlement: Refugee education in Australia. *International Studies in Sociology of Education, 18*, 31–45.

McBrien, J. L. (2005). Educational needs and barriers for refugee students in the United States: A review of the literature. *Review of Educational Research, 75*, 329–364.

McMeekin, A. (2017). L2 Learners of Japanese: Socialization of private assessments in a host family setting. *Canadian Journal of Applied Linguistics, 19*, 107–127.

Montgomery, C. (2012). A future curriculum for future graduates? Rethinking a higher education curriculum for a globalised world. In J. Ryan (Ed.), *Cross-cultural teaching and* learning for home and international students: Internationalisation, pedagogy and curriculum in higher education (pp. 171–195). London, UK: Routledge.

NAFSA. (2018). International student economic value tool. Retrieved from https://www.nafsa.org/policy-and-advocacy/policy-resources/nafsa-international-student-economic-value-tool

Newman, A., Bimrose, J., Nielsen, I., & Zacher, H. (2018). Vocational behavior of refugees: How do refugees seek employment, overcome work-related challenges, and navigate their careers? Journal of Vocational Behavior, 105, 1–5.

Payne-Sturges, D. C., Tjaden, A., Caldeira, K. M., Vincent, K. B., & Arria, A. M. (2018). Student hunger on campus: Food insecurity among college students and implications for academic institutions. American Journal of Health Promotion, 32, 349–354.

Perez-Encinas, A., & Ammigan, R. (2016). Support services at Spanish and US institutions: A driver for international student satisfaction. Journal of International Students, 6, 984–998.

Pierce, S., Bolter, J., & Selee, A. (2018). US immigration policy under Trump: Deep changes and lasting impacts. Retrieved from https://observatoriocolef.org/wp-content/uploads/2018/07/TCMTrumpSpring2018-FINAL.pdf

Robjant, K., Hassan, R., & Katona, C. (2009). Mental health implications of detaining asylum seekers: Systematic review. The British Journal of Psychiatry, 194, 306–312.

Rodriguez, N., Mira, C. B., Myers, H. F., Morris, J. K., & Cardoza, D. (2003). Family or friends: Who plays a greater supportive role for Latino college students? Cultural Diversity and Ethnic Minority Psychology, 9, 236–250.

Sanchez, R. E. C., & So, M. L. (2015). UC Berkeley's undocumented student program: Holistic strategies for undocumented student equitable success across higher education. Harvard Educational Review, 85, 464–477.

Shackleford, N. (2011). Japanese students in a New Zealand homestay programme: Issues of linguistic and intercultural competence. Communication Journal of New Zealand, 12, 71–81.

Silove, D., Sinnerbrink, I., Field, A., Manicavasagar, V., & Steel, Z. (1997). Anxiety, depression and PTSD in asylum-seekers: Associations with pre-migration trauma and post-migration stressors. The British Journal of Psychiatry, 170, 351–357.

Silove, D., Steel, Z., McGorry, P., & Mohan, P. (1998). Trauma exposure, postmigration stressors, and symptoms of anxiety, depression and post-traumatic stress in Tamil asylum-seekers: Comparison with refugees and immigrants. Acta Psychiatrica Scandinavica, 97, 175–181.

Silove, D., Steel, Z., Susljik, I., Frommer, N., Loneragan, C., Chey, T., . . . Bryant, R. (2007). The impact of the refugee decision on the trajectory of PTSD, anxiety, and depressive symptoms among asylum seekers: A longitudinal study. American Journal of Disaster Medicine, 2, 321–329.

Soria, K. M., & Troisi, J. (2014). Internationalization at home alternatives to study abroad: Implications for students' development of global, international, and intercultural competencies. Journal of Studies in International Education, 18, 261–280.

Sossou, M. A., & Adedoyin, C. A. (2012). A qualitative study of problems and parental challenges of resettled African refugee parents. Professional Development: The International Journal of Continuing Social Work Education, 15, 41–54.

Suárez-Orozco, C., Katsiaficas, D., Birchall, O., Alcantar, C. M., Hernandez, E., Garcia, Y., . . . & Teranishi, R. T. (2015). Undocumented undergraduates on college campuses: Understanding their challenges and assets and what it takes to make an undocufriendly campus. Harvard Educational Review, 85, 427–463.

Taylor, S., & Sidhu, R. K. (2012). Supporting refugee students in schools: What constitutes inclusive education? International Journal of Inclusive Education, 16, 39–56.

Terriquez, V. (2015). Dreams delayed: Barriers to degree completion among undocumented community college students. Journal of Ethnic and Migration Studies, 41, 1302–1323.

Thomas, L. (2016). Developing inclusive learning to improve the engagement, belonging, retention, and success of students from diverse groups. In M. Shah, A. Bennett, & E. Southgate (Eds.), Widening higher education participation (pp. 135–159). Waltham, MA: Chandos Publishing.

Thomson, C., & Esses, V. M. (2016). Helping the transition: Mentorship to support international students in Canada. Journal of International Students, 6, 873–886.

United Nations. (1951). *Convention and protocol relating to the status of refugees*. Retrieved from www.unhcr.org/4ae57b489.pdf

University of California-Berkeley. (n.d.). *Five-year strategic plan for Cal's undocumented student program*. Retrieved from http://undocu.berkeley.edu/wp-content/uploads/2016/03/USP_FinalStrategicPlan-1.pdf

USA for UNHCR. (2018). *Refugee statistics*. Retrieved from www.unrefugees.org/refugee-facts/statistics/

US Department of Education. (2015). *Resource guide: Supporting undocumented youth*. Retrieved from https://www2.ed.gov/about/overview/focus/supporting-undocumented-youth.pdf

US Department of Homeland Security. (2018). *Deferred Action for Childhood Arrivals (DACA)*. Retrieved from www.dhs.gov/deferred-action-childhood-arrivals-daca

US Department of State. (2019). *Historical arrivals broken down by region (1975—Present)*. Retrieved from www.wrapsnet.org/admissions-and-arrivals/

Ward, C., & Masgoret, A. M. (2004). *The experiences of international students in New Zealand: Report on the Results of a National Survey*. Wellington, New Zealand: Ministry of Education.

Weine, S. M., Hoffman, Y., Ware, N., Tugenberg, T., Hakizimana, L., Dahnweigh, G., . . . Wagner, M. (2011). Secondary migration and relocation among African refugee families in the United States. *Family Process, 50*, 27–46.

Wiemann, J. M. (1877). Explication and test of a model of communicative competence. *Human Communication Research, 3*, 195–213.

Wilson, R. M., Murtaza, R., & Shakya, Y. B. (2010). Pre-migration and post-migration determinants of mental health for newly arrived refugees in Toronto. *Canadian Issues, Summer*, 45–49.

14 Examining the Intercultural Outcomes of Internationalized Education in the Arabian Peninsula[1]

Marta Tryzna, Mariam Alkazemi, and Fahed Al-Sumait

Introduction

The internationalization of education is a growing area of interest in countries like the United States, which aim to improve international awareness among its citizens and extract benefits from learning about diverse ways of seeing and interacting with the world outside its borders. Such internationalization efforts generally involve bringing global perspectives into local curriculum planning. This study, however, examines the internationalization of education from a somewhat different perspective. Within the Arabian Peninsula, "Western" forms of education have been rapidly introduced in part or whole in an effort to educate local populations into becoming competitive, global-ready graduates. In recent decades, this region has witnessed the largest inflow of international universities and branch campuses in the world, with far-reaching implications. This chapter focuses specifically on the topic of intercultural communication as a key component of internationalization related to the phenomenon of this educational influx. First it explores the degree to which communication programs across the Peninsula exist that offer specific courses tied to intercultural, international or global communication topics. It then provides a close examination of the degree to which internationalized educational systems in general are actually producing tangible intercultural communication competence (ICC) outcomes by examining the country of Kuwait. The following section outlines various factors of relevance to intercultural communication in general, as well as the measurable components used to evaluate ICC outcomes on a sample of more than 800 university students across three universities in Kuwait. The findings indicate that significant ICC outcomes are present and appear to result from a combination of educational, contextual, and personal factors.

Background

Intercultural Communication Competence

Intercultural communication competence (ICC) in diverse environments can play a key role in mitigating cultural differences and fostering mutual understanding and cooperation. Introduced by Byram (1997) in terms of the interplay between cultural competence and interpersonal skills, ICC has been defined from various perspectives. It refers to the communication between people from different cultures (Chen & Starosta, 1998, p. 28) and is perceived as a "symbolic, interpretive, transactional, and contextual process in which people from different cultures create shared meanings" (Lustig & Koester, 2007, p. 46). Fantini (2006) defines it as "a complex of abilities needed to perform *effectively* and *appropriately* when interacting with others who are linguistically and culturally different from oneself" (p. 12, emphasis in original). Catteeuw's (2012) conceptualization also is that effectiveness and appropriateness are fundamental aspects of ICC.

Effectiveness in ICC refers to meaningful interactions, which involve establishing common goals, successful use of verbal and nonverbal strategies, and the deployment of cultural knowledge and sensitivity in order to achieve mutual understanding and shared meaning (Canary, Lakey, & Sillars, 2013; Spitzberg & Cupach, 2002). Appropriateness relies on culture-specific and situation-specific expectations with regard to behavioral patterns that are common to a group. These expectations help build common ground, promoting trust and mutual understanding in communication (Kashima, 2014). Similar to effectiveness, appropriateness can be assessed by the individuals directly involved in a communicative event based on both linguistic and nonlinguistic means (Ting-Toomey & Dorjee, 2015).

Effectiveness and appropriateness in ICC can be reduced to three underlying aspects: affective, behavioral, and cognitive (Ting-Toomey, 1993; Kim, 1991). The *affective* aspect of ICC involves the ability to form emotional connections and relies on intercultural awareness, motivation, and willingness to interact with people from diverse backgrounds, as well as on individual strategies for resolving ambiguity and mitigating anxiety in intercultural contexts (Arasaratnam & Doerfel, 2005). Chen and Starosta (1997) describe affect in terms of positive emotions toward and appreciation of cultural differences. For the *behavioral* aspect to manifest itself, individuals should engage with people from diverse cultural backgrounds in various communicative situations, form relationships, and build heterogeneous personal and professional networks (Arasaratnam & Doerfel, 2005; Kim, 1991). *Cognitive* complexity is the component of ICC responsible for problem-solving and persuasive skills (Arasaratnam, 2009), integrating new information and experiences (Kline, Hennen-Floyd, & Farrell, 1990; Leighty & Applegate, 1991), and perceiving nuance and responding to new stimuli in the environment (Stone, 2006). Cognitive complexity allows individuals to be more effective and appropriate in intercultural encounters by adapting to the needs of others in interactions (Chen & Starosta, 1996) and utilizing personal and cultural norms to relate better to others (Adams-Webber, 2001; Gudykunst & Kim, 2003).

Bilingual and bicultural communicative competence is a steep learning curve, as it requires "no less than reconfiguring one's original worldview" (Fantini & Tirmizi, 2006, p. 11). Linguistic skills can help individuals negotiate meaning across contexts and in various communicative situations (Bialystok, 2017; Fan, Liberman, Keysar, & Kinzler, 2015; Garrett-Rucks, 2016). Previous research shows that bilinguals score higher on the ICC scale as compared to monolinguals (Arasaratnam-Smith, 2016). This study evaluates all three measurable components of ICC in a highly multicultural environment with the Arabian Peninsula, where English-language institutions of higher education have been developing for some time.

ICC Education in the Gulf Cooperation Council

The current study was conducted in an Arab context with the intention of exploring how internationalization of the higher education environment might be connected to specific types of intercultural learning. It assesses the scope of international institutions of higher education present in the six countries comprising the Gulf Cooperation Council (GCC): Kuwait, UAE, KSA, Qatar, Bahrain, and Oman. It also evaluates the possible intercultural, international and global communication offerings taught within these countries. Finally, it provides a closer examination of a single country, Kuwait, to test the degree to which different types of educational institutions and personal experiences impacted student's intercultural communication competence scores.

While the individual GCC countries are distinct, their alliance was conceived based on the relatively high degree of geographic and sociocultural proximity to one another despite different colonial influences. The GCC is also notable for hosting some of the wealthiest per-capita countries in the world and represent one of the largest concentrations of foreign higher educational institutions globally. Qatar, UAE, and Kuwait have the world's highest percentages of expats-to-citizens (89%, 86%, and 70%, respectively) (The World Bank, 2018). In Kuwait, approximately 38% of these work in domestic labor or various educational institutions as instructors and administrators (Kuwait Central Statistical Bureau, 2017). In such a context, the idea of internationalization in education is somewhat flipped around from its original intention. Rather than seeking to introduce more global perspectives into Western curricula, GCC countries seek to introduce Western curricula and English-language education into their localized context. How well countries in the region respond to these challenges using specialized forms of higher education is of central interest to this study.

Method

Given both the efforts to internationalize Western educational systems and the corresponding Westernization of higher education within the GCC states, it is useful to take stock of the degree to which regional universities might facilitate intercultural learning. Since intercultural communication is a subdiscipline of communication studies, it is logical to assume that universities may introduce intercultural concepts in the context of a communication degree. The existence of relevant courses in the curricula can thus serve as a proxy measure of the likelihood with which a given institution is teaching intercultural communication competence skills. The first goal of this study is to survey the existing communication programs across the region and zero in on possible intercultural communication offerings within the existing curricula to answer the first research question:

> RQ_1: What type of Communication Studies programs are available in the GCC states?

To address this question, a list of institutions of higher education compiled by the authors of this study in 2015 to track communication programs in the GCC was consulted. An internet search of universities and other forms of tertiary education at the time revealed that 170 institutions existed in the six Arabian Peninsula states: Bahrain, Kuwait, Oman, Qatar, Saudi Arabia, and the United Arab Emirates. The websites of these universities were examined to determine whether they offered degrees related to communication. The results demonstrated that 40 programs offered degrees, mostly classified within the area of mass communication.

In December 2018 to January 2019, this list was updated, and a total of 42 communication-related programs were reviewed in the six countries of interest. To understand the nature of these programs and the depth to which they might address intercultural communication, online information about their curricula (bulletins, catalogs, major plans, course descriptions, etc.) were analyzed in both Arabic and

English, as well as noting the types of undergraduate or graduate programs they offered. Appendix 1 demonstrates the undergraduate degrees offered, the colleges and universities in which they are situated, and the courses that most explicitly deal with intercultural, international, or global communication topics, as per their course descriptions available online. Appendix 2 shows the postgraduate degrees offered in the selected countries along with the same corresponding information.

The second phase of the study drills deeper into a single nation with the intent of evaluating the presence of intercultural communication competence among students studying in institutions of higher education. A student population was drawn from three predominant universities in Kuwait seen as broadly representative of the social, educational, and economic models of tertiary education found throughout the GCC, including both local and foreign-oriented institutions. These universities are also the only ones in Kuwait offering undergraduate degrees in communication studies. Participants responded to an online questionnaire distributed by email to their professors and instructors. A snowball sampling technique was utilized to recruit 858 respondents from two private and one public institution. Nonstudent respondents were eliminated from the dataset, reducing the total number of respondents to 829 students. Of the total student respondents, 796 responded to all the questions. At 66%, the majority of the respondents were female, which reflects a social trend within Kuwaiti higher education. Similarly, the majority of the respondents were between 20 and 24 years of age (76%).

The measurement instrument that appeared on the questionnaire was the Intercultural Communication Competency Instrument or ICCI (Arasaratnam & Doerfel, 2005; Arasaratnam, 2009). This instrument examines various dimensions of intercultural communication competence by measuring its affective, behavioral, and cognitive dimensions. The affective dimension measures one's ability to build relationships across intercultural contexts, where prior research suggests that low ethnocentrism is associated with high ICC (Neuliep, 2002; Wrench, Corrigan, McCroskey, & Punyanunt-Carter, 2006). Similarly, the behavioral dimension examines one's ability to adapt to intercultural contexts and seek out intercultural encounters (Arasaratnam, 2005, 2009, 2013). Finally, the cognitive dimension examines the extent to which an individual can employ cognitive constructs in intercultural contexts to develop effective communication messages (Adams-Webber, 2001; Arasaratnam, 2005, 2009, 2013; Gudykunst & Kim, 2003).

The English language ICCI was translated into Arabic with a further back-translation technique used to minimize any discrepancies between the two versions. Both languages were provided as options for the respondents. The instrument consists of 13 items from the ICCI plus additional modifications, such as questions inquiring about the impact of the university education on one's intercultural competence. Further, demographic variables included gender, age, parental levels of education, parents' nationality, and international exposure through extensive travel experience. These additional variables were chosen due to the diverse and largely expatriate configuration of the residents, as well as some of the common cultural and educational norms found among the population. These data were used to address our second research question:

RQ_2: How does the university experience in Kuwait affect intercultural communication competence?

To address this question, the average responses to intercultural communication competence measures are described. Then the average responses to questions directly requesting students to judge the impact of their education on their ICC are provided. Next, a correlation analysis explores the relationship between self-reported measures for the university's development of intercultural communication competence across the affective, behavioral, and cognitive dimensions of the adjusted ICCI tool.

Data on a number of additional variables were collected to address the final research question in order to examine the role of demographic variables on students' ICC measures.

> RQ3: How do demographic variables influence students' intercultural communication competence?

Familial background was operationalized by examining the level of parental education, whether one attended a bilingual or English-language school for more than two years before university, and whether students have lived abroad as a child for 6 months or more. Respondents' education in an English-speaking primary or secondary school prior to their university experience was further evaluated, as were student experiences living abroad for 6 months or longer.

Results

The results of this study were broken down into two sections. First, we will explore the communication programs that exist in higher education institutes of the Arab Gulf states. Then we will examine the ICC of students in Kuwait. Finally, we will examine the impact of students' backgrounds on their ICC.

Communication Curricula

The first research question asked about the extent to which communication programs exist in the selected Arabian Peninsula states. Table 14.1 provides a brief overview of the primary findings in this regard. Across the six countries examined, 36 universities (21%) of the 170 institutions had dedicated undergraduate degrees in communication studies, and half of these were located within the United Arab Emirates (UAE). While many ($n = 57$) offered a single degree in communication studies (most commonly within the area of mass communication), several offered further specializations in an "emphasis" or similar nomenclature

Table 14.1 Summary of communication program degrees and ICC-related courses in the GCC

Country	Bahrain	Kuwait	Oman	Qatar	Saudi Arabia	United Arab Emirates
# of universities with BA degrees in communication	5	3	4	3	3	18
# of BA degrees in communication	7	4	10	4	7	25
# of MA degrees in communication	1	1	1	1	1	5
# of ICC-related courses	7	7	4	5	7	25

that were not quantified herein, since they are not independent degrees and may have shared courses with other emphases within the department that would lead to double-counting. For example, a university may offer one degree in mass communication in which students can specialize in such areas as journalism, graphic design, public relations, broadcast production, or other subsumed areas. A class on intercultural communication, for example, could be offered as a core or elective subject for all emphases within the same department, so counting each emphasis as a separate opportunity for independent exposure to ICC concepts would be misleading. The common rationale for such a configuration (a major with multiple emphases) may have to do with such practicalities as resource availability, curriculum mandates, or common accreditation and regulatory practices in the region. An example of the latter is when government ministries and/or "private" advisory councils tied to the government are charged with authenticating all degrees and through which changes to any degree program must go through an elaborate governmental approval process. In comparison to a degree, changes relating to emphases and specializations from within a major may not be subject to the same degree of bureaucratic oversight and are hence easier to adapt and evolve according to the judgments of the program directors and internal university procedures.

Two additional dimensions of this educational review were assessed for their possible relationship to intercultural communication competency. These were the presence of postgraduate degrees in communication studies and the existence of publicly available course descriptions per each major, which contained content related to international, global, or cultural themes. In total, there were ten related master's degree programs, again, with half of them located in the UAE. From the publicly available course listings, 55 of them had potentially related themes or descriptions. Appendix 1 includes a comprehensive list of the universities, colleges, undergraduate and graduate degrees, and emphases/specializations in communication or closely related studies, as well as relevant course listings. Courses in disciplines other than communication studies were not included in the current study, such as anthropology, translation, foreign languages, and so forth. While they may have some relationship to intercultural learning, their scattered distribution and the difficulty of confirming the presence of specific intercultural components precluded them from this study.

ICC Skills of Kuwaiti Students

The second research question asked how the university experience in Kuwait affects ICC. A total of 814 participants responded to the three questions exploring the role of institutions of higher education on ICC. The three items dealt with the affective, behavioral, and cognitive components of intercultural communication competence. Responses were on a 5-point Likert scale ranging from 1 indicating "strongly agree" to 5 indicating "strongly disagree." The affective item was, "As a result of my university experience, I feel a greater sense of respect for people from other cultures" ($M = 2.23$, SD = 0.96). The behavioral item was, "My university experience has improved my ability to deal effectively with people from other cultures" ($M = 2.29$, SD = 0.96). Finally, the cognitive item was, "My university experience has improved my knowledge and appreciation of other cultures" ($M = 2.19$, SD = 0.94). Lower scores indicate a higher influence of students' higher education experience on their ICC.

These measures were then compared to the indices for the affective, behavioral, and cognitive components of ICC scale. The affective component consisted of four items with a 5-point Likert scale used to demonstrate the degree to which one feels close to and comfortable with people from a different culture ($M = 2.51$, $SD = 0.60$). The behavioral component consisted of three items with a 5-point Likert scale used to demonstrate the degree to which one interacts with people from a different culture ($M = 3.05$, $SD = 0.71$). Finally, the cognitive component consisted of three items with a 5-point Likert scale used to demonstrate the degree to which one distinguishes between individual and cultural factors when evaluating people from a different culture ($M = 2.62$ $SD = 0.66$). A lower score indicates more ICC than a higher score.

A Pearson's correlation was used for this step because it examines the strength of a correlation between two variables. Table 14.2 demonstrates the results of the correlations. Of the nine correlations, five were statistically significant at the 0.001 level, and one was statistically significant at the 0.05 level. This indicates that these differences are likely to be found in the greater population with more than a 95% level of confidence. The strength of the correlations is quite low, however. The greatest correlation was 0.198, indicating weak correlations and an absence of multicollinearity. In other words, the two sets of measures for affective, behavioral, and cognitive components of ICC are distinct and loosely related to one another. The fact that all the correlations are positive indicates a relationship whereby greater self-reporting on the influence of university experience on intercultural competence correlates with greater ICC on the affective and behavioral scale. The most notable finding here is the fact that none of the cognitive measures were statistically significant in the correlations.

Finally, it is important to describe the characteristics of the sample from which students were selected. Respondents selected one of five options to describe the number of years in which they have been enrolled in an institution of higher education: less than 1 year (16.5%, $n = 152$), 1 year (10.0%, $n = 92$), 2 years (19.2%, $n = 176$), 3 years (21.3% $n = 196$), and 4 or more years (26.3%, $n = 242$).

Table 14.2 Pearson's correlations between ICC component indices and the university's effect on each component

	Affective Index	Behavioral Index	Cognitive Index
As a result of my university experience, I feel a greater sense of respect for people from other cultures.			
R	0.168	0.118	0.012
p-Value	< 0.001	0.001	0.740
My university experience has improved my ability to deal effectively with people from other cultures.			
R	0.160	0.121	0.027
p-Value	< 0.001	0.001	0.434
My university experience has improved my knowledge and appreciation of other cultures.			
R	0.198	0.091	0.046
p-Value	< 0.001	0.009	0.193

Three univariate analyses of variance were conducted to examine whether the self-reported measures of the university's influence on one's ICC varied with the number of years students were enrolled in an institution of higher education. None of the three statements about the influence of higher education on students' intercultural communication competence were statistically significant. The results for the affective ($F(4,809) = 0.037, p = 0.997$) behavioral ($F(4,809) = 0.189, p = 0.944$) and cognitive ($F(4,809) = 0.077, p = 0.989$) components of ICC did not differ as students' experience in higher education institutions increased.

Another three univariate analyses of variance were conducted to examine whether the ICC indices varied with the number of years students were enrolled in an institution of higher education. While the behavioral ($F(4,819) = 1.144, p = 0.334$) and cognitive ($F(4,819) = 1.346, p = 0.251$) indices did not significantly vary as the students' experience in higher education institutions changed, the affective index ($F(4,819) = 3.419, p = 0.009$) did differ in a statistically significant matter. A Tukey HSD post-hoc analysis showed that students with one year of experience in higher education statistically differed from those with 2 years ($p = 0.015$) and 4 or more years ($p = 0.008$) of experience as a student. In both cases, the mean difference was truncated to 0.23. The positive mean difference implies that students with more experience in higher education felt closer to people from a different cultural background than those with less experience in higher education.

ICC Skills and Student Demographics

The third research question inquired as to whether other demographic variables influence students' ICC. The questionnaire included an item inquiring about the highest level of education achieved by either parent. The majority of the respondents had a parent who achieved higher than a high school degree. The respondents' parents had achieved the following levels of education: high school ($n = 131$, 14.3%), diploma ($n = 106$, 11.5%), bachelor's degree ($n = 367$, 39.9%), master's degree ($n = 114$, 12.4%), and doctoral degree ($n = 84$, 9.1%).

To examine how the parental level of education influences students' experiences in institutions of higher education, three univariate analyses of variance were conducted in relation to the items in which students rated the influence of university experience on their affective, behavioral, and cognitive aspects of ICC. The attribution of affective ($F(4,797) = 2.380, p = 0.050$) and behavioral ($F(4,797) = 2.687, p = 0.030$) components of the ICC to university experience varied with parental level of education but not cognitive components ($F(4,797) = 1.811, p = 0.125$).

Univariate analyses of variance were then conducted to examine the influence of parental level of education on ICC. Although affective ($F(4,797) = 1.383, p = 0.238$) and cognitive ($F(4,797) = 0.404, p = 0.806$) indices were not statistically significant, the results demonstrated statistically significant differences for the behavioral index ($F(4,797) = 3.186, p = 0.013$). A Tukey HSD post-hoc analysis showed the behavioral ICC index was −0.234 lower for students with a parent with a bachelor's degree than those with a parent with only a high school education ($p = 0.012$). Since lower scores indicate more behavioral ICC, this suggests that parents who are more educated are probably better equipped to interact with individuals from different cultural backgrounds in ways that influence their children's behaviors.

Two other dichotomous variables were examined to explore if students' experiences living abroad or attending bilingual schools have impacted their ICC. A majority of the respondents ($n = 526$, 57.2%) did not attend an English-language or bilingual school prior to university experience. Similarly, only a minority of students lived in a foreign country for longer than 6 months as children ($n = 92$, 10.0%). Independent-sample t-tests were conducted to examine how these developmental experiences affected one's intercultural communication competence and one's attribution of ICC to university experience.

Attending an English-language or bilingual school prior to university was an important factor in ICC. Having such an educational experience affected one's attribution of ICC to university experience in affective ($t = (df = 812) = 2.068, p = 0.039$), behavioral ($t = (df = 812) = 3.477, p = 0.001$) and cognitive ($t = (df = 812) = 2.537, p = 0.011$) ways. Similarly, the ICC affective ($t = (df = 822) = -2.565, p = 0.010$) and behavioral ($t = (df = 822) = -4.377, p < 0.001$) indices were significant, although the cognitive was not ($t = (df = 822) = -1.091, p = 0.275$).

Having lived abroad for at least 6 months as a child was also an important factor in ICC, as might be expected. Having such an international experience did not affect one's attribution of ICC to university experience in an affective ($t = (df = 795) = 0.504, p = 0.614$), behavioral ($t = (df = 795) = 1.472, p = 0.141$), and cognitive ($t = (df = 795) = 0.157, p = 0.876$) way. However, the ICC indices were statistically significant for all three components, though at different levels. The affective index ($t = (df = 795) = -2.420, p = 0.016$) was significant at the 0.05 level, the behavioral ($t = (df = 795) = -5.174, p < 0.001$) index was significant at the 0.001 level, and the cognitive ($t = (df = 795) = -1.767, p = 0.078$) index was significant at the 0.10 level. This shows that we can find these differences in the population from which the sample was drawn, but not with the same degree of confidence.

Discussion

The findings of the first research question demonstrate that the number of courses offered that may teach students how to think about intercultural communication in their social environment is rather scarce. This finding is consistent with the findings of Al Nashmi, Alkazemi, and Wanta (2017) that the majority of courses offered in mass communication degrees in the private universities using an American educational system in the Arab world rely on social sciences and liberal arts as electives, while older universities in the Arab world do not require many electives and are vocationally oriented within the discipline. While some universities require students to take a significant number of courses outside their disciplines, many of these electives are related to economics, and there is very little room for students to take intercultural communication courses as electives (Ibid.).

Perhaps one explanation for these findings is that local accreditation standards in the field of communication studies do not seem to require intercultural communication courses, especially when the institutions are branch campuses or Western-style educational institutions. The US-based Accrediting Council on Education in Journalism and Mass Communication [ACEJMC] (2019), for example, includes standards to ensure that some coursework is offered in international communication and that diversity is represented in the curriculum. However, at the time of this study, only four Arab universities, located in the United Arab Emirates and Qatar, are accredited by ACEJMC (ACEJMC, 2019). The inclusion of such standards, with or without accreditation imperatives, would be one step regional programs could take to broaden the influence of intercultural learning in their home institutions.

The results of the second research question, demonstrated in Table 14.2, indicate that cognitive intercultural communication competence is not being enhanced by students' university experience. The analysis of curricula in the first research question could help explain why students are not learning to think of intercultural communication more effectively during their university years. Our analysis demonstrates weak correlations between the affective and behavioral intercultural communication indices and students' university experience, indicating that the university experience is currently only one of many factors that influence students' intercultural communication competence. Other sources that teach students to relate to individuals from other cultures include family influences, personal experiences, and access to global media (McPhail & Fisher, 2015; Miglietta & Tartaglia, 2009; Yang, Wu, Zhu, Brian, & Southwell, 2004). Nevertheless, the fact that affective and behavioral dimensions are statistically significant demonstrates that students may be experiencing growth in university when relating to and interacting with people of different cultural backgrounds.

Another notable finding is that students with more experience in higher education felt closer to people from different cultural backgrounds. Their answers differed by 0.23 points on a 5-point Likert scale. This finding suggests that students' immersion in diverse environments may lead to an emotional response over time that makes them more likely to relate to individuals with different cultural backgrounds. While research shows that exposure to other cultures does not necessarily result in better intercultural competence (Liu, 2014), it may nevertheless foster a positive attitude toward culturally different others, which is a precursor to ICC.

The results of the third research question showed that students with at least one parent who achieved higher levels of education were more likely to demonstrate higher behavioral intercultural competence. One possible explanation for this finding could be that students with more educated parents may learn from their parents how to more effectively interact in intercultural situations. Alternatively, well-educated parents may be better positioned to expose their children to a wider range of intercultural experiences, which may contribute to the development of cultural awareness and sensitivity. While the positive effects of parental education on students' academic achievement are well established (Bernard, 2004; Gustafsson, Yang Hansen, & Rosén, 2013), the authors are not aware of studies that have specifically addressed the link between intercultural competence and parental educational background.

Further, the results of the third research question demonstrate that students who attended English-language or bilingual schools prior to university did not achieve higher scores in the cognitive dimension of intercultural communication competence. While they may have the ability to relate (affect) or interact (behavior) with individuals from different cultures, the results suggest that they do not think (cognition) about the intercultural experiences in a more nuanced way. This finding once again supports the need for greater intercultural communication competence training at the university level regardless of the type of high school from which students entered university. Further, these findings are suggestive of a need to teach intercultural communication in primary and secondary institutions. As outlined in the literature review, many American and European organizations and educators recognize the necessity of early inclusion of cultural diversity training to foster positive attitudes and develop communication skills with culturally different others (Department of Education, Employment and Workplace Relations (DEEWR), 2010; Huber, 2012; Wagner, Perugini, & Byram, 2017). Such lessons would also likely be well headed in an Arab context.

Finally, students who lived abroad as a child for at least 6 months were not likely to attribute their intercultural communication competence to their university experience. One explanation for this finding could be that these students learned to relate to, communicate with, and interact with individuals from different cultures effectively and appropriately at a younger age. Therefore, their university experience provides a space for them to practice their skills rather than to learn them for the first time. This demonstrates the potential power of personal intercultural experiences as an important foundation to ICC. Universities that provide study-abroad opportunities, student exchanges, and other similar international experiences may be able to foster lasting ICC outcomes that capitalize on experiential learning for those students who may not have had such opportunities in their prior education.

The social environment in which these data were gathered is unique because of the large proportion of expatriates in a national environment. The results demonstrate that even in such a mixed cultural environment, ICC skills are not developed naturally. This is consistent with Briscoe-Smith's (2010) findings that children experience natural racist impulses that they absorb from society without noticing it unless an adult teaches the child to unlearn these attitudes. These findings may explain the rhetoric used by elite Kuwaitis, and echoed across the GCC to different extents, that have been generously described as failing to align with a "social justice agenda" (Weiner, 2017, p. 2). Our results demonstrate that the majority of institutions of higher education in the GCC do not offer education in intercultural communication.

Limitations and Future Research

There are limits to the generalizability of all scientific investigations, and this work is no exception. First, it must be noted that data gathered about university curricula were limited to information available online for institutions operating in the Arabian Peninsula. Further, courses that students can enroll in prior to a university program to enhance their understanding of language and culture, often referred to as "Foundations" programs, were not included in this analysis. Finally, the student data gathered for this study were limited to one nation. Students from both private and public universities were included to obtain a sample that may represent patterns that exist more broadly in the region, but this was not tested empirically.

Future researchers should evaluate the role of language and culture programs available to students prior to their university education, as well as other types of courses outside the discipline of communication studies. Each may have contributions to students' ICC. Further, future researchers should compare samples of students from a number of Arab nations. This would be particularly interesting to explore in different regions of the Arab world, as differences in colonial influence, economic situations, and demography all influence the region in a variety of ways.

Conclusion

Overall, courses relevant to intercultural communication in the Arab Gulf state were assessed. The findings demonstrate that the curricula offering courses to help improve ICC components in the GCC are scarce. Further, a survey of Kuwaiti students revealed that students in the GCC are not naturally learning comprehensive ICC skills by virtue of their social environment. Thus, practical implications include the recommendation to introduce more courses in GCC universities that focus on ICC skills and theories. Because our findings show that students who studied abroad had higher ICC scores, study-abroad opportunities should also be considered in developing a workforce that can navigate the unique cultural environment of the GCC.

Note

1. This work was supported by the Kuwait Foundation for the Advancement of Science [grant no. P114–19TT-01].

References

Accrediting Council on Education in Journalism and Mass Communication [ACEJMC]. (2019). *Nine accrediting standards*. Retrieved from www.acejmc.org/policies-process/nine-standards/.

Adams-Webber, J. R. (2001). Cognitive complexity and role relationships. *Journal of Constructivist Psychology, 14*, 43–50.

Al Nashmi, E., Alkazemi, M. F., & Wanta, W. (2017). Journalism and mass communication education in the Arab World: Towards a typology. *International Communication Gazette, 80*(5), 403–425.

Arasaratnam, L. A. (2005). Sensation seeking and international students' satisfaction of experiences in the United States. *Journal of Intercultural Communication Research, 34*, 184–194.

Arasaratnam, L. A. (2009). The development of a new instrument of intercultural communication competence. *Journal of Intercultural Communication, 20*, 1–11.

Arasaratnam, L. A. (2013). Intercultural communication competence. In A. Kurylo (Ed.), *Inter/cultural communication: Representation and construction of culture* (pp. 47–68). Los Angeles, CA: Sage Publications.

Arasaratnam, L. A., & Doerfel, M. L. (2005). Intercultural communication competence: Identifying key components from multicultural perspectives. *International Journal of Intercultural Relations, 29*, 137–163.

Arasaratnam-Smith, L. A. (2016). An exploration into the relationship between intercultural communication competence and bilingualism. *Communication Research Reports, 33*(3), 231–238.

Bernard, W. M. (2004). Parent involvement in elementary school and educational attachment. *Children and Youth Series Review, 26*, 39–62.

Bialystok, E. (2017). The bilingual adaptation: How minds accommodate experience. *Psychological Bulletin, 143*(3), 233–262.

Briscoe-Smith, A. (2010). How to talk with kids about race. In J. A. Smith, J. Marsh, & R. Mendoza-Denton (Eds.), *Are we born racist? New insights from neuroscience and positive psychology*. Boston, MA: Beacon Press.

Byram, M. (1997). *Teaching and assessing intercultural communicative competence*. Clevedon: Multilingual Matters.

Canary, D., Lakey, S., & Sillars, A. (2013). Managing conflict in a competent manner. In J. Oetzel & S. Ting-Toomey (Eds.), *The Sage handbook of conflict communication* (pp. 263–290). Thousand Oaks, CA: Sage Publications.

Catteeuw, P. (2012). A framework of reference for intercultural competence. In *A 21st century Flemish experiment in capacity building in formal education*. Brussels: FARO.

Chen, G. M. & Starosta, W. J. (1996). *Intercultural communication competence: A synthesis, annals of the international communication association, 19*(1), 353–383, doi:10.1080/23808985.1996.11678935.

Chen, G. M., & Starosta, W. J. (1997). A review of the concept of intercultural sensitivity. *Human Communication, 1*, 1–16.

Chen, G. M., & Starosta, W. J. (1998). *Foundations of intercultural communication*. Boston, MA: Allyn & Bacon.

Department of Education, Employment and Workplace Relations (DEEWR). (2010). *Educators being, belonging and becoming: Educators' guide to the early years learning framework for Australia*. Retrieved from https://docs.education.gov.au

Fan, S. R., Liberman, Z., Keysar, B., & Kinzler, K. D. (2015). The exposure advantage: Early exposure to multilingual environment promotes effective communication. *Psychological Science*, 26(7), 1090–1097.

Fantini, A. (2006). Exploring and assessing intercultural competence. *School of International Training*. Retrieved from www.sit.edu/publications/docs/feil_research_report.pdf

Fantini, A., & Tirmizi, A. (2006). Exploring and assessing intercultural competence. In *World Learning Publications*. SIT Graduate Institute and SIT Study Abroad Digital Collections. Retrieved from https://digitalcollections.sit.edu

Garrett-Rucks, P. (2016). *Intercultural competence in instructed language learning: Bridging theory and practice*. Charlotte, NC: Information Age Publishing.

Gudykunst, W. B., & Kim, Y. Y. (2003). *Communicating with strangers: An approach to intercultural communication*. New York, NY: McGraw Hill.

Gustafsson, J.-E., Yang Hansen, K., & Rosén, M. (2013). Effects of home background on student achievement in reading, mathematics, and science at the fourth grade. In M. O. Martin & I. V. S. Mullis (Eds.), *TIMSS and PIRLS 2011: Relationships among reading, mathematics, and science achievement at the fourth grade-implications for early learning* (pp. 183–289). Chestnut Hill: TIMSS & PIRLS International Study Center, Boston College.

Huber, J. (Ed.). (2012). *Intercultural competence for all: Preparation for living in a heterogeneous world*. Council of Europe, Pestalozzi Series 2. Strasbourg: Council of Europe Publishing and Cedex.

Kashima, Y. (2014). Meaning, grounding, and the construction of social reality. *Asian Journal of Social Psychology*, 17(2), 81–95.

Kim, Y. Y. (1991). Intercultural communication competence: A systems-theoretical view. In S. Ting-Toomey & F. Korzenny (Eds.), *Cross-cultural interpersonal communication* (pp. 259–275). Newbury Park, CA: Sage Publications.

Kline, S. L., Hennen-Floyd, C. L., & Farrell, K. M. (1990). Cognitive complexity and verbal response mode in discussion. *Communication Quarterly*, 38, 350–360.

Kuwait Central Statistical Bureau. (2017). *Statistical Bulletin:Population estimates in Kuwait by age, nationality and sex at 1/12017*. Retrieved from www.csb.gov.kw/Pages/Statistics_en?ID = 67&ParentCatID = 1

Leighty, G., & Applegate, J. L. (1991). Social-cognitive and situational influences on the use of face-saving persuasive messages. *Human Communication Research*, 17, 451–484.

Liu, S. (2014). Becoming intercultural: Exposure to foreign cultures and intercultural competence. *China Media Research*, 10(3), 7–14.

Lustig, M. W., & Koester, J. (2007). *Intercultural competence: Interpersonal communication across cultures* (5th ed.). Shanghai: Shanghai Foreign Langue Education Press.

McPhail, R., & Fisher, R. (2015). Lesbian and gay expatriates use of social media to aid acculturation. *International Journal of Intercultural Relations*, 49, 294–307.

Miglietta, A., & Tartaglia, S. (2009). The influence of length of stay, linguistic competence, and media exposure in immigrants' adaptation. *Cross-Cultural Research*, 43(1), 46–61.

Neuliep, J. W. (2002). Assessing the reliability and validity of the generalized ethnocentrism scale. *Journal of Intercultural Communication Research*, 31, 201–216.

Spitzberg, B., & Cupach, W. (2002). Interpersonal skills. In M. Knapp & J. Daly (Eds.), *Handbook of interpersonal communication* (4th ed., pp. 481–524). Newbury Park, CA: Sage Publications.

Stone, N. (2006). Conceptualising intercultural effectiveness for university teaching. *Journal of Studies in International Education*, 10(4), 334–356. doi:10.1177/1028315306287634

Ting-Toomey, S. (1993). Communication resourcefulness: An identity-negotiation perspective. In R. Wiseman & J. Koester (Eds.), *Intercultural communication competence* (pp. 72–111). Newbury Park, CA: Sage Publications.

Ting-Toomey, S., & Dorjee, T. (2015). Intercultural and intergroup communication competence: Toward an integrative perspective. In A. F. Hannawa & B. Spitzberg (Eds.), *The *handbook of communication science: Communication competence* (Vol. 22, pp. 503–538). Berlin, Germany: De Gruyter Mouton.

Wagner, M., Perugini, D. C., & Byram, M. (2017). *Teaching intercultural competence across the age range: From theory to practice*. Clevedon: Multilingual Matters.

Weiner, S. (2017). The politics of Kuwait's Bidoon issue. *Carnegie Endowment for International Peace*. Retrieved April 11, 2019, from https://carnegieendowment.org/sada/73492

The World Bank. (2018). *International migrant stock (% of population) | Data*. Retrieved from https://data.worldbank.org/indicator/SM.POP.TOTL.ZS?end = 2015&start = 1990&year_high_desc = true

Wrench, J. S., Corrigan, M. W., McCroskey, J. C., & Punyanunt-Carter, N. M. (2006). Religious fundamentalism and intercultural communication: The relationships among ethnocentrism, intercultural communication apprehension, religious fundamentalism, homonegativity, and tolerance for religious disagreements. *Journal of Intercultural Communication Research*, *35*, 23–44.

Yang, C., Wu, H., Zhu, M., Brian, G., & Southwell, G. B. (2004). Tuning in to fit in? Acculturation and media use among Chinese students in the United States. *Asian Journal of Communication*, *14*(1), 81–94.

Appendix 1

Table 14.3 Undergraduate communication programs in the GCC States

University	College	Degree & Specializations	Courses Related to Intercultural Communication
Bahrain			
Ahlia University	College of Arts & Science	Bachelor's Degree in Mass Communication & Public Relations (BSMCPR)	N/A
University College of Bahrain	Department Of Communication & Multimedia	Bachelor of Arts in Communication and Multimedia	SBS200 Social/Cultural Anthropology WCS201- Cultural Studies I WCS301- Cultural Studies II CBS205- Communication Skills
Royal University for Women	College of Art & Design	BA in Graphic Design	LAR 112: Human Rights: Compulsory Liberal Arts Course
Applied Science University	College of Arts and Science	Bachelor of Arts in Graphic Design	GDE 328: Psychology & Sociology Design
Bahrain Polytechnic	School of Humanities	Bachelor of Visual Design Bachelor of Web Media Bachelor of Information and Communications Technology	VC6104: Historical Studies in Design
Kuwait			
American University of Kuwait	College of Arts and Sciences	BA in Communication and Media; BA in Graphic Design	COM 425-International Case Studies in Public Relations COM 222- Global Media and Spaces of Identities COM 366: Popular Culture in South Asia: Film COMM 425 International Case Studies in Public Relations
Gulf University for Science and Technology	College of Arts & Sciences	BA in Mass Communication Emphases in PR and Advertising, Visual communication, Digital media production	MCM 253: Visual Culture MCM 341: Case studies in PR/Advertising MCM 205: International Communication

(*Continued*)

Table 14.3 (Continued)

University	College	Degree & Specializations	Courses Related to Intercultural Communication
Kuwait University	College of Arts	Bachelor of Arts in Mass Communication. Emphases in Public Relations and Media Broadcasting	
Oman			
Sultan Qaboos University	College of Arts and Social Sciences	BA in Mass Communication 3 specializations: Journalism & Online Publishing Broadcasting PR & Advertising	MASS2620: International Communication
Bayan University College	Media Studies Department	BA in Broadcasting BA in Public Relations BA in Advertising BA in Journalism	ANTH105 Cultural Anthropology
College of Applied Sciences Rustaq	College of Applied Sciences	Bachelor of Design in Digital Design Bachelor of Design in Graphic Design	N/A
Scientific College of Design	Department of Graphic Design	B.S. Digital Design B.S. Printing Design B.S. Animation	CST201 Cultural Studies I
Qatar			
Qatar University	College of Arts & Sciences	BA in Mass Communication	MCOM 318: Globalization Communication (in Arabic)
Virginia Commonwealth University in Qatar	VCU School of the Arts in Qatar	Bachelor of Fine Arts in Graphic Design	N/A
Northwestern University in Qatar	Medill School of Journalism, Media, Integrated Marketing Communications	Bachelor of Science in Communications Bachelor of Science in Journalism	MIT 212–0: Exploring Global Media MIT 389–0: Global Culture & Communication JOUR 390–0: Global Perspectives in Strategic Communication Also other special topics courses

Saudi Arabia

King Abdulaziz University	Faculty of Communication and Media	5 Departments: Communication Experiential Journalism Marketing Communication Public Relations	COM 307- International Media COM 361- International Public Relations
King Faisal University	College of Arts	Bachelor of Media	N/A
Jazan University	Faculty of Arts and Humanities	Bachelor of Journalism and Media	102: Human Civilizations 101: Introduction to Art and Human Sciences (code missing) International Media

United Arab Emirates

United Arab Emirates University	College of Humanities and Social Sciences	1- BA in Mass Communication, 2- BA in English Literature with a Minor in Film Studies	N/A
American University of Sharjah	College of Arts and Sciences (CAS)	BA in Mass Communication	MKT 309 International Marketing POL 202 Introduction to International Relations COM504 Cross Cultural Communication
Zayed University	College of Communication & Media Sciences	Bachelor of Science in Communication & Media Sciences in four concentrations: Converged Media Film and Video Communication Integrated Strategic Communication Tourism and Cultural Communication	
University of Sharjah	College of Communication	BA in Communication in one of the 5 specializations: public relations, mass communication, graphic design, electronic media, journalism	800100: Cultural and Global Media

(*Continued*)

Table 14.3 (Continued)

University	College	Degree & Specializations	Courses Related to Intercultural Communication
American University in Dubai	The Mohammed Bin Rashid School for Communication	Bachelor of Communication and Information Studies (BCIS)	COM 101: Introduction to Global Media COM 103: Media Culture and Society WLDC 101: World Cultures 1 WLDC 102: World Cultures II
Abu Dhabi University	College of Media and Human Sciences	BA in Mass Communication (English); BA in Mass Communication (Arabic)	MAC 201 Intercultural Communication; MAC 403 International Communication; MAC 316 Communication and Diplomacy
Ajman University for Science and Technology		BA in Mass Communication	660310- Human Rights in the Modern Time 660312 Regional & International Organizations
Manipal University Dubai Campus	School of Media and Communication	BA in Media and Communication	
American University in the Emirates, AUE	College of Media and Mass Communication	BA in Media and Mass Communication 4 specializations: International Relations Integrated Marketing Communication Public Relations (separate degrees in the English & Arabic languages) Radio & TV	
Al Ghurair University	College of Mass Communication	BA in Public Relations	N/A
Middlesex University Dubai Campus		BA Honours Advertising, PR and Media; BA Honours Journalism and media; BA Honours Film	Global Journalism
Al Ain University of Science & Technology	College of Communication and Media	Bachelor of Mass Communication and Media	0603340E International Public Relations

American University of Ras al Khaimah	School of Arts and Sciences	BA in Mass Communication	COMM 222 Intercultural Mass Communication
Murdoch University Dubai		Bachelor of Communications-Journalism; Bachelor of Communications-Strategic Communication	N/A
University of Jazeera	College of Media and Communication Sciences	BMCS-Journalism; BMCS-PR and Advertising; BMCS-Communication Technology	N/A
University of Modern Sciences, UMS	College of Mass Communication	BA in Mass communication—Journalism; BA in Mass Communication- Public Relations	N/A
New York University of Abu Dhabi	College of Arts and Sciences	Minor in Design; Minor in Interactive Media	
Higher Colleges of Technology		Bachelor of Applied Media	N/A

Appendix 2

Table 14.4 Graduate communication programs in the GCC States

University	Name	Graduate Degrees & Specializations	Courses Related to *Intercultural Communication*
Ahlia University	Bahrain	Master's Degree in Mass Communication & Public Relations (MSMCPR)	N/A
Kuwait University	Kuwait	Master's in Public Relations	N/A
Sultan Qaboos University	Oman	MA in Mass Communication	MASS2620: International Communication
King Abdulaziz University	Saudi Arabia	Master in Communication Skills	COM 307- International Media COM 361- International Public Relations
Zayed University	United Arab Emirates	Master of Arts (MA) in Communication Concentration in Strategic Public Relations Master of Arts (MA) in Communication Concentration in Tourism and Cultural Communication	COM504 Cross Cultural Communication
University of Sharjah	United Arab Emirates	MA in Communication	800100: Cultural and Global Media
American University in Dubai	United Arab Emirates	MA in Leadership and Innovation in Contemporary Media	LICM 608: Global Media Leadership LICM 605- Managing the Media Sector: Local vs Global LICM 604: Global Media Economics
Middlesex University Dubai Campus	United Arab Emirates	MA in Marketing Communication	Global Journalism

15 Internationalizing and Decolonizing the Classroom

Ahmet Atay

After a short walk between buildings, I arrived at Kauke Hall, our main academic building that houses most of the humanities and some of the social sciences. I opened the door that leads to the iconic arch of the college and walked into the building. Today, we would be talking about race and racism, and I had tons of questions and hesitations in my mind. The students had been assigned a chapter that focused on three key concepts: race and racism, orientalism, and whiteness. Having these conversations with our students was never easy, especially for those of us who occupied historically marginalized positions. I climbed the stairs. One, two, three, four . . . pause. It was time.

I opened the classroom door and walked in. This was a diverse and supportive group of students. I had done what I was about to do so many times before. So many times, I had unpacked the notions of race and ethnicity and carried on important discussions with our students. So many times, I had felt the same nervousness. As a transnational queer scholar, I have written extensively and taught so many courses on these issues, but even after so many years, I was still nervous. After all, even within these critical classroom environments, our bodies were still politicized and marked by the ideologies that were embodied through our identities and pedagogical approaches. As we decolonized or globalized the curriculum, our bodies occupied center stage. We were in the classroom, and our bodies and identities were visible. We were the curriculum.

Decolonizing the classroom or taking a transnational approach to communication pedagogies demands an understanding of one's positionality. Regardless of how they are marked or read as texts, as instructors, our bodies and identities are often part of our course content and classroom environments. The ways we create our syllabi, assign readings, choose assignments, and teach our classes reflect or embody these positionalities. No matter who we are, our bodies, identities, and positionalities are in the classroom.

I begin this chapter by recognizing positionalities and bodies, especially those of historically marginalized faculty. Who we are matters in the classroom, especially when we challenge, critique, and resist the oppressive power structures and generate difficult conversations around the construction and embodiment of identity markers. We put our bodies on the frontlines in so many ways. This essay is about the efforts required to decolonize and transnationalize the curriculum, which is an emotional labor often performed by marginalized bodies. However, first, I must explain how I use these two terms. By decolonization I mean decentering white,

Euro-American centric ways of teaching and knowing. Hence, through decentering, we could acknowledge and illuminate the value in different ways of teaching, learning, and knowing to challenge the conventional and mainstream discourse (Calafell & Gutierrez-Perez, 2018). Transnational, on the other hand, refers to interconnectivity between people and moving or changing social, economic, and political positions and boundaries of nation-states (Shome, 2013). Hence, by decolonization and transnationalization of the curriculum, I refer to curriculum that decenters white US-centric knowledge production and dissemination in the classroom and recognizes historically rooted power dynamics and how they play out in the classroom. This curriculum also highlights interconnectedness of people and economic and political linkages of nation-states.

In this chapter, I argue that as communication scholars and pedagogues, we need to be focusing on postcolonial and transnational approaches in order to decolonize our classrooms. By postcolonial approaches, I mean approaches that illuminate power structures, historical oppressions of non-Western cultures and their cultural practices and ways of being and knowing. Hence, it aims to empower historically marginalize bodies and their experiences (Atay, 2015; Shome & Hegde, 2002; Mohanty, 2003). Decolonizing and internationalizing the classroom and curriculum can only be achieved if we are able to successfully challenge power structures, decolonize how we teach and mentor our students, and envision educational settings. Both critical communication pedagogy (CCP) and critical intercultural communication (CIC) aim for social change and promote a diversity of voices with micro and macro structures; however, the communication studies as a field and our scholarship neglect to incorporate this postcolonial approach and the impact of globalization in our communication classrooms. Therefore, despite the push to open up spaces for diverse voices to join the dialogue, white and, more significantly, North American perspectives tend to dominate the course content and discussions around diversity. Raka Shome (2013) critiqued this US-centric approach to driving CIC, arguing that

> we often find in critical intercultural communication studies an implicit tendency to territorialize race where race becomes synonymous with the boundaries of the nation-state. Such a framework ends up shoring and maintaining a US centered ethos in our understanding of race.
>
> (p. 149)

Similar tendencies are also apparent in CCP's agenda. Despite honorable efforts, the notions of identity markers are often articulated within and from the US-centric ethos (Yep, 2013). The cultural and economic linkages in the world are also salient because of increased transportation and communication platforms and means and processes. Similar arguments must be made for CCP research, because unfortunately, CCP scholarship does not often recognize globalization processes and how they impact our teaching. Hence, through personal narratives, my goal in this chapter is to articulate the ways in which we, as communication pedagogues, can mindfully decolonize as well as transnationalize our curricula, syllabi, and pedagogical approaches. This process also calls for a better integration of CCP and CIC pedagogies.

Why is decolonizing educational spaces and transnationalization of the curriculum important? Before furthering my discussion, I think addressing this question is crucial. Higher education as an institution plays an important role in our society. It not only shapes our culture but also mirrors it in so many ways. As Toyosaki and Chuang (2018) argue,

> Education is a culturally rich site and context to explore societies, historical institutionalizations, cultures, and people simultaneously. It helps us see how culture and power work simultaneously and often seamlessly in complex, nuanced, and orchestrated manners at the macro-meso-micro levels. These levels all collide in education.
>
> (pp. 227–228)

Therefore, the classroom is, in a way, a reflection of our society. Demographic shifts, cultural changes, and the transnationalization efforts of higher education are, for economic reasons, changing the landscape of higher education. As this landscape changes, we must also change our curricula, curricular commitments, and pedagogical approaches to educate our racially, ethnically, culturally, economically, and linguistically diverse student population. This process begins with decentering the mainstream white-US perspectives, decolonizing the curriculum, and opening spaces for new voices to come to the center. Decolonization and transnationalization as educational efforts are about an epistemological shift and the educational journey to create a cultural shift. This cultural shift hopes to highlight power dynamics and change them to create positive impact. Furthermore, it aims to empower historically marginalized faculty and students to express their voices and perspectives.

> *I wrote three concepts on the board: race, orientalism, and whiteness. Today's class was about the social constructions of the "other" and unpacking how larger cultural and social structures are created and perpetuated by the discourses around us. This was not the first or only time we had discussed these issues. Throughout the semester, we had talked about different aspects of globalization, Marxist and critical theories, postcolonial theory and criticism, and issues around colonization, imperialism, and other systems of oppression. However, in this class period, we isolated these three particular issues, covering them extensively in order to decolonize and decenter whiteness.*
>
> *I hoped the students were willing to discuss race and racism. After a deep breath, I asked, "What is your understanding of 'race'?" Some looked down at their notes, some shied away from my glance, and some took a deep breath, as I had. Finally, one of the students raised her hand: "Race is a social construction, and it was created to differentiate people in order to exercise power." She was a senior and had previously taken three of my courses. In that moment, I was proud. She was able to clearly articulate the power dimensions such as race and nationality in social constructions. We spent more than 20 minutes defining race and discussing the differences between race and ethnicity. The students were on board. They were able to define race. In order to decolonize, we next had to decenter whiteness. Step by step, inch by inch, I began to decenter. After watching 10 minutes of a documentary about the representation of Latina/o individuals in the mainstream US media, I asked them to think about why there are only a few Latinx characters in our mainstream popular culture and why they are often represented negatively, asking "Who benefits from these representations?" The center started to crack, and we began asking critical questions about mediated representations. One of the students quickly raised*

> her hand. She argued that because media makers are often (upper-) middle-class individuals, we often see their stories and lives, not the lives of minorities. The center continued to crack.

***

Bernadette Calafell and Robert Gutierrez-Perez's (2018) arguments on higher education resonate deeply with me. They argue that academic spaces and structures are not designed for minority students and faculty, building on the idea of whiteness and the ways in which whites perpetuate ideologies of whiteness. I must add that in addition to US-based historically marginalized faculty and students, international students and faculty are also often victimized by white US-centric structures and pedagogies. One of the ways this marginalization operates is within the classroom, where curricula and pedagogical approaches play a paramount role in constructing as well as operating these oppressive systems that disadvantage historically marginalized students and the ways in which they interact with others in the classroom and the curriculum itself. Euro-American-centric perspectives continue to dominate how the education system construes particular ideas about how the world operates, how the marginalized groups are defined, categorized, and treated. Take, for example, how US history is taught in high school or even public speaking in higher education. More often than not, the pedagogical approaches used stand to serve perpetuate whiteness and further silence other ways of knowing, learning, and being in the classroom. There are several factors that explain the marginalization of non-Western knowledge. For example, the lack of diversity in pedagogical approaches and assignment choices, the homogenization and multiplicity in reading materials, and finally, the ways in which the classroom as a culture is constructed and operated feeds into the marginalization of international students. International students are often marginalized by other students because of their accents or backgrounds as well as faculty who either grade them or treat them differently. For example, they might be "encouraged" to speak up in the classroom even though this might not be their mode of learning. They might also have less context about certain information or subject, particularly the US-based ones. Pushing them to be differently often further marginalize them in the classroom. Moreover, the English-language hegemony that instructors depend on and perpetuate through cultivating particular cultural expectations contributes to this marginalization and discrimination of international students.

I see four interrelated issues that stand in the way of the successful internationalization of the curricula: (1) curricula that perpetuate US-centric ideas and whiteness; (2) cultural practices that silence and marginalize international faculty and students; (3) curricular exoticization of diverse and international voices and the mistreatment of their work; and (4) the lack of transnational pedagogies and their incorporation into higher education and the classroom in particular (hooks, 1994, 1996, 2001; Toyosaki & Chuang, 2018; Tuck & Yang, 2012). In the following section, I further expand on these issues and offer some suggestions, including decolonizing and internationalizing the curriculum as well as transnationalizing pedagogical approaches to address these problematic roadblocks.

***

> How many more classes will I have to take which still do not include readings from US-based minority scholars or international scholars? As an international student, I did not often see myself in the courses I was taking. Although I

enjoyed all of my course readings, I also wanted to read more from historically marginalized and international scholars. With some exceptions, in class after class, I read the theories and writings of US-based white rhetoric or media scholars and engaged in dialogues about their arguments. Once in a while, we read pieces by queer scholars or other minority scholars, but international voices were widely missing. I could not hear echoes of their voices, yet they could have helped me to articulate my own. Historically, communication studies as a discipline has been predominantly white and US-centric. Faculty of color and international scholars have been marginally visible and often widely absent. As I looked for a role model and a way to articulate my voice, I felt lost.

* * *

Successful and meaningful transnationalization requires a departmental commitment. These commitments should outlined in departmental goals and each individual syllabus should mirror these commitments. Addressing the first issue of successfully transnationalizing the curricula, as several scholars argue (e.g., Warren, 1999; Warren & Hytten, 2004; Shome, 2013; Yep & Lescure, 2018), whiteness occupies the heart of academic life in the US. Considering that US higher education is built on the ideals of whiteness and Eurocentric cultural and philosophical practices, this is not really surprising. Moreover, since the vast majority of us in US higher education are educated in the US, including some international scholars, our ideas and pedagogical perspectives come from this indoctrination. On the other hand, there are international faculty who are teaching in the US academia and were not educated in the US. They too experience difficulty finding their voice and place in US academia, a fact attributed to their "foreignness" or the stereotypical assumption that they do not know how the US system works. There is a danger in ignoring these multiple experiences. Nonetheless, the desire to expand diverse perspectives in the US classrooms is evident in the way the faculty endeavor to engage in different ways of knowing and different pedagogical lenses. There are three recent events that show engagement of faculty of color, international faculty in efforts to internationalize the communication curriculum. The 2019 Central States Communication Association hosted a preconference on Teaching with a Global Mindfulness. Likewise, 2018 National Communication Association hosted a preconference on Decolonizing Communication Studies and 2019 International Communication Association while be hosting CommunicationSoWhite pre-conference. These are valuable efforts and much appreciated. However, there are concerns about ways faculty of color are perceived and treated as documented in a collection of essays titled *Presumed Incompetent: The Intersections of Race and Class for Women in Academia* (Muhs, Niemann, González, & Harris, 2012). In order to decolonize our classrooms, we must have the ability to decenter white and US-centric teaching and pedagogical frameworks, which continue to support dominant and often oppressive educational philosophies. Through the inability to critically examine our actions and choices as well as practice deep self-reflexivity, we perpetuate the ideologies of whiteness in the classroom and in other academic settings and spaces.

The overall departmental curriculum as well as our own syllabi in many ways may embody US-centrism and perpetuate whiteness in the classroom. To decolonize and transnationalize, we have to examine the larger curriculum in terms of its goals and specifically the student learning outcomes. Consequently, the course design, choice of pedagogical approaches, selection of readings, assignments, and finally expertise to teach certain courses aim to decolonize the communication curriculum.

Likewise, the demographics of students and their lived experiences matter in relation to efforts to decolonize and transnationalize the curriculum.

Before I further my discussion, I must define processes of decolonization as postulated by critical scholars and postcolonial scholars. According to Tuck and Yang (2012), there are two schools of thought when it comes to the decolonization processes in the context of higher education: Franz Fanon's and Paulo Freire's. According to Fanon (1963), decolonization of the mind or the cultivation of the critical consciousness is the first step in the decolonization process of cultural practices. Tuck and Young reflect on this process as follows:

> We agree that curricula, literature, and pedagogy can be crafted to aid people in learning to see settler colonialism, to articulate critiques of settler epistemology, and set aside settler histories and values in search of ethics that reject domination and exploitation; this is not unimportant work. However, the front-loading of critical consciousness building can waylay decolonization, even though the experience of teaching and learning to be critical of settler colonialism can be so powerful it can feel like it is indeed making change. Until the stolen land is relinquished, critical consciousness does not translate into action that disrupts settler colonialism.
>
> (p. 19)

They argue that until what is taken is given back, one cannot develop critical consciousness in order to reject or challenge dominant structures and create positive change. The same applies to pedagogy and classroom experiences. We cultivate a critical consciousness by allowing students to have different teaching experiences, other than white- and Euro-American-centric approaches that suppress non-western ways of knowing and being.

Freire's (2000) arguments on critical pedagogy in relation to decolonization is equally relevant. Freire's arguments mainly focused on the liberation of the oppressed, particularly in educational settings. On the other hand, Fanon argues for developing critical consciousness. According to Freire, the liberation of the oppressed means empowering the oppressed to articulate their voices and develop more agency, even in classroom settings. Of this, Tuck and Young write,

> Freire situates the work of liberation in the minds of the oppressed, an abstract category of dehumanized worker vis-a-vis a similarly abstract category of oppressor. This is a sharp right turn away from Fanon's work, which always positioned the work of liberation in the particularities of colonization, in the specific structural and interpersonal categories of Native and settler.
>
> (pp. 19–20)

In the Freirean approach, "it is unclear who the oppressed are, even more ambiguous who the oppressors are, and it is inferred throughout that an innocent third category of enlightened human exists" (Tuck & Yang, 2012, p. 20). In a way, this is a critique of the Freirean approach by pointing out that "oppressed" is a blurry concept since it is not clearly defined who is being referred to. It could be individuals from different socioeconomic classes or racial and ethnic minorities or queers. This blurriness also comes from the fact that Freire was theorizing from his own lived experiences in Brazil. Therefore, creating a critical consciousness and liberating the oppressed require more intense work since they require decolonizing the power structure. To point out the differences in these two schools of thought, Tuck and Young postulate that

> Fanon positions decolonization as chaotic, an unclean break from a colonial condition that is already over determined by the violence of the colonizer and unresolved in its possible futures. By contrast, Freire positions liberation as redemption, a freeing of both oppressor and oppressed through their humanity.
> (p. 20)

To bring the discussion back to decolonization of the curriculum, both in Fanon's ideas of creating a critical consciousness and Freire's ideas on empowerment of the oppressed, classroom, and higher education, I will now articulate what decolonizing the curriculum and decentering the white- and US-centric approaches and pedagogies would look like at the curricular level. Any curriculum, at both the departmental and syllabus level, must decenter white and US-centric approaches and pedagogies in order to become decolonized and transnationalized. This entails incorporating non-US and non-white pedagogies and approaches as the main perspective to the syllabus and curriculum to decenter power structures and also empower historically marginalized groups. For example, I try to transnationalize my Visual Communication and Culture course by consistently showcasing the works of international artists and filmmakers. This allows students to understand that our media landscape, even though it is highly Euro-American-centric, they should be consuming and studying the works of international artists. For example, when we talk about immigrant experiences, I show two films, *East Is East* (1999), featuring a the lives of a multiethnic family in northern England, and Turkish-Italian director Ferzan Ozpetek's (2011) *La Fate Ignoranti*. Both films allows us to create a richer discussion about the discourse of immigration and film making outside of the US immigration discourse.

Diversifying course content recognizes that diversity and inclusion are imperative in higher education, more so in preparing students for a global world. Therefore, diverse international topics should be the centerpiece of courses to be redesigned to reflect the transnational and decolonization pedagogies. Redesigning courses should consider diverse learning resources including international films, documentaries, readings, literature, poetry, and performance pieces authored by transnational scholars. There are some cautions to take to avoid perpetuating the ideologies of orientalism and categorize the units, topics, or readings from historically marginalized researchers and international faculty as the "other." Instructors must not exoticize the readings or other learning materials. For example, in a media or popular culture class, instead of using film and television shows made by the US companies and director to represent the "other" cultures, instead consider using works by transnational directors who engage in larger national and transnational issues from a larger and non-US perspective. For example, Turkish-Italian director Ferzan Ozpetek grapples with issues of transnational movements, immigration, and homosexuality. Similarly, if we teach a course on race, we should be able to take a transnational perspective and talk about race as a transnational construct rather than highly depending and focusing on the US discourse. For example, race is not simply a US discourse, and it is constructed and experiences differently in South Africa, Australia, or different European countries based on historical experiences and relationships.

Through these mindful practices, students would be exposed to learning resources that introduce them to different ways of knowing other than solely or predominantly white- and US-centric ideas, issues, scholars, and publications.

The second main issue with effort to internationalize the curriculum revolves around questions about how to decolonize institutionalized classroom cultures that silence or commodify historically marginalized and international faculty and students. Starting with the curriculum, it is often true that students from diverse backgrounds and international students do not see themselves in the curriculum. The issues pertaining to their lives, experiences, or communities are often glossed over, and in some cases, the subjects are mishandled or inaccurately and partially addressed. This disconnection often silences the students' experiences, particularly international students.

Regarding classroom practices and cultural expectations, not all of our students come from the US. A number of them come from educational backgrounds that privilege certain classroom behaviors. For example, for some international students, participating in class discussions and openly expressing their opinions is difficult. The US classroom practices contradict teaching and learning values of the home educational models. Similarly, public speaking is new to most international students who hail from cultures where listening is preferred to talking. Additionally, English language is not the first language of most of the students. These two facts, among others, could cause the students to remain quiet and suffer in silence. Recognizing the cultural differences of and creating alternative assignments and opportunities for students who come from different backgrounds or learn differently is an effort toward decolonizing classroom practices. It is important to diversify our pedagogical approaches and recognize that there are multiple ways for students to participate, engage in class, and be part of the classroom culture. One way to internationalize the classroom requires rethinking the ways we teach and cultivate classroom culture, and another is to retool how we mentor our historically marginalized and international students to thrive in our institutions.

A third way to internationalize the classroom is to allow the students to see themselves in the curriculum either by mindfully internationalizing the readings or working with them collaboratively to add the readings of their choice. As Fanon suggested, decolonization is creating a critical consciousness, and we have to think critically about our practices.

Part of the internationalization efforts also deal with challenging and changing our institutional and departmental cultures to allow faculty, specifically international and historically marginalized faculty, to be change agents. Making internationalization and global engagement a departmental learning goal and asking that each course mindfully fulfill this requirement would be a positive step in the right direction. The international faculty who specialize in diversity-related areas and topics should be given the space and resources to develop courses in their areas of expertise, subsequently allowing them to shape the curriculum in a way that they would feel comfortable doing. This same faculty should also be provided with resources to add off-campus and international engagement opportunities for their students. These opportunities would help to internationalize the curriculum as well as contribute to the retention of the institution's diverse faculty members by allowing them to engage in the internationalization efforts as they see fit.

The third main issue that must be addressed in order to successfully internationalize the curriculum is challenging the curricular exoticization of diverse and international voices as well as the mistreatment of their work. As I already implied, this is a real problem within internationalization efforts. Since global engagement and internationalization have become academic and curricular buzzwords, most of the universities and colleges in the US have been working on globalizing their curricula. This is a commendable effort; however, it may produce some dire outcomes. If we aim to mindfully decolonize individual course syllabi, we have to rethink the ways in which the larger departmental curriculum is structured. If departments are committed to internationalizing their curricula, all the instructors committed to this agenda must frame their courses within the parameters of this learning goal. Internationalization, however, does not mean simply including courses that use US perspectives to examine other cultures, foreign politics, and global issues but rather diversifying the perspectives and opening new spaces to include authors writing from these different perspectives. However, each syllabus and the departmental curriculum itself should not treat national and international diversity as the "other" or exoticize these materials and authors. True internationalization efforts aim to decenter the mainstream US perspectives. Hence, instead of treating international topics or authors as the "other," internationalization treats the core of the course without calling attention to itself and its place in the curriculum. These efforts require a shift in designing the courses and looking at the departmental curriculum. Furthermore, there is a need to shift the pedagogical tactics or approaches to recenter the "international curriculum" as the new center rather than the "other" or the periphery. Moreover, it is important not to exoticize the international authors whose works are being read or the international faculty who might be teaching these courses from an international perspective. Also crucial is to decolonize the curriculum by decentering Western perspectives and introducing different ways of knowing (Atay, 2018; Maathai, 2004, 2007, 2009; Mutua, 2012; Shome, 2013; Toyosaki & Chuang, 2018; Yueh & Copeland, 2015).

The fourth and the last issue in internationalizing the curriculum revolves around decentering and decolonizing the US-centric ways of teaching and being in the classroom. In order to decolonize and decenter, as instructors, we, historically marginalized faculty and mainstream faculty alike, must question our role in the classroom. Furthermore, we must also be self-reflexive and carefully examine the power positions we occupy. Obviously some faculty have more power than others, but I believe we all have to understand and be self-reflexive about the positions that we occupy in academia. For example, while international faculty might not have power in certain situations, we have power to deconstruct how the US academy represents non-Western knowledges.

Overall, there is a need to shift our mindsets, to embrace diverse and inclusive pedagogues to meet the learning needs of our diverse students. With increasing numbers of international students studying in the US, our classrooms will not be the same. While some see the classroom as a liberating space, others might find it an oppressive and fearful cultural space. If, for example, our students do not wish to orally share their perspectives or stories, we must create alternatives for them to voice their stories. We must also train ourselves and our students to listen well and without judging the accents of international students and faculty. These barriers are socially constructed, and we can have conversations about learning how to listen when we encounter non-US English accents. In regards to considering adaptable writing approaches, instructors should endeavor to diversify in ways that incorporate multiple elements of linguistic and cultural backgrounds to our teaching. For example, writing is difficult for both domestic and international students. Perhaps, we should find ways to encourage students to express themselves in meaningful ways without fear or intimidation.

The Final Story

> Marina was my new advisee. She sent me an email about wanting to talk with me about some issues she was having in one of her classes. Her email was polite and direct, but she did not mention the issue we were to discuss, so I was very curious. She gently knocked on my door two minutes before our appointment. When I invited her in and asked her to sit down, she quietly came in and hesitantly sat down in the black leather office chair. After we exchanged a few pleasantries, I asked her what she wanted to discuss. She sat silently for a bit, then she began telling me that she was fearful of public speaking and had an upcoming presentation in one of her classes in another major. I asked her why she was anxious about her presentation. Instead of looking at me, she directed her gaze at my office carpet. I hesitated to press her and instead gave her some time to collect her thoughts. Finally, she said, "I am an international student, and I feel like my English will not be good enough, and my classmates will not understand my presentation." I asked if she had talked with her instructor about her fears. She said she could not because she had already been penalized by often being on her phone. I asked, "What do you mean?" She replied that the instructor had called her out in class and asked her not to text during the lectures. Immediately, I knew where this conversation was headed. Marina was basically using her phone to look up words or information she was not familiar with because of her lack of cultural references. She was very present in the classroom but trying to learn by using the electronic means available to her in that moment. Her online dictionary was her lifeline to the class content. On the contrary, when she worked in a small group, she could ask her peers about concepts or cases that she was not familiar with. However, the instructor's perceptions about Marina and her presence or absence in the class were working as a barrier that deepened her fears and had negatively influenced her attitude to the class and the instructor.

Marina is only one of those students who might be struggling because of their English-language and cultural competencies. However, the lack of sensitivity and empathy toward international students and their experiences puts a real barrier between the students and the instructors. Pedagogical approaches that invite international students (or any students for that matter) to engage in the class material in different ways are welcome to support transnationalization efforts. In an era of globalization, we stand to empower our students by "globalizing" our curriculum as well. In failing to do so, we continue to support an education system that works to disempower and oppress historically marginalize groups. It is now the time to recognize marginalized voices, experiences, and scholarly works of postcolonial and transnational faculty in US communication studies curriculum.

References

Atay, A. (2015). *Globalization's impact on cultural identity formations: Queer diasporic males in cyberspace*. Lanham, MD: Lexington Books.

Atay, A. (2018). Wangari Maathai's rhetorical vision: Empowerment through education. In E. M. Mutua, A. González, & A. Wolber (Eds.), *Planting the future: The rhetorical legacy of Wangari Maathai* (pp. 83–94). Lanham, MD: Lexington Books.

Calafell, B. M., & Gutierrez-Perez, R. (2018). (Critical) love is a battlefield: Implications for critical intercultural communication pedagogical approach. In A. Atay & S. Toyosaki (Eds.), *Critical intercultural communication pedagogy* (pp. 49–64). Lanham, MD: Lexington Books.
Corsi, T., Ormieres, J-L., & Romoli, G. (Producer) & Ozpetek, F. (Director) (2001). *Le Fate Ignoranti [Motion Picture]*. Italy & France: R&C Produzioni & Les Films Balenciaga.
Fanon, F. (1963). *The wretched of the earth*. New York, NY: Grove Press.
Freire, P. (2000). *Pedagogy of the oppressed*. New York, NY: Continuum.
hooks, b. (1994). *Teaching to transgress: Education as the practice of freedom*. New York, NY: Routledge.
hooks, b. (1996). *Reel to real: Race, class, and sex at the movies*. New York, NY: Routledge.
hooks, b. (2001). *All about love: New visions*. New York, NY: HarperCollins.
Maathai, W. (2004). *The Green Belt Movement: Sharing the approach and the experience*. New York, NY: Lantern Books.
Maathai, W. (2007). *Unbowed*. New York: Anchor Books.
Maathai, W. (2009). *The challenge of Africa*. New York, NY: Pantheon Books.
Mohanty, C. T. (2003). *Feminism without borders: Decolonizing theory, practicing solidarity*. Durham, NC: Duke University Press.
Muhs, G. G., Niemann, Y. F., González, C. G., & Harris, A. P. (2012). *Presumed incompetent: The intersections of race and class for women in academia*. Boulder, CO: Utah State University Press.
Mutua, E. M. (2012). You were not born here. *Women and Language, 35*(2), 91–94.
Ozpetek, F. (2011). *La Fate Ignoranti*. R&C Produzioni.
Shome, R. (2013). Internationalizing critical race communication studies: Transnationality, space, and affect. In T. K. Nakayama & R. T. Halualani (Eds.), *The handbook of critical intercultural communication* (pp. 149–170). Malden, MA: Wiley-Blackwell.
Shome, R., & Hegde, R. S. (2002). Postcolonial approaches to communication: Charting the terrain, engaging the intersections. *Communication Theory, 12*(3), 249–270.
Toyosaki, S., & Chuang, H. Y. (2018). Critical intercultural communication pedagogy from within: Textualizing intercultural and intersectional self-reflexivity. In A. Atay & S. Toyosaki (Eds.), *Critical intercultural communication pedagogy* (pp. 227–247). Lanham, MD: Lexington Books.
Tuck, E., & Yang, K. W. (2012). Decolonization is not a metaphor. *Decolonization: Indigeneity, Education & Society, 1*(1), 1–40.
Wands, A. J. (Producer), & O' Donnell, D. (Director). (1999). *East is East*. United Kingdom: FilmFour & Assassin Films.
Warren, J. T. (1999). Whiteness and cultural theory: Perspectives on research and education. *Urban Review, 31*(2), 185–2003.
Warren, J. T., & Hytten, K. (2004). The faces of whiteness: Pitfalls and the critical democrat. *Communication Education, 53*(4), 321–339.
Yep, G. A. (2013). Queering/quaring/kauering/crippin'/transing "other bodies" in intercultural communication. *Journal of International and Intercultural Communication, 6*(2), 118–126.
Yep, G. A., & Lescure, R. M. (2018). Obstructing the process of becoming: Basal whiteness and the challenge to critical intercultural communication. In A. Atay & S. Toyosaki (Eds.), *Critical intercultural communication pedagogy* (pp. 115–136). Lanham, MD: Lexington Books.
Yueh, H.-I. S., & Copeland, K. D. (2015). The embodiment of intercultural communication through course syllabi. *Intercultural Communication Studies, 24* (2), 135–154.

16 The Value of a Fulbright

Internationalizing Education One Person at a Time

Wendy Leeds-Hurwitz

To internationalize the curriculum means that faculty place what they teach, and also help students place what they learn, into a global context. "Internationalization is about taking the rest of the world seriously, not only one's home country, and can be thought of as the formal term for thinking globally before acting locally. It requires knowing enough about the larger world to act appropriately in a specific context and location, especially when interacting with cultural others."[1] Faculty members are not always considered central to internationalization, but since they design and teach the courses that make up the curriculum, they most certainly should be. At the same time, faculty members not only teach courses, they stand at the center of ever-widening circles of influence. These include their own students most obviously, but also their peers and students of those peers, their administrators and efforts to make internationalization integral to an entire campus, and even community members and organizations, especially in these days of community-based learning and applied communication.

All too often, the model for internationalization has been the weakest form of faculty development, where someone in university administration chooses an appropriate goal and sets about trying to convince the faculty to change the ways they teach. Logically, this is backward: to be effective, changes need to come from the faculty, in this case preferably through international experiences that influence their understanding, and thus their courses. The American Council on Education (ACE) understands this: "As the primary drivers of teaching and research, faculty are the lynchpins of student learning; in order for students to achieve global learning goals, faculty must be globally competent themselves, able to convey their international experience and expertise in the classroom, well prepared to engage effectively with international students, and actively committed to the internationalization endeavor" (2017, p. 38).

It seems completely obvious to assume with ACE that faculty members are central to student learning, and thus the logical starting point for curricular changes such as internationalization (see also Engwall, 2016; O'Hara, 2009; Snow, 2008). We can similarly assume that ACE is correct in suggesting that faculty members need to be globally competent themselves to adequately integrate international content into courses. Thus "the surest road to internationalizing the US faculty is to make sure that they receive some international experience" (Finkelstein, Walker, & Chen, 2013, p. 338). As Eddy (2014) points out, US faculty typically travel abroad far less frequently than their EU counterparts—partly because the US is so large, but partly because not everyone yet understands the value of international experience. Until this changes, internationalization of the curriculum seems likely to lag.

The Fulbright Program

The Fulbright program is the largest, oldest, best-organized, and most effective tool for supporting an extended stay in another country for academic purposes and is thus a significant way to internationalize the curriculum. In 1945, Senator J. William Fulbright introduced legislation establishing the program that now bears his name, and it was signed into law by President Truman in 1946. Lebovic (2013) details the largely forgotten story of how, in the aftermath of World War II, "rotting food and rusting trucks . . . bequeathed to us the world's pre-eminent international exchange program" (p. 281). The US Department of State manages the program through the Bureau of Educational and Cultural Affairs. Today, there are approximately 8,000 Fulbright grants awarded annually, for travel to or from 160 countries, for students, scholars, K–12 teachers, professionals, and groups (https://eca.state.gov/fulbright/fulbright-programs). More than 380,000 awards have been given out since the program's inception (https://eca.state.gov/fulbright/about-fulbright). Traditional Fulbright awards most often entail a year of travel, but Senior Specialist awards last 2 to 6 weeks, providing a new option for those who cannot initially imagine spending a year away from home. Fulbright awards go in two directions: they either bring people to the US or send US citizens to other countries. At least when faculty are involved, both types result in internationalizing the curriculum in the US in a wide variety of often subtle ways, not least as a result of further collaborations between those who met as a result of a Fulbright award. This chapter will focus on faculty members rather than other types of grantees.

Fulbright awards bring about internationalization by starting with individuals. The argument that this is essential has been made often (most recently in Niehaus & Williams, 2016), and even has been made specifically for the discipline of communication. Oliver (1956) provides an early example of proposing Fulbrights as a tool for developing international connections within communication; DeWine (1995) expands this to living abroad more generally. Beebe (1999) argues that communication is an obvious discipline to emphasize internationalization, so that "communication departments should be in the forefront to seek creative ways to initiate and sustain contacts with international scholars" (p. 63). Stohl (2007) summarizes the position concisely: "If we want to internationalize the university, we have to internationalize the faculty" (p. 367). Given these and many other sources published over the last few decades, it is only surprising that more has not already been done and that we are yet again discussing the need for internationalization.

Shute (2002) considers the specific activities that develop interculturally competent faculty; his answers range from hiring those with international experience to providing funding for research/teaching related travel to rewarding those who improve international activities, whether these be leading study abroad programs or international research collaborations (see also Alkarzon, 2016; O'Hara, 2009). These goals fit well with what Fulbright awards offer.

Stories of the Impact of Fulbright Awards on Internationalization

The best way to demonstrate the value of a Fulbright award is to provide specific details based on actual experiences. First, my own stories, since I know them best, followed by those of other Fulbrighters.[2] I have received two Fulbright awards, one to bring an international scholar to my US university and one to travel abroad myself, which gives me experience for how these grants work in both directions. I'll briefly describe each, focusing on the impact on curriculum.

> In 1983, I brought a Belgian colleague, Yves Winkin of the Université de Liège, to the University of Wisconsin-Parkside as a Fulbright Visiting Scholar. Aside from the impact on department colleagues who met him, the students he taught on campus, the talks given to local schools and community groups, and the joint publications we went on to write, all of which might have been predicted, there were unexpected results involving ever more people. I'll describe just one. Winkin led a campuswide faculty seminar on noted French sociologist Pierre Bourdieu, drawing in participants from communication, education, sociology, anthropology, political science, and philosophy. As one of Bourdieu's students, Winkin was quite familiar with his work whereas, at that time, few in the US knew much about it, although they were eager to learn. In addition to content learning, the faculty seminar helped build a community of scholars across disciplines on campus, which led to a wide variety of collaborative projects. Among others, this new community had the side effect of strengthening the international studies program just getting started on campus, clearly an element of internationalizing the entire university curriculum.

This example demonstrates the simplest, least-time-consuming form of involvement in a Fulbright, as well as several related results:

1. Hosting an international scholar at a US institution who introduces international content into courses.
2. Making international connections for US colleagues.
3. Becoming involved in campuswide efforts to internationalize the curriculum.

Several decades later, in 2012, I held a Fulbright Senior Specialist Award to work with the Centro de Inovação e Estudo da Pedagogia no Ensino Superior (CINEP), a teaching center at the Instituto Politécnico de Coimbra, in Portugal.

> I had spent 2011 writing a book intended for a French audience about pedagogy in the US (with Peter Hoff, at Winkin's request), which I mentioned to CINEP's director, Susana Gonçalves. She asked that Peter and I prepare a monograph version emphasizing the most directly relevant parts; this was translated into Portuguese, published, and distributed to faculty on campus. In addition to multiple campus presentations, I served as in-house consultant, working with one group about to visit US teaching centers and another applying for a major grant to improve pedagogy. I prepared a wide variety of documentation for CINEP's use after my stay ended, including a template for peer observation of teaching, a PowerPoint on best practices for blended delivery, a bibliography on math pedagogy, handouts on how to handle plagiarism, and how to socialize students to college.

The new result here is:

4. Showing how international knowledge applies directly to local pedagogy.

Next follow a series of stories from other communication faculty members who also have been Fulbrighters. Donal Carbaugh (University of Massachusetts, Amherst) had the title of Bicentennial Chair of North American Studies and Distinguished Fulbright Professor in Finland and has held Specialist grants as well. He writes:

> When I was in Finland on my first Fulbright, there was a television program broadcast in the US about Finns. It was a segment of the newsmagazine, *60 Minutes*. I heard about it immediately from my Finnish friends and colleagues, as well as from friends in the US. After viewing it, I decided to use it upon my return to my home university, where I showed it to students. They reacted to it by formulating impressions of Finland and Finnish people. At the same time, a colleague in Finland would show it to Finnish students, who formulated impressions about Americans. Then we would have our students share their impressions, thereby engaging in an intercultural discussion about it. Each group was not very pleased about the impressions formulated and would have to figure out why. This sort of exercise proved invaluable as students learned from each other not only, ostensibly, about those on the other side of the Atlantic, but perhaps more importantly about their own limits in developing such an understanding. Many concluded they would not watch the news or televised broadcasts the same way again. We have conducted this sort of cross-cultural exercise for two decades.

From this we can draw several conclusions. First and most central, Fulbright awards frequently result in:

5. US faculty adding international content to existing courses.
6. Developing international connections across student populations.

In addition, Carbaugh mentions that upon his return to the US, he developed connections with a variety of Finnish-American organizations, and that this can lead to:

7. Developing one or more community-based learning activities.

Richard Buttny (Syracuse University) concludes that "The primary benefit from my Fulbright to India and Malaysia has been that the experience allows me to speak with more knowledge about what's going on in those countries for my Intercultural course. For instance, I can tell the story of the ethnic tensions and conflict in Malaysia. Also, of Islamization of the Malays of Malaysia." This provides a further example of how content learned during a Fulbright can be brought into the classroom, probably the most immediate result for most of us.

James Schnell (Ohio Dominican College), a Fulbrighter in both Cambodia and Myanmar, writes:

> I have found that, since my Fulbright experience in Cambodia, I've got cross-cultural dynamics on my mind a lot more than before and that this impacts the content I stress in my courses. I find that in many of my course lectures, when I'm seeking to illustrate communication concepts, I will often stress cross-cultural contexts. I've come to think of this as "cross-cultural dynamics across the communication curriculum" much the way one hears about "writing across the curriculum" or "speaking across the curriculum." I teach a wide range of courses in the communication studies curriculum. Cross-Cultural Communication is one of the courses I teach, and one would expect to find cross-cultural

emphasis in such a class. However, when I teach public speaking, interpersonal communication, organizational communication, and mass media, I find that I will also stress cross-cultural dynamics in those classes as well.

This description provides further evidence of the ways in which new experiences by faculty members influence course content. In addition, Schnell mentions that some of his former students have gone on to teach English in other countries, which can more broadly lead to:

8. Advising and mentoring students.

Learning new content can also lead to the design of entire new courses, as Phillip Glenn (Emerson College), who has held a traditional Fulbright to the Czech Republic and a Specialist award to Moldova, explains:

> I have created a new course, *Intercultural Negotiation*, intended for Emerson's campus in the Netherlands, called Kasteel Well. This course will blend with an existing course in Leadership for a two-course summer experience. Students will reside at Emerson's Kasteel Well. We will travel to nearby sites that are nerve centers for international, intercultural challenges in negotiation and leadership. These will include inter-governmental, governmental, NGOs, for-profit, and non-profit organizations. My work in creating this new course was shaped by my Fulbright appointments in the Czech Republic (1995) and Moldova (2005), by past collaboration with a Polish colleague who was in the US on a Fulbright, and by a recent semester teaching at a university in Barcelona.

This gives evidence for:

9. Introducing new courses into the curriculum.
10. Developing international experiences for US students.

Ted Schwalbe (State University of New York, College at Fredonia), has held both traditional Fulbrights (Bulgaria, Hungary) and Specialist awards (Namibia, Swaziland, and Albania).

> I created two new courses as a result of my Fulbright experiences. One was COMM 385 International Media and the second was COMM 386 International Films. COMM 385 has also become a part of our General Education course options. Interestingly, I have used a mini-variation of the film course during later Fulbright experiences by having community film nights in various countries. I have also incorporated more international media discussion into my existing courses especially the introductory Mass Media and Society course.

His example documents both constructing new courses and updating old ones, as well as suggesting:

11. Introducing global diversity courses as a requirement.

Schwalbe continues: "Due to my Fulbright experiences and understanding what it feels like to live in another culture, I have worked very hard to try and make our international students here at Fredonia get acclimated. In addition to bringing them into classes, I have established a fairly regular Friday coffee hour just to meet and help." This enables:

12. Involving international students in courses while simultaneously facilitating their campus integration.

After describing study-abroad activities taking US students to Bulgaria, he did the reverse by bringing Turkish students to the US. Then, in a third iteration, he brought US students involved in the second experience to Turkey. This leads to:

13. Developing international research collaborations and involving students.

Stacey K. Sowards (University of Texas at El Paso), who has held both a student Fulbright award and a faculty award, describes her experience thus:

> In 2000, I received a Fulbright for my dissertation research in Indonesia. I spent the prior year studying Indonesian and preparing for my research work there. After arriving, I had to spend more time studying Indonesian so that I could do my field research and field interviews. That fluency in Indonesian led to study-abroad programs, a 20-year research trajectory, a million-dollar university partnership grant from USAID, and numerous publications as well as collegial collaborations between Indonesian and US institutions that I was able to lead. I also started studying Dutch so that I could examine how the Indonesian diaspora has been shaped by international forces and patterns of migration. I have spent months, if not years of my life dedicated to becoming fluent in Spanish, Indonesian, Dutch, Portuguese. If it hadn't been for that first Fulbright for my dissertation research, I probably would have only studied Spanish. Such experiences fundamentally change our research trajectories, language experiences, and how we relate those to our students and our US-based institutions.

This leads to:

14. Studying and/or using language in new ways, in and out of the classroom.
15. Establishing one or more forms of international institutional affiliations.

Clearly, this and other stories also provide evidence of the influence that a Fulbright award has on research, although that is not being highlighted here.

Ann Miller (University of Central Florida) has been a Fulbright Africa Regional Scholar and a Fulbright Specialist; she specifically addresses the fit between teaching and research and the way a Fulbright can contribute to both simultaneously.

> Although my Fulbright grant was actually a research award, when I arrived at my Ugandan host institution I was asked if I might additionally co-teach a course in the master's program. My acceptance of that request turned out to be one of the most significant decisions I made, and is, I suppose, proof of C. S. Lewis' contention that "what one calls the interruptions are precisely one's real life." As a result of my involvement with that two-week course, I have returned repeatedly to teach and mentor research at my host institution,

and published multiple journal articles with student and faculty co-authors there. Among many other amazing students, I have taught a blogger who fled the Democratic Republic of Congo in the middle of the night, another who remained as one of the few journalists in South Sudan during the current civil war, yet another whose research passion was to explore the role of radio in reconciling former Lord's Resistance Army fighters with their home communities. Stories like these regularly pop up in my US classes. Also, we now have a departmental Memorandum of Understanding with my host institution that we are currently attempting to expand to include a focus on joint research. Two of my colleagues—Tim and Deanna Sellnow—have now been to visit my host institution, and we are trying to work out a plan for all three of us to teach modules in the new strategic communication master's program.

Beyond providing further examples of the fit between research and teaching, mentoring students, and details about establishing institutional affiliations, this adds a new result:

16. Integrating students into the publication process.

Jeff Kelly Lowenstein (Grand Valley State University) held a Fulbright Specialist award to South Africa. As one set of results,

> I convened a meeting of a half-dozen journalists from Africa, Europe, and the United States at the African Investigative Journalism Conference. We decided to go beyond investigating an individual state or national lottery to shine light on the nearly $300 billion industry. Our team grew throughout the year, eventually comprising more than 40 people from 10 countries. I wanted to present about the investigation I had led and to bring students. I brought two Multimedia Journalism majors with me to the Global Investigative Journalism Conference held in South Africa in 2017. Together the pair wrote, shot video, snapped pictures, and tweeted throughout the four days, as part of the first-ever student newsroom. They were the only American students, together with more than 40 students from throughout South Africa and Germany. Both students had to purchase passports, as neither of them had ever been outside of North America.

This then introduces:

17. Participating in international conferences, including students as possible.

Mara Adelman (Seattle University), has published on English as a second language (ESL), and thus that topic has been directly relevant to her Fulbright Specialist awards.

> When I do Fulbrights I often speak to ESL audiences about integrating cross-cultural with ESL. In China I spoke at such a conference for over 300 ESL teachers. Also, I was asked by Fudan to develop a cross-cultural course that would be required of their undergraduates in English—so I worked hard to adapt my teaching to provide cross-cultural comparisons that were Chinese specific. Second, when I was in Ethiopia, I did workshops for the US Embassy

for Ethiopian politicians (public speaking), journalists (interviewing skills), and PR professionals. Finally, now that I am retired, I do community workshops on "World Travel on a Shoestring" and encourage people to get their ESL certificates. My university was not really interested in promoting cross-cultural communication, but I did speak about the Fulbright Specialist awards for faculty.

Her comments support the prior points about new course development, revising existing courses, and working with the local community but also adds a way to expand the impact of one Fulbright on the curriculum:

18. Encouraging colleagues to apply for Fulbright awards.

Perhaps with a few more Fulbrighters on staff, her department and/or university might more readily recognize the value of internationalization.

Ayseli Usluata (Yeditepe University, Turkey) used her Fulbright award to travel from Turkey to the USA.

> As a Fulbrighter at the University of Kansas, I translated Turkish author Sait Faik's stories and poems into English, which were published in Kansas magazines. Upon my return to Turkey, I taught English at the Preparatory School of Middle East Technical University (METU) in Ankara. After two years, I proposed "Translation" as a new Freshman elective course open to all departments. I talked with colleagues at several international conferences, emphasizing the importance of interpersonal communication to understand the cultures of different countries, and we decided to have our students communicate through the Internet, including using email. I first started with a German friend from Karlsruhe University; the whole semester, students from our two universities exchanged e-mail messages about their culture, daily lives, etc. This international exchange expanded in following semesters to include Canadian, Swedish, and American students. On a visit to Nebraska-Lincoln University, I met Dr. Charles Braithwaite, who talked about his Global Classroom project (to improve students' practical experience with intercultural communication) and expanded from email exchanges to video conferencing between students and from discrete teaching to joint video-conferencing. This collaboration has continued every semester since 2000. I also organized two international conferences at Yeditepe University.

This adds support to new course development, course revision, establishing international collaborations for students, and participation in international conferences. For the first time, it introduces:

19. Publishing translations of academic work for students.

David Altheide (Arizona State University), a Fulbright Specialist in Germany and Portugal, writes:

> One interesting development was contributing to some disciplinary integration. I am a sociologist with a long history of research, teaching, and publishing in mass communication, news and propaganda, and fear communication—all areas that are also associated with communication departments and scholarship. It seemed

that my Fulbright lectures and seminars attracted students and faculty from various disciplines who might not otherwise have much contact. Our conversations, often during meals, etc., occasionally sparked some shared topics of interest that could promote collaborative work in the future in the host institutions.

This demonstrates a final result:

20. Increasing interdisciplinarity so that communication faculty members and/or students collaborate across campus.

Conclusion

Fulbright awards have long proven effective in influencing the way individual faculty members perceive their subjects and teach. Since international travel can be crucial to internationalizing the curriculum, and since Fulbright awards finance a scholar's extended travel to a different country, thereby broadening that scholar's global perspective and adding tools to their teaching arsenal, these awards have, over the decades, profoundly affected courses taught by thousands of individuals. Fulbright awards have the greatest impact on the individual recipient, who receives an opportunity to travel internationally. Since virtually all Fulbright scholars have students and will subsequently have even more, not to mention colleagues, the impact of the program multiplies exponentially. This iconic program that appears on its face to be changing one scholar at a time is in fact capable—through this ripple effect—of internationalizing entire curricula. Chaos theory's most memorable trope, the "butterfly effect," provides one way to describe the impact.[3] As rephrased by Gaiman and Pratchett (2006, p. 136), "A butterfly flaps its wings in the Amazonian jungle, and subsequently a storm ravages half of Europe." Fulbright may have succeeded far beyond his wildest dreams in creating his famous grants program.

Other international exchange programs have comparable effects on faculty members, and thus on internationalization of the curriculum (Tournes & Scott-Smith, 2018; Perna et al., 2014). Some particularly well-known examples include the German Academic Exchange Service, the Japan International Cooperation Agency, and both the ERASMUS and SOCRATES programs in the European Union. In addition, there are now many institutes for advanced study (readily located through organizations such as EURIAS, the European Institutes for Advanced Study), for which US scholars are frequently eligible. Given that fellowships within any of these exchange programs or institutes also involve long-term international stays, they can have similar impact on internationalizing the curriculum as do Fulbright awards.

In 1992, Carter lamented "that so little attention has been written regarding the role of faculty in the implementation of international competence in higher education" (p. 39). Not enough has changed in the past 27 years. The role of faculty members in internationalization efforts is critical. This chapter has emphasized Fulbright awards because they have always been, and remain, one of the easiest and most obvious ways to internationalize the faculty, and thereby the curriculum. Starting with a single faculty member, Fulbright awards, or any international faculty exchange program, can result in substantial influence across an ever-widening group of students, colleagues, and institutions. Fulbrighters stand at the center of multiple circles of influence. The value of a Fulbright is thus the value of the butterfly flapping its wings in the Amazonian jungle: one small change causing larger, often unanticipated, results.

Notes

1. I wrote these words in 2011 and still find them a useful explanation today. This is the opening to "Internationalization," a section of the National Communication Association's website first published in 2012, which I prepared for the organization. The section was revised in 2013 to incorporate content from the task force on internationalization, on which I served. It can be found at: https://www.natcom.org/academic-professional-resources/internationalization
2. My thanks to all the Fulbrighters who were able to make time to share their stories. My apologies for having had to shorten most of them. In particular, nearly everyone wrote about how much their time abroad has influenced them and how pleased they are to have had the experience.
3. The original discussion was put forth by Lorenz in a 1972 conference paper titled "Predictability: Does the flap of a butterfly's wings in Brazil set off a tornado in Texas?" which remained unpublished (though oft cited) until Lorenz (1993).

References

Alkarzon, A. (2016). The influence of faculty exchange programs on faculty members' professional development. *Research in Higher Education Journal, 30*. Retrieved from http://www.aabri.com/manuscripts/152371.pdf

American Council on Education. (2017). *Mapping internationalization on US campuses: 2017 edition*. Washington, DC: American Council on Education. Retrieved from https://www.acenet.edu/news-room/Documents/Mapping-Internationalization-2017.pdf

Beebe, S. A. (1999). International communication education. In W. G. Christ (Ed.), *Leadership in times of change: A handbook for communication and media administrators* (pp. 61–84). Washington, DC: National Communication Association.

Carter, H. M. (1992). Implementation of international competence strategies: Faculty. In C. B. Klasek (Ed.), *Bridges to the future: Strategies for internationalizing higher education* (pp. 39–51). Carbondale, IL: Association of International Education Administrators.

DeWine, S. (1995). A new direction: Internationalizing communication programs. *Journal of the Association of Communication Administration, 3*, 204–210.

Eddy, P. L. (2014). Faculty as border crossers: A study of Fulbright faculty. *New Directions for Higher Education, 165*, 19–30.

Engwall, L. (2016). The internationalization of higher education. *European Review, 24*(2), 221–231.

Finkelstein, M. J., Walker, E., & Chen, R. (2013). The American faculty in an age of globalization: Predictors of internationalization of research content and professional networks. *Higher Education, 66*, 325–340. doi:10.1007/s10734-012-9607-3

Gaiman, N., & Pratchett, T. (2006). *Good omens*. New York: William Morrow.

Lebovic, S. (2013). From war junk to educational exchange: The World War II origins of the Fulbright program and the foundations of American cultural globalism, 1945–1950. *Diplomatic History, 37*(2), 280–312.

Lorenz, E. L. (1993). *Essence of chaos*. Seattle, WA: University of Washington Press.

Niehaus, E., & Williams, L. (2016). Faculty transformation in curriculum transformation: The role of faculty development in campus internationalization. *Innovative Higher Education, 41*(1), 59–74.

O'Hara, S. (2009). Vital and overlooked: The role of faculty in internationalizing U.S. campuses. *IIE Study Abroad White Paper Series: Meeting America's Global Education Challenge: Expanding Study Abroad Capacity at U.S. Colleges and Universities, 6*, 38–45.

Oliver, R. T. (1956). Speech teaching around the world: An initial survey. *The Speech Teacher, 5*, 102–108.

Perna, L. W., Orosz, K., Gopaul, B., Jumakulov, Z., Ashirbekov, A., & Kishkentayeva, M. (2014). Promoting human capital development: A typology of international scholarship programs in higher education. *Educational Researcher, 43*(2), 63–73.

Shute, J. (2002). The influence of faculty in shaping internationalization. In S. Bond & C. Bowry (Eds.), *Connections and complexities: The internationalization of Canadian higher education* (pp. 114–123). Winnipeg, Canada: Centre for Research and Development in Higher Education.

Snow, N. (2008). International exchanges and the US image. *The Annals of the American Academy of Political and Social Science*, 616(1), 198–222.

Stohl, M. (2007). We have met the enemy and he is us: The role of the faculty in the internationalization of higher education in the coming decade. *Journal of Studies in International Education*, 11, 359–372.

Tournes, L., & Scott-Smith, G. (Eds.). (2018). *Global exchanges: Scholarships and transnational circulations in the modern world*. New York: Berghahn.

17 The Three Pillars of Short Course-Abroad Experience

Ismael Lopez Medel

Two years ago, a group of my students at Azusa Pacific University paid a visit to a small creative boutique in Barcelona, where we learned about data-driven marketing strategies to connect Nescafe's Nespresso coffee with Middle Eastern consumers. The creative director carefully and passionately explained the cultural challenges of the project, the innovative approach, and the logistical details that resulted in a successful campaign. My students left the agency overwhelmed by the complexity of the project and amazed at the amount of time and care the creative director had dedicated to them. As we were heading toward our next destination, one of them quietly smiled and announced to the group: "I have now found what I want to do with my life!" At that moment, for that student, the agency visit became a turning point, a moment of confirmation that her degree in public relations was the right one for her. Through experiences like this, a short course-abroad program becomes much more than mere travel for students. Particularly in the field of communication, the exposure to trends, innovation, and international best practices make short study-abroad programs the ideal complement to the academic programs.

Such experiences transpire every year as millions of students worldwide study abroad and encounter one of the landmarks of a well-rounded college experience: internationalization. Every year, a significant number of students travel abroad as part of their academic programs. According to data from the Education at a Glance report from the Organisation for Economic Co-operation and Development (OECD), the number of students traveling abroad has "exploded" from 2 million in 1999 to 5 million in 2018 (OECD, 2018, p. 219). The growth of international mobility has been constant, quantified at 12% each year (Sood, 2012), although it is interesting to point out that US students traveling abroad make up for a rather small percentage of that figure, only reaching 325,339 in the academic year 2015/16 (NAFSA, 2016). However, short course-abroad programs are becoming ever more popular among US university students. According to the 2018 Open Doors Report, almost 40% of the students who choose to study abroad go for short, summer programs that are less than eight weeks in duration (IEE, 2018).

International mobility has increased in the last two decades because of several advantages to the point that the OECD considers it "the key differentiating experience for students" (OECD, 2018, p. 221). Its benefits are multiple. From an academic perspective, it allows students to access quality education in a multicultural setting; it expands the opportunities to embrace knowledge in different contexts, taught with varying styles of learning in different languages. Adding an international component to an academic program enhances it and broadens the horizons of the students participating in it. In addition, multiple studies (University of

California San Diego, 2002; University of Indiana, 2009; University of Georgia, 2010; University of Minnesota, 2009; The Center for Global Education, 2011) have concluded that the students who travel abroad graduate faster and with better grades than those who do not travel abroad.

From a more practical perspective, studying abroad increases the employability of the students and their perception in the marketplace. Studying abroad provides essential skills to succeed in the marketplace, such as leadership, problem-solving capacities, independence, and languages. According to data from the Student Survey from IES Abroad, 90% of students who had participated in international programs had found jobs within six months of graduating, compared to 49% of students who had not traveled abroad (IES, 2016). Results from a report from The American Institute of Foreign Studies (AIFS) indicated that employers are more interested in hiring students who have participated in international education. In particular, global companies are "interested in whether or not a job applicant demonstrates that as a result of his or her international experience, he or she has developed the requisite skills and sensitivity that make him or her stand out as the strongest candidate for a particular job" (AIFS, 2013, p. 3). In Europe, the unemployment rate of students who participated in the Erasmus program is 23% lower than average, according to data from the International Exchange Erasmus Student Network (IEESN, 2014).

Studying abroad is also increasingly affordable and flexible, offering a multitude of formats and possibilities for students to participate. From the perspective of the organizing faculty, summer study-abroad courses present a complicated logistical challenge, a time-consuming effort that undoubtedly includes a degree of frustration, but also an excellent opportunity to offer students a life-changing experience (Deardoff, 2006; Dwyer, 2004; Tarrant, Rubin, & Stoner, 2015).

I have spent my entire academic career involved in the internationalization of the university within the field of public relations and advertising from two different perspectives. I spent the first ten years of my career in Europe actively participating in the internationalization of my university through the European Union's Erasmus programs and initiatives. As the associate dean of the School of Communication at CEU San Pablo University in Madrid, I built international programs, established partnerships with European universities, and promoted student participation and success in international mobility programs. Later on, as I moved to the United States, I continued promoting the internationalization of the curriculum, both incorporating study-abroad semester options to my programs and also designing, directing, and leading short course-abroad programs. I currently direct the undergraduate program of Public Relations at Azusa Pacific University in Los Angeles, California.

Over the last eight years, I have developed a method to organize the study-abroad programs I direct. This design rests upon three main pillars: academic, professional, and cultural. These three pillars are commonly used elsewhere, and they are interconnected and function as a unity, making the entire program cohesive. The academic component is the first element, as it justifies the very existence of the study-abroad program. Connecting a short-term international trip with the educational content of the class also adds value to the students and the institution. The professional pillar aims to bridge the gap between the academic world and the industry. It introduces students, sometimes for the first time, to the reality of the communication industries. Students have the opportunity to meet top professionals in the field and learn about their struggles, successes, and experiences working in the field. In my trips, I try to include both agencies (public relations, branding, digital, traditional advertising) as well as clients to show students the entire process. Lastly, the cultural pillar broadens students' perception of the local cultures, traditions, and customs while allowing students to reflect on their own culture. The presence of these three components can create robust and meaningful short course-abroad experiences for students and bring value to an institution. In this chapter, I will describe in detail how each pillar functions individually in my course-abroad programs.

The Academic Pillar

In this section, I will briefly contextualize the idea of the curriculum integration component of the course abroad, emphasizing its importance, and then explain the logistical implications of the academic pillar for the design process. I will then review the course selection, format, and design.

Institutions offer different formats for international courses. As a reference, we will use the classification provided by the Forum of Education Abroad, which distinguishes six different types: reciprocal exchange programs, integrated university study, faculty-led short- and long-term programs, informal, and other types (FEA, 2015a, p. 20). My institution, Azusa Pacific University, offers four options for international programs: semester-abroad programs organized by the university, programs organized by a third-party, short-term program (called Go Terms), and service-learning courses, called Action Teams. The international life at Azusa Pacific is organized at the Center for Global Learning and Engagement (CGLE) that sets 15 goals for global studies: self-limitation, local rootedness, social solidarity, cultural inquiry, intercultural experimentation, self-awareness, emotional intelligence, perspective taking, language development, global awareness, issue analysis, documentation, ethical reasoning, perspective transformation, and cosmopolitan response (APU, 2019).

The academic pillar rests fundamentally in curriculum integration, which is a practice well researched and documented in the field (Hulstrand, 2012) and a key element in the internationalization efforts of higher education institutions. NAFSA defines it as the "approaches designed to fully integrate study abroad options into the college experience and academic curricula for students in all majors," which Brewer and Cunningham summarize it as "making sure that students can receive the credit towards their degree programs for courses taken abroad (2009, p. 8). Even in the short duration of the summer study abroad, students can gain more knowledge if the content of the course is directly related to the academic content of the course. (Spencer & Tuma, 2008)

The importance of curriculum integration is well accredited as one of the best practices in the field, according to organizations such as the Forum of Education Abroad (FEA, 2015a, p. 5), which places curriculum integration as one of the main concerns for the success of international programs (FEA, 2015b). Similarly, NAFSA specifies that a robust curriculum integration rests on four elements: the support from the institution to develop curriculum integration, the transferability of the lessons learned, the cooperation between cross-campus partnerships, and the outcomes of the program (2015b). The literature in the field strongly supports this argument. For instance, Gayle Woodruff from the University of Minnesota, one of the references in internationalization in higher education in the United States, frames curriculum integration as a process that involves several constituents within the university seeking a response to three questions: "What do you want to see students learning while abroad? How do we want students to complement their undergraduate experience with an experience abroad? How do you advise your students?" (2009, p. 2).

The first question posed by Woodruff helps to frame the context of the course abroad and also connects the learning objectives of the program to the curriculum. In my experience, it is essential to emphasize the international element of the learning objectives. In other words, how is traveling abroad adding specific knowledge to the student that would not be available otherwise? As Goodman and Nevadomski Berdam point out: "study abroad has to be done correctly. It shouldn't be a separate or tangential part of education, but rather an integrated part of the curriculum, incorporating proper cross-cultural preparation and supportive reintegration to help students understand and internalize what they learn" (Goodman & Nevadomski, 2014). The importance of the academic pillar can be summarized in one sentence: without curriculum integration, my institution would not allow the short-term course abroad to exist.

The design process includes careful attention to curriculum integration, specifically in the goal-setting phase of the process, and the desired outcomes. The planning on the trip, including site visits, guest lectures, and activities, is a response to the learning objectives. Students can appreciate the different activities during the country portion of the course because they connect it with specific academic goals and objectives. The daily schedule abroad clearly differentiates between course-related content and free time. In my experience, the academic pillar adds value to the course because it helps students understand theories and experience learning firsthand. It also allows them to reaffirm their commitment to their field of study (I usually travel with public relations, journalism, and communication majors. In many occasions, a visit to an agency is the life-changing experience that confirms their choice of the program). In practical terms, emphasizing the academic pillar builds a solid reputation for the program, educating administration and fellow faculty members. In practical terms, emphasizing the academic pillar builds a solid reputation for the program, educating administration and fellow faculty members. The consequence is that a good academic program attracts students who are more invested, prepared, and engaged.

In order for the course to have a solid academic pillar, it is interesting to point out the role of what Eckert, Luqmani, Newell, Quraeshi, and Wagner (2013) call "the faculty champion," a person who will "have a good relationship with students and be able to sell the program to them, while students must feel that the program is run by a professor with whom they would like to spend a significant amount of time" (2013, p. 441). The "faculty champion" designs the trip, connects it with the academic content of the major, identifies opportunities, engages with students and administration, and becomes one of the critical elements for the success of the program. To implement the academic pillar, I have developed a series of five steps that help me organize the content and structure the courses accordingly.

Finding a Theme

I have found it useful to design each course using an academic theme that becomes the foundation for the content of the class. A theme helps frame the context of the trip, select the readings and assignments, organize the itinerary, and determine the type of visits and guest lectures needed in the schedule. A particular theme is also helpful to promote the course; from a communication perspective, it is easier to explain to students that we are particularly interested in a specific topic and that all the lectures will revolve around the issue. Examples of themes I have used in the past are:

Communicating the City (2008)

A trip organized between CEU San Pablo in Madrid, Spain, and InHolland Hoghescool Diemen in the Netherlands. A group of students from Madrid visited Amsterdam to learn about the rebranding of Amsterdam, and three months later, a group of Dutch students visited Madrid to study the communication efforts of the Spanish capital.

City Branding (2013)

An in-depth exploration of the branding of the city of Barcelona, Spain. Students met with architects, city planners, designers, journalists, and politicians.

Environmental Communication (2016)

Students toured New Zealand for three weeks and explored the role of the environment in the communication of the country and its challenges for the local communities.

Trends in Digital Communication (2018)

As the field of advertising changes rapidly, this trip aimed to explore the latest trends in digital communication in Amsterdam and Berlin.

Course Selection

Once the theme is selected, I choose which courses can be offered. As one of the "faculty champions" of the Department of Communication Studies at Azusa Pacific University, one of my primary responsibilities was to select which courses could be potential candidates to be offered through the course-abroad format. Out of our three undergraduate programs (public relations, journalism, and communication), I selected the following courses:

COMM 230 Small-Group Communication

It studies the dynamics of small-group communication. Students use their small group traveling abroad as a case study to apply the theories of the field.

COMM 260 Intercultural Communication

It covers the fundamental ideas of communication across cultures. Students choose one particular cultural expression to develop their projects abroad.

JOUR 410 Global Journalism

Studies global issues covered by journalism worldwide. It becomes an excellent opportunity for students to prepare culturally for the country visit.

PUBR 450 Public Relations International Experience

Ad-hoc course created to explore the trends and practices of public relations abroad. Students pay attention to the different approaches to strategic communication in other countries.

PUBR 495 Special Topics

Occasionally, we use this course to cover specific content. For instance, in 2018, I taught this course as "creative processes in advertising" because of the theme of that year's trip.

All the above courses are worth three units, a total of 45 contact hours, as in a regular semester. The classes target students from our three majors, and one of them (COMM 260) is a General Education course, attracting other majors within the university. Of course, other faculty may choose to redesign any other class to adapt it to the course-abroad program format. Still I have found that keeping a small pool of courses designated as "international" facilitates promoting the course abroad and helps the "faculty champion" navigate the lengthy approval process quickly.

The course format follows what the Forum of Education Abroad defines as "embedded programs," courses that have a travel component (Forum of Education Abroad, 2015b, p. 14). That is, we do not allow students to travel abroad for three weeks in the summer for the sake of traveling, they must be enrolled in at least one course to participate. I offer two classes per study abroad. Students have to enroll in one of them but can do two if they choose to. One of the ways administration at Azusa Pacific University promotes the internationalization is through significant discounts for summer courses. For many students, it becomes more cost-effective to take two courses in the summer than during the regular semester.

Format of the Course

To meet the academic requirement from Azusa Pacific University of 45 hours, I divide the courses into three phases: 15 hours of face-to-face lecture, 10 hours of online coursework, and 20 hours in guest lectures and agency visits on site. The face-to-face sessions currently start in May and allow me to lecture on the academic content of the trip and also address group dynamics and cultural expectations. I divide the 5-hour sessions into three blocks: lecture, debates, and workshop. The time between the two sessions is designed to cover travel expectations, practical issues, and university policies regarding logistical aspects of the trip. It is a perfect time to share details of the trip, offer advice (I usually bring a student from a former cohort to share her experiences), and review the itinerary of the trip. The small size of the group allows for more intense discussions and exercises, and I take the opportunity also to become more familiar with each student and learn about group dynamics. This week becomes an excellent opportunity to build team spirit, get to know one another and work on team dynamics.

Once abroad, the academic component takes place in the visits to local universities, which provide opportunities for the group to cover the lecture format for students to become familiar with other universities, new professors, and different styles of teaching and learning. Visiting universities in June usually means little or no interaction at all with the local students. However, it still allows the possibility of envisioning what their lives would look like if they were college students abroad.

Designing the Coursework

The last step of the academic pillar is to design the coursework specific to meet the learning goals of each course. As Andrade et al. summarize, it is vital that "the sites to be visited and the activities that occur in and out of the travel have specific learning objectives that tie into and continue the learning objectives of the course on campus before departure" (2019, p. 4). Unless the course is created specifically for a particular program (for instance, a special topic), I always refer to the approved course goals and student learning outcomes. But the particularities of the short-term program allow me to introduce creative elements in the coursework related to the international nature of the course. Over the years, I have designed multiple assignments for different courses, for instance:

PUBR 450 International Experience

We study branding and its connection to culture. We compare Interbrand's top 100 brands report (US-based) with research based on the country of destination.

COMM 260 Intercultural Communication

I teach Hofstede's national dimensions theory and ask students to choose one of the six elements of the theory and apply it to the destination country.

PUBR 450 International Experience

We visited a design studio in Barcelona to study the importance of design in the city. The designer in charge of the lecture gave students ten prompts to find in their cities of origin.

PUBR 495 Special Topics

A creative director at an advertising agency in Madrid explained the ten most important features of the city, divided students into groups, assigned them different areas, and gave them 5 hours to find those ten features and document them.

JOUR 410 Global Journalism

For three weeks, students had to compare specific coverage of global environmental issues as covered by New Zealand and American media.

The course assignments typically include in-class discussions, assigned readings, an online weekly news quiz, movie forums, and a trip diary using the format of a website. Students spend time in the face-to-face week researching, preparing their websites, and planning the data collection while abroad. The students work through our online platform (Canvas), where I create online assignments and discussion forums and share the content of each course.

The Professional Pillar

The second pillar of my course-abroad strategy is the professional component. The central idea is to connect the content of the course to the professional industries where students will eventually work. In this section of the chapter, I cover the importance of adding a professional element to the trip, review the benefits of visiting strategic communication agencies for students, and discuss the practicalities of organizing such visits.

It is well established in the literature of the field that studying abroad increases employability, reduces the time to access the job market, and improves the career development of students engaged in global learning. The amount of research that supports this argument is overwhelming. According to the Institute of International Education (IIE), studying abroad has a positive impact on the professional careers of the students. It expands the career possibilities, adds the skills required to succeed in the workplace, and those skills tend to have a long-term impact on promotion and development (Farrugia & Sanger, 2017). Similarly, Norris and Gillespie (2009) studied the effect of the professional interaction in the perception of study-abroad students, showing that a vast majority of respondents (77%) agreed that the experience had profoundly shaped their professional career (386). The impact of study abroad in the students' professional careers has also increased over time (Dwyer, 2004), and a vast majority of students surveyed connected the skills learned abroad with their career path (Dwyer & Peters, 2012). Students who traveled abroad have better creative, time-management, social, and problem-solving skills (Andrade, Dittloff, & Nath, 2019).

A survey published by IES International reported that the students who had participated in their study-abroad programs were ten points higher in the employability rate compared to students who had not engaged in global studies (IES, 2016, p. 12). The European Commission for Education and Culture offers similar conclusions: studying abroad (in this case through the Erasmus program) has profound impact on employability of students, resulting in higher employability rates, lower unemployment (EC, 2014), although some authors are also warning about the fact that the perceived benefit of study abroad on employability has gray areas. For instance, Erik van 't Klooster, from the Rotterdam School of Management, warns that short-term programs may not have a significant impact as one thought (Klooster, 2014).

The Benefits of Agency Visits

The challenge, then, is how to incorporate this significant benefit of the study-abroad experience to my communication programs. And the solution to this question is professional visits, which have become the absolute cornerstone of my offering and one of the most attractive features of the trip for students. The benefits of visiting professional agencies are three: students understand how agencies work, learn from case studies, and picture themselves as future professionals.

In our ever-changing field, agencies take different shapes and organizational structures, and they are continually evolving. The question of the future of the advertising agency is often debated in professional outlets such as *Ad Age*, *PR Week*, and *Campaign US* and is subject to much debate in the classroom. For students about to enter the workplace, understanding the professional format of the agency is crucial. The professional landscape has changed dramatically in the past decade due to the impact of technology and social media. Agencies have changed their methodologies, adapted to new formats, and shaped new relationships with clients. Many times, the organizational structures described in the textbooks we use in public relations and advertising courses have merely become obsolete due to the fast-paced changes in the industry.

To ensure that students are exposed to different types of agencies, I usually offer three to four professional visits per week. I aim to include large agencies belonging to multinational groups (such as Edelman, TBWA, or Ogilvy) as well as smaller and upcoming agencies, most of the time more specialized such as The Cocktail or 180 Amsterdam. Each agency brings its methodology and structure and shares its creative strategy. The format of the visit typically includes a tour of the agency to show different departments and functions, a short presentation of the agency, and a detailed case study. The end of the visit is reserved for a time for dialogue, which usually translates as students asking details of the speakers' professional careers and their day-to-day experience.

The second benefit of visiting agencies is learning from case studies. I have realized over the years that students are eager to connect the theories and knowledge acquired in the classroom with real-life experiences. For instance, in our public relations lectures, we teach different strategic management processes utilized in the industry, with an emphasis on Cutlip and Center's RACE model (research, action planning, communication, and evaluation), as it is the original model developed in 1963 that serves as the basis for all the updates. When we prepare the visits to the agencies, I remind students of the RACE model and ask them to identify how each agency understands the creative process. Case studies present real-life situations, problems, and challenges that students need to understand to grasp the complexity of professional work. And while most of the agencies tend to concentrate on success case studies, I also ask about failures and lessons learned to offer a more realistic and comprehensive view of the field for the students. Some examples of the case studies developed at agencies are as follows:

Sra. Wilson Barcelona (2012)

We met with the creative director, who shared his experience as a member of the jury of the Laus Awards, a local competition to reward design and creativity. Then he explained an award-winning campaign for a local restaurant that only employed former convicts.

Good Rebels Madrid (2015)

The agency had been recently named Spain's most creative digital agency and had decided to rebrand to surprise the competition. Much of our conversation revolved around this idea. We met with the CEO and the creative director, who shared a recent campaign they had developed for IKEA Spain and explained with details the logistics of the campaign and their relationship with the Swedish company.

Ogilvy Berlin (2018) shared their difficulties branding the Coca-Cola products for a younger generation that is changing consumer habits. They focused on Fanta and explained a campaign where they invited young local artists to develop the creativity of the campaign.

180 Kingsday Amsterdam (2018)

We toured the agency and met with the account director and his executive assistant. They explained the different departments of the agency and how each one of them found a career in advertising. We then met with the creative director to learn about a recent campaign developed by the agency for PlayStation.

Lastly, visiting agencies has a profound impact on students, as it helps them picture themselves as future professionals. In the classroom, students can only imagine what working for an agency may look like. On the trip, as they walk through the doors of the agencies, it immediately becomes a tangible reality. Students must meet the professionals, network with them, see the design of the agency and the profile of the employees, hear how they talk about themselves and their role in the larger structure of the agency. Of course, creative agencies are exciting environments to visit, filled with creative people, and students leave inspired, challenged, and energized.

The Cultural Pillar

Gaining knowledge of other cultures is widely accepted as one of the primary outcomes of the study-abroad experience for students, according to scholarly and industry research. At the same time, the professional associations in the field also indicate intercultural competences as one of the desired skills for students. In this last segment of the chapter, I will briefly discuss the importance of the cultural competencies as the final pillar of my study-abroad programs and offer examples of how this idea translates into specific activities during the travel component of my courses.

The scholarly literature of the field overwhelmingly supports the idea of intercultural competence as one of the benefits of study abroad (Dwyer, 2004; Chieffo & Griffiths, 2004; Shulsinger, 2017; Hadis, 2005; Cisneros-Donahue, Krentler, Reinig, & Sabol, 2012; Rundstrom Williams, 2005; Clarke, Flaherty, Wright, & McMillen, 2009). There are multiple examples of scholars who have surveyed alumni who participated in study-abroad programs, and the results always show the importance of intercultural competences. For instance, Chieffo and Griffiths surveyed alumni from the University of Maryland. They concluded that appreciation of other cultures was the top perceived outcome of the study abroad experience for students (2004, p. 173). Similarly, Cisneros-Donahue et al. (2012) measured five cognitive elements, including knowledge of cultural sensitivity: understanding how language and culture impact the ability to relate to and communicate with individuals of other cultures (p. 170) and discovered that students who had traveled abroad presented higher scores in all elements. In the last decade, professionals in the field of study abroad have also paid attention to assessment to improve the outcome measures of study-abroad programs. Scholars have increasingly noted more nuances to the initially perceived benefit of intercultural competence. For instance, Root and Ngampornchai (2012) focused on the impact of pre-departure and post-departure training in learning experiences abroad. Others, such as Deardorff have questioned the amount of time spent abroad, indicating that "the development of intercultural competence needs to be recognized as an ongoing process and not a direct result of solely one experience, such as study abroad" (2006, p. 259).

At the same time, the leading institutions devoted to promoting study-abroad programs (such as ISA, Open Doors, AIFS, IIE, Study Abroad, Diversity Abroad, and others) publish research reports that corroborate the same idea. For instance, the American Institute for Study Abroad surveyed 1,600 alumni who had participated in international programs, and 98% of the respondents reported that the program had impacted their knowledge of other cultures (AIFS, 2013, p. 10). Similarly, a study published by the Institute for the International Education of Students in 2018 confirms this: "98 percent of respondents said that study abroad helped them to understand better their cultural values and biases, and 82 percent replied that study abroad contributed to their developing a more sophisticated way of looking at the world" (Dwyer & Peters, 2012).

Lastly, the leading professional associations in the fields of advertising and public relations include the developing of intercultural competences as one of the desired skills for students. These organizations—for instance, the American Advertising Association, Interactive Advertising Bureau, Public Relations Society of America, International Association of Business Communication, Association for Education in Journalism and Mass Communication—devote efforts to promote diversity, study cultural factors affecting communication, and in development of intercultural competences as one of the crucial skills for students.

Gaining intercultural competences is, therefore, one of the main benefits of studying abroad. Students who enroll in these programs are seeking the excitement of engaging with new cultures, language, food, and cultural expressions. In the field of communication, cultural competences play a vital role in developing well-rounded professionals, and the literature of the field plays a crucial role in developing a well-rounded professional. The exposure to new cultures, languages, and worldviews permeates the entire trip. Still, I think it is essential to reinforce the intercultural element by strategically thinking about how the interaction with culture meets the learning goals of the different courses offered.

Practical Examples

From a logistical perspective, the program includes different types of experiences: museum visits, guided tours of the cities, musical performances, and gastronomical experiences. It is repeatedly one of the highlights of the trip. Some examples of how cultural activities meet the goals of the course are as follows:

PUBR 450 International Experience

In 2013, I led a program to Barcelona to study the impact of the 1992 Olympic Games in the city. The main goal of the course was to identify places and local areas that had been impacted by the games. To meet the goal, we toured the Olympic Museum, where students learned about the context of the games. Then I arranged a walking tour of Barcelona with a local architect, who showed students specific actions and places and discussed the positive and negative impact of the games on the city.

COMM 260 Intercultural Communication

One of the theories covered in the course is Hofstede's theory of national dimensions of culture. In the face-to-face portion of the trip, we study each dimension, comparing the different countries we will visit. One of the goals of the course is to identify the dimensions in the interactions with locals and their culture. In one of our visits to Berlin, we toured the Museum of German History. I hired a local guide, who showed us the museum not only from a historical and artistic perspective but from the cultural lens as well. The guide helped students identified traces of German culture through the paintings.

PUBR 450 International Experience

In our trips to Spain, I emphasize the role of gastronomy not just as a cultural expression but also as an industry. One of the goals of the course was to identify specific ways in which local brands were communicating their products. In 2015, I had students select ten local food franchises, analyzing their communication efforts, social media presence, and overall experience.

JOUR 410 Global Journalism

One of the goals of the course was to examine the role of media in the branding of New Zealand's tourism and hospitality industry. I designed a day in the program in which students first met with a local professor at the Auckland Institute of Technology, who shared the key points of criticism regarding the *Lord of the Rings* effect in New Zealand. The day after, we toured the location of the movie set of Hobbiton, this time paying attention, not to the production details of the movie but the main impact on the local community.

PUBR 495 Special Topics

In 2018 we visited Amsterdam, and one of the courses offered was a special topic on creative thinking. One of the goals for students was to discover ways in which local companies had reimagined a particular service. During our visit to the city, we had the opportunity to experience how the local chapter of an international nonprofit, Youth With a Mission, had reimagined the walking tour of Amsterdam. Instead of taking people through the Red Light District, this organization had developed a tour of the role of Amsterdam in the human rights movement. It toured the Red Light District from the perspective of the organizations that fight against modern-day slavery and human trafficking.

Conclusion

Higher education institutions agree on the importance of promoting an international agenda. All the industry indicators appreciate its crucial role as an extension of the academic career and as a tool to provide students with intercultural competencies, develop soft and hard skills, improve students' employability, and help universities offer a higher-quality education in an increasingly crowded higher education marketplace. Although these overall benefits are widely accepted, some scholars are also beginning to indicate areas of potential challenges. These include economic and political factors, the cohesiveness of curriculum integration, and the struggle to find effective ways to assess and measure international programs (Andrade et al., 2019).

Short study-abroad programs have all the potential to adjust to these new realities and to become one of the differentiating elements of academic offerings. Study-abroad programs will need to adapt to a changing landscape and do a better job at communicating its many values, beyond what faculty involved already see (Salisbury, 2012).

In the field of communication, short study-abroad experiences are perfect tools to engage students, connect with course content, and learn by doing. The nature of the courses we teach in programs such as communication, public relations, advertising, and journalism is a natural fit for international programs. But if we need to move beyond the association of study abroad as travel, or sometimes vacation, we will need to reinforce the value of our offering.

The three pillars I build my courses upon have allowed me to create meaningful and creative programs that become a natural continuation of the academic content of the degree and offer a unique experience abroad while maintaining the rigor of the semester offering. These pillars reinforce the academic component while connecting the content with the learning objectives of the classes offered. At the same time, they add value to the internationalization of our programs, educate students and administration, and help create experiences that become the highlight of the academic career of our students.

References

American Institute for Foreign Studies (AIFS). (2013). AIFS study abroad outcomes. *A View from Our Alumni, 1999–2010).* Retrieved February 19, 2019, from www.aifsabroad.com/advisors/pdf/AIFS_Study_Abroad_Outcomes.pdf

Andrade, L. M., Dittloff, S., & Nath, L. (2019). *A guide to faculty-led study abroad: How to create a transformative experience.* New York: Routledge.

Azusa Pacific University. (2019). *Global learning at APU.* Retrieved November 11, 2018, from www.apu.edu/global-engagement/learning/

Brewer, E., & Cunningham, K. (Eds.). (2009). *Integrating study abroad into the curriculum: Theory and practice across the disciplines.* Sterling, VA: Stylus.

Center for Global Education (CGE). (2011). *Impact of study abroad on retention and success.* Retrieved October 24, 2018, from http://globaledresearch.com/study-abroad-impact.asp

Chieffo, L., & Griffiths, L. (2004, Fall). Large-scale assessment of student attitudes after a short-term study abroad program. *The Interdisciplinary Journal of Study Abroad, 10,* 165–177.

Cisneros-Donahue, T., Krentler, K. A., Reinig, B., & Sabol, K. (2012). Assessing the academic benefit of study abroad. *Journal of Education and Learning, 1*(2), 169–178.

Clarke, I., III, Flaherty, T. B., Wright, N. D., & McMillen, R. M. (2009). Student intercultural proficiency from study abroad programs. *Journal of Marketing Education, 31*(2), 173–181.

Deardoff, D. K. (2006, Fall). Identification and assessment of intercultural competence as a student outcome of internationalization. *Journal of Studies in International Education, 10*(3), 241–266.

Dwyer, M. (2004, Winter). Charting the impact of studying abroad. *International Educator,* Washington, 13(1), 14–17, 19–20.

Dwyer, M. M., & Peters, C. K. (2012, March 2). *The benefits of study abroad.* Retrieved October 8, 2019, from www.iesabroad.org/news/benefits-study-abroad#sthash.vycIdtgh.dpbs

Eckert, J., Luqmani, M., Newell, S., Quraeshi, Z., & Wagner, B. (2013, July/August). Developing short-term study abroad programs: Achieving successful international student experiences. *American Journal of Business Education,* 6(4).

European Commission, Education and Culture. (2014). *The Erasmus impact study: Effects of mobility on the skills and employability of students and the internationalisation of higher education institutions.* Luxembourg: Publications Office of the European Union. Retrieved April 4, 2019, from http://ec.europa.eu/assets/eac/education/library/study/2014/erasmus-impact_en.pdf

Farrugia, C., & Sanger, J. (2017). Research and impact: Gaining an employment edge: The impact of study abroad on 21st century skills & career prospects in the United States. *IIE Center for Academic Mobility.* Retrieved March 3, 2019, from www.iie.org/en/Research-and-Insights/Publications/Gaining-an-employment-edge-The-Impact-of-Study-Abroad

Forum of Education Abroad, The. (2015a). *Standards of good practice for education abroad.* (5th ed.). Retrieved September 3, 2019, from https://forumea.org/resources/standards-of-good-practice

Forum of Education Abroad, The. (2015b). *2015 state of the field survey report*. Retrieved December 4, 2019, from https://forumea.org/wp./08/ForumEA-2015-State-of-the-Field-Survey-Report.pdf

Goodman, A., & Nevadomski Berdam, S. (2014, May 12). Every student should study abroad. *The New York Times*. Retrieved April 20, from www.nytimes.com/roomfordebate/2013/10/17/should-more-americans-study-abroad/every-student-should-study-abroad

Hadis, B. (2005). Why are they better students when they come back? Determinants of academic focusing gains in the study abroad experience. *Frontiers: The Interdisciplinary Journal of Study Abroad, 11*, 57–70.

Hulstrand, J. (2012, September/October). Curriculum integration: It's a marathon, not a Sprint. *International Educator*, 48–51.

Klooster, E. (2014). Studying abroad benefits employability, but not universally. *Rotterdam School of Management*. Retrieved December 11, 2018, from https://discovery.rsm.nl/operations/article/120-studying-abroad-benefits-employability-but-not-universally/

IES International. (2016). *Career outcomes of study abroad students survey of IES abroad Alumni 2012–2015*. Retrieved December 1, 2019, from www.iesabroad.org/system/files/resources/career_outcomes_of_study_abroad_students.pdf

Institute of International Education (IIE). (2018). *2018 open door report*. Retrieved September 19, 2018, from www.iie.org/Research-and-Insights/Open-Doors/Data/US-Study-Abroad/Duration-of-Study-Abroad

International Exchange Erasmus Student Network. (2014). *The Erasmus impact study: Effects of mobility on the skills and employability of students and the internationalisation of higher education institutions*. Retrieved June 6, 2018, from www.esn.org/erasmus-impact-study

NAFSA. (2016, August 4). *Curriculum integration best practices*. Retrieved from www.nafsa.org/Professional_Resources/Browse_by_Interest/Education_Abroad/Network_Resources/Education_Abroad/Curriculum_Integration__Best_Practices/

Norris, E., & Gillespie, J. (2009). How study abroad shapes global careers: Evidence from the United States. *Journal of Studies in International Education, 13*, 382–397.

OECD. (2018). *Education at a glance*. Retrieved April 13, from https://read.oecd-ilibrary.org/education/education-at-a-glance-2018_eag-2018-en#page7

Root, E., & Ngampornchai, A. (2012). I came back as a new human being: Student desperations of intercultural competence acquired through education abroad experiences. *Journal of Studies in International Education, 17*, 513–532.

Rundstrom Williams, T. (2005). Exploring the impact of study abroad on students' intercultural communication skills: Adaptability and sensitivity. *Journal of Studies in International Education, 9*, 356–371.

Salisbury, M. (2012). A study-abroad experience can do more than improve intercultural skills: If well designed, it can also increase self-awareness and strengthen a commitment to civic engagement. *The Chronicle of Higher Education*. Retrieved February 21, 2018, from www.chronicle.com/article/Were-Muddying-the-Message-on/133211/

Shulsinger, T. (2017). *The unexpected ways studying abroad benefits your education and career. Northeastern University Graduate programs*. Retrieved March 1, 2018, from https://www.northeastern.edu/graduate/blog/study-abroad-benefits/

Sood, S. (2012). The statistics of studying abroad. *BBC Travel*. Retrieved March 11, 2018, from www.bbc.com/travel/story/20120926-the-statistics-of-studying-abroad

Spencer, S., & Tuma, K. (Eds.). (2008). *The guide to successful short-term programs abroad* (2nd ed.). Washington, DC: NAFSA and Association of International Educators.

Tarrant, M. A., Rubin, D. L., & Stoner, L. (2015, Fall). The effects of studying abroad and studying sustainability on students' global perspectives. *Frontiers: The Interdisciplinary Journal of Study Abroad, 26*, 68–82.

Woodruff, G. (2009). *Curriculum integration: Where we have been, where we are going*. Internationalizing the Curriculum and Campus Paper Series. Minneapolis: University of Minnesota Press.

Part III

Internationalization Promising Practices

Sample Syllabi, Critical Incidents, and Activities

18 Connecting Local and Global Communication Contexts in the Classroom
Intercultural Engagements With University and K–12 Students

Eddah M. Mutua

Preamble

The internationalization of the communication curriculum is an opportunity to make students more aware of the interrelationships between global and local contexts. These interrelationships seem to grow at an ever-accelerated rate and raise questions about ways to bring our increasing encounters with diversity into the intercultural communication classroom. This chapter discusses the imperative for connecting local and global communication contexts in the intercultural communication classroom. It presents a semester-long service-learning project popularly known as Communicating Common Ground (CCG), which seeks to enrich intercultural communication pedagogy in the global age. Specifically, the project utilizes learning resources and activities aimed at stimulating mutual understanding between students from disparate cultures in Central Minnesota and Kenya in order to equip them with broader knowledge and skills to navigate the increasingly diverse experiences in their schools and home communities. The pedagogical practices described are grounded in intercultural communication theory, community collaborations, and related organizational procedures to bring international perspectives into the intercultural communication curriculum and also develop civic engagement skills.

The first part of this chapter discusses the communication milieu of the globalization age. The second part considers the importance and feasibility of addressing local and global communication needs in the classroom. The third part describes schematically the basic features of CCG and some of the pragmatic details required for implementing it. Additionally, the relevance of service-learning pedagogy in impacting student learning and the struggle of assessing service learning are discussed. Last but not least, the final part of the chapter offers some procedures for interested parties to design and implement a service-learning project seeking to connect communities locally or globally. The conclusion underscores the value of generating discussions about intercultural communication in the classroom to support efforts to promote mutual understanding, peaceful coexistence, and cooperation in local and global intercultural contexts.

Setting the Context

The communication milieu in the global world is nuanced with questions about how local and global contexts are interconnected, inform each other, inform how we communicate across cultural differences, and engage diverse community members with each other and with those from other parts of the world. For the purposes of this chapter, the process of globalization is understood in the context of globalizing economic, political, migratory, and communicative processes that are increasingly transforming and linking different local contexts around the world. Expanding global trade, mass communication, the global workplace and associated relocations, war, displacements, and the refugee crisis are some of the key happenings calling for new understandings of intercultural interactions in the 21st century.

In its many aspects, globalization presents a picture of a world that is diverse, interdependent, and no longer distanced by time and space (McDaniel & Samovar, 2015). Generally, globalization has facilitated the collaboration of many actors to advance the flow of goods as well as improve lives. Two examples from East Africa suffice. Rwanda, a country ravaged by the 1994 genocide, is making globalization work by collaborating with international and local peace and human rights groups to restore peace and prosperity (Sadara, 2014). In Kenya, the biggest mobile money service, M-Pesa, started as a basic service to transfer money via mobile phone to cater to Kenyans without access to the formal banking network. M-Pesa has now gone global in a deal with Western Union that will allow users to send money all over the world (Miriri, 2018). On the other hand, there has also been both reasoned and reactionary resistance to change. For example, the rural–urban divide and subsequent economic inequalities in developing countries like India generate the tensions associated with globalization (see Watkins, 2006, Economist's View 2006 on India, Infrastructure, and Resistance to Globalization). Becoming aware of the paradoxes of globalization opens an opportunity to understand what is happening for good or for ill. For intercultural communication scholars, it is about understanding the impact of globalization on cultures; how we interact across differences, and the meanings assigned to words and actions about cultures uniting and respecting each other, becoming hostile to each other, or resisting cultural imperialism. Shome and Hedge (2002) observe that cultures have converged variously, in creative, integral ways, and sometimes as homogenized within a growing commodification of cultures. Ahmed Samatar argues against this hegemonic oppression and homogenization by stating that "The emerging logos of our age ought to start with the recognition of the dialectic of multiple differences that cannot be obliterated or wished out of existence, yet they must co-evolve with each other" (Samatar, 2007, p. 7). Therefore, as we continue to witness demographic and cultural changes in the world and in particular our local communities, it becomes a challenging civic obligation to instill our globalizing citizens, including our students, with values and skills to negotiate simultaneous diversity and interdependence of the world. In this regard, it is imperative that intercultural communication theorizing stands strong to meet emerging obligations of preparing students to cope with the uncertainty and anxiety about multiple differences in the era of globalization.

In view of the ongoing changes, communication scholars continue to enrich and reimagine intercultural communication scholarship with new experiences and theoretical models that help us to understand better how diverse cultures interact, clash, unite, and/or mediate belongingness and identity in new cultural contexts (Yep, 2016; Martin & Nakayama, 2018; Chen, 2015; Haydari & Holmes, 2015; McDaniel & Samovar, 2015; Sorrells, 2013). These scholars offer varied approaches to theorizing multiple forms of differences in the global world, identifying specific concepts and approaches that inform ways to connect local and global communication contexts. Chen (2015) proposes that attitudes and practices relevant to "seeking common ground while accepting differences through tolerance are needed to recognize that differences and similarities of cultural values exist at the same time in human societies" (p. 468). In recognition of our diverse identities in the world today, Yep (2015) offers an expanded understanding of the concept of intersectionality and its importance to understanding social and cultural identity in an increasingly global world. His theorizing of thick(er) intersectionalities is valuable to examine the connections between microscopic (e.g., interpersonal relations) and macroscopic forces (e.g., social institutions) in the constitution of identity in cultural, historical, and spatial contexts. Moreover, specific practices are recommended to help us process the challenges of interactions in complex global intercultural contexts. Sorrells (2013) proposes intercultural praxis as "a process of critical, reflective thinking and acting that enables us to investigate the complex and challenging intercultural spaces we inhabit interpersonally, communally and globally" (p. 15). In order to engage in the practice of reflexivity, Jones (2010) proposes intersectional reflexivity. He opines that "we must reflexively engage in a rigorous understanding of intersectionality if we want to begin to explore the complexity of our identities and create possibilities for coalitional activism and social change" (Jones, 2010, p. 121). These concepts lay a good basis for dialogue about the issues integral to the relevance of internationalizing the intercultural classroom in communities experiencing changing cultural demographics.

My understanding of dialogue in the context of this work is informed by a thought-provoking question about how multiple factors impact dialogue in intercultural settings. Haydari and Holmes (2015) want us to consider this question: "[H]ow do the complex dynamics and interplay of history, culture, power, and urgency influence intercultural dialogic processes?" (p. xix). Thus, questions posed to evoke thought about understanding ways that complex dynamics and the interplay of multiple factors impact dialogue are to "strive for dialogue which emphasizes the interplay of different perspectives where something new and unique emerges" (Ellis & Maoz, 2003, p. 225). In a global community, where members seek to "cross the divide of diversity" (Chen, 2015, p. 470), dialogue is to be construed as "a search for deep differences and shared concerns. It asks participants to inquire genuinely about the other person and avoid premature judgment, debate and questions designed to expose flaws" (Ellis & Maoz, 2003, p. 225). At the same time, we need to take note of the fact that dialogue is not always accepted as "the primary means of dealing with conflict in spite of the many valiant efforts on the part of the peacebuilding community" (Broome, 2015, p. 50). Kwame Anthony Appiah (2011) opines that "our starting point with others doesn't have to be dialogue. It can be conversation in the old-fashioned sense of simple association, seeking familiarity around mundane human qualities of who we are" (NPR On Being with Krista Tippett).

Awareness about the impact of local and global factors on interactions between diverse groups reveals the relevance of the three components of intercultural communication competence: namely, motivation, knowledge, and tolerance for uncertainty (Martin & Nakayama, 2010). Similarly, Lustig and Koester (2013) argue that intercultural competence "produces behaviors that are both appropriate and effective and it requires sufficient knowledge, suitable motivations, and the right skills" (p. 63).

The interplay of factors that influence communication theorizing sets the context to consider ways to advance teaching and learning about intercultural interactions in a globalized world. It also clarifies the urgency to partake in scholarly activities and pedagogical practices to bring some of the desired understandings about productive encounters and communication into a global world. In response to these changes, for example, in the US, the National Communication Association (NCA) has invited and supported scholarly activities that actively engage with current issues of increasing diversity in the US and communication in a globalized world. An example is the work of NCA's Fostering International Collaborations in the Age of Globalization Task Force, whose mission is international collaboration on research, teaching using different paradigms, and offering services such as conferences and workshops. Another initiative is the collaboration by the NCA, the Southern Poverty Law Center, Campus Compact, and the American Association of Higher Education to promote Communicating Common Ground, to foster peaceful co-existence between diverse groups in communities facing hate crimes. Likewise, localized efforts that support scholarship about communication in changing environments have now become a priority of the Intercultural Interest Group of the Central States Communication Association (CSCA). Consequently, the group has taken a leading role in championing scholarly deliberations about cultural dynamics within the Upper Midwest communities being transformed by increasing numbers of refugees, immigrants, and migrant workers.

These perspectives about theory and praxis of intercultural communication in the global world allow us to see new insights about reimagining communication in the 21st century. For scholars seeking to internationalize the communication field, the challenge may entail recognizing how local and global contexts stand to influence intercultural communication research, pedagogy, and associated community service in our time. The service-learning project discussed in this chapter is illustrative of innovative, active learning pedagogy adopted to connect local and global communication contexts in an intercultural classroom.

Communicating Common Ground Exemplifying Active Learning in Intercultural Contexts

Gonçalves (2015) argues that "globalization requires change in learning spaces where the Other is not the alien but ourselves" (p. 68). This view sets the expectation that a multicultural society requires of us to learn about each other by taking into consideration the view of how local and global contexts influence each other in shaping communication needed to promote peaceful co-existence. One of the ways to transform "foreignness" or the notion of an "alien" is to come into contact with each other. Literature in intergroup contact posits that diverse groups of people can develop mutual understanding and empathy and learn about each other's background (Allport, 1954; Pettigrew, 1998). Specifically, Pettigrew (1998) has exemplified the importance of cross-group friendships in reducing prejudice. Efforts to bring diverse groups together continue to be theoretically embedded in Gordon Allport's (1954) presumption that contact between diverse groups is important in improving social relations under certain conditions. According to Everett (2013), we continue to see this view enshrined in policy making all over the globe in explicit moves for greater contact improving social relations between races in the United States, in improving relationships between Protestants and Catholics in Northern Ireland, and in encouraging a more inclusive society in postapartheid South Africa. This theoretical framework sets the backdrop of my effort to connect local and global communication contexts by bringing diverse students together to address intercultural problems encountered in their communities.

Communicating Common Ground (CCG) exemplifies active learning by adapting use of pedagogical practices that welcome active participation of students in a structured, semester-long service-learning project. For the purposes of this chapter, the understanding of service learning draws on the definition that explains how service learning as a pedagogy incorporates credit-bearing courses to include reflection activities that connect the student's experience with course content and the wider discipline (Bringle & Hatcher, 1995, cited in Steinke & Fitch, 2007b, p. 24). Service learning is the preferred pedagogical approach to meet the goals of CCG in ways that it "inherently teaches the kind of thinking skills and knowledge application necessary for success outside academia" (Steinke & Fitch, 2007b, p. 24). I have adopted service learning as a pedagogy in internationalization of communication studies in order to open opportunities for new experiences and provoking questions that stimulate understandings of diversity in an increasingly interconnected world. Additionally, this pedagogy allows students to be in contact with each other in a space that has the potential to enable and facilitate opportunities to learn about each other in a less stereotypical manner.

What is requiring change in learning spaces in Minnesota? The increasing number of immigrant and refugee communities has initiated the move to expand diversity and inclusion education in schools, colleges, and universities. According to the Immigrant Law Center of Minnesota, since 1979, Minnesota has welcomed refugees from more than 100 countries. This makes Minnesota the state with the highest number of refugees per capita in the US (Shaw, 2018). In 2012, it was estimated that 30% of preschool-age children are minorities. Children under age 5 are the most diverse of all age groups in Minnesota (Shah, 2012). I believe that the efforts in place to educate students about these changes seek to reimagine a Minnesota that is not simply a place of strangers. Specifically, CCG creates a learning space in which participating high school and university students are, in the words of John Dewey, "learning by doing." They engage in well-structured activities built on understanding concepts such as finding common ground, intergroup contact, intercultural praxis, intersectional reflexivity, thicker intersectionalities, dialogue, and conversations.

Goals and Learning Outcomes

Overall, CCG is contextualized within the following settings: (i) NCA's outcome to utilize communication to embrace difference and (ii) the macro and micro factors impacting communities in Central Minnesota and Kenya at the time the Skype interactive sessions were conducted between 2013–15.

CCG synthesizes the above stated NCA learning outcomes with the rubric of the domains of global learning provided by the Association of American Colleges and Universities (see AAC&U Global Learning VALUE Rubric. www. aacu.org).

Following are the specific goals formulated for CCG:

- To enhance students' learning about effective communication across differences
- To enable students to apply intercultural communication principles, knowledge, and skills by participating in local and global experiences
- To provide opportunities for students to develop leadership skills to promote understanding and peaceful co-existence in their local communities

The anticipated learning outcomes are:

- To demonstrate an awareness of the interrelationship between local and global experiences as relevant to promoting peaceful co-existence among diverse communities

- To identify the causes of intercultural and interracial conflicts and to recognize their own responsibility to take an ethical stance
- To demonstrate capacity for perspective—taking from learning about the experiences of others different from their own
- To demonstrate an ability to apply principles, knowledge, and skills of intercultural communication in peacebuilding activities

Content

Akin to many service-learning projects, CCG's learning activities are developed to connect students' experiences with the course content, and the goals of the wider discipline (Bringle & Hatcher, 1995 cited in Steinke & Fitch, 2007b). While the content is primarily rooted in intercultural communication scholarship and education, contemporary political and sociocultural problems experienced by participating students are also discussed. It explores ideals of peaceful co-existence through learning about shared experiences and concerns. The driving force behind intercultural and interracial tensions due to demographic changes in Central Minnesota and ethnic tensions in Kenya are explained in context of events happening elsewhere in the world. For example, the impact of war and subsequent forced migration of communities in East Africa illustrates the political instability in the region that has forced some citizens to flee their countries to Kenya and the United States as refugees. Another problem discussed is the impact of terrorism on the US and Kenya. These shared experiences of conflicts due to cultural, religious, and ethnic diversity help students find an entry point to start conversations about peace. These experiences from two diverse communication contents are connected in a classroom in Minnesota through pedagogical practices such as small-group dialogue sessions (face to face and via Skype), guest speakers, storytelling, case studies, videos, role plays, peer-to-peer mentoring sessions, and selected topics for structured discussions. Additionally, the learning is enriched by personal experiences of some of the participating students in Central Minnesota, who include ethnic Somali students born in Kenya who still maintain strong ties with families and friends left behind.

Participants

Since its inception in 2007, participants have comprised 70 diverse groups of students in Central Minnesota and university students enrolled in an upper-division intercultural communication course taught during the spring semester. For three years (2013–2015), 15 high school students in Kenya were part of the project but had to discontinue participation due to logistical problems. The university class meets once a week for 2 hours and 45 minutes (3–5:45). The title of the course, *Problems in Intercultural Communication*, focuses on theoretical content and case studies relevant to seeking ways to promote intercultural understanding in an increasingly diverse world. In addition to the "standard" content set to meet the goals of the course, I have developed additional learning material to meet the goals of the service-learning activity. The topics include sequences of thematic areas relevant to structuring the service-learning dialogue sessions. Some examples of the topics geared to supporting students' efforts to understand the communication milieu in a global world, as well as their role to promote understanding across differences, include the concepts of becoming the change you wish to see in the world, understanding self/I and other/we, embracing differences, interbeing, youth leadership, effective intercultural conflict management skills, compassionate communication, and intercultural alliances, among others. Throughout the semester, university students engage in academic activities intended to meet the goals for the course as well as the service-learning component of the course. They learn about theories, skills, and practices of intercultural communication and world events and interact with guest speakers. This academic preparation not only informs the work university students do with the high school students but also equips and guides them to reflect on their experiences in journals and group presentations at the end of the semester.

This project has become increasingly multilayered, as evidenced by the practice followed in the last 5 years. In the first layer, university students engage in intercultural dialogue sessions with high school students in Minnesota and Kenya. The sessions with the students in Minnesota are conducted face to face and the sessions with those in Kenya via Skype. The second layer consists of supervised Skype conversations between high school students in Minnesota and Kenya. In the third layer, high school students put into practice what they are learning from the university students in their communities. Students from one of the participating high schools are working with a fifth-grade class about respect for differences. Additionally, university students interested in honing their skills in intercultural dialogue facilitation and peer-to-peer mentoring have volunteered to work with local middle school students about peace and community building across cultures.

Assessment of Service-Learning Projects

I begin this section by highlighting the struggle of assessing service learning in view of the national debate on assessment in higher education and the paucity of research in assessing service learning. Despite these challenges, there are efforts to increase research efforts in this area. For example, service-learning pedagogues continue to lead efforts to increase the quality and quantity of service-learning assessment that focuses on cognitive outcomes, including critical thinking and problem solving (Steinke & Fitch, 2007b, p. 24). This is a step toward owning efforts to engage in assessment for its proper uses and not to merely respond to calls for accountability that focus increasingly on economic issues rather than on helping students become thoughtful citizens and lifelong learners (Linkon, 2005). Moving forward with the resolve to design innovative teaching strategies to internationalize the communication curriculum is a good rationale for faculty to demonstrate the positive impact that these pedagogies can have on student learning about the world as it is today. Personally, I have given considerable thought to ways that can make assessment apolitical, less standardized, and nonthreatening. My assessment plan for CCG focuses on assessing cognitive outcomes of the service-learning experience. There are questions that I often ask myself to inform what I want to assess and how to do it, such as "How do I know that students are learning? What are they doing in class and outside the classroom (in the community) that is indicative of their understanding of the goals and objectives of CCG? What are the high school students reporting back to us about what they are doing in their school?"

In most cases, responses to these questions are reflected in the multiple approaches to service-learning assessment measures and protocols adopted to assess the impact of CCG experience on student learning. I create my own assessment tools in the form of assignments for the service-learning component of the course which is 50% of the overall grade. The graded components of the service-learning activity consist of journal entries, dialogue session outlines, response to guest speakers, and a simple three-question survey administered to high school students at the end of the semester: "What did you learn? What would you like to learn more? What can we do differently to improve what we do together?" I have also used pre– and post–service-learning questionnaires provided by the service-learning office on campus. Student feedback on assignments and surveys, as well as unsolicited feedback, informs ways to support the achievement of the expected learning outcomes.

While there are many approaches to assessment measures and protocols, there are also many diverse views about the essence of assessment in higher education. Despite the dissenting view that assessment is "overburdening everyone with a never-ending proliferation of paperwork and bureaucracy" (see Christopher Nelson, 2014), whatever we do, the goal should be directed at preparing students for the global world. For example, the Association of American Colleges and Universities Association (AAC&U) report titled *Employers More Interested in Critical Thinking and Problem Solving Than College Major* (2013) states that "No matter what careers students seek, their college education must equip them with intercultural skills, ethical judgment, and a sophisticated understanding of the diversity of our society and of any successful business or organization." It is my hope that leading scholars in service-learning pedagogy research, notably Pamela Steinke and Peggy Fitch, will continue to advance research in service-learning assessment. Developing tools useful to improve the quality of service-learning assessment would help educators realize the benefits of this pedagogy. Below is a list of a few service-learning assessment resources that give good leads to learning more about assessing service learning.

>Steinke and Fitch (2006). Cognitive Learning Scale (CLS).
>
>http://departments.central.edu/psychology/files/2011/07/Service-Learning-Cognitive-Learning-Pre-Post-Scale.pdf
>
>Fitch and Steinke (2013). Tools for Assessing Cognitive Outcomes of Experiential Learning.
>
>Paper prepared for the 2013 NCA HLC Annual Conference on Quality in Higher Education
>
>http://departments.central.edu/psychology/files/2011/07/HLC-2013-Paper-Fitch-Steinke.pdf
>
>Steinke, P. & Fitch, P. (2007). Assessing Service-Learning. Research and Practice in Assessment. Volume 1, Issue 2 June 2007, 24–29.
>
>www.nvcc.edu/assessment/_docs/step3/assessingservicelearning-08222013.pdf
>
>Steinke, P. & Buresh, S. Cognitive Outcomes of Service-Learning: Reviewing the Past and Glimpsing the Future. Michigan Journal of Community Service-Learning. Volume 8, Spring 2002.
>
>https://quod.lib.umich.edu/m/mjcsl/3239521.0008.201?rgn=main;view=fulltext

Guidelines for Implementation

This final section outlines some procedures for interested parties to design and implement a service-learning project seeking to connect communities locally or globally.

Initial Preparation

- As initial preparation, one should present the plan and obtain whatever support is available from the chair, dean, and other colleagues in the department and college.
- Develop collaborative partnerships with local school districts, international universities, or schools. Determine that there is a basic compatibility and complementarity between the instructor's pedagogical goals and outcomes and those of the participating institutions and teachers, for example, regarding diversity education. Secure necessary agreements.
- Endeavor to learn what participating teachers consider to be the major communication needs of their students and the communities they live in. Also determine how they recruit students to participate in the program.
- The understanding of the needs of local and foreign students forms the basis of the development of a specific set of thematic foci for the discussion sessions. The idea is to ensure that diverse experiences are presented. Other topics to be discussed with foreign and local teachers fall under logistics, including the introductions of teachers via email or Skype, parental consent slips for student participation, and dates/times for the various kinds of interactive and Skype sessions. It is important to take into consideration meeting times based on the time zones (locally and overseas).
- Under logistics for local students are considerations such as the means and costs of transportation to different venues where face-to-face sessions are held, the provision of meals and snacks, debriefing, and so on.
- Overall, plans for the overseas segment of the program become clearer and further develop as one gains experience with the activity.

Learning Resources

The instructor must determine that learning resources meet the set goals and outcomes of the course and the service-learning experience.

- Find books, articles, documentaries, and community members as guest speakers to effectively communicate the desired content.
- Identify suitable activities such as stimulation exercises and role-plays. One might consider other methods to engage students, such as storytelling or art education.
- Check the compatibility of such resources with the educational needs and requirements of participating institutions.
- Consider both the effectiveness and availability of technological delivery methods for the different communities of students.
- Perhaps allocate times in class for university students to prepare for their tasks in facilitating dialogue with the high school students.

Introducing the Activity to Students

University Students

- On the first day of class, introduce the service-learning activity as an integral part of the course, and provide a basic overview of what it will involve.

- Help students understand how the civic skills cultivated in the activity are vital to becoming a good communicator in the global world.
- Explain tasks and roles, procedures, expectations, and deadlines of the activity.
- Instruct students in the basics of engaging in dialogues with the high schools students. These include creating a welcoming space for all students, collaborating to set ground rules, and talking and listening with a purpose.
- Explain logistics of getting to and from the high schools, carpooling, or riding in a van if funds for that are available.
- Set aside time for questions and answers. Encourage students to ask questions.

First Day of Dialogue Session With High School Students

Students are often anxious to learn how the activity will proceed. The instructor should engage them in ways that make the space safe and welcoming. It is important for the instructor to outline an agenda for the session with reasonable timelines. Allow opportunities for extended exchanges to enable students to bond. Sessions usually improve as students become more proficient, comfortable, and interested in the tasks. This is how the first class is usually structured:

- 15 minutes: Arrival of students and teachers
- 15 minutes: Snacks
- 15 minutes: Welcoming remarks and introduction to the session
- 1 hour: Dialogue session about selected topics
- 30 minutes: Each group reports back to the class and reflects on what they have learned.

Skype Session

The Skype sessions can be structured based on the time available.

- Usually, each session lasts for about an hour.
- Encourage students to have questions to ask well in advance to save time.
- Let students understand access to the internet may be limited, especially if your partners are from some countries in the global South.
- Technology can be unreliable even in the US. Have a Plan B.

I have provided a detailed discussion about the project in terms of its planning, implementation, outcomes, successes, and challenges (see Mutua, 2017b) as part of the efforts by Kellet and Matyok (2017) to promote communication and conflict transformation through local, regional, and global engagements.

Conclusion

As globalization in its many ramifications continues in the 21st century, the need to generate discussions about intercultural communication pedagogy in classrooms cannot be overstated. The literature reviewed speaks to the reality of the communication milieu of the globalization age. As such, the service-learning project discussed serves as an exemplar of a local effort to bring both local and international perspectives into the communication curriculum. It involves creating opportunities for students to talk with one another locally and globally. There must also be local and international collaboration among administrators, teachers, and parents to support such an endeavor. As illustrated in a modest way by the activity described, intercultural communication is not merely a theory but also a form of what John Dewey called "learning by doing." Students have an opportunity to experience, firsthand, different ways to navigate an increasingly diverse and interconnected world. Perhaps this effort should be what inspires intercultural communication scholars to endeavor to connect local and global communication contexts in the 21st-century classroom.

References

Allport, G. W. (1954). *The nature of prejudice*. Cambridge and Reading, MA: Addison-Wesley.

Appiah, K. A. (2011). Sidling up to difference: Social change and moral revolutions. *On Being with Krista Tippett. NPR*. Retrieved March 24, 2011, from https://onbeing.org/programs/kwame-anthony-appiah-sidling-up-to-difference-social-change-and-moral-revolutions/

Association of American College and Universities (AAC&U). *Global learning VALUE Rubric*. Retrieved from www.aacu.org/value/rubrics/global-learning

Association of American Colleges and Universities Association. (2013). *Employers more interested in critical thinking and problem solving than college major*. Retrieved from www.aacu.org/press/press-releases/employers-more-interested-critical-thinking-and-problem-solving-college-major

Broome, B. (2015). Dialogue across the divide: Building the separation in Cyprus. In N. Haydani & P. Holmes (Eds.), *Case studies in intercultural dialogue* (pp. 39–56). Dubuque, IA: Kendall Hunt Publishing Company.

Chen, G.-M. (2015). Seeking common ground while accepting differences through tolerance: US-China intercultural communication in the global community. In L. Samovar, R. Porter, E. McDaniel, & C. Roy (Eds.), *Intercultural communication: A reader* (14th ed., pp. 465–471). Boston, MA: Cengage Learning.

Economist's View. (2006). *India, infrastructure, and resistance to globalization*. Retrieved from https://economistsview.typepad.com/economistsview/2006/02/india_infrastru.html

Ellis, D., & Maoz, I. (2003). Dialogue and cultural communication codes between Israel Jews and Palestinians. In L. Samovar & R. Porter (Eds.), *Intercultural communication: A reader* (pp. 223–230). Belmont, CA: Wadsworth Publishing.

Everett, J. (2013). Intergroup contact theory: Past, present, and future. Magazine Issue 2/Issue 17. Retrieved from www.in-mind.org/article/intergroup-contact-theory-past-present-and-future

Global Learning Outcomes. Retrieved from www.aacu.org/global-learning/outcomes

Gonçalves, S. (2015). Multiculturalism, contact zones, and the political core of intercultural education. In N. Haydari & P. Holmes (Eds.), *Cases in intercultural dialogue* (pp. 57–71). Dubuque, IA: Kendall Hunt.

Haydari, N., & Holmes, P. (2015). Introduction: Contextualizing "intercultural dialogue" and the "case study." In N. Haydari & P. Holmes (Eds.), *Cases in intercultural dialogue* (pp. xix–xxxi). Dubuque, IA: Kendall Hunt.

Jones Jr., R. G. (2010). Putting privilege into practice through "intersectional reflexivity": Ruminations, interventions, and possibilities. *Reflections: Narratives of Professional Helping*, 16(1), 122. Retrieved February 3, 2019, from https://open.lib.umn.edu/communication/chapter/8-4-intercultural-communication-competence/

Kellett, P. & Matyok (Eds.) (2017). *Communication and conflict transformation through local, regional, and global engagement*. Lanham, Maryland: Lexington Books.

Linkon, S. (2005, July–August). Rethinking faculty work. *Academe*, 91(4). Retrieved from www.clark.edu/tlc/outcome_assessment/documents/Sherry_Lee_Linkon_How_CanAssessment_Work_for_Us.pdf

Lustig, M.W & Koester, J. (2013). *Intercultural competence: Interpersonal communication across cultures*. Seventh Edition. Upper Saddle River, NJ: Pearson.

Martin, J. N., & Nakayama, T. K. (2018). *Intercultural communication in contexts* (6th ed.). Boston, MA: McGraw-Hill.

McDaniel, E., & Samovar, L (2015). Understanding and applying intercultural communication in the global community: The fundamentals. In L. Samovar, R. Porter, E. McDaniel, & C. Roy (Eds.), *Intercultural communication: A reader* (14th ed., pp. 5–15). Boston, MA: Cengage Learning.

Miriri, D. (2018). UPDATE 1-Kenya's Safaricom takes M-Pesa global with Western Union. *Reuters*. Retrieved November 6, 2018, from www.reuters.com/article/kenya-safaricom-western-union/update-1-kenyas-safaricom-takes-m-pesa-global-with-western-union-idUSL8N1XH5ZI

Mutua, E. (2017a). Internationalizing students' intercultural conversations: Experiences from Central Minnesota and Kenya. *Spectra*. The Magazine of the National Communication Association May 2017, 53(2), 24–27.

Mutua, E. (2017b). Students talk, listen and act to transform conflict: A case study of service-learning project in Central Minnesota, United States, and Kajiado, Kenya. In T. G. Matyok & P. Kellett (Eds.), *Communication and conflict transformation through local, regional and global engagements* (pp. 269–287). Lanham, MD: Lexington Books.

Nelson, C. (2014). Assessing assessment. *Inside Higher ED*. Retrieved November 24, 2014, from www.insidehighered.com/views/2014/11/24/essay-criticizes-state-assessment-movement-higher-education

Sadara, S. (2014). The globalization of human rights in Post-Genocide Rwanda. *Bridges*, 8(Spring), 55–62.

Samatar, A. (2007, Spring). Musings on global citizenship. *Macalaster Civic Forum*, 1(1), 7–17. Retrieved from http://digitalcommons.macalester.edu/cgi/viewcontent.cgi?article=1006&context=maccivicf

Shah, A. (2012, July 21). May 18: Census shows the changing face of Minnesota. *Star Tribune*. Retrieved from www.startribune.com/local/151981455.html

Shaw, B. (2018). *Minnesota has the highest refugee per capita in the U.S. will that continue?* Twin Cities Pioneer Press. Retrieved from www.twincities.com/2018/01/13/the-not-so-welcome-mat-minnesota-winces-at-refugee-cutbacks/

Shome, R., & Hedge, R. S. (2002). Postcolonial approaches to communication: Charting the terrain, engaging the intersections. *Communication Theory*, 12(3), 249–270.

Sorrells, K. (2013). *Intercultural communication: Globalization and social justice*. Los Angeles: Sage Publications.

Steinke, P. & Buresh, S. (2002). Cognitive outcomes of service-learning: Reviewing the past and glimpsing the future. *Michigan Journal of Community Service-Learning*. 8, Spring 2002. Retrieved from https://quod.lib.umich.edu/m/mjcsl/3239521.0008.201?rgn=main;view=fulltext

Steinke, P. & Fitch, P. (2006). *Cognitive Learning Scale (CLS)*. Retrieved from https://departments.central.edu/psychology/files/2011/07/Service-Learning-Cognitive-Learning-Pre-Post-Scale.pdf

Steinke, P., & Fitch, P. (2007a). *Using goal-based learning to improve cognitive learning outcomes: The case of service-learning*. Unpublished manuscript. Retrieved fromhttps://departments.central.edu/psychology/files/2011/07/HLC-2013-Paper-Fitch-Steinke.pdf

Steinke, P. & Fitch, P. (2007b). Assessing service-learning. *Research & Practice in Assessment*. Volume Two: Summer 2007, 24–29. https://files.eric.ed.gov/fulltext/EJ1062690.pdf

Steinke, P. & Fitch, P. (2007c). Assessing service-learning. *Research & Practice in Assessment*. Volume Two: Summer 2007, 24–29. https://files.eric.ed.gov/fulltext/EJ1062690.pdf

Pettigrew, T. F. (1998). Intergroup contact theory. *Annual Review of Psychology*, 49(1), 65–85.

Watkins, K. (2006). When globalization leaves people behind. *New York Times*. Retrieved from www.nytimes.com/2006/02/12/opinion/when-globalization-leaves-people-behind.html

Yep, G. (2015). Intersectionality. *Key Concepts in Intercultural Dialogue*, 49. Available from: https://centerforinterculturaldialogue.files.wordpress.com/2015/02/key-concept-intersectionality.pdf

Yep, G. (2016). Towards thick(er) intersectionalities: Theorizing, researching, and activating the complexities of communication and identities. In K. Sorrells & S. Sekimoto (Eds.), *Globalizing intercultural communication: A reader* (pp. 86–94). Sage Publication, Inc.

19 Internationalizing the Communication Classroom via Technology and Curricular Strategy

Pedagogical Takeaways From a Three-Way Online Collaboration Project

Rita Koris, Sushil K. Oswal, and Zsuzsanna B. Palmer

Introduction

The idea of setting up an international collaborative project aided by the Internet comes from an increasingly significant line of research on global collaborations that teach students intercultural communicative competence (Anderson, Bergman, Bradley, Gustaffson, & Matzke, 2010; Davison, Panteli, Hardin, & Fuller, 2017; Guth & Helm, 2010; O'Dowd & Lewis, 2016). Several innovative pedagogical approaches also have been published, particularly in education, information design, and professional communication, fields that support teachers to incorporate disability and accessibility into their curricula (Foley & Ferri, 2012; Oswal, 2015, 2018; Palmer & Palmer, 2018). While most of these projects have succeeded in increasing awareness of disabilities in the classroom on a local level, there is a lack of research about pedagogical projects that support inclusivity with global implications. To fill this lacuna, we devised a three-way collaboration involving business planning, web design, and disability and accessibility theory. The purpose of the project was to create an accessible website for the businesses proposed by the student teams from Hungary while availing the disability and accessibility expertise of the Washington graduate students.

With the help of the results of preproject and postproject surveys, we have assessed whether and to what extent such international collaborations can influence students' preconceived notions about intercultural communication, disability, and technology that allow access to information for all users in digital environments (Blanchard, 2010; Meiselwitz, Wentz, & Lazar, 2010). The preliminary survey results show that this project was successful in teaching intercultural communication skills and in increasing awareness of disability and accessibility. Our intercultural communication–centered project connects business planning and web design pedagogy to communication-oriented fields and the academy's stress on accountability to society and all its members.

Three-Way Online Collaboration Project

Our pedagogical project is based on the online interactions among students enrolled in three different courses at three universities: one in Hungary and two in the United States, in Michigan and Washington, respectively. We wanted to gain a more complete understanding of what best practices would or would not work when simultaneously teaching intercultural communication values and skills, web design principles, and accessible design from the perspective of disabled and elderly users. While our intercultural communication emphasis was on acquiring linguistic and social proficiency by working with student groups situated in locations far apart from one another, our own academic locations as faculty in different disciplines coming together to collaborate on this international project co-incidentally created another layer of interactions that were both interdisciplinary and intercultural. To bring together our differing backgrounds, courses, and programmatic bearings, we designed a collaboration project for ourselves and our students that would (1) permit us to deliver our standard curriculum for our particular course and meet the programmatic requirements, (2) provide opportunities to our students to substantively interact with the other two classes through engagement with their respective course content, and (3) create incidental sites of cultural interactions and collaboration.

While our students contributed differing cultural and linguistic backgrounds, we ourselves also added to the diversity of thought and content through our own peculiar backgrounds. For example, our Hungarian partner—a faculty member of business English—teaching in Hungary in a program rooted in the European applied linguistics tradition offered Hungarian–English bilingual perspective on workplace writing through her combined European graduate and U.S. workplace training. Likewise, our Michigan partner teaching a professional communication course situated in a rhetorically oriented writing studies program presented her Hungarian–English language background on the U.S. soil while combining her Hungarian and U.S. graduate training. Our Washington partner, located in an interdisciplinary school and teaching a graduate course in disability studies came from a mixed academic background in environmental science and studies, human-centered design, and more recently disability studies while drawing on his Indo-English background and US graduate training. While the participating Hungarian students were studying business English in the context of international studies, the Michigan students from computer and information sciences and writing studies were taking this course to fulfil their major's requirement for a professional communication course. The Washington student group further added to this diversity with their status as graduate students and primarily hailing from social sciences and studying disability methods and theory. Thus, the three collaborating faculty had to develop a situation-specific, novel model of collaboration among ourselves and our students within the curricular boundaries of our programs and the requirements of our individual courses. Additionally, each of us had our own professional and pedagogical priorities and agenda: the Hungarian faculty was keen to promote students' English language proficiency, the Michigan teacher engaged in integrating the values of access for the disabled in web design instruction, and the Washington instructor have students practice their newly acquired knowledge of disability and accessibility theory (Oswal & Palmer, 2018).

With these constraints and agenda in view, we had our students—each class split into eight groups—work in tandem on interrelated and overlapping projects and collaborate in business and web design skill building, gaining insights into disabled and elderly customers' and users' interactions with businesses, websites, and overall access to the services offered by an entrepreneurial venture. Each of the eight Hungarian groups developed an entrepreneurial business plan, the Michigan groups designed websites for their linked Hungarian clients, and the Washington groups supplied know-how, educational information, and one-on-one assessment about the accessibility of the entrepreneurial businesses and their respective websites. At the end of the project, each of the Hungarian groups delivered a finished entrepreneurial venture plan, the Michigan groups produced an accessible website that would meet their clients' business needs, and the Washington groups offered support and project evaluation to the aforesaid with their accessibility know-how.

Use of Technology for International Collaboration

Besides students and faculty using equipment in the computer lab, their personal laptops, and hand-held devices for ideational, writing, and design activities, we orchestrated the interactions and collaborative work among students and ourselves via email. We chose this low-tech medium due to our students' varying skill levels in technology use, unavailability of our university's learning management systems for collaboration beyond our campuses, and to escape from what Griffiths calls, "the tyranny of the leading edge" (2003, p. 7). Besides students exchanging information through email messages and sharing their project drafts and know-how advisories via email attachments, the Michigan groups employed free online wireframe tools to design the mockups of websites and then develop web pages on free content-management platforms such as Wix, Weebly, and WordPress. The instructors here and there also discussed collaboration matters over the phone. Eventually, the three instructors had a face-to-face meeting at a U.S. conference venue to discuss the aftermaths of this project and to plan the next iteration of this collaboration.

Curricular Strategies

During the preparation and design phase of the collaboration project, we aimed at internationalizing the internal curricular core of each of the three academic courses. Each instructor determined a designated part of the syllabus that was incorporated into the collaboration project. Consequently, the international project was embedded into the curricular core of each course to ensure that the remaining frame of the syllabi could be dedicated to meeting the programmatic requirements of the individual courses. This curricular strategy also allowed time and space for the instructors to prepare their students for the collaboration, guide them through the necessary background material, and broaden their disciplinary knowledge and expertise necessary for their successful participation in the project assignments. Hungarian students learned about how to prepare, design, and write a business plan for their start-up venture; Michigan students learned about business communication, web design and accessibility of websites; and Washington students learned to teach disability theory and principles of accessibility and inclusion. Thus, our approach guaranteed that all student groups were provided with the necessary knowledge, information, and skills to participate in the project effectively and make the most out of their intercultural collaboration.

The design elements of the collaboration brought together the three disciplines of the local teams. The students practiced collaboration skills through complementary roles that their teams assumed while working with others toward common goals and learning from constant interaction and communication among the international teams (World Economic Forum, 2016). As these students came from various academic backgrounds, they were in possession of different areas of expertise and made different contributions to the project deliverables. The major challenge of interdisciplinary collaboration projects is to design activities that complement each other, so that the various student groups can draw on their own discipline, providing an input into the teamwork. Another key element of interdisciplinarity is to find the connecting points that bring together the various academic fields and allow students to create a shared, collective outcome by relying on each other's expertise.

Our framing of business planning and web design within the theories of disability and access enhances social accountability in teaching and learning on part of instructors and students. Our model of international collaboration also challenges the traditional notions of interactions by having students function within an intercultural space that is also populated with highly interdisciplinary content aimed at teaching and learning for diverse goals: planning, design, and disability access framework (Oswal & Palmer, 2018). Our peculiar contextualization of the three classes' projects notably moves the historically marginalized disabled and elderly users and their accessibility needs to the center while asking students to learn to view their workplace roles from the lens of equity and inclusion.

Designing, planning, and implementing interdisciplinary projects might be more challenging, but such projects yield considerable advantages for the students. On the one hand, interdisciplinarity extends students' foci and perspectives beyond their own discipline, and on the other, it stretches their imagination and skill sets for solving broader human problems. Projects like the one described in this chapter tend to simulate workplace environments in which future employees will have to work in global teams, potentially with colleagues from other business areas, and they will need to build on each other's expertise and input to solve problems, including the problems of their disabled and elderly customers. Our project also promoted client–provider relationship and students using the genres of international business communication associated with it. Global interconnectivity and collaborative communication is an essential component of business communication competence in today's business world (Waldeck, Durante, Helmuth, & Marcia, 2012). Through the simulation of global business communication, thus moving away from designing and writing only for their instructors, students were given the opportunity to write to and for various audiences and apply appropriate communication strategies.

Another motivation behind the collaboration project from a pedagogical perspective was to give students the opportunity for learning-by-doing to gain experience in business and technical communication work (Hager, Lee, & Reich, 2012). Having relevant experience of working in global culturally different teams is highly valued by future employers (Milhauser & Rahschulte, 2010). While defining the concept of "interculturality," Arasaratnam points out that "in intercultural spaces, our implicit assumptions are confronted, and the concepts that we may have reified are exposed" (Alexander et al., 2014, p. 16). During this collaboration, for example, Oswal registered that his graduate students were amazed by the Hungarian students' intimate knowledge of the US material spaces, popular culture, and their general awareness of a country several thousand miles away and physically separated with a vast ocean in between. Even greater was the consternation over their own knowledge gaps about the basic facts about Hungary, its people, and cultures even though each class had access to similar online information resources. Elsewhere, Arasaratnam emphasizes that navigating intercultural spaces involves "flexibility," "humility," and "mindfulness," and we as teachers are glad to report that our students definitely experienced some of these moments (Alexander et al., 2014, p. 16). Preliminary results of our surveys indicate that students' intercultural awareness and intercultural communication competence improved as a result of participating in the project.

Furthermore, students were given the opportunity to develop and practice skills essential for surviving in the 21st century, including more common decision making, creative thinking, problem solving, and collaboration skills in a global economy (World Economic Forum, 2016). The project also contributed to the increase of students' awareness of accessibility and disability. In the case of students who were nonnative speakers of English, their English-language proficiency and professional communication competence improved considerably. Cumulatively, our course content and delivery mechanisms demonstrated what would be called, "best practices" for teaching international, intercultural, and transcultural values in action (Palmer, 2013).

Challenges of International Collaboration

As mentioned in the previous sections, the coordination of online intercultural projects can be challenging and often requires extensive planning. Most of the challenges stem from coordinating activities between different geographical locations. While technology most of the time helps with bridging the gap over large distances, it can fail and can cause delays and necessary readjustments of the project schedule. Also, large distances often come with different time zones. In the case of our collaboration project, there was a total of nine hours' time difference between all the groups. For this reason, synchronous activities were very difficult to schedule, and thus email was used as the primary method of keeping everyone connected. In addition to the time zones, class meetings in each location took place on different days of the week on different academic schedules (semester/trimester/different holidays), and deliverables had to be coordinated between these disparate meeting times. As for the best practice in planning this project, we worked on preparing a complex project schedule that was broken down into weekly or even daily activities of the student teams including interim deadlines of the project assignments and deliverables. Not only did activities of in-class meetings have to be thoroughly planned, but we also had to orchestrate the execution of project tasks outside of class and the communication flow among the various student teams. The implementation of the project required continuous monitoring of the student teams' activities and performance, as well as instant tackling of unexpected difficulties or problems.

Another area of possible challenges is also connected to large geographical distance and more specifically to different cultural values. This can be an issue especially in language use and word choice during online communication between students at different locations but can be mitigated with the help of instructors by turning each misunderstanding into a teachable moment. For example, Hungarian students enjoyed incorporating wordplay into their proposed website text, and the Michigan students had to work hard to convey to their Hungarian partners that some of these texts were confusing for the reader. Misunderstandings can also happen within local teams, as is often the case with any kind of a team project, and also require instructor involvement for resolving conflicts. Additional challenges result from coordinating course learning outcomes and deliverables between the classes involved. Each instructor has to ensure that their learning outcomes are met, which can result in changes to the project and deliverables that are already subject to different assessment standards. For this reason, while we all worked together, each of us had to advocate a somewhat different approach in order to maintain the original goals of our own course. The key to overcoming all of these challenges, thus the most important best practice in coordinating online collaboration projects, is early and frequent communication between instructors before the project and flexibility during the project. Careful planning and scheduling can ensure timely submission of the deliverables to partner teams, and communicating unexpected delays and issues with partner instructors in a timely manner during the project is crucial for readjusting the original schedule.

Pedagogical Takeaways and Conclusion

Online collaboration projects such as the one described in this chapter are very effective for connecting students from different parts of the world. To ensure that the collaboration is successful, the project has to be situated in a discussion of intercultural communication principles and practices in face-to-face and online communication environments. Through these discussions, students learn to appreciate the similarities and differences in the communication practices of different cultures. In addition to this framing activity, each assignment needs to be scaffolded by exposing students to existing documents in the same genres of their deliverables and by modeling the planning and design activities in the class. Students also incorporate assigned readings into their writing and design process, as many of these readings not only focused on explaining the larger concepts (i.e., user experience, business planning and start-up management, and accessible design), but also provided practical strategies (i.e., how to create wireframes, how to write a marketing plan, and how to draft an advisory document for other teams lacking the knowledge of disability theory and accessible design for completing the final product). At the end of the course, students presented their teams' deliverables and the results of the project in their own classrooms. In these presentations, not only did they focus on their own assignments, but they also briefly drew on the work of their partner cohorts at the other two universities. For example, the presentation of the Hungarian teams included the detailed plan of their own start-up venture, the details from the presentations of the websites designed by the Michigan students, and the accessibility solutions worked out by the Washington students. All three courses concluded with class discussion and feedback on the students' project experiences, recognition of the learning curve involved in such interdisciplinary work, and a review of the takeaways for their future academic and professional endeavors. Underlying our client–provider–based, stacked design of this international, intercultural collaboration on three disparate projects on different locations—business planning, website design, and disability and accessibility advisory for the aforesaid two—was the curricular strategy of experientially demonstrating to all our students that global workplace teams do not function in discrete and tidy disciplinary or professional groups. Yet they often perform in tandem or simultaneously with other teams in diverse and distant locations and quite regularly provide and receive feedback from each other to develop the overall project, keep it on track, and serve as quality-control resources for one another's work.

Researchers claim that "educators engaging constructively in producing different cultural knowledges, by increasing the active participation of educators from different linguistic and cultural backgrounds, and by building a cosmopolitan transnational identity among all students and educators" can advance the goals of global citizenship (Palmer, 2013; Singh, Kenway, & Apple, 2007, p. 13). By assigning diverse readings aimed at inculcating cosmopolitan values and modeling different stages of the intercultural and interdisciplinary activities, online collaboration projects can be adapted to different courses as long as the accompanying documents and the final product are aligned with some of the course's international learning outcomes. Regardless of the specific project elements, international online collaboration projects are always a great way to introduce students to the intricacies of intercultural communication in online environments, a skill that will not only be necessary for their professional success in the globalized, networked world but also crucial for them to be at home in a heterogeneously structured future.

Acknowledgment

The three authors contributed equally to this chapter.

References

Alexander, B. K., Arasaratnam, L. A., Avant-Mier, R., Durham, A., Flores, L., Leeds-Hurwitz, W., & Halualani, R. (2014). Defining and communicating what "intercultural" and "intercultural communication" means to us. *Journal of International and Intercultural Communication*, 7(1), 14–37.

Anderson, P., Bergman, B., Bradley, L., Gustaffson, M., & Matzke, A. (2010). Peer reviewing across the Atlantic: Patterns and trends in L1 and L2 comments made in an asynchronous online collaborative learning exchange between technical communications in Sweden and in the United States. *Journal of Business and Technical Communication*, 24(3), 296–322.

Blanchard, E. G. (2010). Adaptation-oriented culturally-aware tutoring systems: When adaptive instructional technologies meet intercultural education. In H. Song & T. T. Kidd (Eds.), *Handbook of research on human performance and instructional technology* (pp. 413–430). Hershey, PA: IGI Global.

Davison, R. M., Panteli, N., Hardin, A. M., & Fuller, M. A. (2017). Establishing effective global virtual student teams. *IEEE Transactions on Professional Communication*, 60(3), 317–329.

Foley, A., & Ferri, B. A. (2012). Technology for people, not disabilities: Ensuring access and inclusion. *Journal of Research in Special Educational Needs*, 12(4), 192–200.

Griffiths, S. (2003). Low-tech: Escaping the tyranny of the leading edge. In J. Batgchi et al. (Eds.), *Sarai reader 03: Shaping technologies* (pp. 7–11). New Delhi, India: Centre for the Study of Developing Societies.

Guth, S., & Helm, F. (Eds.). (2010). *Telecollaboration 2.0. language, literacies and intercultural learning in the 21st century*. Bern: Peter Lang.

Hager, P., Lee, A., & Reich, A. (2012). *Practice, learning and change: Practice-theory perspectives on professional learning*. Dordrecht: Springer.

Meiselwitz, G., Wentz, B., & Lazar, J. (2010). Universal usability: Past, present, and future. *Foundations and Trends® in Human—Computer Interaction*, 3(4), 213–333.

Milhauser, K. L., & Rahschulte, T. (2010). Meeting the needs of global companies through improved international business curriculum. *Journal of Teaching in International Business*, 21(2), 78–100.

O'Dowd, R., & Lewis, T. (Eds.). (2016). *Online intercultural exchange: Policy, pedagogy, practice*. New York: Routledge.

Oswal, S. K. (2015). Physical and learning disabilities in OWI. In B. Hewett & K. Depew (Eds.), *Foundational practices of online writing instruction* (pp. 253–290). Anderson, SC: Parlor Press.

Oswal, S. K. (2018). Can workplaces, classrooms, and pedagogies be disabling? *Business and Professional Communication Quarterly*, 81(1), 3–19.

Oswal, S., & Palmer, Z. B. (2018). Can diversity be intersectional? Inclusive business planning and accessible web design internationally on two continents and three campuses. In L. A. Whittle (Ed.), *2018 Conference Proceedings* (p. 23). Association for Business Communication. Retrieved from www.businesscommunication.org/page/conference-proceedings

Palmer, Z. B. (2013). Cosmopolitanism: Extending our theoretical framework for transcultural technical communication research and teaching. *Journal of Technical Writing and Communication, 43*(4), 381–401.

Palmer, Z. B., & Palmer, R. H. (2018). Legal and ethical implications of website accessibility. *Business and Professional Communication Quarterly, 81*(4), 399–420.

Singh, M., Kenway, J., & Apple, M. W. (2007). Globalizing education: Perspectives from above and below. In M. W. Apple, J. Kenway, & M. Singh (Eds.), *Globalizing education: Policies, pedagogies, & politics* (pp. 2–29). Bern, Switzerland: Peter Lang.

Waldeck, J., Durante, C., Helmuth. B., & Marcia, B. (2012). Communication in a changing world: Contemporary perspectives on business communication competence. *Journal of Education for Business, 87*(4), 230–240.

World Economic Forum. (2016). *New vision for education: Fostering social and emotional learning through technology*. Geneva: World Economic Forum. Retrieved January 15, 2019, from www.weforum.org/reports/new-vision-for-education-fostering-social-and-emotional-learning-through-technology

20 Translating Tasks for International Classrooms

Rebecca M. Townsend and Trudy Milburn

Introduction

Internationalizing communication curriculum can mean partnerships among universities. The particular context in which we are working is a US-based private university in partnership with a Polish private university awarding master's degrees. While Polish public universities have been around for centuries, Polish private universities are relatively new, developing since the 1990s. They are increasing, with more than 300 private schools (Siwinska, 2011), and have the highest enrollment among private European universities. As teaching-based institutions, private universities in Poland focus on degree completion. Most students are not able "to win places on prestigious, free-of-charge study programmes at state universities" (Vasagar, 2011) and are working to support themselves and their families. While some have criticized Poland's slower pace to internationalization (Grove, 2014), the particular university in which we have taught has moved explicitly toward internationalization since 2004.

American professors bring their ways of teaching to the Polish university. Half of the students are native Poles, and half are from all over the world. Studies are taught in English. Poles and international students collaborate on team projects. The master's degrees students will receive an American degree. When we were asked to teach, we learned they valued American-style-teaching, which places value on practical knowledge from theoretical bases (Chetro-Szivos, 2010). Discussions and skill-based learning are important. Additionally, we value independent work and citation of sources. Citation practices vary by place; they have a certain "plasticity," and some "standards" from many places may be judged as "not as rigorous as those in the United States" (NYU School of Law, 2006, p. xiii). Given this context, we believed that the American norms of classroom interaction and presentation of individuals' original work would prevail here.

This case study is based on two professors' assignment of a similar task for the students in this Polish university: translating "key concepts in intercultural dialogue" for publication on the Center for Intercultural Dialogue's website (2018). Although each instructor taught a different course, Organizational Communication and Intercultural Communication, we recognized the importance of including the expertise of students in class exercises. The ethnic and national composition of students in our Polish classrooms was extremely diverse, with students from China, France, India, Ivory Coast, Japan, Jordan, Nepal, Pakistan, Poland, Russia, Saudi Arabia, Spain, Ukraine, Vietnam, and Yemen. Therefore, their native languages created what we had initially supposed was a ground of expertise from which to draw.

One problem of translation is the translation of expectations. We were surprised to discover several students used Google Translate to complete the tasks.

Intercultural Communication and Translation

The roots of intercultural communication grew out of earlier work done for US Foreign Service diplomat training (Leeds-Hurwitz, 1990). The need for applied learning, rather than from theoretical understanding of conceptual bases of knowledge, mirrors our international graduate students' goals. By earning this degree, they hope to learn practical skills they can put to immediate use in their workplaces and lives.

Even though we taught different courses, the two authors share similar research traditions. When we reflect upon what we do as instructors and communication scholars, we frequently differentiate "cultural communication" from "intercultural communication." The distinction is useful for teasing out the emergent nature of how both culture and communication come into being. According to Carbaugh (2007), from a cultural discourse perspective, one examines "communication as a practice and culture as emergent in practice" (p. 169). This is important because intercultural communication can sometimes be mistaken for the practice of transferring knowledge or understandings from one culture to another within interaction.

Although translation scholars (Babaee, Wan Yahya, & Babaee, 2014; Dávila-Montes, 2017; Pavan, 2013; Saito, 2015; Evans & Ringrow, 2017; Horváth Futó & Hózsa, 2016; Masi de Casanova & Mose, 2017; Waisbord, 2016; Yang, 2015; Yu, 2017) describe the act of translation as an interpretive exercise whereby one must know and address the meaning of any particular phrase or sentence, we had different goals. We provided the translation assignment in the spirit of what Carbaugh (2007) has referred to as the descriptive mode of analysis. Rather than focus on the differences of meaning present in an interpretive exercise, the descriptive mode focuses on "what is." When we initially assigned this translation exercise, we expected students to take the key concepts at face value and to "simply" translate them into their first language. We did not discuss levels of translation, such as the micro-, macro-, or extra-linguistic situations to which concepts or terms might be put (e.g., Horváth Futó & Hózsa, 2016).

Our primary concern in this chapter is the exploration of the case studies as examples of international education, or more precisely, engagement. The study of translation practices is a secondary focus for us. We acknowledge that there exists a wide body of literature on the concept of translation. Our concern with the use of translation as a pedagogical tool will rely upon those scholars who have studied this (e.g., Yang, 2015).

Two Case Examples

Due to the way the degree program was structured, both authors shared many of the same students. In Intercultural Communication, students were learning about intercultural communication through communication theory. Students could develop their comprehension through discussion and structured application of theories to their experiences. Some of the goals for the class involved understanding "the multiple perspectives" of intercultural communication; being able to "identify the assumptions about human action and communication that influence the ways scholars and practitioners conceptualize" it. As an option to a standard project researching a scholar's professional bibliography, students could translate one of the key concepts.

In Organizational Communication, students learned how to recognize how organizations are formed in and through communication. After examining basic structures, roles, and responsibilities of managers and employees, the class explored several ways that different communicative practices could lead to different outcomes, at times producing solutions or conflict. As a final bit of extra credit, the professor proposed that students who chose to do so may opt to translate designated key concepts.

The Center for Intercultural Dialogue's need for translations presented an opportunity for the students to be able to share their skills in their own native language and at understanding English in a way that would provide them with a tangible public accomplishment they could add to their resumes. We had assumptions about the nature of translation and about educational goals and meanings of tasks. We assumed that students are competent as readers, speakers, and writers in their first language. We credited students for their undertaking study in an alternate language as a recognition of their competence. Students were already engaged in translation in order to participate in our courses. None who participated had English as their first language. We additionally assumed that if learning about a new concept has occurred sufficiently, one could "back-translate" those concepts to one's first language.

Regarding educational goals and tasks, we assumed that extra credit is considered optional and can be undertaken by a student who feels competent to choose it (however, the students who most likely "needed" extra credit were not the strongest students). Finally, we assumed that students would interpret the opportunity to have their work published as a value in and of itself. We assumed students would prepare their work in the ways we directed and show deference to the editor of the website. In some situations, these were not shared assumptions, as we shall demonstrate in the cases below.

The Assignment

In the Intercultural Communication class, students were given a choice of assignments. They could research a concept or scholar and write a seven-page essay about how that concept has been studied or about what areas that researcher has developed over the years. The alternate assignment was to translate one of the key concepts into their native language. This option was developed late in the course's development, ostensibly as a way to provide students seeking credentials with an added value to their work. We assumed that students would value the additional accomplishment on their resumes. In hindsight, the professor's educational goals were insufficiently developed for such a task. The assignment would receive either a pass/fail, based on whether work was done or not done.

In the Organizational Communication course, students had the option of completing an extra-credit assignment that involved translating one of five key concepts, concepts most relevant to the content of the course: conflict management, conflict transformation, intractable conflict, moral conflict, and negotiation. The limitation of concepts was further stipulated so as not to cause too much overlap with the assignment in the Intercultural Communication course (we had briefly discussed the idea of including this assignment before the classes began). The extra-credit assignment would be submitted via Moodle or email. The format had to conform to the format of the key concepts that were already available including, "What it is," "Who uses the concept?" "Fit within intercultural dialogue," and "What work remains?" The professor requested that students have a "native speaker" of the translated language "sign off" on the translation and include the name and email address of that person with their submitted assignment in case we needed verification. Finally, students were told that if the concept was chosen to be published, the editor would be in touch with them directly.

The task called for translations to be shared via email in a Word document with the editor of the website. Another native speaker of that language would review the work as a quality check. The editor and the reviewer would make suggested changes to the draft, and the translator would make those changes and resubmit the work. Finally, the editor would send the final proofs to the translator for approval. Upon receipt of that approval, the translation would be published, with credit given to the translator. Following our last day of class, each instructor sent the editor a set of the translated documents.

Successes

When the process worked well, the editor was able to confirm the translation by a same-language peer reviewer. Upon corresponding with each student via email, the student responded quickly to the editor's queries. In 11 cases, the process worked well, and the student's translation was published. One such term was "moral conflict." A Polish student from Intercultural and a Vietnamese student from Organizational each had their translation approved and accepted.

Missteps

Unfortunately, several reviewers discovered that 50% or more of a translation was prepared using the software Google Translate. While helpful for simple phrases, the software does not catch nuances of usage. Additionally, if a student used it, they would not be responsible for the work of translation—the software did the work for them. Both the American professors and the editor place value on original work. The norm against others' writing (even if the other is software) being presented as a student's original work resulted in instructors having to discuss this with students. In such cases, students were emailed for their responses and a second chance, but they often did not respond to email requests. In two cases, the authorship of the translation was difficult to discern, as the submitted work did not correspond with the student submitting the work.

For instance, the key term "conflict management" was submitted in Hindi, Igbo, and Arabic. Each reviewer believed Google Translate was used. The one in Hindi left out a major section of the work, and the one in Igbo was found inadequate as a translation (even after the student requested the work be reexamined). We did not notice any patterns to why some students succeeded and why others used Google Translate or did not respond to emails.

Lessons Learned

Although our own scholarship draws upon the ethnography of communication, in the practical application, we learned what others have often articulated: "cultural members are not always capable of articulating complex systems of cultural competence on which they rely regularly in their daily lives" (Sprain & Boromisza-Habashi, 2013, p. 183). Borrowing the reflexive categories described by Carbaugh, Nuciforo, Molina-Markham, and van Over (2011), we use "interpretive reflexivity" to note that we did not share students' meaning regarding this assignment. We use "comparative reflexivity" to highlight the distinct cultural perspectives that students had when encountering such a translation assignment and the way that their own learning is assembled and experienced that may hinder the completion of what an instructor may perceive as a straightforward exercise. Finally, it behooves us to consider this case from a "critically reflexive" position and call into question our "explicit ethical stance(s)" (p. 162). For in some ways, our students' goals, which included fulfilling expectations to earn a passing grade to continue to be eligible to work in Poland, was a burden that we bore in creating and marking assignments based on assumptions that may have not been shared.

We would change at least three things: preparation, instructions, and feedback. Because not all concepts can be learned from reading only, we would work with students to consider the historical background regarding how and under what conditions key concepts in the field of intercultural dialogue came into being. We would consider the context whereby the terms could be used in places around the world. We would now use the resources of the translated concepts to discuss any differences between the English and translated versions.

We would revise the way we provide instructions for this and other assignments. We must be more explicit in our discussion of the appropriate use of software tools such as Google Translate. Given its pervasive use and perhaps its place as a key enabler for students to enter into new cross-cultural or international scenes, we need to consider its role in the communication classroom.

Finally, we must spend more time discussing the role of audience in written communication. When a concept is written and when it is translated, asking "for whom?" is a question that cannot go unanswered. The audience one imagines to read one's work may be very different from a local, vernacular community. This is especially true for internet publications, especially one that focuses on having readers from a variety of countries. The use of in-class exercises that encourage collaboration or teamwork can help students to understand how others are hearing and interpreting what is said and written. This feedback, along with feedback from an editor outside the classroom, can help students to recognize the impact of their work on a broader group of people. Having published work can help newcomers to our field to understand a concept in their own language.

Other ideas for feedback include presenting models that chunk the work into more manageable pieces. Working with concepts that are common to more cultures or languages can help scaffold a one-page translation exercise into workable units that can be discussed and debated before providing an evaluation.

Conclusion

In reflecting on these assignments, we have come to appreciate how our own translation limitations hindered our ability to provide guidance on this project. The ways that students encountered us and the assignment encouraged us to include more translation mini (and ungraded) exercises throughout our courses in the following year.

Instructors who teach outside their native countries must be reflective and adaptable, approaching the international classroom in respectful ways. We must also be mindful of our assumptions about scholarly work or demonstrations of academic knowledge and the forms in which it should and should not be transmitted, about assumptions for our purposes, and what students expect from us. Where the students are international as well, our charge to be reflective is compounded. As teachers ourselves, we offer this "reflexive utterance" (Carbaugh, 1988/89) to remind ourselves that while we are there to provide the American way of teaching, we reflect about what that means and how it positions us. We must remember that we are also students of our own experiences and learn from them. We cannot fully anticipate all the twists and turns the experience will take, but we must anticipate that there will indeed be paths we had not expected.

We agree with Saito (2015), who cited the important contribution John Dewey made when he articulated the way education begins "at home." This is particularly important to keep in mind in international classrooms.

References

Babaee, S., Wan Yahya, W. R., & Babaee, R. (2014). Creativity, culture and translation. *English Language Teaching*, 7(6), 14–18. http://dx.doi.org/10.5539/elt.v7n6p14

Carbaugh, D. (1988/89). Deep agony: "Self" vs. "society" in Donahue discourse. *Research on Language and Social Interaction*, 22, 179–212.

Carbaugh, D. (2007). Cultural discourse analysis: Communication practices and intercultural encounters. *Journal of Intercultural Communication Research*, 36(3), 167–182.

Carbaugh, D., Nuciforo, E. V., Molina-Markham, E., & van Over, B. (2011). Discursive reflexivity in the ethnography of communication: Cultural discourse analysis. *Cultural Studies <=> Critical Methodologies*, 11(153), 153–164. http://dx.doi.org/10.1177/1532708611401334

Center for Intercultural Dialogue. (2018). *Key Concepts in Intercultural Dialogue – by number*. Retrieved December 26, 2018, from https://centerforinterculturaldialogue.org/publications/key-concepts-in-intercultural-dialogue-by-number/

Chetro-Szivos, J. (2010). Cross-border tertiary education: The challenges and opportunities for intercultural understanding. *Journal of Intercultural Management*, 2, 5–22.

Dávila-Montes, J. M. (2017, May). Translation as a rhetoric of meaning. *Poroi*, 13(1), 1–28.

Evans, J., & Ringrow, H. (2017). Introduction: Borders in translation and intercultural communication. *TranscUlturAl*, 9(2), 1–12. Retrieved from http://ejournals.library.ualberta.ca/index.php/TC

Grove, J. (2014, March 6). Shrinking enrollments in Poland. *Inside Higher Ed*. Retrieved December 27, 2018, from www.insidehighered.com/news/2014/03/06/universities-poland-struggle-shrinking-enrollments

Horváth Futó, H., & Hózsa, E. (2016). Divergent cultural environment: Translator authenticity, Acta Universitatis Sapientiae. *Philologica*, 8(2), 7–20.

Leeds-Hurwitz, W. (1990). Notes in the history of intercultural communication: The Foreign service institute and the mandate for intercultural training. *Quarterly Journal of Speech*, 76(3), 262–281. http://dx.doi.org/10.1080/00335639009383919

Masi de Casanova, E., & Mose, T. R. (2017). Translation in ethnography: Representing Latin American studies in English. *Translation and Interpreting Studies*, 12(1), 1–23. http://dx.doi.org/10.1075/tis.12.1.01dec

New York University School of Law. (2006). *Journal of international law and politics guide to Foreign and international legal citations*. New York: New York University. Retrieved from www.law.nyu.edu/sites/default/files/upload_documents/Final_GFILC_pdf.pdf

Pavan, E. (2013). The Simpsons: Translation and language teaching in an EFL class. *Studies in Second Language Learning and Teaching*, 3(1), 131–145.

Saito, N. (2015, March). Philosophy as translation and understanding other cultures: Becoming a global citizen through higher education. *Educational Studies in Japan: International Yearbook*, 9, 17–26.

Siwinska, B. (2011, October 16). Poland: Private higher education under threat. *University World News*. Retrieved December 27, 2018, from www.universityworldnews.com/post.php?story=20111015213651212

Sprain, L., & Boromisza-Habashi, D. (2013). The ethnographer of communication at the table: Building cultural competence, designing strategic action. *Journal of Applied Communication Research*, *41*(2), 181–187.

Vasagar, J. (2011, April 6). Poland's students go private in force. *The Guardian*. Retrieved December 27, 2018, from www.theguardian.com/world/2011/apr/06/poland-universities-private-public

Waisbord, S. (2016). Communication studies without frontiers? Translation and cosmopolitanism across academic cultures. *International Journal of Communication*, *10*, 868–886.

Yang, P. (2015). Enhancing intercultural communication and understanding: Team translation project as a student engagement learning approach. *International Education Studies*, *8*(8), 67–80. http://dx.doi.org/10.5539/ies.v8n8p67

Yu, X. (2017, August). An analysis of English translation of Chinese classics from the perspective of cultural communication. *Theory and Practice in Language Studies*, *7*(8), 651–656. http://dx.doi.org/10.17507/tpls.0708.07

21 Contact and Context(s)
Cultural Discourse Analysis of Internationalized Activities in a Blended Media Studies Course

Barbara Ruth Burke and LieneLočmele

Introduction

In joining the recent debate within the discipline of communication, on whether globalization allows for scholarly cultures and ideas to meet or, in fact, perpetuates the preexisting power dynamics stemming from national intellectual politics and US-based thematic interests (Waisbord, 2016), we offer a description, analysis, and evaluation of an international academic partnership that offers a partial response. While acknowledging the presence of the elements belonging to the latter (e.g., the choice of textbooks and language dynamics, since the language of instruction corresponds with the native tongue of some), we argue for the former and suggest working toward meeting points. Our chapter highlights elements and examples that may not be present in all classroom Cultural Discourse Analysis (CuDA). Nonetheless, the study may be useful for furthering a conversation about similar mixed cultural experiences in virtual classrooms.

The wide range of purposeful learning experiences we created by using common readings and writing prompts, by putting students into blended, international and intercultural classrooms through online technologies, and by having students writing experience reflections connected our institutions and our Media and Society course students.

Together we learned many things.

Theoretical Frame

Understanding how classroom communication builds a specific learning environment and how factors of identifiable difference may influence the culture were of concern to us as we considered our experiences of and evaluated the virtually blended course. Several studies explore diverse student populations and compulsory education contexts (e.g., Ungemah, 2015), apply pedagogical arguments offered by Foucault regarding forms of neoliberalism, student self-management, and control (Besley & Peters, 2007), or integrate Freire's ideas regarding allowing student freedoms (Micheletti, 2010).

Because we know people will perform culturally and socially constructed roles based upon their understandings and interpretations of a relational situation, we thus assert the classroom has communication-rich situations and settings that are well understood by students and instructors. Furthermore, research shows that the customary assortment of classroom discourse patterns is familiar and predictable, involving the shared understandings of negotiated positions, relationships and values that make up the learning environment (Cazden, 2001). It is also understood that participants perform within the context of institutionally predefined opportunities and possibilities (e.g., Cameron, 2000), where teacher-lecturing courses using "ordinary classroom talk" sometimes have the tendency to replicate hegemonic processes and reinforce power relationships (e.g., Alexander, 1999; Braswell, 2015; Damrow, 2014; Maybin, 2013).

A few education research studies apply the perspective of Hymes's (1962) Ethnography of Communication (EC; Damrow, 2014; Duff, 2002; and Zhu & Bargiela-Chiappini, 2013). However, our project moves the description and analysis into the related theoretical and methodological modes of CuDA (Carbaugh, 2007), to contribute to the understanding of university-level education contexts (e.g., Boromisza-Habashi, Hughes, & Malkowski, 2016; Covarrubias, 2008;Ločmele & Burke, 2017). Furthermore, we are influenced by Carbaugh (1996) and Carbaugh (2005), who used CuDA to study the cultural differences in communication experienced by exchange students upon interacting with counterparts at their host countries. Those situations are ideologically specific to a particular national context in which the studied communication takes place. Our work moves the questions forward to the 21st century by focusing on communication that has no singular physical place of existence, since the communication between our students (from ViA and UMM) is a product of technology-mediated real-time interaction. This communicated construction foregrounds a potentially creative and negotiated set of cultural norms.

To conduct our analysis, we extended ideas from Cultural Discourse Analysis (CuDA), which defines culture as a "potentially integrative and changeable system of symbols, symbolic meanings and forms that are mutually intelligible, commonly accessible, deeply felt and historically grounded" (Carbaugh, 1990, 2007). CuDA offers the systematic understanding of how culture is a part and product of discursive systems, seeing historically transmitted expressive systems of communicative acts, events, and styles that consist of symbols, symbolic forms, norms, and meanings. It treats discourse as "culture in conversations," understood as meta-communication about *preferred* ways of being a person, acting, relating, feeling, and dwelling (Carbaugh, 2005, 2007).

When doing CuDA, a scholar identifies, describes, and formulates rules and norms about a particular communication practice/pattern. In the case of intercultural communication, the focus is primarily on those communication moments when two or more cultures are played out by interlocutors (Carbaugh, 1990). Here, instead of focusing only upon how a certain communication practice is a cultural phenomenon, the analyst's task is to explore several sides of "the story" relevant to the studied interaction. This is exactly what we do when examining the variety of contexts students bring to the joint learning interaction. Thus, CuDA approaches intercultural encounters by focusing on conversations, contexts, distinctive cultural features, and meanings, instead of on idealized situations or seeing intercultural meetings as a move toward "competencies" favoring assimilation toward one way of interaction.

After establishing our approach *theoretically* regarding the notion of culture, communication, and meaning, we turn to the *description* of particular instances of communication and an analysis of student interactions, without a singular physical place of existence and without instruction specifically about the intercultural aspects of the experience. We thus find instances in which students engage in comparing perspectives on the discussed media course theme based on their understandings of how the perspective of the other group might be different from theirs. To create the *interpretative* mode, we then investigate ways the observed phenomenon embeds meaning and significance, since communicatively, participants say things literally but also culturally (Carbaugh, 2007).

Our analysis is *comparative* in the sense that in the interpretative mode, we also compare and contrast the variety of available perspectives that students brought to our blended learning space. Via extrapolation of the cultural premises of value, we point at a variety of potential inequalities informed by professional/institutional contexts of the participants.

Analysis

CuDA and EC would claim that all meaning is contextual. In that sense, one cannot *discover* a context, since it is always there for us to provide a variety of meanings that are available for our participants for interpreting the communication at hand. The blended classroom is a "place created by and through discourse"—students visit then revert "home," reflect and write, and finally reenter in subsequent scheduled connection times. As ethnographers of communication, we approached our data theoretically informed, but not assuming the existence of certain patterns. In this case, we observed our students directly and indirectly describing each other's media uses and media content interpretative strategies, building upon the sensibilities of the contexts to which they belong. We saw this discourse as being worth further examination, since it emerged from the variety of types of data that we directly gathered. By describing the related meanings and investigating the norms and values enabling their use by our students, we arrived at recognizing the intersections of various contexts present in our students' interaction. For the sake of clarity, the following analysis demonstrates the most reader-friendly excerpts of our data, which stand for the larger pattern but, by far, are not the only excerpts illustrating that pattern.

Professional/Institutional Context(s)

The following excerpts point at similarities and differences identified by students in their virtual class discussions as well as used in their suggestions of possible additions and improvements of the class.

> What was surprising was that there [on the Latvian side], there seemed to be a more focused mindset [meaning more "serious" topics and connections of media and politics] when it came to the lectures and lessons from class, and that their class was more ready to answer questions [and to give practical examples about news] than our class was.
>
> (UMMjournal17)[1]

> If some [students] from ViA use video sharing website YouTube for education and to get to know some actual information, then UMM students use it for fun and to watch different bloggers. I do both of these things—I watch some educational videos, but I like to watch bloggers and videos about some things that I am interested in just for fun.
>
> (ViAjournal3)

The meanings associated with media content are organized around the dichotomy "educational/entertaining" since students in several instances speak about media content as generally divided into "pop culture" and "serious content/news." While examining the differences in their preferences, consumption and interpretation of both types of content are seen as valuable, but with respect to their hierarchical relationship and associated normative values. The former manifests itself more in ViAjournal3 talk and media consumption patterns and for UMMjournal17 signals the presence of "more focused mindset" and being "ready to answer questions"— characteristics that are preferred in the academic setting in comparison to doing things "just for fun."

The popular discourse about young people and media in Latvia, along with the design of ViA3 study programs, has to be considered as an enabling force for such hierarchy to be present in our virtual classroom. ViA journalism instructors often are professionally affiliated with media, and their feedback on papers encourages students to develop media consumption habits that would benefit their understanding of social, economic, and political affairs instead of "just having fun" online. Moreover, as students of *professional* higher education programs, ViA students are expected to complete compulsory internships in journalism, so a correspondence with the job market and ability to tailor competencies to its needs from the institutional perspective is seen as an essential marker of study quality. By contrast, UMM is a liberal arts college, which aims to expose students to a breadth of topics they integrate when they graduate and seek occupations.

Therefore, the cultural logic brought to the virtual classroom by ViA students operates on the following premises of existence and value: (1) media content has either entertainment *or* education function; (2) one can tell which of the functions a particular content fulfills; (3) in the hierarchy of these functions, education is preferred over entertainment; and (4) a future communication professional should prioritize media content associated with educational function. Thus, ViA students symbolically engage in a morally loaded performance recognizing professional and institutional expectations. By openly admitting enjoying entertainment media, the future communication professional threatens one's professional identity, hence students may not highlight that interest within a classroom discussion. By contrast, UMM counterparts may envision a professional, highly regarded career in entertainment media and for assignments and discussions have been told that the study of entertainment is a valuable enterprise and that popular culture analysis is a scholarly activity. Hence, these students consume mostly entertainment media and consider it seriously. The ViA students also enjoy entertainment, but, in the absence of a strong industry, do not choose to discuss entertainment in class in front of instructors and, when doing so, see it as somewhat trivial.

The difference in the cultural logic between both groups of students lie around the premises of value. While all participants could most likely agree on separation between the educational and entertainment functions of media, as well as ability for a person to identify which content serves each of the functions, for UMM students, the hierarchical relationship between both functions and the prioritization of educational content in association with professional identity, while recognized, is not so clear-cut. The presence of this dynamics in the blended classroom has consequences for the content, flow, and learning during joint discussion sessions.

In practice, the ways different media are discussed are communications infused with symbolic meanings, borrowed from the professional and institutional contexts that enable/disable the legitimacy of certain media types, content, and use, since this nature of communication is linked to our students' professional identity performances. In our situation, because learning contemporary media theory involves familiarity with recent studies on video gaming, social media and pornography, which the identified normative meanings stigmatize, the presupposed hierarchies become deconstructed as a part of a joint task for both groups of students in order to create mutual awareness and open up the potentiality to safely debate all kinds of media content. The exploration of media functions beyond the dichotomous (entertainment/educational) raises several additional discussion topics. We as scholars see this distinction as arbitrary, made by students, yet useful as part of a teachable moment.

Local Context(s)

Here the observed pattern is related to the discussion fragments where insider knowledge about local communication styles as well as outsider interpretations of them were brought into being in the blended classroom. The following excerpt is a part of a transcribed oral discussion in a blended class, wherein ViA and UMM students directly exchange views on a particular style of politeness employed by characters of the TV series filmed in Minnesota:

> I thought the politeness [observed in the TV series] was too crazy, it can't be true. Is it wrong [the offered interpretation], or is it really how it is, that polite. Saying "oh, sorry, oh sorry" and all this polite stuff?
> (ViAdiscussionIVstudent1)

> It's not like perceived as so polite, but it's called Minnesota Nice. And, it's a way that no one is willing to say that something is wrong but it's sort of passive-aggressive. We hint at it. So, everyone just kind of skirts around problems. They hope that you notice what you are doing wrong and stop doing it, instead of calling each other out about it.
> (UMMdiscussionIVstudent6)

ViAstudent1 brings to our attention two kinds of interpersonal politeness. When she labels observed acts of politeness as exaggerated or "too crazy," she builds upon common perceptions of "American" ways of interacting, which, in comparison to "Latvian," is generally associated with significantly higher amount of smiling, small talk, and verbal exchange of pleasantries. Openly referencing the common view might be risky due to its generalized and stereotypical nature, so with her comment that is initially devoted to communication style observed in media, the student indirectly tests whether interpersonal communication in reality is "that polite" as a TV series as well as a common perception of "American" communication tells. Therefore, the culturally bounded connections between what is said and is meant puts "American" performance into the scrutiny of "Latvian" eyes. For the former ("American"), exchanges of pleasantries function as a "social glue"—as a way to establish relationship, acknowledge other's presence, and keep the conversation going—while for the latter ("Latvian"), the preferred performance involves exchanging sincere information (state what you mean or remain silent). Additionally, UMMstudent6 introduces the third kind of interpersonal politeness that functions as a form of social sanctioning of undesirable behavior within the performance of "Minnesota nice." He identifies that the behavior that ViAstudent1 sees as exaggerated is, in fact, locally known as a "passive-aggressive" way of noting an undesirable behavior.

The cultural logics regarding verbal performance of polite behaviors from "Latvian" perspectives can be formulated in the following premises of existence and value: (1) difference exists between what one says and what one means; (2) saying polite things to others might have another meaning than just being polite; (3) to be appropriately polite, one should maintain a balance between the amount of verbal politeness and the sincerity of the content of one's words; (4) the one who uses too many polite phrases without sincere content cannot be honest.

The difference in the cultural logics of these kinds of interpersonal politeness lies upon aspects of the interaction—the amount of verbal input in general; the desirable level of being "truthful" in one's polite speech; and the social actions such as apology, creating and/or maintaining social relationships, or the sanctioning of an "undesirable"—that this kind of verbal politeness can accomplish in its local contexts. While participants may possibly agree on a premise differentiating between verbal politeness and its meaning, the rest of the listed elements vary. In our previous research, we illuminated cultural differences between UMM and ViA students in terms of the amount of verbal participation in learning activities and the identity risks for ViA students that are associated with social pressures to contribute unique information (Ločmele & Burke, 2017). Here we also see how the amount of verbal interaction, in this case, along with the desired level of "truth" that the meanings of words stand for, adds to our understanding of how interpersonal interaction can be interpreted as polite, dishonest, or controlling.

Thus, available interpretations of interpersonal politeness observed and discussed about fictional others served a variety of learning purposes, both interpersonal and media theory related. Firstly, participants gained access to a variety of symbolic meanings in relation to what counts as "polite" for the range of students as well as to creative uses of "politeness" in social interaction. Secondly, the discussion itself also served as a relatively safe space for testing generalized assumptions one might have, in this case, about "American" communication. Thirdly, via this discussion, participants directly witnessed how culture enables us to interpret the same media content in a variety of ways and how these interpretations are linked to cultural resources participants brought to their interaction. As a benefit of the joint course, participants added to each other's interpretation, extending the repertoire available at our single virtual locality. These could be systematically used to learn about media theory, (e.g., active audience, cultural imperialism) but also for sensitizing participants to their local communication patterns and habits, since without comparing and contrasting, they usually are taken for granted. While investigating media content, our classroom discussions simultaneously contain indirect meta-commentary about culturally specific ways and meanings of communication.

Conclusions and Implications: International Blended Classrooms and Merged Contexts

Media uses/consumption are conceived of as the ritualized activities of social and culturally specific "communities" (Carey, 1989). For us, understanding globalized availability, differences and similarities in interpretations, and media habits thus needs to be considered not merely based on the clarity of message delivery of the transmission model(s) of communication. Instead, we focus on ways (inter)cultural understandings are taught and practiced by layers of strategy.

Scrutinizing and investigating the pervasiveness of Western-centered or US-driven methods of communication studies and instruction, certain ideological dynamics became highlighted within the analysis of this blended learning activity. In some instances, one might expect that communication "success" would derive from building interactions so that the Latvians were successful communicators when they became more like the American communicators. In this situation, we found instead that there is much more at play than just the locations and educational backgrounds of instructors and students in our media theory courses. Rather, there is a particular classroom culture that develops with each set of students, and that attention to context(s) matters. In the development of students' curiosity about media theories, our students engaged in thinking about their current and future possibilities and about ways of living and communicating in the world (Sorrels & Sekimoto, 2016).

In review of our blended classroom experience, we observed students: (1) forming connections across disciplines and locations; (2) applying skills, knowledge, and methods from a media studies course to a different task, namely building an enhanced intercultural repertoire. Throughout the extended semester-long partnership, with the variety of parallel assignments, writing exercises, electronic journal exchanges, and connected and not-connected class discussions, we came to recognize that "knowledge, learning and meaning-based activities" created an enriched understanding of networked social processes (Siemens, 2005).

Traditionally EC and CuDA's contribution is associated with foregrounding communication as the object to be studied in its own right. If we compare our work with primary-level education research projects, wherein scholars often seek to understand learning styles, use of technology, and/or problem-based learning with a focus on technologies selected by instructors as preconditions for success, here we have instead an examination of the *communication* of adult students, at a university level, in moment-to-moment interactions, in which we and they recognize that the experience is allowing for creativity, inclusion, and the co-construction of their unique learning environment. Through the study and analysis of their communications, CuDA can thus illuminate these potentials along with, for instance, potential for clashes and conflicts. As we attempted to understand our students, they enhanced their proficiencies at recognizing contexts they did not have/did not know about before the class and became more comfortable with articulating positioned, specific considerations. How could students begin to get connected to/within contexts in order to generate more robust zones of contact and become even more cosmopolitan? For future projects between two universities, planning faculty should predominantly start with the study of the shared course topics and then also address how partnerships:

- elucidate the contexts and design future assignments to get them more prominent;
- discuss intersections that create more nuanced understandings;
- use technology to make this happen.

Students entered into the learning experience with a sensibility that there might be a "national culture" with norms and values. They came to recognize that generalizations do not reflect their realities and therefore should not be applied to others without scrutiny. In part, this is because as illuminated through CuDA, the blended classrooms have willingly participated in their conversations about conversations, forming their contexts and specific cultures. Kim (2007), citing Fougere and Moulette's (postcolonial) criticism (2007), unpacks and responds to Hofstede's "national" dimensions and categories studied in other classes. Following this logic, through our activities, students instead used guided-discourse experiences to foster greater awareness of diversity within groups. This new perspective, aligned with Waisbord's (2016) view of cosmopolitanism, is a positive outcome of education.

Furthering Livingstone's (2015) arguments, we find translation and "cosmopolitanism" require deliberation and practice in communication processes, because to recognize and productively engage differences is the goal of genuine academic internationalization. Thus, moving beyond acknowledging and tolerating nationally different others, with other disciplinary interests, translation requires activity to "cultivate zones of contact and to engage with others and supersede cultural differences" (p. 881). Fulfilling this interest was an underlying, important goal behind the planned internationalization of our Media Studies courses.

Note

1. Our attribution style for quotes from participants, in this document: (schoolsource (journal or discussion)person#).

References

Alexander, B. K. (1999). Performing culture in the classroom: An instructional (auto)ethnography. *Text & Performance Quarterly, 19*(4), 307.
Besley, T., & Peters, M. A. (2007). *Subjectivity & truth: Foucault, education, and the culture of self* (Vol. 303). New York: Peter Lang.
Boromisza-Habashi, D., Hughes, J. F., & Malkowski, J. A. (2016). Public speaking as cultural ideal: Internationalizing the public speaking curriculum. *Journal of International and Intercultural Communication, 9*(1), 20–34.
Braswell, G. G. (2015). Observations of representational practices by Indian-descent children in a US preschool classroom: Connections among people, spaces and artifacts. *Early Childhood Education Journal, 43*(2), 135–142.
Cameron, D. (2000). *Good to talk? Living and working in a communication culture*. Thousand Oaks, CA: Sage.
Carbaugh, D. (Ed.). (1990). *Cultural communication and intercultural contact*. Hillsdale: Lawrence Erlbaum.
Carbaugh, D. (1996). *Situating selves: The communication of social identities in American scenes*. Albany, NY: SUNY Press.
Carbaugh, D. (2005). *Cultures in conversation*. Mahwah, NJ: Lawrence Erlbaum.
Carbaugh, D. (2007). Cultural discourse analysis: Communication practices and intercultural encounters. *Journal of Intercultural Communication Research, 36*, 167–182.
Carey, J. W. (1989). *Communication as culture*. New York: Routledge Publications.
Cazden, C. B. (2001). The language of teaching and learning: The language of teaching and learning. *Communication, 80*(3), 348–369.
Covarrubias, P. O. (2008). Masked silence sequences: Hearing discrimination in the college classroom. *Communication, Culture & Critique, 1*(3), 227–252.
Damrow, A. (2014). Navigating the structures of elementary school in the United States and Japan: An ethnography of the particular. *Anthropology & Education Quarterly, 45*(1), 87–104.
Duff, P. A. (2002). The discursive co-construction of knowledge, identity, and difference: An ethnography of communication in the high school mainstream. *Applied Linguistics, 23*(3), 289–322.
Hymes, D. (1962). The ethnography of speaking. In T. Gladwin & W. C. Sturtevant (Eds.), *Anthropology and human behavior* (pp. 15–53). Washington, DC: Anthropological Society of Washington.

Kim, Y. Y. (2007). Ideology, identity, and intercultural communication: An analysis of differing academic conceptions of cultural identity. *Journal of Intercultural Communication Research*, 36(3), 237–253.

Livingstone, S. (2015). Active audiences? The debate progresses but is far from resolved. *Communication Theory*, 25, 439–446.

Ločmele, L., & Burke, B. R. (2017). The contribution of technology to an undergraduate international learning partnership: The ritual perspective. *Society, Integration, Education: Proceedings of the International Scientific Conference*, (3), 528–538.

Maybin, J. (2013). Towards a sociocultural understanding of children's voice. *Language & Education: An International Journal*, 27(5), 383–397.

Micheletti, G. (2010). Re-envisioning Paulo Freire's "Banking concept of education." *Inquiries Journal*, 2(2).

Siemens, G. (2005). Connectivism: A learning theory for the digital age. Retrieved from www.itdl.org/journal/jan_05/article01.htm

Sorrels, K., & Sekimoto, S. (2016). *Globalizing intercultural communication*. Los Angeles: Sage.

Ungemah, L. D. (2015). Diverse classrooms, diverse curriculum, diverse complications: Three teacher perspectives. *Anthropology & Education Quarterly*, 46(4), 431–439.

Waisbord, S. (2016). Communication studies without frontiers? Translation and cosmopolitanism across academic cultures. *International Journal of Communication*, 10, 868–886.

Zhu, Y., & Bargiela-Chiappini, F. (2013). Balancing emic and etic: Situated learning and ethnography of communication in cross-cultural management education. *Academy of Management Learning & Education*, 12(3), 380–395.

22 Internationalizing Interpersonal Organizational Communication

Ann Rogerson and L. Celeste Rossetto

Introduction

The large numbers of international students who study beyond their home borders present opportunities for educators to leverage linguistic, cultural and learning background differences between students to enhance curriculum and assessment, particularly in the area of cross-cultural interpersonal communication. Leveraging these opportunities develops individual student skills and better prepares them for future employment in a globalized workforce in which differences in cultural and language backgrounds are the norm. Integrating "real-world" interpersonal communication situations into class and assessment activities helps students to develop capabilities in accommodating language and cultural differences. By developing academic capacities beyond knowledge, students experience the complexity of cross-cultural communication and encounter acquisition in a safe and collaborative learning environment (Kolb & Kolb, 2005). In addition, students have opportunities to develop their skills in cross-cultural communication through collaborative problem-solving–based assessments, as well as enhancing their academic language, literacy, and research capabilities.

This chapter demonstrates how the effective integration of group and individual activities with a focus on developing cross-cultural communication skills into curricula can be achieved. The discussions and outlines here are written to assist educators to replicate the assessments and activities in their own classrooms. The examples presented and discussed are drawn from a cross-cultural postgraduate management subject in a master of international business (MIB) degree in a regional Australian university. Explicit teaching activities were designed to utilize the inherent diversity in our student populations to achieve learning outcomes and replicate workplace experiences. The number of international students at our university mirrors Australia's higher education sector (Norton, Norton, & Shannon, 2013, p. 24) where English is the only language of commonality. International students studying in Australia are required to have a minimum skill level in English (written, spoken, and comprehension) in order to gain entry into a program of study; however competence, confidence, accents, and experiences with English vary between individuals and within cohorts.

Curricula Design

Curricula and the related assessments and activities were planned through an integrated approach that considered the relationship between learning design and the processes and actions necessary for students to achieve the outcomes of the subject, improve their cross-cultural communication skills, and develop skills transferable to workplaces. Consequently, we used the approach outlined in Rogerson's (2015) model (see Figure 22.1), which depicts an integrated process guiding the consideration and design of appropriate assessments and activities to underpin assessments tasks.

Design Considerations

Design considerations comprised the approved learning outcomes, an identified need to embed academic skills within assessment tasks while developing individual interpersonal communication skills relevant to globalized workforces. We used backward planning, also known as backward design (Wiggins & McTighe, 2012), as we knew the learning outcomes we wanted to achieve in summative assessments.

Learning Outcomes

Of the three learning outcomes for this subject, two specifically focused on cross-cultural and interpersonal communication skills in individual and teamwork contexts. For example, Learning Outcome 2 required students to be able to "demonstrate cross-cultural knowledge and interpersonal skills to manage and work with individuals, teams and organizations in a variety of cultural and global contexts," while Learning Outcome 3 specifically mentioned the development of cross-cultural communication skills. It is important that interpersonal and communication skills are explicitly stated so educators can highlight the relationship between the learning outcomes, assessments, and assessment activities. Students should be made aware of why assessment tasks and related activities are designed the way they are and the benefits of embracing the educational opportunity on offer. In addition, if students can understand how the learning skills developed during the subject relate to their future beyond their degree, they may be motivated to sustain this approach to learning in similar situations (sustainable learning; Boud, 2000; Boud & Soler, 2016). Being explicit about the structure and purpose of learning activities addresses potential or actual student concerns. For example: some students may feel uncomfortable about their differing levels of language and academic competencies being exposed in a group work situation (Levinsohn, 2007). However, discussing this

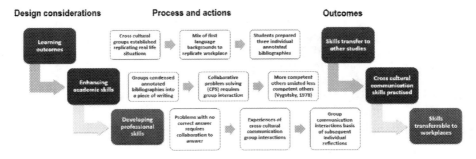

Figure 22.1 Designing for development of cross-cultural communication for higher education and future employment.

acknowledges and normalizes their discomfort as a natural part of building cross-cultural communication competencies.

Embedding Academic Skills

There is often an assumption that students who enroll in a university to complete a postgraduate degree will already be familiar with the higher education environment. While this may be true for some domestic students, our experience suggests that the majority of enrollments in our faculty postgraduate degrees are international students with different educational backgrounds. There is a perception that students coming from overseas have little to contribute (Gale, 2012), and their previous learning experiences may not equip them for postgraduate study in Australia, so we offered the students the opportunity to contribute, and they accepted the challenge. International students do benefit from explicit teaching around assignment requirements that also assists with the culture shock that many international students experience. For instance, Canning (2010) notes that teaching staff should design initial tasks around existing competencies before introducing strategies and activities that will enhance student learning. Therefore, our focus was to consolidate students' capabilities in academic study areas while tacitly introducing them to cross-cultural communication experiences.

Developing Individual Interpersonal Communication Skills

The best way to achieve this is to mandate that students move into mixed first-language groups with group work tasks facilitated by the lecturer or tutor. This can be implemented in two ways. First, the lecturer or tutor determines group composition (size/mix) prior to the first class. This ensures that there is a mix of cultural and language backgrounds based on enrollment information before announcing group allocations to the class as a foregone conclusion. Secondly, using the enrollment information, the lecturer or tutor determines the mix of students (and any dominant national groups) and allows groups to self-select around a specific set of rules/guidelines. Both methods provide a mix of students and reduce the impact of cultural clusters in which students tend to congregate with others from a similar cultural/language background. Based on our previous experiences using both methods, the second achieves the best results as an interactive activity to promote intercultural communication, but this may need to be varied dependent upon the class composition. For example, you may need to ask the class what language they usually speak at home to draw on family language backgrounds and migration patterns if there is only one dominant language group.

The guidelines used for intercultural/cross-language group formation used in this case are presented in Table 22.1.

Assessments and Activities

Three assessments were specified for students to successfully complete the classes: a group work task, an individual reflective report, and a final examination. The primary focus here is to discuss how the group work assessment and related tutorial activities promote the development of cross-cultural communication skills. The design of the reflective report and activities assist students to understand what they have experienced and learned in the group work communication interactions.

Table 22.1 Cross-cultural group formation guidelines

Step 1	Step 2	Step 3	Step 4	Step 5	Step 6
Determine cultural background/potential language mix through enrollment records. For example: Domestic versus International enrollments, country of origin. Determine group size (ideally minimum 3, maximum 5) to promote interactions.	Introduce the group formation activity as preparation for the group work assessment. Make the connection to both subject content and how working with people from other cultures and language backgrounds is a key factor for success in a globalized business environment.	Get the class to stand. Ask all students from the dominant background to stand to one side of the class, and ask the others to form a certain number of groups (Total students divided by the 3–5 range = number of groups required for the class). Ideally, this should be no more than three people.	Invite students from the dominant background to join one of the groups (not exceeding the maximum number you determined in Step 1).	Have students sit in their new groups and allow them time to introduce themselves to each other.	Unpack the group work assessment task, giving students the key points that need to be determined such as tasks for each week, and encourage them to share contact information.

Group Work Assessment Task

The group work assessment task comprised two components. The first, three short pieces of individual writing (maximum 250 words for each piece), are then condensed into the second component, where the individual pieces of writing are crafted by the group into a literature summary of 350 to 500 words. The group work was structured in this way to mitigate some of the difficulties evident in feedback about group work assessments where some of the more capable students have to compensate for the less capable or lazy students to avoid having their grades adversely affected (Smith, 2018). By addressing this factor in the assessment design, one of the expected objections about group work is overcome, allowing students to focus on the task while learning through their interactions. In addition, instead of setting group work that requires students to organize their interactions outside the classroom, the content and time allocations were flipped. This meant that reading and preparation took place outside of lecture and tutorial time, and the group work interactions were conducted in an extended tutorial.

Individual Written Component of Group Work

For the individual component, students had to choose three peer-reviewed research articles on a given cultural dimension, which in this class was collectivism versus individualism (Hofstede, 1983). The lecturer selected the topic or theoretical area relevant to the subject matter, changing it from session to session—thus making assessment tasks difficult to copy from previous sessions and incorporating the principles of assessment design to reduce instances of contract cheating (Rogerson, 2017). Students could select the context of the theoretical area for search purposes, for example, a study related to their own or another country, or a specific population (students, workplaces, occupations). They had to read, summarize, and present them to their group. As cross-cultural communication is not an individual task, if students had chosen identical articles, they had to negotiate selections, further developing their communication experiences related to actual workplaces.

Group Written Component of the Assessment Task

The group work component offered opportunities to learn together through collaborative exercises in which students had to communicate orally with each other to integrate their individual pieces of writing into a summary of the literature reviewed by the group. Not only did students explore the subject matter, but they also developed ways to communicate what they learned from their individual journal selections. The level of engagement increased as this cohort of students exchanged ideas and comments about what they had read. Students learned how to evaluate and compare the ideas, definitions, study populations, and methodologies in academic journals that focused on their topic. This approach was influenced by the social constructivist theories of Vygotsky (1978) that claim learning in a social environment is valuable, as learners share what they know and together create further knowledge. The teacher becomes less central to the learning process and morphs into a facilitator of learning.

Students were given templates that offered them a clear map of how to examine the literature and determine what was important for their topic as support for their discussions and efforts to combine and condense individual pieces of writing into an integrated literature summary. The template assisted students in grouping together similarities and differences in order to compare and analyze their selections critically. It also provided groups with an actual record of what they did and how they progressed during the trimester.

Facilitating Group Work by the Lecturer/Tutor

The group work was conducted in class time, allowing for facilitation of the assessment task. The lecturer/tutor would introduce activities to support the assessment task then ask the groups to work on the activities. Throughout the tutorial, the lecturer/tutor observed group interactions, answered questions that were raised, and intervened when observing that the group members were struggling to understand a concept or task. Where similar questions were asked, the lecturer/tutor gained the attention of all groups to avoid repeating answers. This demonstrated to students how to and when to ask questions and normalized the lack of understanding about an area but encouraged shared learning. Further, more capable students were comfortable in assisting less capable students, as they were aware that the greater proportion of their grades would be earned through their individual component. Facilitating group work in tutorial time also reduced the pressure on groups to complete the assessment task effectively outside of class. Students found this sped up their ability to complete tasks, as they also knew there was support immediately available from the lecturer/tutor to address concerns and provide clarifications.

Individual Reflective Assessment Task

The second assessment was a reflective individual report requiring a comparison and reflection on cultural and communication differences. This task first required students to compare themselves to the relevant cultural classifications under Hofstede (1983). This assisted them in developing critical analysis skills. Students developed an understanding of how they could challenge ideas using evidence to support their arguments where their own experiences differ from those published. Secondly, students had to reflect on their cross-cultural communication experiences during the group interactions from assessment one. Reflection can generate a conscious acknowledgment of the impact of experiences while developing understanding of how those experiences can influence (in this case) future interpersonal interactions. However, not all students have experienced a reflective task, so to stimulate their thinking, we posed questions such as what went well, what did they learn, and how might they apply this in the future (Canning & Callan, 2010). In this way activities were included to support students learning how to construct their own reflections while exposing them to examples of poor and better reflections and how reflections can be aligned to immediate and future experiences. This follows the principles of heutagogy (Hase & Kenyon, 2007; Kenyon & Hase, 2001), in which students are prepared to apply learning for both future known and unanticipated situations.

Tutorial Activities

In Australian universities, there is a push for students to become independent learners which is an aspiration that needs to be translated into application and learning. With this in mind, we constructed scaffolded activities around the assessment tasks in which students collaboratively learned how to identify different types of writing, how to select critically relevant journal articles, and how to read them, identify pertinent information, and cite correctly. The tutorial time was used to allow students to share articles, discuss their meaning and contribution.

Many students did not have research skills, so they were given explicit teaching around accessing and then evaluating their selected literature. Introductory activities included unpacking an abstract so that students do not waste time on irrelevant reading. They were unused to reading academic journals in English and so needed to understand the structure of journals to guide their expectations, improve their vocabulary, and learn how to analyze critically and then communicate this to their peers. In this way, they could apply what they had learned together. As acknowledging sources is part of academic integrity in research, understanding and applying the mechanics of a prescribed citation system was also embedded in their learning.

In Summary

This chapter outlines some of the approaches to class, lecture, and tutorial activities that integrate cross-cultural learning as part of the curriculum. Leveraging the inherent characteristics of the student cohort and educational backgrounds can provide opportunities to enhance curriculum and learning. In order to achieve the learning outcomes, design and timing of activities and facilitation of group work dynamics are crucial as students encounter ways of learning that are often new to them. The heutagogical approach can be uncomfortable for students (and some lecturers) as they struggle with the challenges of this new way of learning that requires more self-efficacy but generates transformation (Canning & Callan, 2010). Reflective activities allow students to understand how they have both managed and overcome interactional challenges to achieve positive results.

References

Boud, D. (2000). Sustainable assessment: Rethinking assessment for the learning society. *Studies in Continuing Education, 22*(2), 151–167.

Boud, D., & Soler, R. (2016). Sustainable assessment revisited. *Assessment & Evaluation in Higher Education, 41*(3), 400–413.

Canning, N. (2010). Playing with heutagogy: Exploring strategies to empower mature learners in higher education. *Journal of Further and Higher Education, 34*(1), 59–71.

Canning, N., & Callan, S. (2010). Heutagogy: Spirals of reflection to empower learners in higher education. *Reflective Practice, 11*(1), 71–82.

The Foundation for Young Australians. (2018). *The new work reality*. Melbourne: The Foundation for Young Australians.

Gale, T. (2012). Towards a southern theory of student equity in Australian higher education: Enlarging the rationale for expansion. *International Journal of Sociology of Education, 1*(3), 238–262.

Hase, S., & Kenyon, C. (2007). Heutagogy: A child of complexity theory. *Complicity: An International Journal of Complexity and Education, 4*(1), 111–118.

Hofstede, G. (1983). National cultures in four dimensions: A research-based theory of cultural differences among nations. *International Studies of Management & Organization, 13*(1–2), 46–74.

Kenyon, C., & Hase, S. (2001). *Moving from Andragogy to Heutagogy in vocational education*. Paper presented to Research to Reality: Putting VET Research to Work, Adelaide, 28–30 March, 2001. Retrieved from www.avertra.org.au/PAPERS%202001/kenyon%hase.pdf

Kolb, A. Y., & Kolb, D. A. (2005). Learning styles and learning spaces: Enhancing experiential learning in higher education. *Academy of Management Learning & Education, 4*(2), 193–212.

Lai, E. R., & Viering, M. (2012). *Assessing 21st century skills: Integrating research findings*. The National Council on Measurement in Education, Vancouver.

Levinsohn, K. (2007). Cultural differences and learning styles of Chinese and European trades students. *Institute for Learning Styles Journal, Fall*(17), 13–22.

Norton, L., Norton, B., & Shannon, L. (2013). Revitalising assessment design: What is holding new lecturers back? *Higher Education, 66*(2), 233–251.

Rogerson, A. M. (2015). *Designing assessments to develop academic skills while promoting good academic practice and limiting students' use of purchased or repurposed materials*. Paper presented to Assessment in Higher Education, Birmingham, 16–18 June, 2015.

Rogerson, A. M. (2017). Detecting contract cheating in essay and report submissions: Process, patterns, clues and conversations. *International Journal for Educational Integrity, 13*(1), 1–10.

Smith, A. R. (2018). Managing the team project process: Helpful hints and tools to ease the workload without sacrificing learning objectives. *The e-Journal of Business Education & Scholarship of Teaching, 12*(1), 73–87.

Vygotsky, L. S. (1978). *Mind in society: The development of higher psychological processes*. Cambridge: Harvard University Press.

Wiggins, G., & McTighe, J. (2012). *Understanding by design guide to advanced concepts in creating and reviewing units*. Alexandria: Association for Supervision and curriculum Development.

23 Introduction to the Course Face-to-Face Communication

Tessa van Charldorp, Marije van Braak, and Aranka Akkermans

The course Face-to-Face Communication is part of the bachelor program in Communication and Information Sciences at Utrecht University, the Netherlands.[1] The course is taught in Dutch and is aimed at Dutch-speaking first-year university students. In this course, students are introduced to pragmatics, specifically "talk in interaction." Students learn (1) about pragmatic theories concerning how we get things done in talk; (2) how one's cultural background and speaking in a second language influence interactional understanding; and (3) how to do research on intercultural interaction in formal and informal settings. In order to achieve these three goals, students not only read a textbook on conversation analysis and papers on studies concerning intercultural face-to-face communication, but they also experience talking to international students themselves. Students start with a research project in the first week of class and are guided through several phases of doing research on intercultural interaction.

In this chapter, we would like to present the **syllabus** of the course, including a list of topics discussed, reading materials, course assignments (such as reflective diary assignments and in-class activities), and a step-by-step explanation of the various phases of the research project in which students learn to do research on intercultural interaction. We will end this chapter with a reflection on internationalizing the face-to-face communication curriculum.

The Course Schedule Week by Week (10-Week Course, 210 Hours)

In the table below, the 10-week course is outlined, including the topics discussed, the literature students read, and the assignments, papers, and exams that are part of the course (see section 3 for more detail). The course consists of one lecture and two seminars per week (6 contact hours per week). Lectures take place in a big lecture hall, whilst seminars take place in smaller groups with a maximum of 25 students.

Internationalizing the Face-to-Face Communication Curriculum

The following four sections further explain what literature, assignment(s), and activities contribute to achieving the course goals, particularly focusing on the intercultural learning goal through internationalizing the face-to-face communication curriculum.

Internationalizing the Face-to-Face Communication Curriculum Through Literature

An overview and short description of the literature contributing to the intercultural course aim is presented in Table 23.2. The main book we use for this course is A. C.

Table 23.1 Course outline

Week	Lecture/Seminar	Theme	Reading material (read material before lecture or seminar)	Assignment (due before seminar)
1	Lecture 1	Face-to-face communication from 1960 until 2019 and beyond		
	Seminar 1.1	Introduction to pragmatics	Murphy, B. & Neu, J. (1996). My grade's too low: the speech act of complaining.	Diary & reading assignment 1
	Seminar 1.2	Recording (natural) interaction		
2	Lecture 2	Face, politeness, introduction to conversation analysis	Garcia chapter 1 + 2 + 3	
	Seminar 2.1	Face, politeness, introduction to conversation analysis	Nakane, I. (2006). Silence and politeness in intercultural communication in university seminars. Bailey, B, (2000). Communicative behavior and conflict between African-American customers and Korean immigrant retailers in LA.	Diary & reading assignment 2
	Seminar 2.2	Learning to transcribe	Garcia chapter 4	
3	Lecture 3	The "technique" of conversation 1	Garcia chapter 5 + 6 + 7	
	Seminar 3.1	Adjacency pairs, preference	Garcia chapter 8 + 9	Diary & reading assignment 3
	Seminar 3.2	Transcribing your own data		
4	Lecture 4	The "technique" of conversation 2	Garcia chapter 11 + 12	
	Seminar 4.1	Topical continuity, storytelling		
	Seminar 4.2	Data session + choosing a phenomenon	Pomerantz, A. & Fehr, B. J. (1997). Conversation analysis: an approach to the study of social action as sense making practice.	Transcript assignment
5	Lecture 5	Institutional interaction 1: Police interaction and 911 (and 112) calls	Garcia chapter 14 + 15 + 16	

	Seminar 5.1	Police interaction and 911 (and 112) calls	
	Seminar 5.2	Making a collection and formulating a research question	Diary & reading assignment 4
6	Lecture 6	Institutional interaction 2: Medical interaction	
	Seminar 6.1	Doctor–patient interaction with and without an interpreter	Garcia chapter 18 + 19 Bolden, G. (2000). Towards understanding practices of medical interpreting: interpreters' involvement in history taking.
	Seminar 6.2	Working on collection	
7	Lecture 7	Summary	Diary & reading assignment 5
	Seminar 7.1	Group feedback session	
	Seminar 7.2	Group feedback session	
8–10	–	Exam/office hours/final paper due	

Table 23.2 Course literature addressing intercultural communication

Course week	Literature	Literature description
1	Murphy, B. & Neu, J. (1996). My grade's too low: The speech act of complaining. In Gass, S.M. & Neu, J. (Eds.), *Speech Acts Across Cultures: Challenges to Communication in a Second Language* (191–216). Berlin/New York: Mouton de Gruyter.	The speech act set "complaining" as performed by American native speakers of English and by Korean nonnative speakers of English are discussed and compared as well as the ways in which American native speakers perceive Korean nonnative speakers' performance of the complaint speech act set.
2	Nakane, I. (2006). Silence and politeness in intercultural communication in university seminars. *Journal of Pragmatics*, 38, 1811–1835.	This paper reports on an analysis in which the politeness orientation of participants with Japanese and Australian backgrounds is related to speech and silence in a university classroom setting.
	Bailey, B. (2000). Communicative behaviour and conflict between African-American customers and Korean immigrant retailers in Los Angeles. *Discourse & Society*, 11(1), 86–108.	This paper reports on the analysis of videotaped service encounters involving both African-American and immigrant Korean customers in Los Angeles. The author argues that the contrasting communicative patterns are the result of cultural and linguistic differences as well as social inequality and therefore becomes a source for further intercultural tensions between African-Americans and immigrant Koreans.
6	Bolden, G. (2000). Toward understanding practices of medical interpreting: interpreters' involvement in history taking. *Discourse Studies*, 2(4), 387–419.	In this paper, the role of medical interpreters in structuring the interaction between doctors and patients is examined.
1–6	Garcia, A.C. (2013) *An Introduction to Interaction: Understanding Talk in Formal and Informal Settings*. New York: Bloomsbury Academic.	This textbook provides an elaborate introduction to the theoretical perspectives and methods of conversation analysis, an approach to the study of talk in interaction. It provides plenty of examples and teaches readers how to analyze conversations in both informal and formal settings.

Garcia's textbook, *An Introduction to Interaction: Understanding Talk in Formal and Informal Settings*, which not only contributes to the intercultural course aim but also introduces the methodology of conversation analysis and teaches students how to apply this method to all sorts of interaction.

The majority of the literature contributes to the intercultural aim of this course by addressing communication between people from different (language) cultures. Garcia (2013) also addresses interaction between people from different *sub*cultures (e.g., laypersons and professionals). The mainly American examples in Garcia (2013) of, for example, medical interaction or 911 calls were often contrasted with Dutch examples of visiting the local doctor or calling the Dutch emergency services during class. The literature and the corresponding preparatory reading assignments stimulate students to reflect on what makes intercultural communication different from same-culture communication, how interactional rules can differ from culture to culture, and how this might influence face-to-face communication. It also familiarizes students with researchable phenomena within intercultural communication and with transcription and presentation of translated intercultural communication.

Internationalizing the Face-to-Face Communication Curriculum Through Diary Assignments

As part of this course, students write weekly diary reflections in an online environment (only visible to the instructors). In these diary assignments, students reflect on their own and other people's actions and gather examples of everyday interactions. The main aim of the diary assignments is to make students aware of unwritten interactional practices that make it possible to live together in a society. A short description of these diary assignments is presented in Table 23.3.

Apart from the broader aim of letting students explore unwritten interactional norms in society, each diary assignment has a more specific aim. Assignment 3, for example, contributes to the intercultural aim of the course by exploring differences in turn-taking rules and overlap between subcultures. In this way, assignment 3 stimulates students to reflect on how interactional rules can differ from (sub)culture to (sub)culture and the effects this may have on face-to-face communication.

Internationalizing the Face-to-Face Communication Curriculum Through Seminar Activities

The course includes a variety of seminar activities that address intercultural face-to-face communication. An overview and short description of these is presented in Table 23.4.

In general, the activities discussed in Table 23.4 address either one of two types of intercultural communication: communication between people from different linguistic cultures (activities 1–8, 12) or communication between laypersons and professionals (activities 9–11, 13). Together, these activities contribute to the intercultural course aim by:

- stimulating students to reflect on what makes intercultural communication different from same-culture communication. Communication entails norms that we abide by, but what are those norms, and what are their interactional consequences for intercultural communication?

Table 23.3 Diary activities addressing (intercultural) face-to-face communication

Diary assignment number	Diary assignment description
1	**Introduction to face-to-face communication** Observe your own behavior during a whole day. Describe at least ten situations (where you were, with whom, what you did), and describe what you "got done" in those situations through face-to-face communication.
2	**Breaching experiments** Find a partner from your seminar group and search for two breaching experiments on YouTube that you feel comfortable with (1) or think of two breaching experiments yourself. Perform the breaching experiments together. Describe clearly what happened during the experiment: A. What did you do? B. What expectations did you breach? C. How did people around you respond? D. How did it make you feel to carry out this experiment?
3	**Subcultures and turn taking** Garcia (2013:49–50) writes that people from different cultural (or social) backgrounds organize the exchange of turns at talk differently. We can understand culture in a broad sense—a group of people with a shared way of doing things or interests. You are probably part of all sorts of different (sub)cultures. A family culture, a student culture, a soccer, dance, or tennis culture, a faith culture, an animal lover culture, a Utrecht culture, a Frisian culture, etc. Describe three conversations you have recently had with people from your own different subcultures that you belong to. Describe: a. With whom did you have the conversation, and to which subcultures did you belong? b. To which turn-taking rules did you adhere? How smoothly did it go? Did the use of turn-taking rules differ per subculture, and if so, how? c. Was there a lot of overlap? When, or when was there not? How did overlap differ between the three conversations?
4	**Technology in face-to-face communication** Technology plays an important role in (face-to-face) communication within all sorts of institutional settings. 911 operators, for example, pass on the caller's information directly via a dispatch system to get the right aid to the right place. Police officers type up the police report while they interrogate suspects. And GPs search for information in the computer system while listening to the patient. Observe an institutional setting of your choice in which technology plays a role in the interaction. Describe in about 200 words what this setting is, what kind of interaction takes place, how technology plays a role, how technology influences the conversation and vice versa. Just like an ethnographer, try to describe very precisely and objectively what you see and hear.

Table 23.4 Seminar activities addressing intercultural communication

Course week	Activity number	Activity description
1	1	**Assignment Murphy & Neu (1996)** In groups of 3–4 students: Discuss your answers to the preparatory questions about this paper. Use your answers to prepare a 2-minute presentation in which you (1) summarize the article and (2) situate the summary within pragmatics and speech act theory.
	2	**Speech acts across cultures** In duos: 1. Think of three situations (in the Netherlands, in Dutch) in which you would give a compliment in distinct ways. 2. What cultures would be interesting to compare with regard to the speech act of complimenting? Explain your idea. 3. How could you design a study to find out whether people from these different countries compliment differently?
	3	**Introduction transcription** 1. Individually: Make a representation of the audio fragment you are hearing (presented in class). The interaction took place between international students and is in English. 2. Plenary: Teacher discusses the students' experiences and any difficulties in representing interaction before introducing Jeffersonian transcription conventions.
2	4	**How was your week?** Introductory activity. Teacher gives random students a piece of paper with one of various communication styles, e.g., "In your culture, it is polite to speak very softly," "In your culture, people are used to touching each other while speaking," and "In your culture, people appreciate having little space between people they talk to." Students were blind to each other's communication style. 1. In groups of 2–3: Discuss your week while applying your assigned communication style. 2. Plenary: Teacher discusses students' experiences, focusing on norm violation and cultural differences in interactional norms.
	5	**Assignment Nakane (2006) and Bailey (2000)** In groups of 3–4: Choose one of the two articles. Prepare two mini-presentations: 1. a scientific summary 2. a summary in everyday language for everyone to understand
	6	**Transcribe a conversation between international students**
3	7	**Closings in different cultures** Students are given a handout with closings of several Dutch telephone calls. 1. Individually: (a) describe how a routine closing is done in this Dutch example and (b) describe how the elements of this routine closing differ from how a routine closing in American telephone calls is done (see examples in Garcia). 2. Plenary: Discuss results.

(Continued)

Table 23.4 (Continued)

Course week	Activity number	Activity description
4	8	**Analyze your own data set** In research project groups: Analyze one extract of your own data set by applying the steps described in Pomerantz & Fehr (1997). The data set includes conversations between international students.
5	9	**Analyze layperson/professional interaction (1)** 1. In duos: Discuss your answers to the preparatory question about two problematic 911 calls (Garcia). 2. Plenary: Discuss "where things went wrong" in the calls.
	10	**Analyze layperson/professional interaction (2)** 1. Plenary: Watch a 112 call (Dutch 911). 2. Teacher assigns each phase of 112 calls to a different group of 2–3 students. Instruction: Note where your assigned phase starts and ends, and describe the routine elements of your assigned phase that you recognize in this 112 call. 3. Plenary: Discuss phases and routine elements.
6	11	**Interpreting vs. translating** Introductory activity. Plenary: Discuss the difference between interpreting and translating. How can interpreting affect the conversation?
	12	**Analysis of Bolden (2000)** Following up on the previous activity: 1. In groups of 2–3: In Bolden's (2000) analysis, find examples of the six dimensions relevant to institutional conversation analysis (turn-taking organization, overall structure of the organization of the interaction, sequence organization, turn-design, lexical or word choice, epistemological, and other forms of asymmetry). 2. Plenary: Discuss students' findings.
	13	**Doctorability Mr. Kool** 1. Plenary: Listen to the Dutch GP consult fragment between Mr. Kool and his GP (layperson/professional interaction). 2. In groups of 3–4: Construct a short analysis of the phenomenon "doctorability," using the steps of Pomerantz & Fehr (1997) as a guideline. 3. Present your analysis to the group.

- introducing students to reported analyses of intercultural communication. Students get an idea about possible phenomena for research in intercultural communication and familiarize themselves with transcription and presentation of translated intercultural communication.
- having students experience transcribing actual intercultural communication. These activities present a valuable opportunity to discuss with students the difficulties of transcribing nonnative conversation and the importance of the transcription to later analysis.
- practicing analyzing intercultural communication. The complexity of these assignments increases throughout the course.
- stimulating students to think about ways to conduct intercultural communication research. As this activity was situated very early in the course, students mainly proposed to conduct interview or survey research. Discussing their proposals in relation to Murphy and Neu's (1996) approach provided students with an interesting start to their journey of discovering intercultural communication analysis.

Internationalizing the Face-to-Face Communication Curriculum Through the Research Project

Students start with the research project in the first week of the course. Related seminar activities guide students through several phases of doing research on intercultural interaction.

Data collection takes place in course week 1 and 2. Students are instructed to make two 5-minute recordings, one of a Dutch interaction between Dutch students and one of an English interaction between students in which at least one student is an international student. In this phase, students experience being part of an intercultural conversation, arrange ethical approval, and record (Skype) conversations for analytic purposes. Next, students prepare the data for analysis by transcribing the conversations according to conversation analytic standards (week 3). In this phase, students experience the difficulties that can arise when transcribing conversation in a nonnative language (and in most cases by nonnative speakers). In weeks 4 and 5, we focus on data analysis. Students learn to select sequences, identify actions, and build a collection by doing data sessions. Each group chooses a phenomenon for analysis and is stimulated to think about comparative analyses. Students analyzing English interaction learn to look beyond "X is done differently in English." Students conducting comparative analyses learn that features of interaction can be very different depending on the language spoken but especially depending on the intercultural character of the interaction. Each individual student hands in an analysis of one extract from their group's collection before week 7. They receive feedback on these analyses from their teacher during a consultation hour, in which the teacher and group members together discuss the analyses and formulate a research question. Finally, students read additional literature to frame and underpin their analyses. Each group collaboratively writes a research paper, for which they are instructed to use Bolden's (2000) article as an inspiration. Students receive guidance during the seminars and office hours.

In sum, once students hand in their final report in week 9 of the course, they have gained considerable knowledge about and experiences with conducting interaction analysis in an intercultural context. Their fine-grained analyses of everyday interaction opened many eyes to the minute details that together construct intercultural interaction.

Reflection

In their evaluation of the course, students positively evaluated the course content's strong link with real life. Students found it fascinating how the *literature* showed that cultural differences in interactional rules could lead to awkward or even hostile situations. Interestingly, in their exam answers, some students showed that they could relate "divergent" communicative behavior with cultural differences, whereas others labelled these behaviors as "wrong."

Nearing the end of the course, we asked a selection of students to evaluate the *seminar activities*. In general, students very much valued the repeated listening to and analysis of a variety of interaction fragments from different settings. A considerable number of students referred to the communication styles introductory activity (activity 4) as the most instructive activity of all. At the same time, students did not explicitly mention the intercultural communication aim when we asked them what was the most important thing that they had learned.

Reflecting on the contribution of the *research project* to the intercultural communication course aim, two issues are important for consideration. First, although we stimulated students to conduct a comparative analysis of a phenomenon in Dutch and English interaction, the number of groups that chose to do so was limited. Groups mainly selected a phenomenon for investigation in Dutch interaction. Possibly, analysis of interaction in a language that was not their mother tongue held them off. At the same time, students often noticed specific linguistic features that were salient in the international conversations and intuitively felt that these features had an effect on the interaction—a topic that indeed some students discussed in their research projects (for example, the frequent use of "yeah" and continuers such as "hmhm" in the international student talk). Second, the transcription and analysis of *intercultural* interaction seems to add value to the research project. Students experienced difficulties in transcribing the interaction, which appeared to be an excellent starting point for discussion about the value of accurate representation for later analysis.

In sum, a face-to-face communication curriculum can be "internationalized" by carefully choosing literature, guiding students through a research project for which they gather real conversations in both a local and international setting, encouraging students to reflect on their own and other people's intercultural interaction in diary assignments, and designing interactive seminar activities focusing on intercultural communication. Through this curriculum design, students learn about, experience, and do research on face-to-face communication beyond their own culture, language, and context.

Note

1. The course was developed by the first author and taught by all three authors in 2018–2019. The first author would like to thank her former colleagues Marca Schasfoort and Joyce Lamerichs, with whom she developed similar courses at VU Amsterdam, and Marloes Herijgers for helping shape and finalize the course in its current form in 2017–2018.

References

Bolden, G. (2000). Toward understanding practices of medical interpreting: interpreters' involvement in history taking. *Discourse Studies*, 2(4), 387–419.

Garcia, A. C. (2013). *An introduction to interaction. Understanding talk in formal and informal settings*. New York: Bloomsbury.

Murphy, B. & Neu, J. (1996). My grade's too low: The speech act of complaining. In Gass, S. M. & Neu, J. (Eds.), *Speech acts across cultures: Challenges to communication in a second language* (pp. 191–216). Berlin/New York: Mouton de Gruyter.

24 Thriving in the Globalized Communication Environment
Teaching Resilience to Digital Culture Shock

Kate Dunsmore

This chapter explains an example of problem-based learning curriculum for a junior-level international and intercultural communication course of 25 to 30 students. Problem-based learning provides an excellent means for students to become comfortable with the discomfort of interacting with other cultures through navigating the digital divide. When an information-gathering process is in service to applying a theoretical framework explaining qualities of culture, it can also demonstrate the complexity of achieving intercultural understanding.

The problem students confront in this semester-long project is to analyze a conflict in another country and identify options opposing stakeholders may have to reduce conflict or at least reinforce whatever stability does exist. This analysis requires them to dispassionately evaluate opposing viewpoints, infer values both from the culture in general and from the issue specifically, and suggest culturally appropriate conflict resolution strategies. Through the structuring of a series of low-stakes assignments, the students are compelled to confront their assumptions about representation of other cultures and about cultural values, norms, and preferences that are greatly at variance with their own worldview. Practice confronting the resulting sense of dislocation and disquiet normalizes persistence and resilience in the face of culture shock, digital or otherwise.

To make the process manageable for the students, considerable scaffolding is employed, working from lower-level cognitive tasks toward critical thinking. I have found it most effective to choose a broad policy area that students will explore in the single country they choose. Each country can only be chosen by one student. This greatly limits the temptations of plagiarism. Changing the focal topic each semester serves the same purpose. Topics I have chosen include agricultural policy, treatment of animals, choosing national leaders, K–12 education, water rights, microentrepreneurship, and rights of prisoners/detainees. I have sometimes brought world maps into the classroom to remind students of the many countries that do, in fact, exist. The countries must meet the following criteria:

- The country must be included on the list the Hofstede Center provides at www.hofstede-insights.com/product/compare-countries/. This ensures they will have measures for power distance, individualism/collectivism, and uncertainty avoidance/uncertainty tolerance. I have found using just these three dimensions offers sufficient challenge.
- The country cannot be in North America or Europe; nor can they choose Australia, New Zealand, Great Britain, or Ireland. These limits increase the chance they interact with the global South or face other challenges such as different alphabets. I discourage students from choosing countries engulfed in

civil war, as there have been cases when it was difficult to find information on anything except the warfare.

Students choose a country by posting to a discussion board. I do not make the board available until after the class meeting when I explain the process (otherwise students become focused on "claiming" a country, and valuable class time is wasted). While I encourage students to consider their choice carefully and even seek out some information about possible choices, students tend to post a choice nearly immediately. The choice is often based on places they have vacationed, their own ethnicity, or having a friend from a particular country. As the assignments proceed, very often those who have chosen based on these personal factors enjoy a moment of sudden awareness that the culture of the country is actually unknown to them in important ways. In other cases, students opt to change countries. The structure of several low-stakes exercises and assignments makes this feasible even later in the semester.

The next step is a series of exercises to get students used to searching non-consumer-oriented websites. These exercises could have many kinds of prompts. This is the first one I assign for searching the United Nations' website:

> Find out what the United Nations offers as resources to understand the issue in your focal country or its region. Post two links on the discussion board. Along with each link, write a sentence or two to describe what information each webpage provided about the topic. For example, what kind of issues arise? What kind of solutions? And so on.

I supplement this instruction with topically relevant links on the United Nations website and reminders that each body of the UN has its subwebsite requiring separate searches from the main UN.org site. Students usually find this website structure quite frustrating, since they are used to consumer-oriented sites where the search field could reach any section of the website. This exercise also introduces them to the idea of following links like breadcrumbs in order to find the information they need.

Follow-up exercises ask students to locate websites *from* their chosen country as opposed to *about* their chosen country. I usually ask that one of the websites be that of the country's government to help normalize that other countries have governmental structures and not just bus crashes and earthquakes. Political communication research has thoroughly established the limited range of international news US audiences receive. Students must explain what features of the websites they found suggest that they are from their chosen country. This begins strengthening their situational awareness, countering the tendency to accept search results uncritically.

Other exercises begin to focus their attention on identifying a conflict related to the semester's topic area. By finding websites of parties involved in the topic, students develop a set of sources for the first graded assignment. This stage also introduces the concepts of conflict resolution, focusing on identifying values of stakeholders as well as being able to discuss different perspectives in a neutral manner.

I spend one class session early on explaining the digital divide as an uneven distribution of resources—in social structures as well as infrastructure—that results in widely differing quality of representation on internet-based media. At several points in the course, I make class time into a workshop on finding information internationally on the Internet. Below is an example of the class schedule:

Week	Topics
Weeks 1, 2, and 3	Lecture on concepts and theories related to the nature of culture and intercultural communication
End of week 3	**Focal country choice due**
	In this and subsequent weeks, discuss digital divide and challenges for information seeking.
Beginning of week 4	**Navigating UN Site exercise due**
End of week 4	**Locating Websites exercise due**
Beginning of week 5	**Identifying Project exercise due**
End of week 5	Exam over initial set of concepts
Week 6 and 7	Lecture on cultural preferences for forms of communication, reasoning, and persuasion
Beginning of week 7	**Background Research Prep exercise**
End of week 7	Exam over cultural preferences for communication, persuasion, and reasoning
Week 8	Spring recess—no class
Beginning of week 9	Lecture on cultural preferences for decision making and managing conflict
End of week 9	**Background Research due**
Beginning of week 10	Exam on terminology related to conflict resolution. (This incentivizes learning the terminology so it can be used in the later analyses and discussions.)
End of week 10	Begin applying terminology. Workshop on identifying statements of stakeholders.
Beginning of week 11	**First Perspective due**
	Continue applying terminology to examples provided to the class
End of week 11	Hand back the First Perspective assignment. Workshop to address any problems and to prepare for Second Perspective assignment.
Beginning of week 12	**Second Perspective due**
	Exercises to adopt the perspective of stakeholders and to infer values from statements
End of week 12	Exercises to infer values from statements
Beginning of week 13	**Values Analysis due**
End of week 13	Exercises to apply concepts to negotiation scenarios
Beginning of week 14	**Communication Assessment Prep exercise**
	Analyzing intercultural interaction
End of week 14	Analyzing intercultural interaction
Beginning of 15	Exam requiring analysis of cases and statements. The rationale for inferences demonstrates comprehension of course concepts.
End of week 15	**Communication Assessment due**

The first major assignment (Background Research) requires them to identify a specific conflict within the broad topic area. They identify several stakeholders, at least one of which must differ in perspective from the others. All the stakeholders must have been raised in and still live in the chosen country. Students must also provide a bibliography of their sources so I can advise them on their search strategies.

Sometimes students seize on prominent expatriates from somewhere else now living in the chosen country. In these cases, I explain that these individuals may be in some sense rebels from their own culture but are not actually from the culture of the chosen country. Because of this, they cannot speak for the members of the chosen country's culture.

Expatriates of the chosen country may sometimes be acceptable stakeholders, especially if they are refugees fighting to return to their homeland. Discussion of these situations lets students see the impact of culture as the source of values, norms, attitudes, and behaviors. It helps them see culture as a real factor in how people view the world.

The second and third major assignments (First Perspective and Second Perspective) require the students to find quotes from opposing stakeholders. I have divided this task into two assignments so that I can give feedback on their results for one perspective before they begin searching for quotes from a second perspective. This intervention has been effective with most students, overcoming the most common problematic assumptions.

Although explicitly directed to find quotes that express opinion or interpretation, students show a preference for the relative "safety" of quotes conveying factual material. Shifting student attention to statements that provide a basis for inferring values is also a process of shifting them from an arm's-length observation of other cultures toward a more dialogic engagement with other cultures. Requiring them to find statements directly from members of the chosen country's culture reinforces the need to listen to the authentic voice of culture members in order to understand their viewpoint.

Students often assume that the first search results are the best and become frustrated that these results do not include rich quotes by stakeholders from the chosen country. From the first day of the course, I foreground that intercultural interaction may involve emotional, psychological, and logistical problems and that a major objective of the course is to learn how to persist in the face of discomfort.

As students begin to research conflicts within their chosen country, the sense of discomfort intensifies. I use this as an opportunity to repeat the course objective of learning to be resilient in addressing obstacles. I model how to do this with examples from the experiences of the students. I encourage them to gain from having solutions brainstormed in class. This approach is to foster a growth mindset, which I make explicit.

As students speak up, I ask "who else has encountered something similar?" Sometimes I do not have a ready solution in the form of a suggested search term or in response to some specific element of the particular conflict going on in a particular country. In these cases, I think out loud so students can see that, again, it is normal to struggle with a situation in which there is not a pre-determined answer.

As these applied exercises and assignments proceed, several concepts are being presented and tested by exam. In addition to three Hofstede dimensions, I discuss how culture prioritizes values and thus influences attitudes and behavior. I specifically discuss cultural preferences for information forms and sources (low context/high context) and for decision-making processes. This prepares them for the next assignment, when they analyze the quotes previously found in order to infer values of the stakeholders (Values Analysis).

The Values Analysis assignment is a solid test of how much progress students are making in setting aside their own cultural values—for a moment—and adopting the viewpoint of people from a different culture. Very frequently, at this stage, students must return to the web to identify a more specific conflict, more clearly opposing stakeholders, and quotes that point to values (as opposed to quotes conveying facts). This is the point at which I will have a workshopping day in class to help students appreciate the cultural and socioeconomic realities of their chosen countries and how this gives rise to issue-specific values. Having a single broad topic area makes it possible for me to come up to speed on the range of issues likely to arise. Even so, there are always surprises. In those instances, I let the students see how I go about finding the needed information.

To keep them moving toward a growth mindset, I use examples from other complex things such as sports, performing music, and dancing to demonstrate that it is possible for them to move past the discomfort of learning to coordinate a number of different skills, such as understanding the impact of the digital divide, employing strategies to move past the consumer-oriented haze, applying multiple concepts from a theoretical framework, maintaining a neutral stance, and writing clearly.

In the final third of the course, students learn specific conflict resolution and negotiation approaches. They apply these to the question of how to improve understanding between their opposing stakeholders (Communication Assessment). This requires bringing together several kinds of concepts, specific information, and inferences about values. Then they critically assess all they have learned and answer questions such as:

- What are the concerns of each participant regarding honor in the context of this negotiation? What would you recommend to assist in preserving the honor of all participants?
- What are the concerns of each participant regarding fairness in the negotiation process? What would you recommend to help all participants feel the negotiation process was fair?
- What are the preferences the participants may have for how the meeting is reported to the public?

Although this assignment is challenging, students are invariably able to do at least part of the communication assessment correctly. It is quite difficult to predict which parts will give the most trouble to any particular student. With this assignment, they are under the most pressure from engaging with another culture and often seek recourse within their own cultural framework. To assist with shifting out of their home viewpoint, I have them do a preparatory exercise that amounts to a rough draft of part of the final assignment, timed so I can give them feedback and also have an in-class workshop.

As can be seen from the above description, this is a writing- and reasoning-intensive project. It is highly demanding of the instructor because it is not possible to know exactly what obstacles students will face. In general, the most common obstacles have been:

- Accepting the first search results as the final word, which is seldom useful in finding information about other countries and, particularly, finding information *from* other countries. I emphasize the need to find the actual voice of members of a culture.
- Seizing on the first conflict that turns up in the search and being unable to move on to an appropriate conflict. I provide multiple opportunities for feedback so they can get on track without doing great damage to their final grade. Assignments (and exams) are never more than 8% to 10% of the final grade.
- Treating the project like a conventional research paper rather than a means of transforming their own viewpoint. Again, having multiple attempts (in essence,

drafts) makes it possible to shift students toward being immersed in a culture rather than distantly reporting on the culture.
- Assuming that negotiations would be between whoever is the most prominent in news coverage. This overreliance on search results makes it hard for students to commit to considering the full range of stakeholders and their representatives.
- Having limited understanding of political, social, or economic issues, even within a US context. As initial examples, I use domestic issues for which they have an understanding of the dynamics involved. Then we have a base from which to extend that understanding to another country.

Other demands on the instructor include:

- Acquiring a basic knowledge of a new topical area each semester.
- Allocating time to score and return the exercises and assignments within one or two class meetings.
- Allocating class time to enable individual conversation with students at least twice through the semester. (This is in addition to answering questions from the class as a whole or in the context of discussion.)
- Reframing assignments and exercises to account for ongoing changes in how algorithms return results and in how material finds its way to the internet. For example, 2018 was the first year that students made wide use of Twitter as a source of quotations from other countries.

The demands on the instructor are similar to those arising from any problem-based curriculum. The advantage of this method is that it drives student comprehension forward on multiple fronts simultaneously. By persisting in solving problems of finding websites from countries on the disadvantaged side of the digital divide, students learn firsthand of the limitations the digital divide imposes. They also form an appreciation of the narrowing of perspective that comes from the consumer-oriented dominance of algorithms as the web is experienced from US servers. Discussion of the internet as fundamental to international communication is absorbed more readily in the process of solving the problem of finding information using the internet.

By insisting that students stay focused on the communication issues involved in bringing stakeholders in their chosen country more into alignment, students begin to see how communication is a factor in a range of issues. While there is a single broad topic for each semester, within that are a wide range of specific issues. Through class discussion, students become familiar with the specific issues others are analyzing. Students see the adjustments necessary to account for varying local conditions.

The approach explained here could be used in a range of courses where an international element would be desirable. For example, in courses focused on organizational communication, small-group communication, or business communication, students could work with actual cases of companies needing to have cohesive international teams or needing to negotiate with governments.

Students frequently comment subsequent to completing the course that the project—while uncomfortable—proved useful in internships and full-time jobs in which they encountered members of other cultures. This outcome provides some support for expending the additional effort needed to set up and carry out the curriculum.

Contributors

Seokhoon Ahn is an assistant professor of the Department of Communication at Central Washington University. Dr. Ahn earned his MA and PhD from University of Wisconsin-Milwaukee. His main research interests range from acculturation to cultural differences.

Aranka Akkermans is currently working as a PhD student at the Amsterdam UMC. She conducts research on how doctors and surrogate decision makers communicate about the possible redirection of care in the neonatal, pediatric, and adult intensive care unit. Her research interests are in the fields of communication and argumentation.

Mariam F. Alkazemi is an assistant professor of public relations at Virginia Commonwealth University. She is an international media scholar, with a focus on the Middle East. Her publications involve a range of topics including censorship, terrorism, and honor-based violence. Previously, she served as a faculty member at Gulf University for Science and Technology and a Carnegie fellow at University of North Carolina Chapel Hill.

Fahed Al-Sumait is the Vice President for Academic Affairs at the Gulf University for Science and Technology in Kuwait. His research concerns international, strategic communication with a concentration on the Gulf region of the Middle East. He has served as a Fulbright-Hays dissertation fellow, a postdoctoral research fellow at the National University of Singapore, and a research fellow at the London School of Economics. He holds a PhD in communication from the University of Washington.

Ahmet Atay is an associate professor of communication at the College of Wooster. His research revolves around cultural studies, media studies, and critical intercultural communication. In particular, he focuses on diasporic experiences and cultural identity formations of diasporic individuals; political and social complexities of city life, such as immigrant and queer experiences; the usage of new media technologies in different settings; and the notion of home. He is the author of *Globalization's Impact on Identity Formation: Queer Diasporic Males in Cyberspace* (2015). He holds a PhD from Southern Illinois University-Carbondale.

John Baldwin is a professor of communication at Illinois State University, where he has worked since 1994. He studies and teaches about domestic and international diversity, identity, and intolerance. His research includes studies on sexual harassment, ethnic stereotypes and communication, as well as cross-cultural adaptation and cross-cultural differences in teaching styles. He has written summary chapters for books on Western communication, communication and relationships, prejudice in communication, and the history of intercultural communication. His co-edited book, *Redefining Culture*, analyzes the notion of "culture" from several different disciplinary perspectives.

Soumia Bardhan is an assistant professor at University of Colorado Denver. She earned her BA (with Honors) in English Literature from the University of Calcutta, her MA in Communication from University of Madras, and her PhD in Communication from the University of New Mexico. Her research interests are informed by intercultural/international communication and Islamic/religious studies and she has conducted grant-funded fieldwork in Egypt, Turkey, Morocco, and India. Her research has appeared in peer-reviewed journals and books by leading academic presses. Soumia has directed seven travel study courses in Spain, France, Morocco, and India. She serves as a director on the board of the International Communication Association and is chair of its Intercultural Communication Division (2019-2021). She also served on the National Communication Association's Task Force on Fostering International Collaborations in research, teaching, and service.

Marije van Braak is an educational scientist interested in interactional approaches to learning and education. Having obtained a BA in linguistics and a MSc in educational sciences at Utrecht University, she is currently working on her PhD research about teacher facilitation at the Dutch Training for General Practice. Besides doing research, she teaches courses in interaction analysis to students of communication and a course in teaching to third-year GP residents.

Barbara Ruth Burke is an associate professor of communication, media, and rhetoric at the University of Minnesota Morris. Her research interests include explorations of media messages and understandings of identity and the ways that culture is thus shaped by mediated and interpersonal communication. Burke earned her MA and PhD degrees in American studies from Purdue University and her MA in telecommunication arts from the University of Michigan.

Tessa van Charldorp is an assistant professor at Utrecht University. She is the coordinator for the Culture, Communication and Diversity track within the Communication and Information Sciences program. Her current research projects concern face-to-face interaction in various institutional domains. She has a background in communication studies and linguistics. She completed her PhD project about face-to-face interaction among police officers and suspects in 2012.

Janet Colvin is a communication studies professor at Utah Valley University. She is serving as the associate dean for the College of Humanities and Social Sciences. Her research focuses on diversity, mentoring, and intercultural communication. Her current projects center around women refugees and how they navigate and adapt to a new culture. She has written a book as well as numerous book chapters and journal publications. She has received campus-wide awards for her scholarship and teaching.

Andrew Jared Critchfield has worked in China, Japan, Mongolia, Nigeria, and Taiwan and has presented his research at regional, national, and international

286 Contributors

conferences. At Howard University, he was a Sylff (Ryoichi Sasakawa Young Leaders Fellowship Fund) Fellow.

Stephen M Croucher is Professor and Head of the School of Communication, Journalism, and Marketing at Massey University. He is also the Wellington Regional Director of the Massey Business School. He researches immigrant cultural adaptation, religion and communication, statistics, and conflict. He has also explored how religion influences communication behaviors. He has authored more than 85 peer-reviewed journal articles, co-edited 10 books, and given keynote addresses in more than 20 nations. He has/held/holds various leaderships positions in the National Communication Association, International Communication Association, the World Communication, and holds honorary Professorships at the University of Jyväskylä, Universidade Aberta, and the Universidade de Coimbra. He earned his PhD from the University of Oklahoma.

Maria De Moya, PhD, is an associate professor of public relations in DePaul's University College of Communication, where she also serves as academic director of the master's program in public relations and advertising, and director of the Latino Media and Communication program. She holds a PhD in mass communication from the University of Florida and an MA in business and economic journalism from New York University, where she was a Fulbright scholar. Her research interests centers on international and ethnic public relations, with a specific focus on questions of community, identity, and advocacy.

Qingwen Dong is a professor and Director of Graduate Program in the Department of Communication at University of the Pacific, where he is a recipient of their highest teaching and research honor---the Award for Eberhardt Teacher/Scholar, their highest honor for scholarship---the Award for Faculty Research Lecturer, and their highest honor for service---the Award for Excellence in Undergraduate Research Mentoring. Currently he is serving as Pacific Provost Faculty Fellow as well as Director of Pacific Summer Institute. He serves as two distinguished professorships and multiple visiting professorships in China and his research focuses on the relationship between socialization and various media.

Kate Dunsmore is an associate professor of communication studies at Fairleigh Dickinson University's Florham Campus, where she is also Director of the MA in Communication program. Bringing together concepts in political communication, discourse analysis, and international relations, she studies contemporary and historical public discourse including news and entertainment genres. Her most recent publication is *Discourse of Reciprocity: The Role of the Press in the US-Canada Alliance*. Dr. Dunsmore earned her PhD and MA in communication at the University of Washington, Seattle campus.

Elizabeth M. Goering is a professor of communication studies at Indiana University Purdue University Indianapolis (IUPUI). She currently serves as the Director of Undergraduate Studies and the Director of Online Learning in the Department of Communication Studies. Dr. Goering earned her MA from Wichita State University and her PhD from Purdue University.

Alberto González is Distinguished University Professor in the School of Media and Communication at Bowling Green State University. He is a co-editor of The Rhetorical Legacy of Wangari Maathai: Planting the Future (2018) and Our

Voices: Essays in Culture, Ethnicity, and Communication, 6th edition (2016). He earned his PhD from The Ohio State University.

Stephen J. Hartnett is a professor of Communication at the University of Colorado, Denver. He served as the 2017 president of the National Communication Association. His most recent book is the co-edited *Imagining China: Rhetorics of Nationalism in the Age of Globalization*.

Amy N. Heuman is an associate professor in the Department of Communication Studies and a Women's & Gender Studies Affiliate faculty member at Texas Tech University. Her research can be found in publications such as the *Journal of International and Intercultural Communication*, *Journal of Intercultural Communication Research*, *Health Communication*, *Qualitative Research Reports in Communication*, *The Discourse of Special Populations* (Routledge), and *Working in the Margins* (Peter Lang). She earned her PhD from Bowling Green State University.

Tracey Quigley Holden is an assistant professor in the Department of Communication, academic director of the Middle East Partnership Initiative Student Leaders Program, and an affiliate faculty member with the Center for Political Communication at the University of Delaware. She also served on the National Communication Association's Task Force on Fostering International Collaborations in research, teaching, and service. Holden earned her PhD from the Pennsylvania State University.

Rita Koris is a senior lecturer at the Institute of International Studies of Pázmány Péter Catholic University, Hungary. She is also involved in training university educators to develop and implement international virtual exchange projects. She has given several presentations and held workshops on the internationalization practices and virtual online collaboration in higher education. Her research interests include the use of technology and online collaboration practices in higher education and the development of 21st-century skills and competences.

Wendy Leeds-Hurwitz is Director of the Center for Intercultural Dialogue, Professor Emerita of the University of Wisconsin-Parkside, and Associate Faculty at Royal Roads University (Canada). She has been Fulbright Senior Specialist at the Instituto Politécnico de Coimbra (Portugal), as well as holding a variety of visiting positions in Paris and Lyon (France), Beijing and Macau (China). She has published 13 books and is known for contributions to intercultural communication, language and social interaction, social construction theory, semiotic theory, ethnography of communication, and disciplinary history. She earned her PhD from University of Pennsylvania.

Lance R. Lippert is professor of communication at Illinois State University. He is the Program Coordinator for the Communication Studies Program in the School of Communication. Recently, he completed six years as the Coordinator of the University's Civic Engagement and Responsibility Minor. His research interests include effective workplace communication, health communication, organizational culture, civic engagement pedagogy, and appropriate and therapeutic humor use. Over the last 25 years, he has consulted for various public, private, and governmental organizations including health care, small business, large and small corporations, education (higher education and K-12), and non-profits to help them improve organizational effectiveness.

LieneLočmele works as a lecturer at Vidzeme University of Applied Sciences in Latvia, where she teaches a variety of courses on communication. With the support of a Fulbright student fellowship, she is now in the final stage of dissertation research at the University of Massachusetts–Amherst.Ločmele's research interests include the cultural aspects of human communication in a variety of contexts, e.g., the university classroom interaction. She holds a master's degree in intercultural communication from the University of Jyväskylä, Finland.

Ismael Lopez Medel is an associate professor of communication at Azusa Pacific University, California, where he directs the undergraduate program in public relations. Previously he served as Associate Dean of the School of Communication at CEU University in Madrid and has combined academic and administrative positions in Spain and the United States, as well as visiting teaching experiences across Europe. His research in the fields of advertising and public relations has been published internationally.

Sònia Mas-Alcolea is a postdoctoral researcher at the University of Lleida, where she is currently conducting research on the internationalization of higher education, academic mobility, and intercultural and multilingual practices at university. She is a member of the CLA (Cercle de Lingüística Aplicada) group at the Department of English and Linguistics. Her research interests lie within the field of discourse analysis, identity, interculturality, and multilingualism. She earned her PhD from University of Lleida.

Trudy Milburn is Assistant Dean of the School of Liberal Arts and Sciences. Her academic work examines the ways membership categories are enacted and displayed. She co-edited *Engaging and Transforming Global Communication Through Cultural Discourse Analysis: A Tribute to Donal Carbaugh* with Michelle Scollo; edited *Communicating User Experience: Applying Local Strategies Research to Digital Media Design*; co-authored *Citizen Discourse on Contaminated Water, Superfund Cleanups, and Landscape Restoration: (Re)making Milltown, Montana*; and wrote *Nonprofit Organizations: Creating Membership through Communication*.

Juan Mundel is an assistant professor of advertising in the College of Communication at DePaul University. He teaches graduate and undergraduate courses in advertising (Advertising Campaigns, Advertising and Society, Advertising Foundations, Creativity and Portfolio Building), consumer behavior, and insights. From an interdisciplinary background, his research includes media psychology, health communication, consumer behavior, and social media advertising.

Eddah M. Mutua is a professor in the Department of Communication Studies at St. Cloud State University, Minnesota. She teaches and researches in the area of intercultural communication with a special interest in intercultural and interethnic conflict, postconflict peace communication, and African culture and communication. She coordinates an award-wining service-learning project nationally recognized for its efforts to promote internationalization of intercultural communication curriculum. She also served on the National Communication Association's Task Force on Fostering International Collaborations in research, teaching, and service. Dr. Mutua earned her PhD from University of Wales, Aberystwyth.

Taryn K. Myers is a doctoral student in the Department of Communication, Culture and Media Studies program at Howard University with an expected graduation date of May 2020. Her research asks questions that seek to understand how marginalized populations have historically re-centered their experiences within the public sphere.

Sushil Oswal is an associate professor of human-centered design in the School of Interdisciplinary Arts and Sciences and an affiliate associate professor of disability studies at the University of Washington, Seattle. His research focuses on human centered design and the accessibility of digital technologies and built environments. His interdisciplinary research has appeared in *Communication Design Quarterly*, *Journal of Business and Technical Communication*, *Kairos*, *Work: a Journal of Prevention, Assessment, and Rehabilitation*, and in edited collections.

Donna Oti has worked as a journalist, professor, student media adviser, and organizational development consultant. She was a Fulbright Visiting Professor at the University of Jos, Nigeria, where she conceptualized their eLearning Fellowship program. Donna has also worked in Guyana, South Korea, and St. Lucia. She consults on strategic communication and organizational development and has received top paper awards from the Association for Education in Journalism and Mass Communication and the Eastern Communication Association.

Zsuzsanna Palmer is an assistant professor in the Writing Department at Grand Valley State University, where she teaches courses in professional writing. Her research interests include intercultural communication, visual rhetoric, and website accessibility. Her research has been published in edited collections, in the *Journal of Technical Writing and Communication*, and in *Business and Professional Communication Quarterly*.

Esther Quintero is Associate Director of Global Initiatives and adjunct at DePaul University. Previously she held various positions in international business, PR, and marketing at various multinational corporations. She also serves on boards of cultural and community organizations, such as International Latino Cultural Center, Catholic Charities, and Mexican Professionals Abroad, among others. Fully aware of the importance of preparing students to think globally, she has supported faculty to create meaningful educational experiences.

Ann Rogerson is Associate Dean (Education) and an associate professor of management in the Faculty of Business at the University of Wollongong, Australia. She holds postgraduate qualifications in both management and higher education, and also chairs the Academic Integrity Advisory Group at UOW. Her doctoral thesis examined how demographic differences are accommodated in managerial conversations in Australian workplaces.

L. Celeste Rossetto is an academic language and literacy senior lecturer who has worked closely with the Faculty of Business at the University of Wollongong, Australia, for more than a decade. She holds postgraduate qualifications in TESOL education. Her research interests include internationalization of the curriculum, curriculum and assessment design.

Babalwa Sibango is a PhD candidate at the Department of Communication Science at the University of South Africa, where she also teaches undergraduate and early postgraduate level. Her research interests includes; intergroup polarization, with specific focus on interracial polarization, (social) media and polarization and subjective perceptions of media bias and their implications for interracial relations.

Laura A. Stengrim is an assistant professor in the School of Communication and Director of the Speaking Center at the University of Southern Mississippi. She earned her PhD from the University of Illinois, Urbana-Champaign, with areas of research and teaching that include rhetorical pedagogies, rhetorical histories, and contemporary and historical critiques of neoliberal globalization.

Wei Sun is graduate faculty in the Department of Communication, Culture and Media Studies at Howard University in Washington, DC. Her research interests include race and culture, health communication, and new media studies. Her scholarly works have been published in refereed journals and academic books.

Morafe Tabane is a PhD candidate at School of Business Leadership in South Africa and also a lecturer at the Department of Communication Science at the University of South Africa, where she teaches public relations research, and organizational dynamics, at undergraduate and early postgraduate level. Her research interests include corporate governance, developmental finance, and business communication. She previously practiced as a business journalist with the South African Broadcasting Corporation (SABC).

Maureen Taylor is a professor in the School of Communication at the University of Technology Sydney. Taylor's public relations research has focused on civil society, dialogue, and engagement. In 2010, Taylor was honored by the Institute for Public Relations as a Pathfinder. She serves as editor of *Public Relations Review*. In 2018, she was elected as a Fellow in the International Communication Association.

Helena Torres-Purroy is an associate professor in the Department of Catalan Language and Communication at the University of Lleida. She is conducting research on the impact of university internationalization policies on the communication of multinational scientific research teams as part of her PhD. Her research interests are multimodal communication, communication in communities of practice, critical discourse analysis, and the internationalization of higher education.

Rebecca M. Townsend is an assistant professor of communication in the Humanities Department of Hillyer College, University of Hartford, in Connecticut. Her MA from Indiana University Bloomington focused on rhetoric and public memory, and her PhD from the University of Massachusetts Amherst focused on ethnography of rhetorical deliberation. Her research is on political communication across a variety of contexts, from town meeting legislatures in the USA to public memory and national identity in Poland. The White House awarded her the 2012 Champions of Change Award for Transportation Innovation for her scholarship on public engagement of underserved populations.

Marta Maria Tryzna is an assistant professor of linguistics at Gulf University for Science and Technology (GUST) in Kuwait. Previously she served as the writing program coordinator in the English Department at GUST and as a faculty senate president. Dr. Tryzna earned her PhD and MA in linguistics from the University of Iowa.

Paaige K. Turner is Dean of the College of Communication, Information, and Media at Ball State University. She was the recipient of the NAFSA: Association of International Educators Region IV 2012 Dorothy Brickman Outstanding New Professional Award and a 2013 Fulbright-Nehru International Education Administrators Award to India. For the past six years, she has co-led the Campus Internationalization Track at the Institute for Campus and Curriculum Internationalization. She has been an external reviewer for the American Council of Education: Center for Internationalization and Globalization Internationalization Laboratory and served as the program coordinator for the AIEA: Association of International Education Administrators Senior Advisor Program. She also served on the National Communication Association's Task Force on Fostering International Collaborations.

Joseph P. Zompetti is a professor of communication at Illinois State University, where he teaches courses in communication and social issues, classical rhetoric, and political communication. He is internationally known for his research and teaching of argument, critical thinking, and political rhetoric, as he has taught these and similar subjects in nearly 30 countries, including three Fulbright grants. Dr. Zompetti's research interests include the rhetoric of critical cultural studies and the rhetoric of civic engagement. His work has appeared in *Theory and Critique*, the *Journal of Promotion Management*, and *Argumentation: An International Journal of Reasoning*. He is the author of *Divisive Discourse: The Extreme Rhetoric of Contemporary American Politics*, *Essential Readings on Rhetoric*, and (with J.R. Blaney) *The Rhetoric of Pope John Paul II*.

Index

Note: Page numbers in italics indicate figures; page numbers in bold indicate tables.

academic literacies 106–107
Accrediting Council on Education in Journalism and Mass Communication (ACEJMC) 173
acculturation, international communication 26
Ad Age 214
Adelman, Mara 202–203
Africanist epistemologies 91–93
Africanized public relations, South Africa 148–149
agency visits, benefits in study abroad 214–216
Allport, Gordon 226
Altheide, David 203–204
American Advertising Association 217
American Association of Higher Education 226
American Council on Education (ACE) 196
American Institute for Study Abroad 216
American Institute of Foreign Studies (AIFS) 208
Arabian Peninsula 166, 175; states of 167; *see also* Gulf Cooperation Council (GCC)
Argentina: International Social Marketing (course): academics 136; foreign languages 137; key positives 138; location rationale 136; major challenges 138; on-site arrival and orientation 137–138; overview 136–139; program evaluation 138; recommendations for future iterations 139; recruitment 137; student evaluation 139; travel details 137
Argumentation and Advocacy (journal) 26, 27
Aristotle 84, 85
Association for Education in Journalism and Mass Communication 217

Association of American Colleges & Universities (AAC&U) 38, 43, 52, 227, 230
Association of International Educators 4
Azusa Pacific University 207–208, 209, 211, 212

Backward Course Design (BCD) 55–56
Bahrain: degrees and courses 169, **169**; graduate communication programs in GCC states **184**; undergraduate communication programs in **179**; *see also* Gulf Cooperation Council (GCC)
Bakhtin, Mikhail 93
Beebe, Steve 11
Belgian Royal Museum for Central Africa 91
Bernays, Edward 124
blended classroom: implications for international 255–257; local contexts for ViA and UMM students 254–255; professional and institutional contexts of 252–254; theoretical frame of 250–252
Blood Diamond (film) 93
Bourdieu, Pierre 198
Braithwaite, Charles 203
Bridges to the Future (Association of International Educators) 4
Buber, Martin 7
Bureau of Educational and Cultural Affairs, Fulbright program 197
Burke, Kenneth 84, 93
butterfly effect 204, 205n3
Buttny, Richard 199

Calafell, Bernadette 188
Campaign US 214

Campus Compact 226
Carbaugh, Donal 17, 198–199
Center for Global Learning and Engagement (CGLE) 209
Center for Intercultural Dialogue 18, 243, 245
Center for Intercultural New Media Research (CINMR) 19
Central States Communication Association (CSCA) 189, 226
Chávez, César 87
chaos theory 204
China: face-saving culture 115; media ownership and control 121
China Agricultural University 17
Cicero 76, 82
citation game, science communication 105
civil society organizations (CSOs) 92
classroom *see* blended classroom; decolonizing the classroom; translation tasks
class schedule **280**
Clinton, Bill 94
collaboration *see* international collaboration
Collaborative Online International Learning (COIL) Center, State University of New York (SUNY) 14
coloniality 144, 148
Colorado State University 17
Communicating Common Ground (CCG) project 223; assessment of service-learning projects 229–230; content of 228; exemplifying active learning 226–227; globalization 224, 232–233; goals and learning outcomes 227–228; guidelines for implementation 230–232; initial preparation 231; intercultural communication scholarship 224–225; introducing to students 231–232; learning resources 231; local and global factors influencing communication 225–226; participants 228–229; setting context 223–227; Skype session 229, 232
communication: globalized environment 278–283; internationalization and 3–4; scientists' multimodal 100–102; stakeholders of internationalization 12; *see also* intercultural communication; interpersonal organizational communication; strategic communication
communication basic course 64, 67–68; external outcomes 71–72; intercultural communication competence training in community colleges 65, 68; internal outcomes 70–71; internationalization of 67–72; internationalization of community colleges 65–66; knowledge, comprehension and skills 70; Metro Community College 68–69; respect, openness and curiosity 69
communication center 76–77; discipline of 81–82; idea of 77–79; internationalization's local histories 80–81; translingual paradigm 79–80
Communication Competence Model 67
communication curricula/courses: area studies 13; concerns and commitments 19–20; foreign language learning 13; global learning 37–38; intercultural competence 40–41; international content in 12–14; internationalization of curriculum 39–40; international research 18, 19; travel and exchange programs 15–17
Communication Education (journal) 26, **27**
Communication Monographs (journal) 26, **28**
Communication Privacy Management Center 60
Communication Quarterly (journal) 26, **28**
Communication Reports (journal) 26, **28**
Communication Research Reports (journal) 26, **28**
Communication Studies (journal) 26, **28**
communication studies curriculum: aligning departmental global learning goals with learning outcomes in communications (LOCs) 58–59; assessing global learning opportunities in department 59–60; case study of internationalizing 56–62; defining department–level global learning goals 57, 59; embedding global learning infused LOCs throughout major 61
communication studies major: assessment and evaluation 43–46, **44**; background on 36–37; global learning 37–38; implementation of international training 41–43; intercultural competence 40–41; internationalization of 40; internationalization of curriculum 39–40; learning goals and outcomes 42–43
Communication Theory (journal) 26, **28**, 32
community colleges: globalization and internationalized campuses 64; intercultural communication competence training in 68; internationalization

and intercultural competence 65–66; internationalization of campuses 64–65
conflict management, term 246
Confucian Work Dynamism 116
Council of Communication Associations 18
Council on International Educational Exchange (CIEE) 17, 18
critical communication pedagogy (CCP) 186
critical diversity, concept of 147
critical intercultural communication (CIC) 186
Critical Studies in (Mass) Media Communication (journal) 26, **29**
cultural discourse 88
Cultural Discourse Analysis (CDA): blended classroom 252; classroom 250; Ethnography of Communication (EC) and 252; theoretical frame 251
culture: analysis of 25; Cultural Discourse Analysis (CDA) defining 251; dimensions of 117; impact on relationships 114–117; individualism *vs* collectivism 114, 115; indulgence *vs* restraint 116; interdisciplinary definition of in public relations 146–147; long-term *vs* short-term orientation 116; masculinity *vs* femininity 114, 115–116; power distance 114–115; public relations and 144–146; study abroad experiences 216–218; uncertainty avoidance 114, 116
Cultures and Languages Across the Curriculum (CLAC) 13
Cultures and Organizations (Hofstede) 119
curricula: class schedule example **280**; internationalizing the 191–193, 196; strategies for international collaboration 237–239; successful transnationalization of 189–190; *see also* communication curricula/courses; decolonizing the classroom; international collaboration
Curtin, Patricia A. 119

decolonizing the classroom 185–193; diversifying course content 191; empowering marginalized faculty and students 187–188; Fanon's approach 190, 191; Freire's approach 190–191; internationalizing the curriculum 191–193; landscape of higher education 187; orientalism 183, 187; postcolonial and transnational approaches to 186; race 183, 187; story of Marina 194; transnationalizing the curricula 189–190; US perspectives in 191–193; whiteness 185, 187–188
Deferred Action for Childhood Arrivals (DACA) 155
Degree Qualifications Profile (DQP) 50
DePaul University 139; developing faculty-led study-abroad programs 135–136; engagement with Latinx and Latin American communities 132–133, 139; faculty-led study–abroad programs 135–136; internationalization at 131–132; Latino Media and Communication Program 131, 133, 134; *see also* Argentina: International Study Marketing (course)
Developmental Model of Intercultural Sensitivity, Bennett 156
Dewey, John 227, 233, 248
doing global 6–7; transformational approaches to 7–8

East is East (film) 191
Ebola outbreak 60
economic subsidy 122
ELL (English language learner) 79
English as a lingua franca 100
epistemicides 148
ERASMUS program 204, 208
ESL (English as a second language) 79
EURIAS (European Institutes for Advanced Study) 204
European Humanities University, Belarus 14
European Union: United Kingdom voting to leave 5
exchange programs: for faculty 17; for students 15–17; tips to enhance rigor of short-term 16; travel and 15–17

Facebook 16, 123
FaceTime 14
Face-to-Face Communication: course outline **268–269**; course schedule 267; curriculum through diary assignments 271; curriculum through research project 275; curriculum through seminar activities 271, 275; diary assignment description **272**; internationalizing 267; internationalizing curriculum through literature 267, 271; literature addressing intercultural

communication 270; reflection on 276; seminar activities 273, 274
faculty: exchange programs 17; international research 18
Faik, Sait 203
family backgrounds: diversity of 153–156, 160; practical programs for students from 158–160; refugee families 154–155; theoretical models 156–158; transnational families 155–156; undocumented families 155; *see also* students
Fannon, Franz 190, 191
feminism, transnational 89
financial resources, studying abroad 19
Fisher, Walter 93
foreign language learning, communication curricula 13
Foreign Service Institute (FSI), US Department of State 24, 80, 244
Forum of Education Abroad 209
Fostering International Collaborations in the Age of Globalization Task Force 226
Freire, Paulo 190–191
Freitag, Alan R. 119
Fulbright, J. William 197
Fulbright Foreign Student Program 17
Fulbright program 197; Adelman, Mara 202–203; Altheide, David 203–204; awards 197; butterfly effect 204; Buttny, Richard 199; Carbaugh, Donal 198–199; Glenn, Philip 200; impact of awards on internationalization 197–204; influence on internationalizing curricula 204; Lowenstein, Jeff Kelly, 202; Miller, Ann 201–202; Schnell, James 199–200; Schwalbe, Ted 200–201; Senior Specialist awards 197; Sowards, Stacey K. 201; traditional awards 197; Usluata, Ayseli 203; Winkin, Yves 198
Fulbright Scholar Program 17
Fulbright Visiting Scholar Program 17

Gaither, Kenn 119
genuine reciprocity 8
German Academic Exchange Service 204
Ghent University 18
Gillespie, Susan 8
Glenn, Philip 200
global and international learning outcomes (GILOs) 52–53, 55; Backward Course Design (BCD) 55–56; integrating learning outcomes in communication (LOCs) and 55–56, **58**
global citizen: definition 52; education competencies 53; elements in frameworks **54**; knowledge **54**; motivation/mind-set **54**; skills **54**
global citizenship, higher education 53, 55
Global Health Communication Center 60
global learning 37–38; growing interest in 50–51
Global Public Relations (Freitag and Stokes) 119
global socio-political issues, scientists' communication 104–106
Global Voices Speakers 59, 60
glocal, term 6
Golden Rule 80
Gonçalves, Susana 198
Good Neighbor policy 80
Google Translate 246, 247
graduate students, international research 18
Green Belt Movement 92
Gulf Cooperation Council (GCC) 166, 175–176; academic achievement of students' parents 169, 174; communication curricula 169–170; curricular analysis 167, 173; graduate communication programs in GCC states **184**; ICC skills and student demographics 172–173; ICC skills of Kuwaiti students 170–172; intercultural communication competence (ICC) education in 166–167; method for analysis 167–169; Pearson's correlations of variables **171**; students living abroad as children 169, 175; students' university experiences 168–169, 173–174; summary of degrees and courses in **169**; undergraduate communication programs in GCC states **179–183**
Gutierrez-Perez, Robert 188

H&M store 147
Hall, Edward 25
Harding Sandra 8
Hartnett, Stephen 11, 94
Harvey, David 80
higher education, globalization and internationalized campuses 64
Hoff, Peter 198
Hofstede, Geert 114–117, 119

Hosein, Everold 59
Howard Journal of Communication (journal) 26, **29**, 31, 32
Huerta, Dolores 87
Human Communication Research (journal) 26, **29**
humanism 149
Hungarian students *see* international collaboration

I and Thou, Buber's concept of 7
identity, international communication 26
IKEA 113
Immigrant Law Center of Minnesota 227
Indiana University Purdue University Indianapolis (IUPUI): communication faculty 56; communication studies 59; Global Learning Goals 57
individualism *vs* collectivism, culture dimension 114, 115
indulgence *vs* restraint, culture dimension 116
information subsidy, term 121–122
Instagram 123
Institute of International Education (IIE) 4, 14, 214; Center for International Partnerships in Higher Education 15
Integrated Model of Intercultural Communication Competence (IMICC) 40
Interactive Advertising Bureau 217
intercultural communication 23–24; findings on 31–32; frequently occurring words 33 key words in journals (2000 to 2017) 27–31; origin and evolution of field 24–26; quantitative analysis of 26–27, **27–31**; state of affairs in 32–34
intercultural communication competence (ICC) 165–166; affective aspect of 166; appropriateness in 166; behavioral aspect of 166; cognitive complexity 166; effectiveness in 166; framework 53; future research of 175; linguistic skills in 166; model 40–41; theories on 66–67, 69; *see also* Gulf Cooperative Council (GCC)
Intercultural Communication Competency Instrument (ICCI) 168, 169
Intercultural Competence Model, Deardorff 67, 69, 72, 157
Intercultural Sensitivity Model 156–157
intergovernmental organizations, international public relations 144
International Academic Partnership Program 15

International Association of Business Communication 217
International Association of Business Communicators 125
International Association of Universities 3; Global Survey 11
international collaboration: challenges of 239–240; curricular strategies 237–239; Internet assistance in 235; pedagogical takeaways of 240–241; three-way online project 235–237; use of technology for 237
International Communication Association 17, 189
international conferences 17
International Encyclopedia of Intercultural Communication 27
internationalization: of campuses 64–65; communication and 3–4; of curricula 191–193, 196; definition 143; definition of 5; designing educational curricula 11; doing global 6–7; resources 14–15; rise and fall of 4–8; stakeholders in 12; stories of impact of Fulbright awards on 197–204; term 130; transformational approaches to doing global 7–8; *see also* Fulbright program
internationalization of higher education (IoHE) 99–100, 107–108
Internationalization of the Curriculum (IoC), definition 39
International Organisation for Economic Co-operation and Development 4
international public relations 143, 144; Africanisation of PR curriculum in South Africa 148–149; culture and 144–146; future direction for research 149–150; interdisciplinary definition of culture 146–147; power and 147–148, 149–150; theory of 143, 150; *see also* public relations
International Public Relations (Curtin and Gaither) 119
International Public Relations Association 125
international research: faculty and graduate students 18, 23; resources 19
international students, transnational families 155–156
Internet, international collaborative project 235
interpersonal organizational communication: cross-cultural communication for higher education and future employment 260;

cross-cultural group formation guidelines 262; curricula design 259–261, 260; embedding academic skills 261; group work assessment task 263–264; individual reflective assessment task 264; learning outcomes 260–261; skill development 261; tutorial activities 264–265
inter-rhetorical reflexivity 90
Introduction to Interaction, An (Garcia) 271

Japan International Cooperation Agency 204
Journalism and Mass Communication Quarterly (journal) 26, 30
Journal of Applied Communication Research (journal) 26, 29
Journal of Broadcasting and Electronic Media (journal) 26, 29, 32
Journal of Communication (journal) 26, 29
Journal of Intercultural Communication Research (journal) 26, 30, 31, 94
Journal of International and Intercultural Communication (journal) 26, 30, 31, 32
Journal of International and Intercultural Research (journal) 95

Kansas State University 17
Kennedy, John F. 93
Kenyatta, Jomo 88
Klooster, Erik van`t 214
Kruckeberg, Dean 119
KSA *see* Gulf Cooperation Council (GCC)
Kubota, Ryoko 81
Kuwait 165, 166; degrees and courses 169, **169**; graduate communication programs in GCC states **184**; intercultural communication competence (ICC) skills of students 170–172; undergraduate communication programs in **179–180**; *see also* Gulf Cooperation Council (GCC)
Kuwait Foundation for the Advancement of Science 176n1

La Fate Ignoranti (film) 191
Lao Tzu 88
Latin American Institute 80
Latino Media and Communication Program, DePaul University 131, 133
Latinx and Latin American Communities 131; DePaul's engagement with 132–133; *see also* DePaul University

learning outcomes in communication (LOCs) 51–52; aligning global program learning with 55–56; integrating global and international learning outcomes (GILOs) 55–56
Leeds-Hurwitz, Wendy 17, 80
Lewis, C. S. 201
licensing of public relations 123–124
literacy brokers 107, 108
long-term *vs* short-term orientation, culture dimension 116
Lowenstein, Jeff Kelly 202
Lumina Foundation 50, 51

Maathai, Wangari 92, 93
MALM series furniture 113
masculinity *vs* femininity, culture dimension 114, 115–116
Matsuda, Paul Kei 76
Matthew effect, communication function 105
Mbeki, Thabo 93
media: ownership and control of 121–122; traditional 122; transparency 122; *see also* social media
Mediated Communication (Napoli) 122
Michigan students *see* international collaboration
Miller, Ann 201–202
Milstein, Tema 17
Mohanty, Chandra 89
Moon, Dreama 25
M-Pesa money service 224
multilingual 79
multinational corporations (MNCs), culture and public relations 144–145

NAFSA Resources for Internationalizing Teaching and Learning (report) 14
National Center for Education Statistics 77
National Communication Association (NCA) 51, 68, 189, 205n1, 226; Fostering International Collaborations in the Age of Global Task Force 11; Summer Conference on Intercultural Dialogue 17; Task Force on Internationalization 11
nationalism: United Kingdom leaving EU 5; United States 4–5
New London Group, inclusive pedagogies of 160
New York Times (newspaper) 94
Nike 113

non-governmental organizations (NGOs), international public relations 144
Nydegger, Melvin 80

Obama administration 155
Occupy Wall Street (2011) 77
Ogilvy Berlin 215
Oman: degrees and courses 169, **169**; graduate communication programs in GCC states **184**; undergraduate communication programs in **180B**; *see also* Gulf Cooperation Council (GCC)
online courses, global delivery of for-credit 14
Organisation for Economic Co-operation and Development (OECD) 50, 207
Orientalism (Said) 91
Oxfam Development Education Program 52
Ozpetek, Ferzan 191

Parrish-Sprowl, John 59
peer-support programs, students from diverse family backgrounds 159–160
Penn State 17
Pepsi 113
Petronio, Sandra 59
Philosophy & Rhetoric (journal) 26, 30
plagiarism 278
Plato 84, 85
Polish university: American-style teaching in 243; *see also* translation tasks
postcolonial studies 90–91
power: culture and public relations 145; imbalances between cultural groups 146, 149–150; public relations and 147–148
power distance, culture dimension 114–115
Presumed Incompetent (Muhs *et al*) 189
Process Model, Deardorff 157–158
professional associations: codes of ethics 125; public relations 124–125, **126**; systems of accreditation 125
PR Week 214
public relations: conceptual foundations of international 114–117; courses and objectives **120**; culture impact on relationships 114–117; globalization and technology for communication 113–114; international 143, 144; social media and 122–123; traditional media and 122; *see also* international public relations

public relations as global academic subject 117–127; creating dedicated international course 119; initiatives to internationalize education 118–121; internationalizing content in existing courses **120**; licensing of 123–124; media and social media 121–123; ownership and control of media content 121–122; professional associations 124–125, **126**; role in society 125–127; social media and 122–123; social media platform users *123*; systems of accreditation 125; traditional media 122; writing courses 118
Public Relations Society of America 124, 125, 217
publishing practices, internationalization of scientists' 106–107
Putin, Vladimir 94
Pyramid Model of Intercultural Competence, Deardorff 67, 69

Qatar: degrees and courses 169, **169**; undergraduate communication programs in **180**; *see also* Gulf Cooperation Council (GCC)
QQ 123
Qualitative Research Reports in Communication (journal) 26, 30
Quarterly Journal of Speech (journal) 26, 31, 95

RACE (research action planning communication and evaluation) model 215
Reagan, Ronald 94
recession (2008) 77
refugee families, students from 154–155
resources: internationalization 14–15; study abroad and exchange program 18
Rhetoric & Society Quarterly (journal) 95
rhetorical legacy, notion of 85
rhetorical studies 84–85; Africanist epistemologies 91–93; international contexts and 93–94; postcolonial studies 90–91; three cross-national perspectives for 89–93; tradition 85; traditions 87–88; working against national rhetoric 85–87
Rhetoric of Western Thought, The (Golden *et al*) 85
Roh Tae-woo 88
Rotterdam School of Management 214

Rubin, Jon 14
Russia, media ownership and control 121

Said, Edward 91
Samatar, Ahmed 224
Sapir-Whorf hypothesis 25
Saudi Arabia: degrees and courses 169, **169**; graduate communication programs in GCC states **184**; undergraduate communication programs in **181**
Schnell, James 199–200
School for International Training (SIT) Graduate Institute 19
Schwalbe, Ted 200–201
science: communication models 101; constructing and representing facts 102–104; cultural authority of 105–106; digital era of presentations 103; literacy brokers 107, 108; mystification of 100; political aspects of 101–102; world system theory 106
scientific star system 105
scientists: communication and IoHE 99–100, 107–108; gatekeepers for resources 105; globalization of communication 99–100; global socio-political issues in communication 104–106; internationalization of publishing practices 106–107; laboratories studies 102, 103; multimodal communication 100–102, 106; science and technology studies (STS) 103
Self-Perceived Communication Competence Skills Measurement 66
Sellnow, Deanna 202
Sellnow, Tim 202
sense of belonging, New London Group 160
service-learning project 223; assessment of 229–230; resources for 230, 231; *see also* Communicating Common Ground (CCG) project
Shome, Raka 186
Sina Weibo (China) 123
Skype 14; Communicating Common Ground (CCG) project 229, 231, 232
Snapchat 123
social media: Instagram 123; networking platforms 123; platform users *123*; public relations and 122–123; QQ 123; Snapchat 123; Twitter 123, 283; Viber 123; Wechat 123; YouTube 123, 252, **272**; *see also* media

Society for Cross-Cultural Research (SCCR) 19
SOCRATES program 204
South Africa, Africanisation of PR curriculum in 148–149
Southern Communication Journal (journal) 26, **31**, 32
Southern Poverty Law Center 226
Sowards, Stacey K. 201
stakeholders in internationalization 12
Standard American English (SAE) 81
Stanford Center for Opportunity Policy in Education 50
State University College at Purchase (NY) 14
State University of New York (SUNY), Collaborative Online International Learning (COIL) Center 14
Stokes, Ashli Quesinberry 119
strategic communication 130–131; course overview for Argentina: International Social Marketing 136–139; DePaul's engagement with Latinx and Latin American communities 132–133; developing faculty-led study-abroad programs 135–136; internationalization at DePaul University 131–132; internationalization of curricula 133–135
students: challenges facing 160; diverse backgrounds of international 153–156; diversity committee for inclusivity 158; intercultural competence of 157–158; Intercultural Sensitivity Model 156–157; New London Group's guidelines for inclusive pedagogies 160; peer-support programs 159–160; practical programs for diverse familial background 158–160; problem-based learning 278; from refugee families 154–155; theoretical models for addressing diversity challenges of 156–158; from transnational families 155–156; from undocumented families 155; University of California-Berkeley's Undocumented Student Program (USP) 158–159; *see also* Communicating Common Ground (CCG) project
Study Abroad 18; academic pillar of 208, 209–213; benefits of agency visits 214–216; course format 212; course selection in 211–212; cultural pillar of 208, 216–218; designing coursework 213; experiences for students 207; global learning experiences 61; global learning experiences for students 38,

300 Index

207, 218–219; institutions promoting programs 216–217; international mobility in 207–208; organization of programs 208–209, 219; professional pillar 208, 213–216; theme for 210–211
Sustainable Development Goals, United Nations 4, 7
Sutton, Susan Buck 7–8

Tao Te Ching (Lao Tzu) 87–88
technocratic elite 100
Text and Performance Quarterly (journal) 26, **31**
transformational partnerships 8
transformative learning, New London Group 160
translation tasks: assignment 245–246; case examples 244–247; Google Translate 246, 247; intercultural communication and 244; lessons learned 246–247
translingual 79
translingualism 79
translingual paradigm 79–80
transliteracy 79
transnational families, international students from 155–156
transnational feminism 89
transnationalization, successful, of curricula 189–190
Transparency, Public Relations and the Mass Media (Tsetsura and Kruckeberg) 119
travel and exchange programs: faculty exchanges 17, 18; student programs 15–17; study abroad and exchange program resources 18
Truman, Harry 197
Trump, Donald 4–5
Tsetsura, Katerina 119
Tuning, Degree Qualifications Profile (DQP) and 50
Turner, Paaige 17
Twitter 123, 283

UAE (United Arab Emirates) *see* Gulf Cooperation Council (GCC)
Ubuntuism 149
uncertainty avoidance, culture dimension 114, 116
undocumented families, students from 155
Undocumented Student Program (USP), University of California-Berkeley 158–159
United Arab Emirates (UAE): degrees and courses 169, **169**; graduate communication programs in GCC states **184**; undergraduate communication programs in **181–183**
United Farm Workers 87
United Nations (UN): Sustainable Development Goals 4, 7; website 279; UN Educational, Scientific and Cultural Organization (UNESCO) 52
United States: international issues impacting 11–12; Trump administration 4–5
universities: collaboration of three 235–237; diversity committee for inclusive environment 158; recruiting international students 3; *see also* international collaboration
University of California–Berkeley, Undocumented Student Program (USP) 158–159
University of Colorado Denver 17
University of Minnesota 209
University of South Africa 148
University of Southern Mississippi 80
Uppsala University 18
US Civil Rights Movement 86
US Consumer Product Safety Commission 113
US Department of State: Bureau of Educational and Cultural Affairs 17; Foreign Service Institute (FSI) 24, 80, 244
Usluata, Ayseli 203

Viber 123
Vkontakte (Russia) 123

Washington students *see* international collaboration
Wechat 123
Western Journal of Communication (journal) 27, **31**
What's App 123
Whyte, William 25
wild-geese families 156, 160
Winkin, Yves 198
Women's Studies in Communication (journal) 27, **31**
Woodruff, Gayle 209–210
World Communication Association 17
World Health Organization 59
World Pulse 90
World Trade Organization (WTO) 130
World War I 80
World War II 5, 80, 197

YouTube 123, 252, **272**